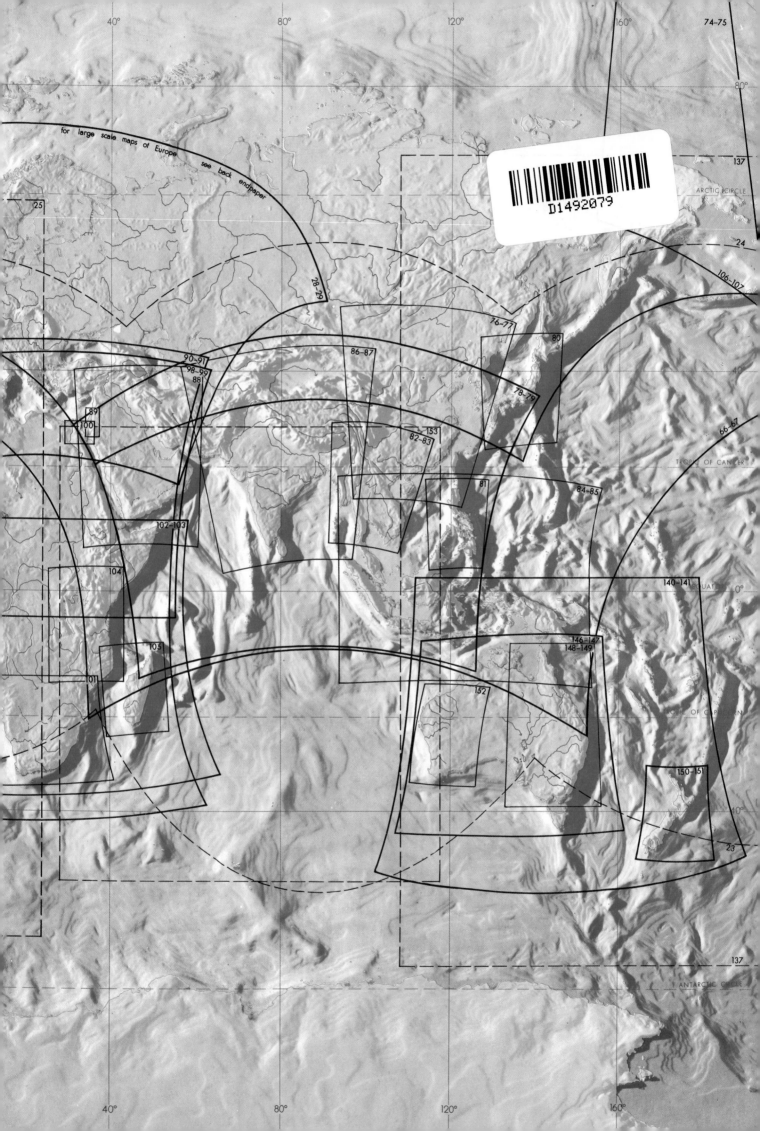

for large scale maps of Europe see back endpaper

28-29

90-91
98-99
88
89
100
102-103
104
105
101

86-87

76-77
80
78-79
153
82-83
81
84-85

140-141
146-147
148-149
152
150-151

25

D1492079

40°   80°   120°   160°   74-75

80°
137
ARCTIC CIRCLE
24
106-107
40°
66-67
TROPIC OF CANCER
EQUATOR 0°
TROPIC OF CAPRICORN
23
40°
137
ANTARCTIC CIRCLE

40°   80°   120°   160°

HAMLYN'S
NEW RELIEF
WORLD ATLAS

HAMLYN'S
NEW RELIEF
WORLD ATLAS

Paul Hamlyn/London

Editor: Shirley Carpenter, M.A., F.R.G.S.
Designer: Romek Marber, A.R.C.A.

Consultants:
Nomenclature: H. A. G. Lewis, assistant I. Dawson
Space: Colin Ronan
Climate: Professor Gordon Manley
Original map technique: Professor Frank Debenham, O.B.E.
(late professor of Geography, Cambridge University)

Institutes consulted:
Institute of Oceanography
Royal Geographical Society
Scott Polar Research Institute

© Geographical Projects, London, 1966
Printed in Holland by Senefelder
Photographs courtesy:
Ronan Picture Library p. 14, p. 15 bottom
Mt. Wilson and Palomar Observatories p. 15 top
Novosti Press Agency (APN) Moscow p. 16 left
United States Information Service p. 16 right

Designed and produced by

Geographical Projects
(Aldus Books Limited)

Contents

Shadow relief maps

This is the first Atlas to use exclusively special shadow relief maps which have a three-dimensional effect. Each map is based on an actual model of its particular area or continent. These models have been constructed from the most up-to-date information and by the most precise techniques in order to ensure a high degree of accuracy. On every model the vertical scale is identical for the elevations of the land and the depths of the sea floor so that it is possible to compare accurately the relief of, say, a mountain range and an ocean deep.

Each model has been photographed under special lighting conditions and the resulting shadow relief maps are used as a basis for the maps in the Atlas. This has ensured that every map is a true picture of the terrain it represents; it enables the user to relate the positions of artificial features such as cities and routes, and natural features such as rivers, to the relief of the country; and it assists the user in the complete study of the geography of the area covered by the map.

Colouring systems

Excluding the special distribution maps of the world, four types of colouring have been used in the Atlas:

Relief colouring

Where shades of green denote the low ground, the darkest green being the areas below sea-level, and shades of brown the high ground, the highest peaks of all being a very dark brown.

Political colouring

Where each political unit is shown by a special colour.

Natural colouring

Which is based on climatic and vegetation factors and gives a general picture of the land—whether it is hot or cold, wet or dry, barren desert or luxurious tropical forest. Thirteen divisions have been used in all, though naturally not all maps necessarily have all these divisions. These 'natural colouring' divisions are:

a   Ice caps—areas permanently under snow or ice.
b   Tundra—areas mainly cold with a permanently frozen subsoil, only stunted vegetation of mosses and lichens.
c   Mountain and moorland—areas in high altitudes not so cold as the Tundra but only stunted vegetation and often bare rocky surfaces.
d   Coniferous Forests—the regions of the 'cold' forests and conifers, long cold winters and many months when the ground is snow covered.
e   Deciduous Forests—areas which are not so cold or dry as the Coniferous Forests, areas in more temperate latitudes with over fifty per cent tree cover, mainly deciduous in type.
f   Temperate Grasslands—the areas in the middle latitudes with no great extremes of temperature or rainfall, luxuriant grasslands with many areas of mixed woodland.
g   Prairie or Steppe—areas of more continental climate, greater extremes of heat and cold, the great grasslands now used for grain production or stock rearing.
h   Mediterranean—those areas which have a typical 'Mediterranean' climate, warm wet winters and hot dry summers, the lands of the citrus, the olive, and the vine.
i   Savanna—the dry tropical grasslands, the areas in the tropical latitudes with high temperatures and a marked dry season. Tall tropical grasses and some low trees.
j   Tropical Forests—the area of the jungle in the tropics, regions of great heat and moisture and luxuriant vegetation cover.
k   Desert—the barren areas with very little, if any, rainfall and great extremes of temperature both daily and seasonally. Very sparse vegetation cover, often only in small areas and existing for short periods after some rain, areas of sandy wastes and bare rock or stony stretches.
l   Semi-desert—the areas bordering the true deserts with a little more rainfall but only enough to support a scant vegetation of scrub, salt bush, and xerophytic plants.
m   Fertile Lands—those areas which because of irrigation or underground water supplies are not semi-desert but have been densely populated and cultivated—the Nile and Tigris-Euphrates valleys, the oases of the deserts.

Ochre colouring

In which the shadow relief is printed in ochre to serve as a background for the vast amount of detail such as place names, routes and natural features, which are superimposed in blue.

In both maps with relief and with natural colouring, the relief of the sea floor is also shown. On the maps with political and ochre colouring the relief of the sea floor is not shown and the sea (and other water) areas are represented by a flat blue tint.

Scope of the Atlas

In this Atlas each continent has been treated in a similar manner: a map of the whole continent in relief colouring and one in political colouring; a map of each major division of that particular continent in natural colouring; and maps at a larger scale of the more important countries, regions or spheres of interest, in ochre colouring. Naturally the continent of Europe is treated in the greatest detail and there is a special section devoted to maps of our own country, including a map of the whole of the British Isles in natural colouring.

Included in each group of continental maps—Europe, Eurasia, Africa, North America, South America and Australasia— is a series of line maps designed to give specific geographical, economical, climatic, and historical information. One set of these maps is devoted to climate: the average temperatures for January and July in degrees centigrade (with a conversion key for fahrenheit); the average rainfall for the two six-monthly periods November-April and May-October in centimetres (again with a conversion key for inches); the average number of days which are likely to be frost free and the areas of permanent ice; the average number of hours sunshine per year and the most frequent paths of tropical storms. Accompanying these climate maps are tables for eight towns on each continent giving more precise information about temperatures, rainfall, and humidity. These towns have been selected to give examples from the various climatic regions as plotted on the World Map on pages 20–21.

A second set of line maps embraces the economic factors—soils, land use, power resources, population density, and religions. The third set, which is designed to lead up to the present-day political scene, shows the development of the continent at various stages throughout recent historical times since the 'Great Age of Discovery'.

To add to this very complete coverage of the world are maps of the four oceans— Arctic, Atlantic, Indian, and Pacific—each of which is accompanied by a cross-section taken through the major features; a map of Antarctica incorporating the most recent results acquired during the International Geophysical Year and the subsequent scientific programmes; and a number of world maps giving some concept of the physiography, the climatic regions, the population distribution, the structure, and the historical development.

Terms of reference

A great deal of thought and careful study has been devoted to the nomenclature and the systems of spellings of place-names which should be adopted. The editor has been advised by a member of the Permanent Committee on Geographical Names and an expert in the various languages which have a non-Roman alphabet such as Russian, Arabic, and Chinese. Wherever possible the local names and spellings have been used and if an anglicised version exists, then, where space permits, this is given in brackets underneath. For the information of readers a glossary of terms in the various languages is given at the beginning of the Index on page 161.

The following are the main features concerning the content of the individual maps and these can be divided into artificial (that is man-made) and natural features.

Artificial features

Towns are shown by a solid black square or dot depending upon the number of inhabitants:

ABCDE Abcd — On all maps (except those with political colouring) towns with over 1,000,000 inhabitants are shown in a heavier and larger typeface with a black square town symbol

ABCDEF Abcd — On all maps (except those with political colouring) towns with over 500,000 inhabitants are shown in the following typeface with a large black dot

ABCDEF Abcde — On all maps with relief and natural colouring towns with over 250,000 inhabitants are shown in the following typeface with a black dot

ABCDEFG Abcde — On all ochre maps towns of over 100,000 inhabitants are shown in the following typeface with a black dot

ABCDEFG Abcdef — All other towns—towns of administrative importance, route centres, ports, places of historical interest—are denoted by a smaller typeface and a smaller black dot

Abcdef — On the maps with political colouring only capital towns are shown

O ABCDEFGH — Ancient sites of particular interest are shown by a lighter typeface in capitals and an open circle

ABCDEF — Mountain peaks are denoted with medium typeface in capitals with a small black dot to mark the actual peak

123456 — Heights are in feet where feet is the normal unit of measurement, and in metres where the metric system is in current use

123456 (654321) — On maps of continents, such as North America, where some countries use the metric system and others feet, then heights are given in metres with the equivalent in feet in brackets

123456 — Depths are shown in metres with a black dot denoting the actual position (where possible they are also named)

✱ — International airports are those airports to which there are services from numerous countries

— International boundaries are marked in red on those maps which have relief or natural colouring, in black in political maps and in blue on the ochre maps

— International boundaries under dispute are denoted differently

— Internal boundaries, such as county boundaries

— Air routes are shown by red lines on the continental and ocean maps

— Arterial roads are shown in red on those maps with natural colouring

— Main shipping lines are shown by a blue line on maps with relief colouring

— Railways are shown by a black line on maps with natural colouring and a blue line on maps in ochre colouring

Natural features

— Rivers are shown by a blue line

— Seasonal rivers, that is those rivers which are not always full of water, are shown by a blue dashed line

— Rivers which drain into inland basins have an arrowhead to mark the direction of flow

— Canals are blue lines with cross lines

— Lakes which are permanent have a blue sea tint and either solid black or blue coastline

— Lakes, whose coastline varies from season to season, are shown by a dashed black or blue line with a blue sea tint

— Lakes which are seasonal, that is they are not always filled with water, are shown by a blue or black coastline with blue or black broken lines over the lake area

— Waterfalls and rapids are shown by a blue line at right angles to the river line

— Mountain passes are shown by black or blue parallel lines

A map projection is a means of representing the lines of latitude and longitude of the globe on a flat surface. Any such representation is termed a 'projection'. The actual network of lines is often referred to as the 'graticule'. On looking through any atlas one will notice numerous different projections. In some the lines of latitude and longitude will be straight, in others they will be curved; or there may be a combination of both, say, straight longitudes and curved latitudes. It is also obvious to the reader and user of an atlas that some countries look 'better' on some projections than on others.

The Greeks, who first realised that the earth is round, also knew that it is impossible to represent accurately a curved surface on the flat. However, it is possible to choose a projection which shows with reasonable accuracy the system of latitudes and longitudes for some given area of the globe, and which maintains certain properties. These properties are preservation of area, preservation of shape (orthomorphism), preservation of scale, and preservation of bearing. No one projection can have all these properties and, depending on the function of the map for which it is used, it will pay greatest attention to either area, shape, scale, or bearing or a combination of some of these factors.

How the earth can be 'projected' on to a flat piece of paper can be understood if one imagines rays of light passing through a number of points on the globe and continuing in straight lines until they touch the paper. Where they touch will depend upon:

    i) Where the source of light is relative to the globe

and ii) where the piece of paper is placed and whether it is in the shape of a cone, a cylinder, or a flat plane.

Choice of projection

There are three main considerations which must be borne in mind when the choice of projection is made for any particular map. These are: the purpose of the map; the position on the globe of the area covered by the map, whether it is in tropical, polar, or middle latitudes; and the extent of the area, whether it is large or small, and whether it covers a large area north-south or has its greatest extent latitudinally.

It is obvious that if the map is to show some form of distribution, such as population density, then the property to which most attention must be paid is that of preservation of area. On the other hand, if the map is to be used for navigational purposes then the first consideration is the preservation of direction, that is bearing. Quite often, though, it is necessary to compromise when preparing maps for atlases or series and to ensure that all the properties are preserved as far as is possible. It is for this reason that 'mathematical projections' are frequently used, as they attempt to compensate and to map the areas, shapes, bearings, and scale with as little distortion as possible.

Zenithal projections

Projections made on to a plane surface are called 'Zenithal' projections. The plane may touch the globe at a point, and, depending upon whether the point is one of the Poles, on the Equator, or between the Poles and the Equator, the projection will be called a 'Normal', 'Equatorial', or 'Olique' Zenithal projection. All these are 'perspective' projections, and their construction can easily be understood if one imagines the source of light as being either at the centre of the globe, at the opposite end of the diameter to that at which the plane touches, or at infinity. But the source of light can of course be moved to any other position in order to obtain certain advantages, and modifications can be made to maintain correct areas or distances. Projections made in this way are termed 'non-perspective' projections. All Zenithal projections have the property of maintaining true bearings from the centre of the map.

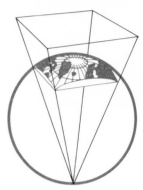

A projection made on to a plane surface.

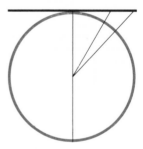

Source of light at the centre of the globe.

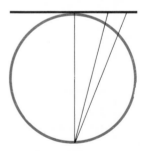

Source of light at the opposite end of the diameter to the plane of projection.

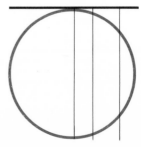

Source of light at infinity.

Cylindrical projections

When the surface is a cylinder, which again is later unrolled, then the projection is called a 'Cylindrical' projection. The cylinder can touch the globe round the equator, along a line of longitude, or in any oblique position. But it is the equatorial case which is most useful and most common. The main disadvantage of the Cylindrical type of projection is that it is likely to give a great exaggeration north-south and therefore it is often modified and adapted. It is of greatest use for maps of the equatorial areas and for some world maps.

Conical projections

If the surface is changed from a plane to a cone, which can later be unrolled, then the projection is a 'Conical' one. Clearly the cone can be placed on the globe in as many positions as can the plane, but it is the normal case which is the most useful. In this the axis of the earth, when produced, becomes the axis of the cone and the cone rests along a line of latitude. Sometimes, however, the cone is made to 'cut' the earth, in which case it cuts the earth along two lines of latitude. Modifications can be made to the simple conical projection in order to maintain certain properties. Conical projections are most suitable for temperate latitudes which do not have too great an extent north-south.

Calculated or Mathematical projections

It is often the case that one of the three basic types of projection—Zenithal, Conical, or Cylindrical—becomes greatly modified as attention is paid to one property or another. The result can be termed a 'Calculated' projection. Again, it is possible to calculate mathematically a system of latitudes and longitudes, an arrangement of the graticule, that will fulfill one of the properties of a projection. This 'Mathematical' projection cannot be directly related to any of the three types mentioned. Calculated and Mathematical projections—of which Gall's projection and the International projection are examples—are most important; many world maps are hased on them.

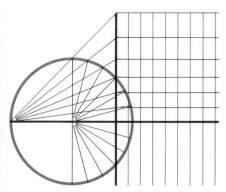

Projection surface in the shape of a cylinder.

Projection surface in the shape of a cone.

Oblique Mollweide projection: the equator and the central meridian, 0° and 180°, form two similar circles.

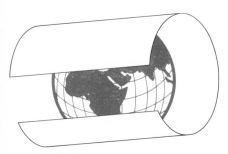

Source of light at the centre of the globe which results in great exaggeration north-south.

The blue tint is the area on the globe between two longitudes which is represented on the cone (the projection surface) by the grey tint.

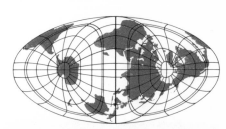

Transverse Mollweide projection: the equator of the normal Mollweide projection becomes the central meridian.

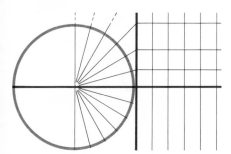

Source of light at the end of one diameter (the equator) and the north-south exaggeration is less marked.

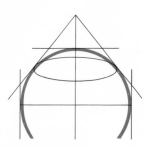

The cone touches the globe along a line of latitude.

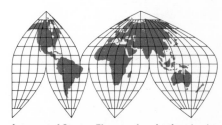

Interrupted Sanson Flamsteed projection: breaks are made in the projection in those areas which are not required in order to lessen the distortion.

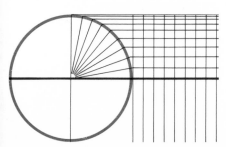

Source of light at infinity.

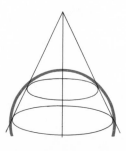

The cone 'cuts' the globe along two lines of latitude.

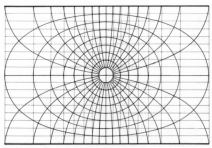

Transverse Mercator projection: in the normal Mercator projection the cylinder, on which the projection is made, touches the globe along the equator, in the Transverse Mercator the cylinder touches along any meridian.

The Solar System

The Solar System consists of one star (the Sun) and nine planets, together with lesser bodies such as moons, minor planets or asteroids, comets and meteors. The outermost planet, Pluto, is not shown, but its orbit lies for the most part beyond that of Neptune, although once each revolution it comes closer than Neptune does to the Sun. The orbits of the planets all lie in nearly the same plane, unlike the more elliptical orbits of the comets (some of which are also shown).

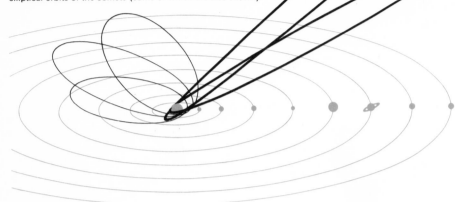

The Earth

At the centre of the Earth is a core of highly compressed material, probably mainly iron and nickel. Surrounding this is an outer core, believed to be molten. The main bulk of the Earth is its mantle, probably composed of compressed iron and magnesium silicates. The very thin outer crust is formed of the rocks that we know.

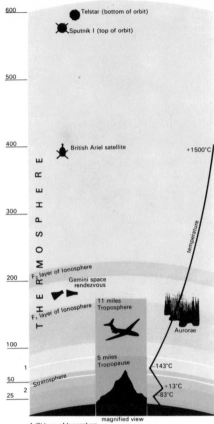

600 — Telstar (bottom of orbit)
Sputnik I (top of orbit)

500 —

400 — British Ariel satellite   +1500°C

300 —

200 — F₂ layer of Ionosphere
Gemini space rendezvous
11 miles Troposphere
F₁ layer of Ionosphere
Aurorae

100 —
5 miles Tropopause   −143°C
1 Stratosphere   +13°C
50 —
2 —   −83°C
25 —
magnified view

1 'E' layer of Ionosphere
2 'D' layer of Ionosphere

The Atmosphere

Surrounding the Earth is the atmosphere, approximately 600 miles deep and becoming progressively thinner with height. Most weather changes take place within five miles of the ground. Temperature alters with height, falling to below −83°C at a height of 10½ miles and beyond this rising to above 1500°C at 50 miles; yet since the air is so thin at this height we should experience no sensation of heat. The atmosphere protects us on the Earth from deadly X-rays, cosmic rays, and other forms of radiation from outer space.

The Moon

The Moon, with a diameter of 2,160 miles, is a little more than one quarter the size of the Earth, about which it orbits once a month at an average distance of 238,955 miles. It is our nearest neighbour in space. It has no water and no atmosphere of any kind, and its surface is barren and rocky. The dark patches are huge plains, the circular features are craters ringed by mountains and sometimes with a mountain in the centre. There are also a number of mountain ranges rising to over 20,000 feet.

The Galaxies

Our Solar System is very small compared with the distances of the stars from it or with the sizes and distances of galaxies. The Sun itself has a diameter of 965,000 miles and a surface temperature of 5000 °C. The nearest planet to the Sun is Mercury, which orbits at an average distance of 36 million miles. We, on our Earth, orbit at a distance of 93 million miles. Mars orbits at 142 million miles, the giant Jupiter at 484 million miles, and Pluto, the most distant planet from the Sun, at about 3,670 million miles. Yet these are small distances in space, for the nearest star to the Sun (which is itself a star) lies at a distance of 25,284,000,000 miles. The largest known star has a diameter 2,300 million times greater than that of the orbit of Uranus round the Sun.

Star distances are often expressed in light-years. One light-year is the distance that light travels in one year, that is 5,880,000,000,000 miles. The next nearest star to the Sun is $4\frac{1}{3}$ light-years away and other stars are far more distant still. All the stars we see in the night sky are part of a huge star-system, called a Galaxy. Our own Galaxy is spiral in shape, is about 100,000 light-years in diameter (the Sun is about 30,000 light-years from the centre of our Galaxy), and contains dust and gas as well as stars. From out in space it would look rather like the Galaxy in the lower picture, which is a photograph of a Galaxy in the constellation of Andromeda. Millions of spiral galaxies like our own or the Andromeda galaxy, are known to exist. There is also another type of galaxy, containing little or no dust or gas, which is elliptical in shape. Both elliptical and spiral galaxies are shown in the upper picture.

Galaxies are mostly found in groups, which may contain as many as a hundred or more separate galaxies. The nearest galaxies to us are the irregularly shaped ones known as the Nubeculae, or Magellanic Clouds; they form part of the local group of Galaxies to which our own Galaxy belongs. Galaxies are usually many millions of light-years apart and some have been observed at distances of thousands of millions of light-years.

1	Sun
2	Mercury
3	Venus
4	Mars
5	Neptune
6	Saturn
7	Jupiter
8	Uranus
9	Earth
10	Pluto

Our knowledge of our own Solar System is now being increased by our ability to fire probes into space. These shots fall into two broad categories; observation probes, which are satellites designed to carry complex instruments and to radio information back to Earth; and manned shots, which are designed to carry both instruments and people. Manned shots yield information about the reactions of the human body to the extreme conditions of space, giving us knowledge that may enable us in the future to land men on some of the other planets or moons. In 1957 the Russians launched the first satellite, which was an observing one, and in 1961 they first put a man into orbit.

Mars probe

On July 14–15, 1965, the American probe Mariner IV came close to Mars after a journey of 7½ months and 325 million miles. Weighing 575 pounds, it carried a television camera and other equipment and made scientific measurements during its long journey. When close to Mars, it transmitted television pictures back to Earth, and the one below shows that Mars has craters and seems to possess a surface much like the Moon. However, Mars has a very thin atmosphere and the white patches may be caused by frost on high ground. There is a possibility that plants of a simple kind exist on Mars.

The picture covers an area on Mars of 44 miles by almost 39 miles and was taken at a distance of 7,800 miles from the surface of the planet. Since its close approach to Mars, Mariner IV is now in permanent orbit round the Sun.

Venus probe

There have also been space probes to Venus and measurements from these indicate that Venus is a hot planet, probably too hot for life to exist there. After approaching Venus, a space probe, like Mariner IV, goes into orbit round the Sun.

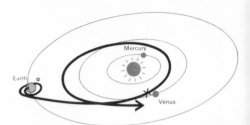

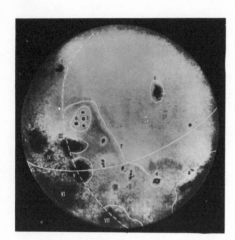

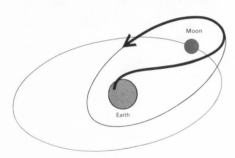

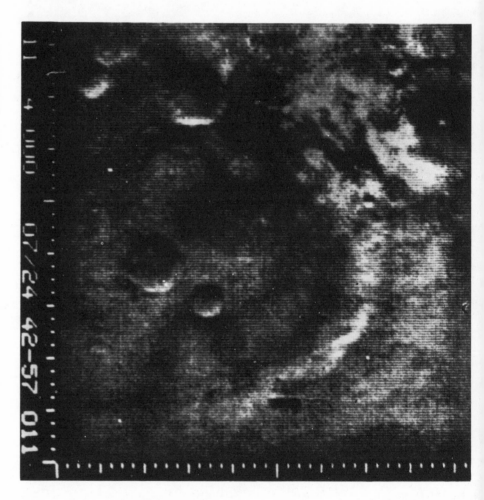

Moon probe

In October 1959, the Russian space probe Lunik III orbited the Moon and took photographs of its far side. Since the Moon rotates once on its axis every time it orbits the Earth, the same side is always facing us and the far side of the Moon cannot be observed from Earth. Lunik III (above) travelled in a curved path, going 'below' the Moon and then moving round it and appearing again 'above' the Moon. The photograph below was radioed back to Earth and shows that there are far fewer dark plains on the Moon's far side than on the side exposed to Earth.

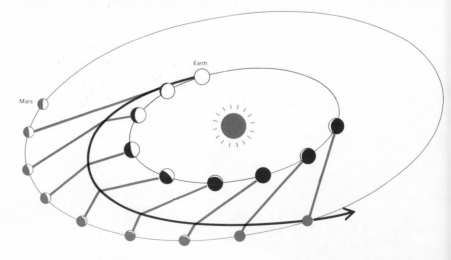

© Geographical Projects

Projection: Gall

Scale : 1 : 46,100,000 equatorial scale

Miles

| 0 | 500 | 1000 | 1500 |

Kilometres
| 500 | 1000 | 1500 | 2000 |

20

ARCTIC CIRCLE

TROPIC OF CANCER

EQUATOR

TROPIC OF CAPRICORN

ANTARCTIC CIRCLE

© Geographical Projects

4 Polar climates

4a Polar

4b Ice caps

5 Mountain climates

5 Mountain climates

The main factor controlling climate is the varying amount of solar energy that can reach the earth's surface. Because the earth is round the sun's rays hit its surface at different angles. When the rays are slanting to the earth the amount of heat received spreads over a larger area. This happens north and south of the tropics where the sun is never overhead, or in equatorial latitudes just after sunrise and before sunset each day. The total effect is to make the climate hotter near the equator and colder near the poles.

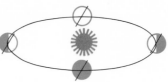

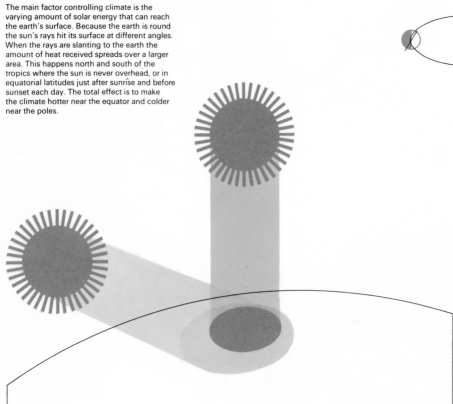

Summer solstice: northern hemisphere: sun is overhead at the Tropic of Cancer on June 22.

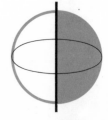

Spring and autumn equinoxes: sun is overhead at the Equator on March 21 and September 23.

Winter solstice: northern hemisphere: sun is overhead at the Tropic of Capricorn on December 22.

Polar easterlies: moving out of polar high pressure area

Low pressure belt of middle latitudes

Westerlies: winds of variable force and direction

Subtropical high pressure belt with variable winds

Trade winds: movement of air towards equatorial low pressure belt

Doldrums: equatorial low pressure belt

Tradewinds: movement of air towards equatorial low pressure belt

Subtropical high pressure belt with variable winds

Westerlies or 'Roaring Forties' of constant direction

Low pressure belt of middle latitudes

Polar easterlies: moving out of polar high pressure area

Pressure is an important property of the earth's atmosphere. At sea level the weight of the air above is greatest and pressure is highest, higher up the pressure becomes lower. In addition, warm air is lighter than cold air and therefore exerts less pressure. It is these differences in air pressure which cause the air to move, thus producing the winds. In general, warm light air from the equatorial regions rises and colder heavier air moves out from the higher pressure areas nearer the poles. The pattern of winds thus formed is complicated by three important factors: the spin of the earth which deflects wind to the right in the northern hemisphere and the left in the southern hemisphere; the tilt of the earth's axis which means that the sun is not always overhead at the same latitude; and the unequal distribution of land and sea which causes contrasts in the air temperatures.

Areas where the atmospheric pressure is high are called highs (or anticyclones) and where it is low depressions (or cyclones). In addition to the permanent pattern of high and low pressure bands round the earth, systems of anticyclones and cyclones also move across the earth, lasting for different lengths of time and being of varying intensity. In an anticyclone the air is sinking and gives rise to a period of relatively stable conditions, clear skies and often extremes of heat and cold.

In a cyclone the warm air rises and the cold air moves in to take its place causing unstable conditions, cloud and rain. The boundary zones between the different masses of air (dashed lines) are called fronts. Between the advancing cold air and the warm air it is termed the cold front and between the warm air and the cold air over which the warm air is being pushed it is termed the warm front.

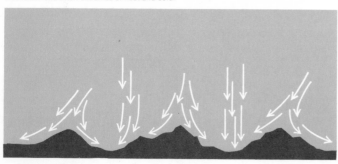

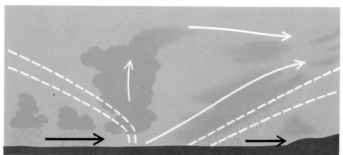

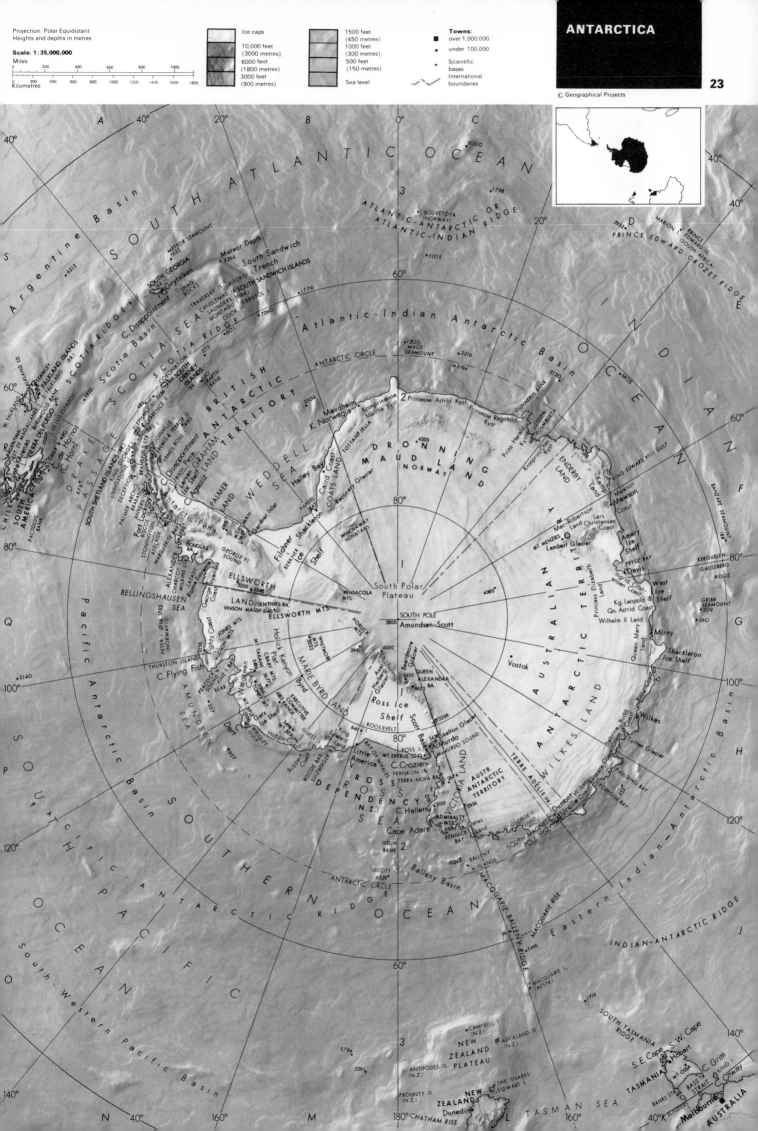

Projection: Polar Equidistant
Heights and depths in metres

Scale: 1:35,000,000

Miles
0   200   400   600   800   1000
Kilometres
0 200 400 600 800 1000 1200 1400 1600 1800

Ice caps

10,000 feet (3000 metres)
6000 feet (1800 metres)
3000 feet (900 metres)

1500 feet (450 metres)
1000 feet (300 metres)
500 feet (150 metres)
Sea level

Towns:
■ over 1,000,000
● under 100,000
• Scientific bases
International boundaries

ANTARCTICA

23

© Geographical Projects

ARCTIC OCEAN

Projection: Polar Equidistant
Heights and depths in metres

Scale: 1 : 30,000,000

Miles
0   200   400   600   800   1000

Kilometres
0   200   400   600   800   1000   1200   1400   1600

Ice caps

10,000 feet (3000 metres)
6000 feet (1800 metres)
3000 feet (900 metres)

1500 feet (450 metres)
1000 feet (300 metres)
500 feet (150 metres)
Sea level

International boundaries
Major air routes
Major sea routes

24

© Geographical Projects

A   Arctic Ocean

2000
Sea level 0
2000
4000

A   Atlantic Ocean

2000
Sea level 0
2000
4000
5000
8000

January:
Mean monthly temperatures

	over 30 C			over 86 F
	20 to 30			68 to 86
	10 to 20			50 to 68
	0 to 10			32 to 50
	0 to 10			14 to 32
	10 to 20			4 to 14
	below 20			below 4

July:
Mean monthly temperatures

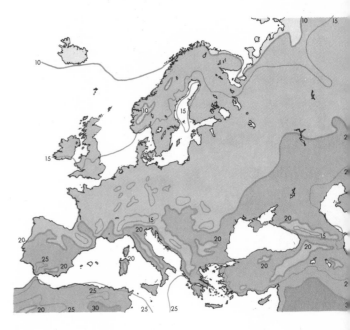

November–April:
Average seasonal rainfall

	over 100 cms			over 40 inches
	75 to 100			30 to 40
	50 to 75			20 to 30
	25 to 50			10 to 20
	12 5 to 25			5 to 10
	less than 12 5			less than 5

May–October:
Average seasonal rainfall

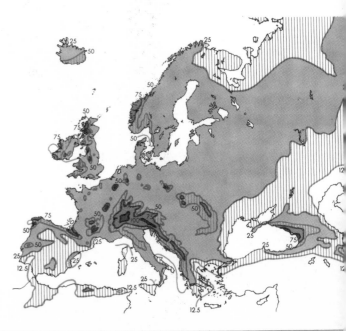

Europe has almost everywhere a sufficiently reliable rainfall and enough warmth to support a great variety of crops and trees and the climate as a whole is unusually favourable for human activity. Along the Mediterranean rain falls mostly during winter and summers are dry, hot and sunny, particularly inland in Spain, Italy, Bulgaria and Greece. Winters are mild beside the Mediterranean and Atlantic shores but become steadily colder inland, especially eastwards into Russia, and northwards into Sweden and Finland, although even in these northern countries the summers are warm. To the north of the Alps the prevailing winds are westerly and barometric disturbances bring the Atlantic air far into the continent in summer. Summer rainfall is much the same in amount from Oxford to Moscow. Cloud, rainfall and snowfall increase in the mountain regions, especially in autumn and winter on the western coasts and highlands in Scotland, Norway and the western Alps. The risk of spring frosts increases northwards, because Arctic air masses are liable to affect the whole of northern Europe up to the end of May. Occasionally warm air from the south-east may reach northern Europe and give a few days of very high summer temperatures, but such heatwaves are usually shortlived. In winter, east winds occasionally bring prolonged spells of severe cold to the western coasts.

Average number of days per year when frost is unlikely to occur

less than 60	
more than 60	
more than 90	
more than 120	
more than 180	
more than 240	
occasional frost	

Average number of hours sunshine per year

over 3000 hours	
2000 to 3000	
1000 to 2000	
less than 1000	

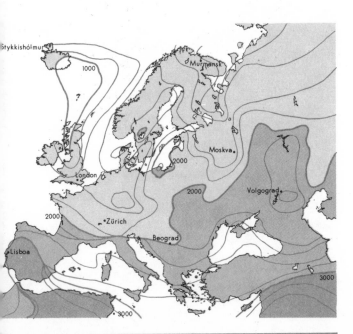

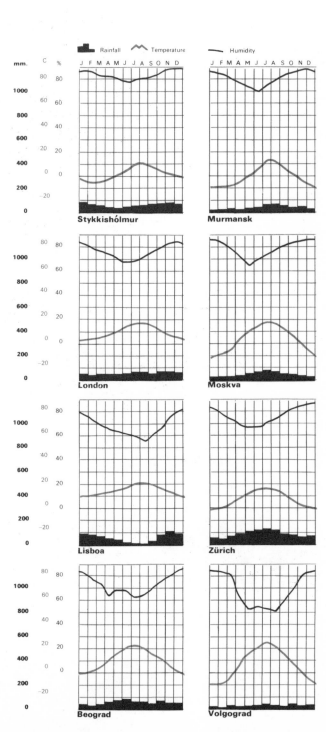

Rainfall   Temperature   Humidity

Stykkishólmur   Murmansk

London   Moskva

Lisboa   Zürich

Beograd   Volgograd

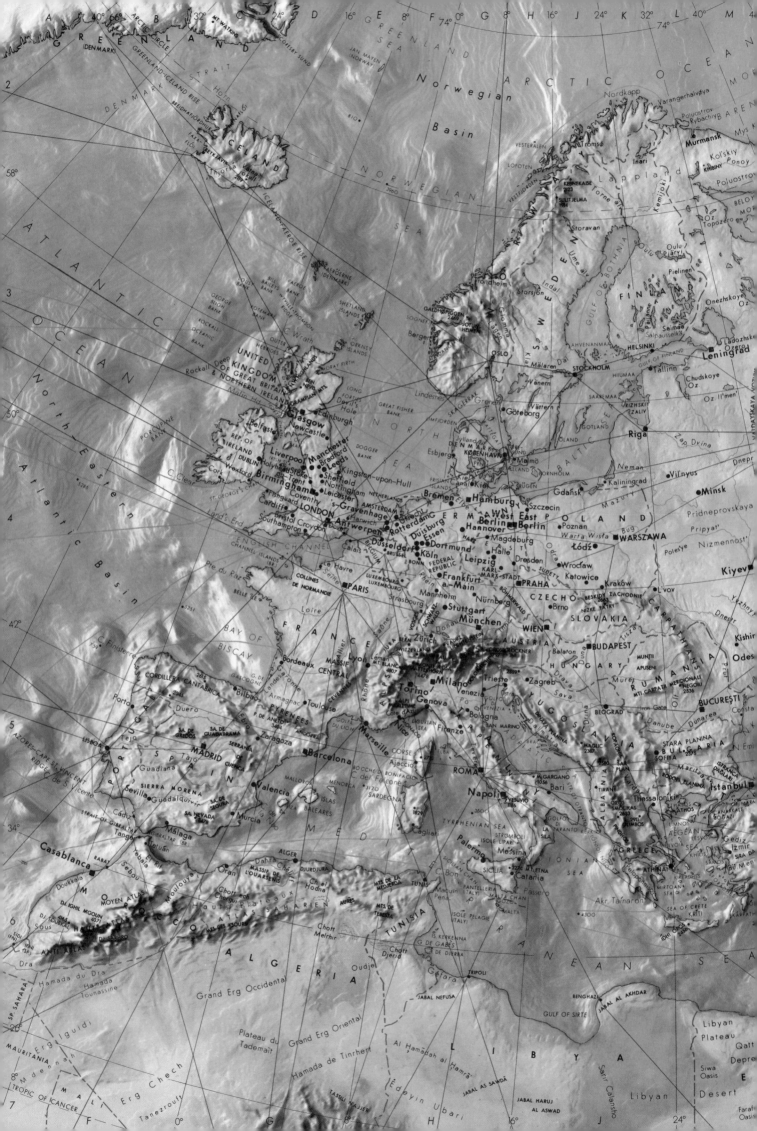

© Geographical Projects

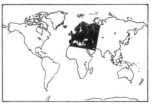

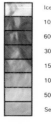

Ice caps

10,000 feet (3000 metres)

6000 feet (1800 metres)

3000 feet (900 metres)

1500 feet (450 metres)

1000 feet (300 metres)

500 feet (150 metres)

Sea level

Towns:

■ over 1,000,000

● over 500,000

● over 250,000

• under 250,000

 International boundaries

Boundaries under dispute

Major air routes

Major sea routes

Scale: 1 : 17,400,000

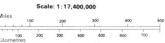

Miles | 100 | 200 | 300 | 400 | 500

Kilometres | 100 | 200 | 300 | 400 | 500 | 600 | 700

Projection: Azimuthal Equidistant
Heights and depths in metres

© Geographical Projects

Soils

■	Permanent ice	
▨	Yellow soils	*Pedalfers (non-lime accumulating soils) in humid, tropical regions, lateritic soils, soils of incomplete leaching*
▢	Podsols	*Pedalfers in sub-tropical and humid, temperate regions, podsolic soils, soils of incomplete leaching*
▤	Grey & brown forest soils	
▨	Terra Rossa	*Pedocals (lime-accumulating soils) in drier, subtropical regions, soils of impeded leaching*
▤	Grey soils	
■	Chernozems	*Pedocals in more temperate, less arid regions, soils of impeded leaching*
▨	Brown and chestnut soils	
↓↓	Tundra soils	*Pedocals in polar regions*
⁙	Mountain soils	*Intrazonal soils*
▨	Alluvial soils	
🌴	Oasis soils	
░	Sand – mainly dunes	

Land use

▢	Unproductive areas
■	Industrial & urban areas
▥	Hunting & gathering
▢	Stock rearing & ranging
▨	Intensive & specialised agriculture
▢	Mixed farming
▨	Forest lands
⌐	Lumbering
↕	Grain production predominant
Ψ	Nomadic economies
░	Deep sea fishing
⋯	Coastal fishing

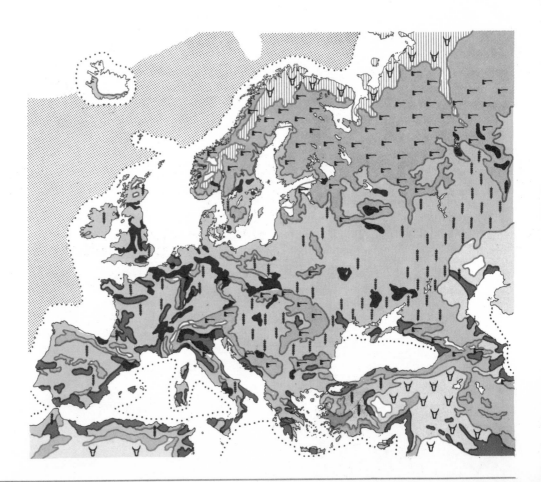

Power resources

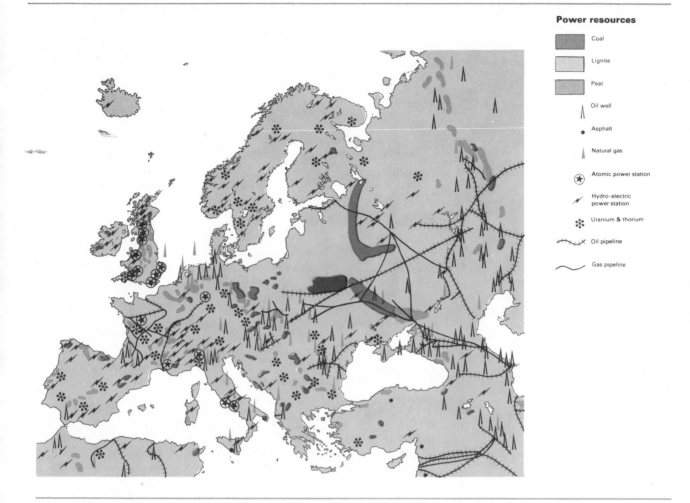

	Coal
	Lignite
	Peat
	Oil well
	Asphalt
	Natural gas
	Atomic power station
	Hydro-electric power station
	Uranium & thorium
	Oil pipeline
	Gas pipeline

Population density & Religions

	over 250 per sq. mile / over 100 per sq. km
	125 – 250 / 50 – 100
	60 – 125 / 25 – 50
	25 – 60 / 10 – 25
	2 – 25 / 1 – 10
	less than 2 / less than 1
	Roman Catholic
	Protestant
	Eastern Orthodox
	Judaism
	Muslim
	Tribal & others

© Geographical Projects

Projection: Azimuthal Equidistant

Scale: 1 : 20,300,000

Miles
0   100   200   300   400   500   600   700

Kilometres
0   100   200   300   400   500   600   700   800   900   1000   1100

• Capital cities

ARCTIC OCEAN

URAL'SKIY KHREBET

UNION OF SOVIET SOCIALIST REPUBLICS

CASPIAN SEA

BELOYE MORE

Sev. Dvina

Onezhskoye Ozero

Ladozhskoye Ozero

Chudskoye Ozero

FINLAND

Helsinki

GULF OF BOTHNIA

Moskva •

Don

Dnepr

Dnestr

Volga

Zap. Dvina

BOL'SHOY KAVKAZ

Kura

Tigris

Euphrates

Baghdad

SYRIA

LEBANON

Beirut

TURKEY

Ankara •

Tuz Gölü

CYPRUS • Nicosia

BLACK SEA

AZOVSKOYE MORE

Wisła

Warszawa •

POLAND

Odra

CZECHOSLOVAKIA

CARPATHIANS

RUMANIA

Bucureşti •

Donau

BULGARIA

Sofiya •

YUGOSLAVIA

Beograd •

Sava

Budapest •

HUNGARY

Wien •

AUSTRIA

Tiranë •

ALBANIA

GREECE

Athinai •

AEGEAN SEA

IONIAN SEA

Kríti

ARCTIC CIRCLE

NORWAY

SWEDEN

Stockholm •

Oslo •

Vänern

GOTLAND

BALTIC SEA

BORNHOLM

DENMARK

København •

NORTH SEA

NETHERLANDS

Amsterdam •

GERMANY

Elbe

EAST GERMANY

Karl-Marx-Stadt

Praha •

FEDERAL REPUBLIC

Bonn •

Rhein

BELGIUM

Brussel •

LUXEMBOURG

Luxembourg •

SWITZERLAND

Bern •

Vaduz

LIECHTENSTEIN

ALPS

Donau

MONACO

SAN MARINO

ITALY

Roma •

CORSE

SARDEGNA

TYRRHENIAN SEA

SICILIA

PANTELLERIA

Valletta •

MALTA

ISOLA PELAGIE

MEDITERRANEAN SEA

FRANCE

Paris •

Seine

Rhône

ANDORRA

PYRENEES

SPAIN

Madrid •

Duero

Tajo

ISLAS BALEARES

PORTUGAL

Lisboa •

Gibraltar (Br.)

MOROCCO

Rabat •

ALGERIA

Alger •

TUNISIA

Tunis •

HAUT ATLAS

ATLANTIC OCEAN

NORWEGIAN SEA

ICELAND

Reykjavík •

FAROE ISLANDS (DENMARK)

SHETLAND ISLANDS

UNITED KINGDOM OF GREAT BRITAIN & NORTHERN IRELAND

London •

REPUBLIC OF IRELAND

Dublin •

Land's End

ENGLISH CHANNEL

BAY OF BISCAY

C. Finisterre

ARCTIC CIRCLE

ADRIATIC SEA

1500–1650

ICELAND
Danish

FAERÖERNE
Danish

BRITISH ISLES

RUSSIA

Dan.
1570–1645

EAST
PRUSSIA

REP. of
UNITED
PROVINCES

SPANISH
NETHERLANDS

HOLY
ROMAN
EMPIRE
1648

KINGDOM
of POLAND

KINGDOM
of
FRANCE

SWISS
CONFEDERATION

IMPERIAL
HUNGARY

Span.
ITALIAN
STATES

PAPAL
STATES

MONTE-
NEGRO

PORTUGAL

SPAIN

CORSICA
Genoa

SARDINIA
Span.

K. of the
TWO
SICILIES
Span.

Venice

OTTOMAN EMPIRE

Tangier Ceuta Span. 1580
Port.
1471

Oran

MOROCCO

MALTA
Span.

CRETE
Venice

1650–1763 (Treaty of Paris)

ICELAND
Danish

FAERÖERNE
Danish

BRITISH ISLES

RUSSIAN
EMPIRE

UNITED
PROVS.

FRANCE

HOLY
ROMAN
EMPIRE

KINGDOM
of POLAND

SWITZERLAND

K. of
HUNGARY

ITALIAN
STATES

PAPAL
STATES

MONTE-
NEGRO

PORTUGAL

SPAIN

Gibraltar
Br. 1704

MINORCA
Br. 1713

CORSICA
Genoa

SARDINIA
Savoy 1720

Austrian 1714–20

K. of the
TWO
SICILIES
Austrian 1720
Span. 1735

Venice

OTTOMAN EMPIRE

Tangier
Br.
1662

Ceuta Span.

MOROCCO

ALGIERS
Ind. 1710

TUNIS

MALTA
Knights of
St. John

CRETE
Turkish 1669

1763–1830

ICELAND
Danish

NORWAY
Ind. Kingdom
1815

FINLAND
to Russia
1808

FAERÖERNE
Danish

UNITED KINGDOM
of GT. BRITAIN
& IRELAND

Act of Union 1801

KINGDOMS
of
NORWAY
& SWEDEN
1816

DENMARK

K. of the
NETHER-
LANDS

RUSSIAN
EMPIRE

PRUSSIA

BELGIUM
1830

GERMAN
CONFED.

FRANCE

Russia
1812

SWITZERLAND

AUSTRIAN EMPIRE

PORTUGAL

SPAIN

ITALIAN
STATES

K. of SARDINIA

PAPAL
STATES

Fr.
1768

MONTE-
NEGRO

Gibraltar
Br.

Span.

K. of the
TWO
SICILIES

OTTOMAN EMPIRE

Algiers
Fr. 1830

MOROCCO

TUNIS

MALTA
Br. 1800

Br.
1809–14

GREECE
1830

1830–1878 (Congress of Berlin)

ICELAND
limited home
rule 1874

FAERÖERNE
Danish

UNITED KINGDOM
of GT. BRITAIN
& IRELAND

KINGDOMS
of
NORWAY
& SWEDEN

DENMARK

NETHER-
LANDS

RUSSIAN
EMPIRE

LUXEMBOURG
Netherlands

PRUSSIA
GERMAN
EMPIRE

BELGIUM

FRANCE

AUSTRIAN EMPIRE

SWITZERLAND

SAVOY
Fr. 1860

BOSNIA
Austrian
Prot. 1878

SERVIA
Ind.
1878

RUMANIA
Ind.

BULGARIA
Principality 1878

E. RUMELIA
Aut. prov. 1878

NICE
Fr. 1860

ITALY
unification
1859–1870

PORTUGAL

SPAIN

Gibraltar
Br.

MOROCCO

ALGERIA

TUNIS
Fr.
Prot. 1881

MALTA
Br.

GREECE

OTTOMAN EMPIRE

CYPRUS
Br. Prot. 1878

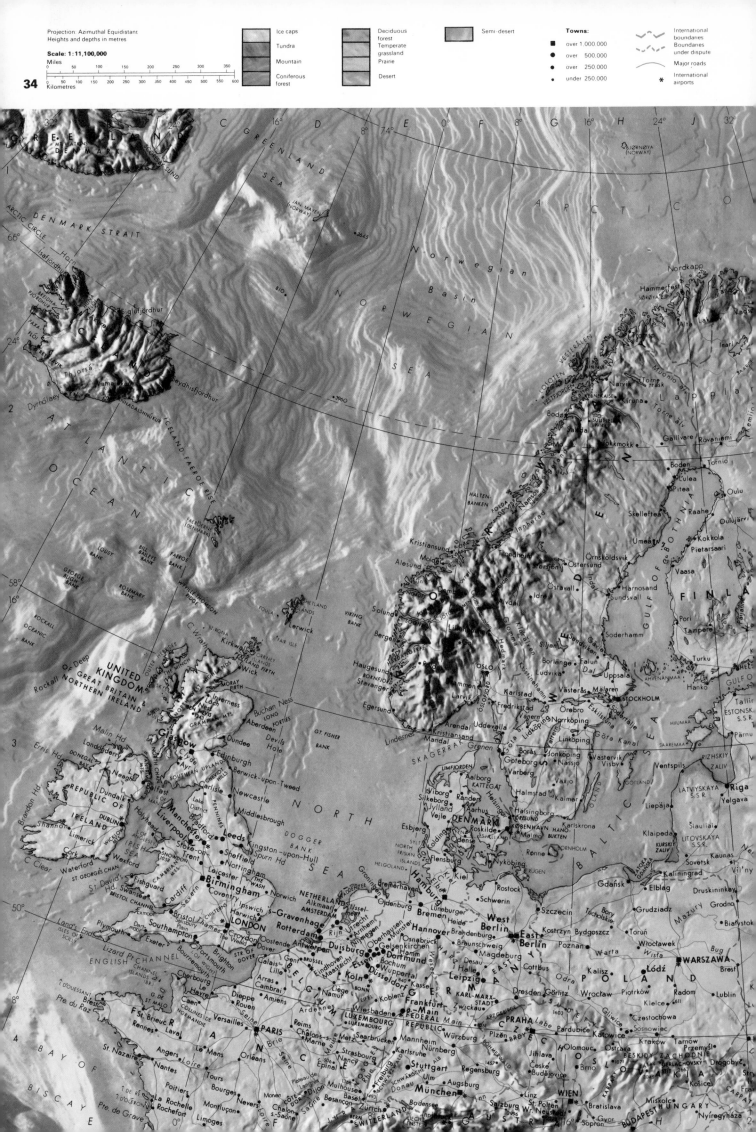

Projection: Azimuthal Equidistant
Heights and depths in metres

Scale: 1:11,100,000

Miles
0   50   100   150   200   250   300   350
0 50 100 150 200 250 300 350 400 450 500 550 600
Kilometres

34

Ice caps
Tundra
Mountain
Coniferous forest

Deciduous forest
Temperate grassland
Prairie
Desert

Semi-desert

Towns:
over 1,000,000
over 500,000
over 250,000
under 250,000

International boundaries
Boundaries under dispute
Major roads
International airports

2

MORE

BARENTSOVO MORE

NOVAYA ZEMLYA

KARSKOYE MORE

PECHORSKOYE MORE

BAYDARATSKAYA GUBA

OSTROV KOLGUYEV

CHESHSKAYA GUBA

Mys Kanin Nos

Poluostrov Kanin

•Murmansk

Arctic Circle

Nar'yan Mar

Pechora

Amderma

Yugorskiy Pov.

Ob'

Vorkuta

•Berezovo

Khanty-Mansiysk

Irtysh

80°

72°

66°

P

Q

KOL'SKIY Poluostrov

CHIBINY 1240

Kirovsk

Kandalaksha

KANDALAKSHSKAYA GUBA

Mezen'

Izhma•

Ukhta

Sosnogorsk

Yarega

•Kozhva

•Kadzherom

Usa

KRYAZH CHERNYSHEVA

PRIPOLARNY. URAL

G.NARODNAYA 1894

Ivdel

Tura

Turinsk

Tavda

•Tyumen'

Yalutorovsk

Ishim

58°

72°

Topozero

BELOYE MORE

Arkhangel'sk

Pinega

Mezen'

Pechora

Zheleznodorozhnyy

SREDNIY URAL

G.DENEZHKIN KAMEN' 1492

Kal'ya•

Severoural'sk

Krasnotur'insk

Serov

•Sos'va

Severnaya Sev. Sos'va

Tobol'sk

Belomorsk

DVINSKAYA GUBA

ONEZHSKAYA GUBA

Severodvinsk

Onega

Severnaya Dvina

Sol'vychegodsk

Vychegda

Syktyvkar

Krasnovishersk

Cherdyn•

Borovsk

Karpinsk

Nizh. Tura

Verkh Tura

Nizhn'iy Tagil

Alapayevsk

Artemovskiy

Bogdanovich

Kamensk-Ural'skiy

Shadrinsk

Kurgan

Petukhovo

KARELO-FINSKAYA S.S.R.

Nadvoitsy

Belomorsko-Baltiyskiy K.

Kotlas

Velikiy Ustyug

Sukhona

Sozimskiy•

Kirs•

Solikamsk•

Berezniki

Kizel•

Gubakha

Chusovoy

Lys'va

Nizhniy Tagil

Sverdlovsk

Asbest

Revda

•Pervoural'sk

Artl

Sergi

Medvezh'yegorsk

Onezhskoye Ozero

Pudozh

Kargopol•

Konosha•

Vel'sk•

Glazov•

Krasnokamsk

Perm

Kungur

Krasnoufimsk

Nyazepetrovsk

Zlatoust

Chelyabinsk

Kopeysk

Shumikha

Petrozavodsk

Ladozhskoye Ozero

Syas'

Vytegra

Kharovsk•

Slobodskoy•

Nolinsk•

Sarapul•

Satka•

Bakal

Miass

Korkino

Troitsk

Kustanay

Podporozh'ye

Lodeynoye Pole

Belozersk•

Kirov•

Novo-Vyatsk•

Votkinsk•

Izhevsk•

Birsk•

Min'yar

Chernikovsk

Yuryuzan'

Beloretsk

Magnitogorsk

Kartaly

Priozersk

Nov Ladoga

Volkhov

Vologda•

Buy•

Kotel'nich•

Vyatka

Kama

Menzelinsk•

Ufa

Oktyabr'skiy

Davlekanovo

Mednogorsk

Orsk

50°

Vyborg

Leningrad

Pavlovsk

Tikhvin

Cherepovets•

Rybinskoye Vdkhr.

Rybinsk

Kostroma

Kineshma

Gor'kovskoye Vdkhr.

Yoshkar Ola•

Naberezhnyye Chelny

Bugul'ma•

Buguruslan•

Buzuluk•

Orenburg

Luga

Oz. Il'men

Bologoye•

Vyshniy-Volochek

Yaroslavl'•

Vichuga

Cheboksary

Kazan'

Meleess

Bol. Kinel'

OBSHCHIY SYRT

Ural

Staraya Russa

VALDAYSKAYA VOZVYSHENNOST'

Kalinin

Rostov•

Ivanovo

Shuya

Gor'kiy

Volga

Kuybyshevskoye Vdkhr.

Ulyanovsk

Kuybyshev

Chapayevsk

Aktyubinsk

Pskov

Ostrov

Taldom•

Teykovo•

Kovrov

Dzerzhinsk

Sergach•

Alatyr'•

Syzran'

Ural'sk•

Velikiye Luki

Rzhev

Vladimir•

Murom

Saransk•

Penza•

Vol'sk

MOSKVA

Kuntsevo

Lyublino

Yegor'yevsk

Meshchorskaya Nizina

Kuznetsk

Balakovo

Nevel'

Zap Dvina

Vyaz'ma•

Noginsk

Kolomna

Oka

Ryazan'•

Morshansk•

Sura

Engel's

Saratov

Polotsk

Vitebsk•

Smolensk•

Kaluga•

Tula

Stalinogorsk

Okso-Donskaya

Michurinsk

Tambov

Lipetsk

Rasskazovo

Serdobsk•

Atkarsk•

BELORUSSKAYA S.S.R.

Orsha•

Kirov

Roslavl'•

Bezhitsa

Bryansk

Orel

Donskaya Nizmennost'

Khopër

Balashov•

Novo Uzensk•

Minsk

Mogilev•

Klintsy•

Yelets•

Borisoglebsk•

Uryupinsk•

Kamyshin

PRIVOLZHSKAYA VOZVYSHENNOST'

KASPIYSKAYA Nizmennost'

Bobruysk•

Novozybkov•

Voronezh

Liski•

Nikolayevskiy•

Pesk

Slutsk•

Gomel•

Shostka•

Kursk•

Don

SREDNE-RUSSKAYA VOZVYSHENNOST'

Volgograd

Gur'yev

Kul'sary

Pripyat'

Mozyr'•

Chernigov•

Bakhmach

Konotop

Sumy•

Belgorod•

Kalach na-Donu

Astrakhan'

Kiyev

Berdichev•

Zhmerinka•

Priluki•

Poltava•

Khar'kov

DONETSKIY KR.

KAZAKHSTANSKAYA S.S.R.

YERGENI

Kuma

CASPIAN SEA

Poluostrov Buzachi

56°

40°

48°

L

M

2

3

4

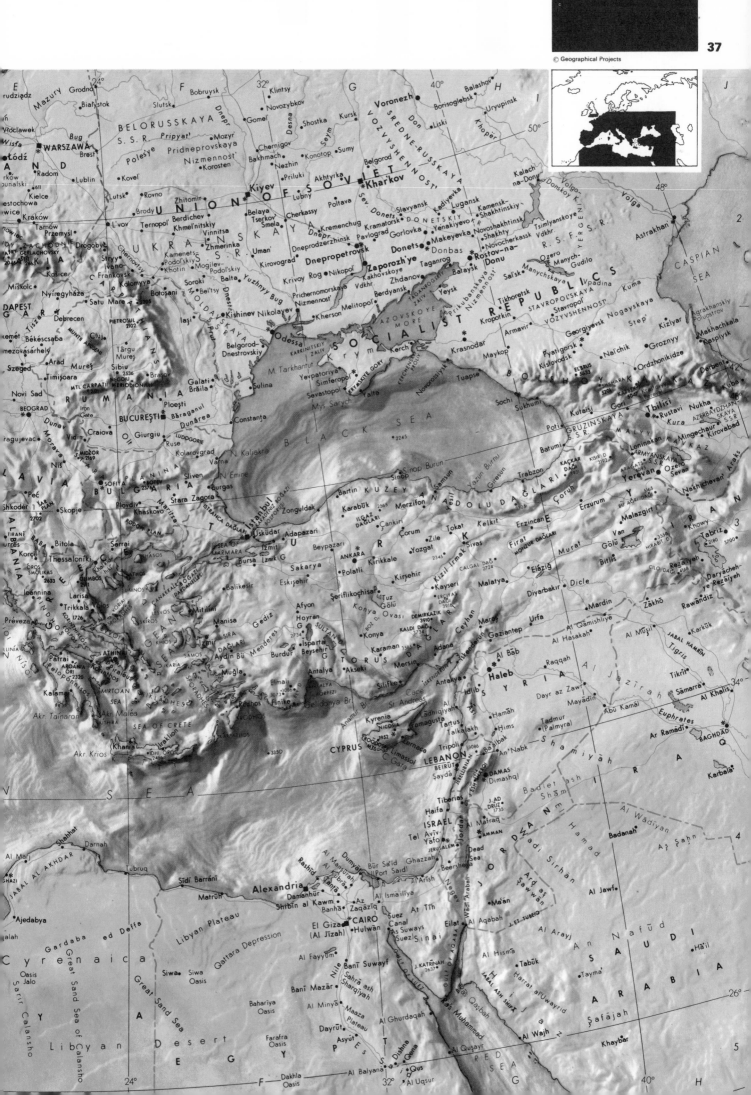

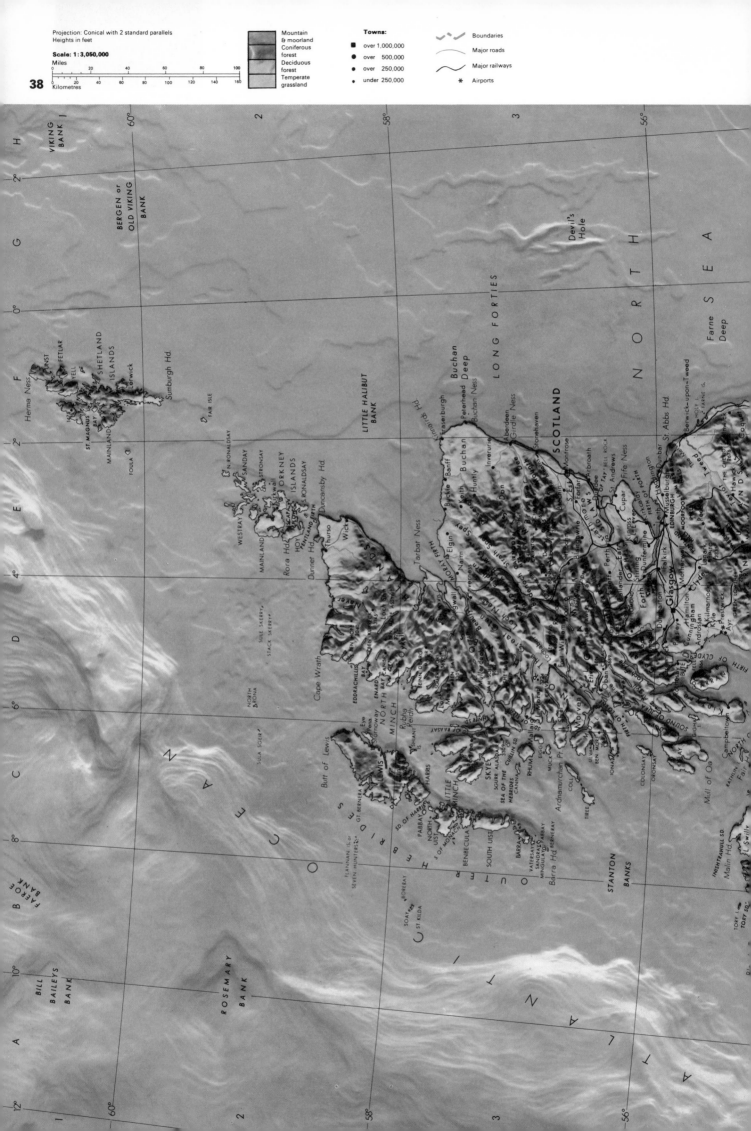

Projection: Conical with 2 standard parallels
Heights in feet

Scale: 1 : 3,050,000

Miles
0   20   40   60   80   100

0   20   40   60   80   100   120   140   160
Kilometres

Mountain
& moorland

Coniferous
forest

Deciduous
forest

Temperate
grassland

Towns:

■ over 1,000,000

● over 500,000

● over 250,000

• under 250,000

〰️ Boundaries

Major roads

Major railways

✳ Airports

VIKING BANK I

BERGEN or
OLD VIKING
BANK

Devil's
Hole

LONG FORTIES

N O R T H   S E A

Farne
Deep

LITTLE HALIBUT
BANK

SCOTLAND

Buchan
Deep

Fraserburgh
Peterhead
Buchan Ness

Aberdeen
Girdle Ness
Stonehaven

Montrose
Arbroath

St. Andrews

Fife Ness

Berwick-upon-Tweed

HOLY IS.
FARNE IS.

St. Abbs Hd.

Dunbar
Haddington

EDINBURGH

Peebles
Hawick

SHETLAND
ISLANDS

Herma Ness
UNST
FETLAR
YELL

ST. MAGNUS
BAY
MAINLAND
Lerwick

FOULA

Sumburgh Hd.

FAIR ISLE

N. RONALDSAY
SANDAY
STRONSAY

WESTRAY
MAINLAND
Kirkwall
HOY
S. RONALDSAY
ORKNEY
ISLANDS

Rora Hd.
PENTLAND FIRTH
Duncansby Hd.
Dunnet Hd.

Thurso
Wick

Tarbet Ness

MORAY FIRTH
Elgin
Nairn
Inverness

Forres
Keith
Banff
Huntly
Inverurie

Spey

Don
Dee

Cape Wrath

SULE SKERRY
STACK SKERRY

NORTH
RONA

SULA SGEIR

Butt of Lewis

Eye
Pena
Stornoway

LEWIS

HARRIS

SD. OF HARRIS

PABBAY
NORTH
UIST

BENBECULA
SOUTH UIST

BARRA
VATERSAY
SANDRAY
MINGULAY
BERNERAY
Barra Hd.

FLANNAN IS. or
SEVEN HUNTERS

SOAY
BORERAY
ST KILDA

SKYE
SCUIR ALASDAIR
CUILLIN SD.
SEA OF THE
HEBRIDES
CANNA

RHUM
EIGG
MUCK

COLL
TIREE

Ardnamurchan Pt.

IONA
COLONSAY
ORONSAY

Mull of Oa
Campbeltown
RATHLIN I.
Fair Hd.

STANTON
BANKS

INISHTRAHULL SD.
Malin Hd.

TORY I.
TORY SD.
L. SWILLY

Glasgow
Hamilton
Motherwell
Lanark
Paisley
Cunningham
Ardrossan
Kilmarnock
Kyle
Ayr
Prestwick

BUTE
ARRAN

FIRTH OF CLYDE

FIRTH OF LORNE
SOUND OF JURA

Oban
Morven

Mallaig

MULL

O U T E R   H E B R I D E S

N O R T H   M I N C H

LITTLE
MINCH

RAASAY
OF RAASAY

Rubha
Reidh

ENARD
BAY

NORTH
BAY

EDDRACHILLIS
BAY

A T L A N T I C   O C E A N

ROSEMARY
BANK

FAEROE
BANK

BILL
BAILEY'S
BANK

Stirling
Dunfermline
FIRTH OF FORTH
Falkirk

Perth
Dundee

Forfar

Blairgowrie

Ballater
Braemar

Callander

Crieff

Dumbarton

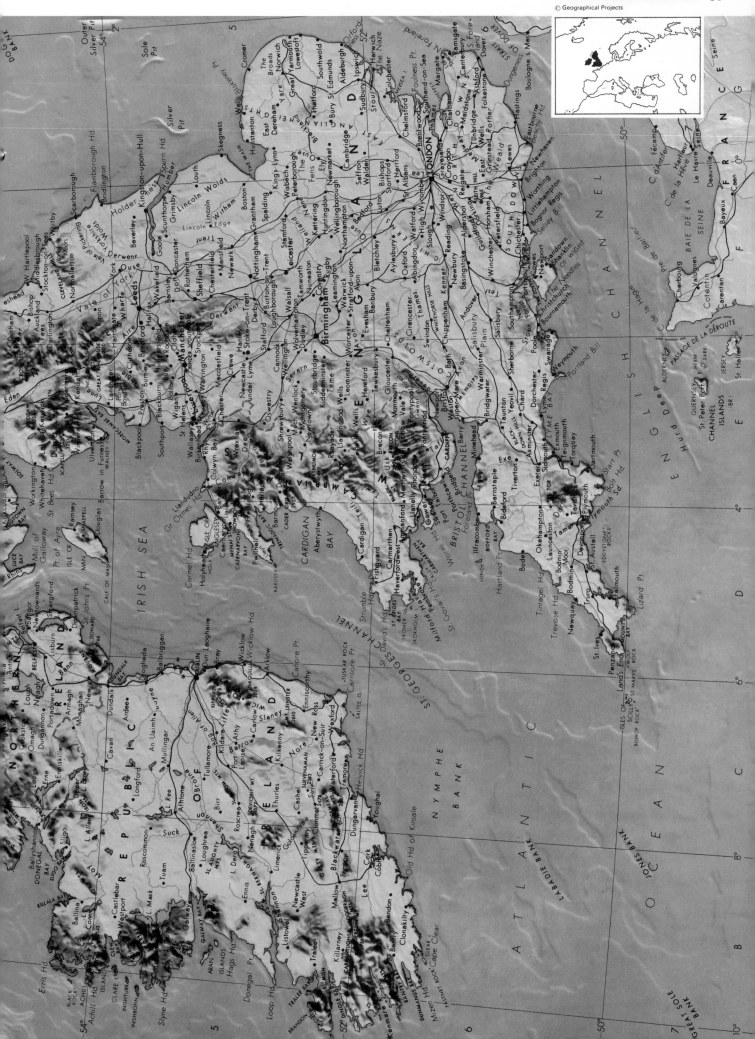

Soils

Podsols	*Pedalfers in humid, temperate regions, podsolic soils, soils of in- complete leaching*
Gleys	
Brown forest soils	
Acid brown soils	
Calcareous soils	*Pedocals in temp erate, less arid regions, soils of impeded leaching*
Mountain and upland soils	*Intrazonal soils*
Warp and warp gley soils (alluvial)	
Peat	

Power resources

Coal	
Peat	
Oil well	
Shale oil well	
Natural gas	
Atomic power station	
Hydro-electric power station	
Peat-fired power-station	
Uranium	

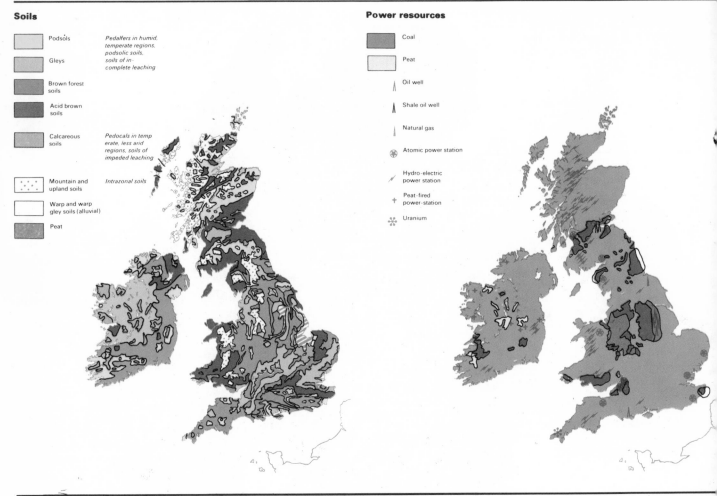

Land use

Unproductive areas	
Industrial & urban areas	
Intensive & specialised agriculture, orchards	
Mixed farming	
Meadowland	
Rough pasture	
Forest lands	
Grain production predominant	
Deep sea fishing	
Coastal fishing	

Population density

Over 500 per sq. mile	
250—500	
125—250	
60—125	
30—60	
15—30	
less than 15	

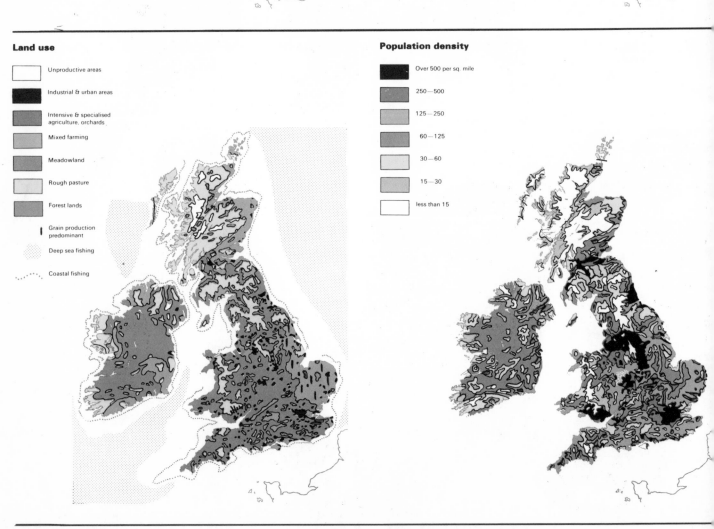

Projection: Conic
Heights in feet

Scale: 1: 810,800

Miles
0   5   10   15   20   25

Kilometres
0   5   10   15   20   25   30   35

Towns:
● over 100,000
• under 100,000

▨ Greater London area

County boundaries
Major railways
Cross-Channel ferries
✳ Airports

© Geographical Projects

Projection: Conical with 2 standard parallels
Heights in feet

Scale: 1:1,430,000

Miles
0   10   20   30   40

Kilometres
0   10   20   30   40   50   60   70

Towns:
● over 500,000
● over 100,000
• under 100,000

〰 National boundaries
〰 County boundaries
〰 Major railways
✳ Airports

2°   G   1°   H   0°   J   1°   I   2°

SCOTLAND   56°

St. Abbs Head
Eyemouth
Greenlaw
dstream
Kelso
Whiteadder
Berwick-upon-Tweed
HOLY I.
FARNE IS.
2
Wooler
Belford
THE CHEVIOT 2676
Till
Coquet
Alnwick
Rothbury
NORTHUMBERLAND
Morpeth
Wansbeck
Blyth
Tyne
llingham
Blyth
North Shields
Whitley Bay
Tynemouth
South Shields
Corbridge
Newcastle
Jarrow
altwhistle Hexham
Tyne
Gateshead
Sunderland
Team Valley
Chester le Street
Seaham Harbour
Allendale Town
Derwent
Consett
Hetton-le-Hole
Easington
Durham
Peterlee
DURHAM
Stanhope
Wolsingham
Crook
Spennymoor
Ferryhill
Hartlepool
St. John's Chapel
Bishop Auckland
West Hartlepool
FELL
Middleton in Teesdale
W. Auckland
Sedgefield
Redcar
opleby
Barnard Castle
Newton Aycliffe
Saltburn
Loftus
Stockton on Tees
Middlesbrough
Whitby
WESTMORLAND
Darlington
Thornaby
Guisborough
Brough
Kirkby Stephen
Yarm
Egton
Robin Hood's Bay
Reeth
Richmond
Stokesley
CLEVELAND HILLS
Swale
Catterick
Northallerton
Yorkshire Moors
Leyburn
Middleham
Kirby Moorside
Scarborough
Wensleydale
Bedale
HAMBLETON HILLS
Pickering
Hawes
Thirsk
Helmsley
Vale of Pickering
Filey
WHERNSIDE 2414
Masham
Hunmanby
GT. WHERNSIDE 2310
Ripon
Nidd
Y O R K
Malton
EBOROUGH
Pateley Bridge
Ure
Easingwold
Yorkshire Wold
Flamborough Head
Settle
Boroughbridge
Bridlington
als
Airi
Ripley
Great Driffield
BRIDLINGTON BAY
Knaresborough
yland
Gap
Wharfedale
Harrogate
Dewent
York
Hornsea
Skipton
Ilkley
Otley
Wetherby
Pocklington
Holderness
Keighley
Wharfe
Tadcaster
Beverley
Clitheroe
Bingley
Horsforth
Aberford
Market Weighton
Nelson
Colne
Shipley
Leeds
Sherburn in Elmet
Kingston-upon-Hull
Burnley
Bradford
Pudsey
Castleford
Selby
Withernsea
Accrington
Halifax
Birstall
Morley
Ouse
Patrington
ingden
Todmorden
Brighouse
Batley
Ferrybridge
Goole
Barton
urn
Elland
Wakefield
Knottingley
Snaith
Immingham
Humber
Spurn Head
awtenstall
Littleborough
Pontefract
Grimsby
bottom
Rochdale
Huddersfield
Crowle
Scunthorpe
Cleethorpes
wich
Bury
Heywood
Kirkburton
Isle of Axholme
Brigg
N. Somercotes
Radcliffe
Middleton
Penistone
Barnsley
Epworth
Caistor
Saltfleet
orth
Salford
Oldham
Doncaster
Kirton
LINCOLN WOLD
Louth
igh
Ashton under Lyne
Mexborough
Bawtry
Gainsborough
Market Rasen
Mablethorpe
rincham
Stalybridge
Rotherham
Wragby
Alford
Sale
Manchester
Glossop
Sheffield
East Retford
Lincoln
Horncastle
Burgh le Marsh
Knutsford
KINDER SCOUT 2088
Worksop
Branston
Spilsby
Skegness
Northwich
Chapel-en-le-Frith
Dronfield
Eckington
Ollerton
Tuxford
Wainfleet
Gibraltar Point
Macclesfield
Staveley
DERBY
Chesterfield
Mansfield
Southwell
Newark
Tattershall
53°
Middlewich
Buxton
Bakewell
Sherwood Forest
Congleton
Leek
Longnor
Matlock
Alfreton
Wirksworth
Belper
Cranwell
Sleaford
Boston
Hunstanton
Wells
Blakeney Point
Sheringham
Crewe
Nantwich
Tunstall
Burslem
Hanley
Ashbourne
Ripley
Hucknall Torkard
Heanor
Southwell
NOTTINGHAM
Swineshead
NORFOLK
Holt
Cromer
Newcastle under Lyme
Cheadle
Ilkeston
Nottingham
Sleaford
Holbeach
THE WASH
Mundesley
Longton
Stoke-on-Trent
Derby
Long Eaton
Bottesford
Grantham
Donnington
Holbeach Marsh
NORFOLK EDGE
Fakenham
East Dereham
North Walsham
Stone
Uttoxeter
Trent Junction
Colsterworth
Long Sutton
King's Lynn
Wensum
Aylsham
The Broads
Eccleshall
Abbots Bromley
Tutbury
Repton
bourne
Spalding
Yare
Norwich
Gt. Yarmouth
Stafford
Rugeley
Ashby de la Zouch
Loughborough
Melton Mowbray
Market Deeping
swaffham
NORTH SEA

55°
54°
2° 3° 4° 5°

SCOTLAND

© Geographical Projects

Towers:
- ● over 500,000
- ● over 100,000
- • under 100,000

- National boundaries
- County boundaries
- Major railways
- ✳ Airports

Scale: 1:1,430,000

Projection: Conical with 2 standard parallels
Heights in feet

IRELAND

Towns:

- over 500,000
- over 100,000
- under 100,000

National boundaries

County boundaries

Major railways

* Airports

Scale: 1:1,430,000

Miles
0 10 20 30 40

Kilometres
0 10 20 30 40 50 60

Projection: Conical with 2 standard parallels
Heights in feet

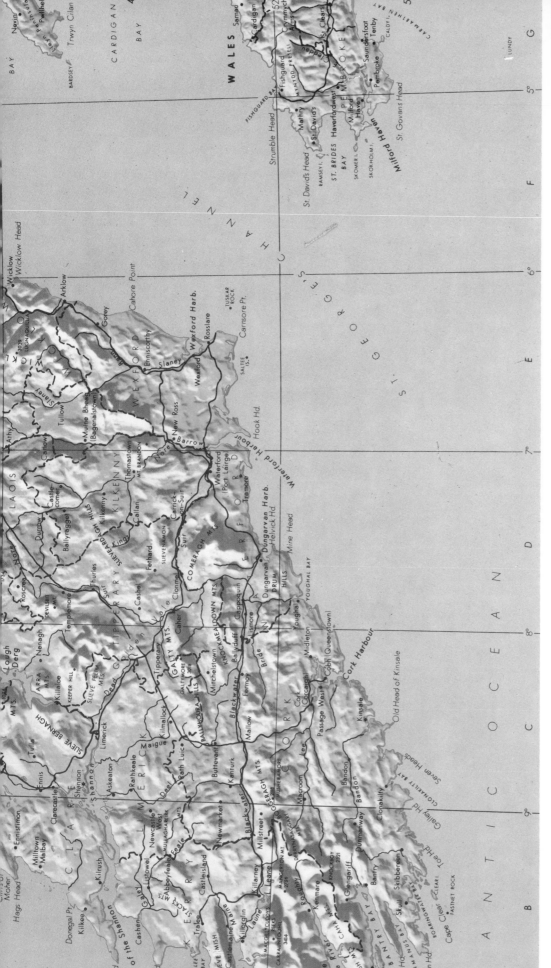

Towns:

- ■ over 1,000,000
- ● over 500,000
- ● over 100,000
- • under 100,000

 International boundaries

Major railways

Ferry

✳ Airports

Scale: 1 : 6,100,000

Miles
0 20 40 60 80 100 120 140 160 180

Kilometres
0 20 40 60 80 100 120 140 160 180 200 220 240 260 280

Projection: Conic
Conical Orthomorphic
Heights in metres

SPAIN & PORTUGAL

53

© Geographical Projects

Towns:

- ■ over 1,000,000
- ● over 500,000
- ● over 100,000
- • under 100,000

〜〜 International boundaries

〜 Major railways

✳ International airports

Scale: 1:3,250,000

Miles
0 20 40 60 80 100

Kilometres
0 20 40 60 80 100 120 140

Projection: Modified Polyconic
Heights in metres

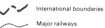

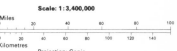

HOLLAND & BELGIUM

© Geographical Projects

Projection: Conic
Heights in metres

Scale: 1:2,000,000

Miles
0 10 20 30 40 50 60 70

Kilometres
0 10 20 30 40 50 60 70 80 90 100 110

Towns:
● over 500,000
● over 100,000
● under 100,000

〜 International boundaries
〜 Major railways
〜 Polders under construction
✳ International airports

NORTH SEA

NETHERLANDS

EAST FRISIAN ISLANDS

WANGEROOGE SPIEKEROOG LANGEOOG BALTRUM NORDERNEY JUIST BORKUM ROTTUMEROOG

Oster Ems Wester Ems Wester Eems Oster Ems

NORDERNEY Norden Harlinger Land Aurich Ostfriesland Emden Ammerland Westerstede Leer Saterland DOLLARD Ammerland

TERSCHELLING AMELAND SCHIERMONNIKOOG ROTTUMERPLAAT BOSCHPLAAT SIMONSZAND ROTTUMEROOG

BOOMKENSDIEP AMELANDER GAT PINKE GAT FRIESCHE GAT GRONINGER WAD

VLIELAND TERSCHELLINGER WAD FRIESCHE WAD LAUWERS ZEE

ENGELSMANPLAAT WAARD GRONDEN

Franeker Dokkum Leeuwarden Groningen Helpman Delfzijl Bedum Reit diep Eemskanaal Hoogezand Winschoten GRO... Leer Saterland Arenberg

Harlingen Huizum Drachten FRIESLAND

WADDEN-ZEE

TEXEL Den Helder Schagen Wieringer-meer Medemblik Workum Bolsward Sneek Joure Heerenveen Tjonger Assen O.-Musselkanaal Meppen Quakenbrück

SCHULPENGAT MARSDIEP Koegras Balgzand IJsselmeer Staveren De Lemmer Wolvega DRENTHE Emmen Hoogeveen Coevorden Lingen Nordhorn Bramsche

Alkmaar Hoorn Enkhuizen (Zuiderzee) Noordoost-polder Steenwijk Meppel Almelo Oldenzaal Osnabrück Ibbenbüren Lengerich

NOORD HOLLAND Markerwaard Kampen Zwolle Hengelo Enschede Gronau Burgsteinfurt

Volendam Edam Zaandam MARKEN Oostelijk flevoland Harderwijk OVERIJSSEL Lochem Ahaus Münster

Noordzeekanaal IJmuiden Haarlem Weesp Zuidelijk flevoland Veluwe Apeldoorn Deventer Zutphen Coesfeld Warendorf

AMSTERDAM Amsterdam-Rijnkanaal Naarden Bussum Laren Baarn Amersfoort Rheine Münsterland

Noordwijk aan Zee Leiden Alphen aan de Rijn Hilversum Utrecht Zeist Doorn Arnhem Rheden Groenlo Aalten Winterswijk

's-Gravenhage (The Hague) Voorburg Gouda Oude Rijn UTRECHT GELDERLAND Velp Zevenaar Bocholt Borken Haltern

Scheveningen Delft IJssel Lek Renkum Waal Nijmegen Emmerich Kleve Rees Wesel Recklinghausen Lünen

R. Hoek van Holland Rotterdam Schiedam Culemborg Leerdam Tiel Oss Maas Goch Rhein Dinslaken Gladbeck Bottrop Werne Hamm

ZUID HOLLAND Haringvliet Dordrecht Gorinchem 's-Hertogenbosch Uden Geldern Hambom Oberhausen Hellweg Unna

Grevelingen GOEREE OVERFLAKKEE Amer Mark NOORD BRABANT Boxtel Venraij Horst Viersen Krefeld Duisburg Mülheim Essen Bochum Ruhr Dortmund

SCHOUWEN ND. BEVELAND THOLEN Roosendaal Breda Tilburg Helmond De Peel Venlo Mönchengladbach Neuss Düsseldorf Wuppertal Remscheid

OOSTERSCHELDE ZEELAND Goes Bergen-op-Zoom Eindhoven Weert Roermond Rheydt Solingen Ebbegeb.

WALCHEREN Middelburg ZD. BEVELAND Westerschelde Honte ANTWERPEN Herentals Geel Mol Kempenland Maaseik Roer Köln (Cologne) Mülheim Bergisch-Gladbach Olpe

Vlissingen Knokke Terneuzen Antwerpen (Anvers) LIMBURG Genk Sittard Heerlen Eschweiler Jülich Düren Siegburg

Blankenberge Brugge Maldegem Eeklo St. Niklaas Lokeren Mechelin Aarschot Diest Hasselt Maastricht Aachen Aix-la-Chapelle Euskirchen BONN GERMANY

Oostende Sint-Andries Torhout OOST-VLAANDEREN Gent (Ghent) (Gand) Dendermonde Aalst Demer Leuven St. Truiden Tongeren Heerlen LIEGE Eupen HONE...

Nieuwpoort De Panne Veurne Diksmuide Tielt Leie Schelde Ninove BRUSSEL (Bruxelles) Halle Tienen LIÈGE Liège Verviers Herve

Dunkerque WEST-VLAANDEREN Roeselare Izegem Ieper Kortrijk Menen Oudenaarde Ronse Geraardsbergen BRABANT Wavre Braine-l'Alleud Nivelles Gembloux Hesbaye Huy Meuse HONE

Gravelines Ijzer Poperinge Tourcoing Roubaix Mouscron Ath Leuze Soignies Mons La Louvière Binche NAMUR Andenne Condroz Tailles SCHWARZER MANN

St. Omer Bailleul Hazebrouck Armentières Lille Tournai Antoing HAINAUT Charleroi Namur Sambre Dinant Marche-en-Famenne St. Vith Prüm

Bruay-en-Artois Béthune Carvin Orchies Saint-Amand Douai Leuze Binche Thuin Beaumont Philippeville FAGNES Grotte de Han La Roche-en-Ardenne Saint-Hubert Bastogne Wiltz

Noeux-les-Mines Liévin Lens Hénin-Liétard Valenciennes Denain Maubeuge Avesnes Bois de Chimay Chimay Fourmies Bouillon LUXEMBOURG LUXEMBOURG Birburg Bitburg

Collines d'Artois St. Pol Arras Cambrai Escaut Le Cateau Hirson Revin Neufchâteau Forêt d'Anlier Ettelbruck Sauer Bernkastel-Kues Bad Kreuznach

Cache d'Artois Authie Doullens Albert Péronne Guise Oise Saint-Michel Charleville Mézières Signy-l'Abbaye Forêt de Mortagne Arlon LUXEMBOURG Diekirch Trier HUNSRÜCK

Amiens Somme St. Quentin Thiérache Vervins Rethel Vouziers Bastogne Longwy Differdange Bettembourg Saarlautern Zweibrücken

Beauvais Montdidier Laon La Fère Serre Aisne Vesle Aire Reims Montmédy Verdun Longuyon Thionville Metz Saarbrücken Homburg Kaiserslautern

Clermont Compiègne Forêt de Compiègne Soissons FRANCE Vouziers Montfaucon Conflans-en-Jarnisy Briey Boulay Forbach Fénétrange Erbesrück

Creil Valois Senlis Ourcq Château-Thierry MONTAGNE DE REIMS Châlons Sainte-Menehould Meuse Toul Pont-à-Mousson Château-Salins Sankt Wendel Ottweiler Neunkirchen

Pontoise Oise

Projection: Conical with 2 standard parallels
Heights in metres

Scale: 1:1,500,000

Miles

Kilometres

Towns:
- ■ over 1,000,000
- ● over 500,000
- ● over 100,000
- · under 100,000

--- International boundaries

Major railways

✱ International airports

GERMANY & AUSTRIA

© Geographical Projects

Towns:

- ■ over 1,000,000
- ● over 500,000
- ● over 100,000
- • under 100,000

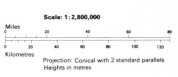

International boundaries

Boundaries under dispute

Major railways

* International airports

Scale: 1 : 2,800,000

Miles 20 40 60 80

Kilometres 0 20 40 60 80 100 120

Projection: Conical with 2 standard parallels
Heights in metres

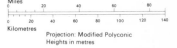

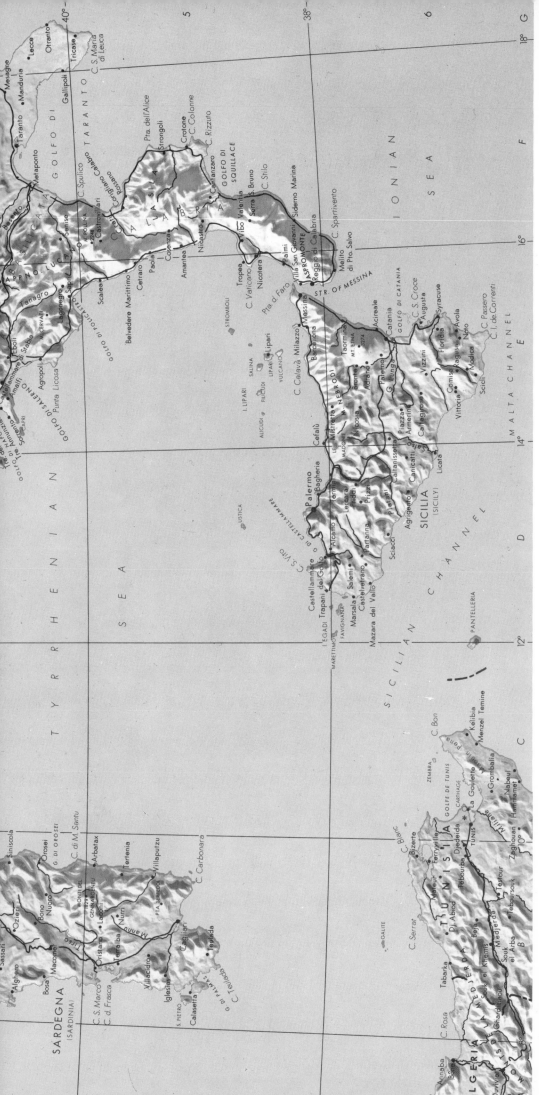

Towns:

■ over 1,000,000

● over 500,000

● over 100,000

• under 100,000

〰 International boundaries

〰 Major railways

✳ International airports

○ Ancient sites

Scale: 1 : 2,900,000

Miles
0   20   40   60   80

Kilometres
0 20 40 60 80 100 120

Projection: Modified Polyconic
Heights in metres

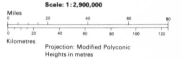

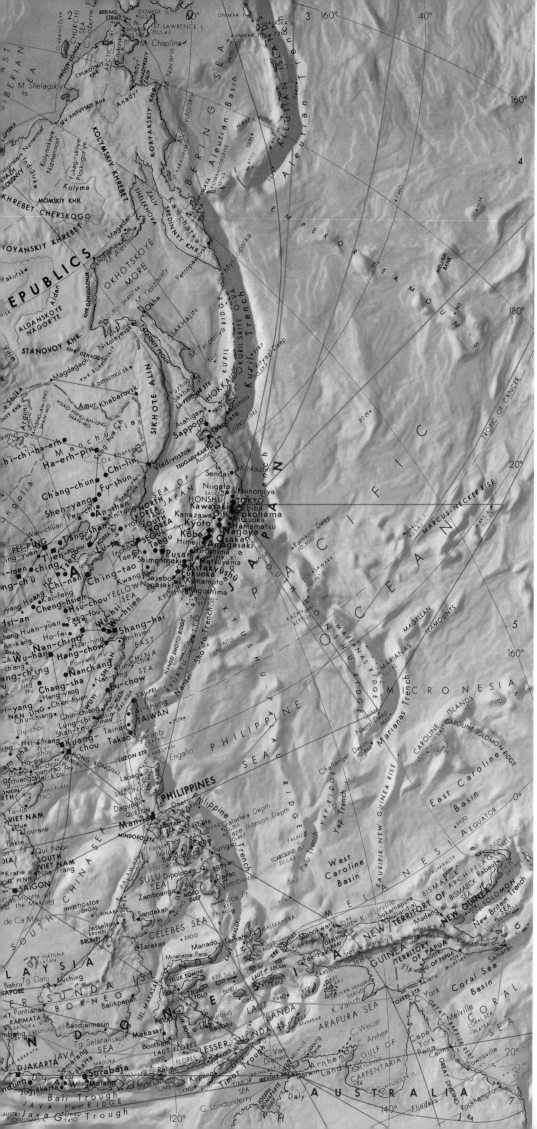

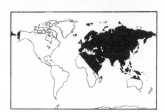

EURASIA

67

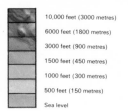

10,000 feet (3000 metres)
6000 feet (1800 metres)
3000 feet (900 metres)
1500 feet (450 metres)
1000 feet (300 metres)
500 feet (150 metres)
Sea level

Towns:

■ over 1,000,000

● over 500,000

● over 250,000

· under 250,000

∿∿ International boundaries

⌇⌇ Boundaries under dispute

⌣ Major air routes

⌣ Major sea routes

Scale: 1:37,400,000

Miles
0   200   400   600   800   1000
Kilometres

Projection: Lambert's Azimuthal Equal Area
Heights and depths in metres

68

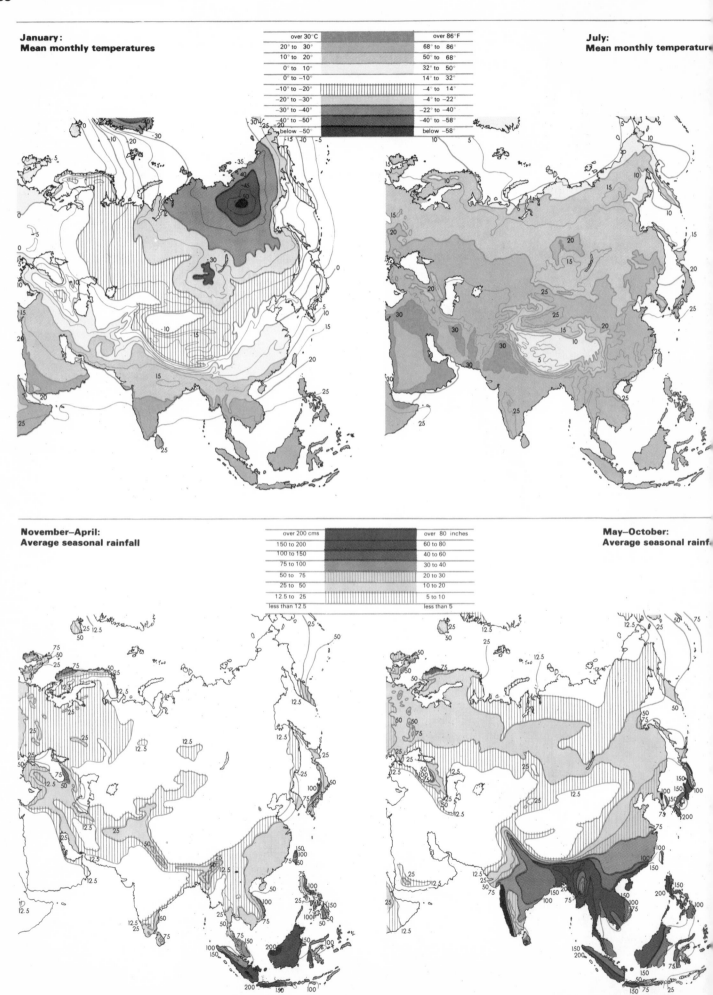

January:
Mean monthly temperatures

	over 30°C		over 86°F
	20° to 30°		68° to 86°
	10° to 20°		50° to 68°
	0° to 10°		32° to 50°
	0° to −10°		14° to 32°
	−10° to −20°		−4° to 14°
	−20° to −30°		−4° to −22°
	−30° to −40°		−22° to −40°
	−40° to −50°		−40° to −58°
	below −50°		below −58°

July:
Mean monthly temperatures

November–April:
Average seasonal rainfall

	over 200 cms		over 80 inches
	150 to 200		60 to 80
	100 to 150		40 to 60
	75 to 100		30 to 40
	50 to 75		20 to 30
	25 to 50		10 to 20
	12.5 to 25		5 to 10
	less than 12.5		less than 5

May–October:
Average seasonal rainfall

Asia, the largest of the continents, shows also the greatest climatic contrasts. Southern India, coastal Burma, Thailand, Malaysia and Indonesia are very warm or hot throughout the year with, for the most part, a seasonal alternation from rainy and very humid to dry and rather humid. Central and northern India have a longer dry season and are very hot in early summer. Central China has a similar, but rather wetter, climate. The high mountains and plateaus of Central Asia are sunny with very dry summers and bitterly cold winters. In northern China winters are cold for the latitude—because of the spread of cold air from Siberia—and summers are hot. Northern Japan resembles northern China, but is more snowy and its summers are humid as well as hot. Siberia itself has short but very warm summers and intensely cold, mainly dry, clear winters. This region of north-east Asia has the coldest winters of any inhabited part of the world, although even here trees can still grow nearly as far north as the shores of the Arctic Ocean. South-west Asia, however, is for the most part dry or very dry, with intensely hot summers.

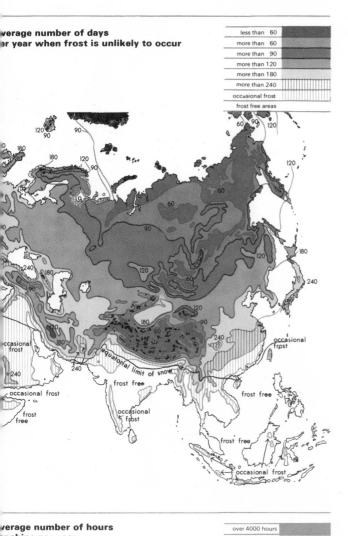

Average number of days per year when frost is unlikely to occur

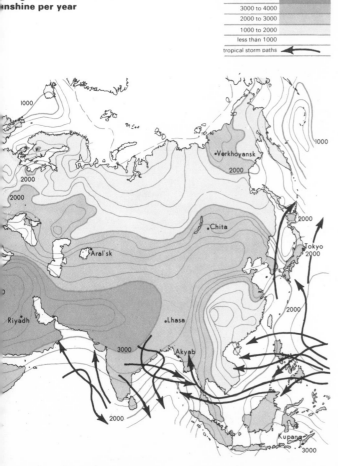

Average number of hours sunshine per year

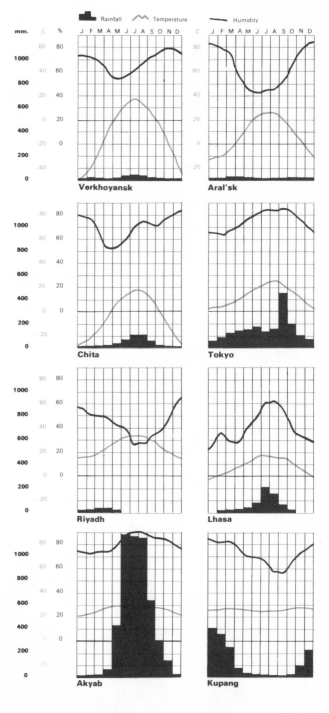

Verkhoyansk · Aral'sk · Chita · Tokyo · Riyadh · Lhasa · Akyab · Kupang

© Geographical Projects

Projection: Lambert's Azimuthal Equal Area

Scale: 1 : 48,700,000

Miles
0   200   400   600   800   1000   1200   1400   1600

Kilometres
0   200   400   600   800   1000   1200   1400   1600   1800   2000   2200   2400   2600

● Capital cities

TROPIC OF CANCER

PACIFIC OCEAN

ARCTIC OCEAN

BERING SEA

OKHOTSKOYE MORE

ALEUTIAN ISLANDS (USA)

EAST SIBERIAN SEA

Kamchatka

M. Lopatka

KURIL'SKIYE O-VA

SAKHALIN

HOKKAIDO

SEA OF JAPAN

HONSHU

J A P A N

NORTH KOREA

SOUTH KOREA

Pyong

Seoul

KYUSHU

RYUKYU RETTO

EAST CHINA SEA

YELLOW SEA

TAIWAN

Tai-pei

TAI-WAN HAI-HSIA

Hong Kong (Br.)

Macau (Port.)

HAINAN TAO

PHILIPPINES

Quezon

LUZON

MINDANAO

CAROLINE ISLANDS (USA)

MARIANAS (USA)

PALAU IS
CAROLINE IS

CORAL SEA

TERRITORY OF NEW GUINEA

PAPUA

NEW GUINEA

HALMAHERA

CELEBES

SULAWESI

BRUNEI (Br.)

KALIMANTAN

BORNEO

M A L A Y S I A

Kuala Lumpur

Singapore

SUMATRA

Djakarta

DJAWA

I N D O N E S I A

SOUTH CHINA SEA

NORTH VIET NAM

Hanoi

SOUTH VIET NAM

Saigon

LAOS

Vientiane

CAMBODIA

Phnom Penh

T H A I L A N D

Bangkok

B U R M A

Rangoon

ANDAMAN IS (INDIA)

NICOBAR IS (INDIA)

BAY OF BENGAL

Mouths of the Ganges

C H I N A

Pei-ping

HUANG HO

CHIN-LING SHAN

Ch'ang (Yangtze Kiang)

NAN LING

NAN SHAN

ALTAY

M O N G O L I A

Ulan Bator

Oz. Baykal

Ch'ing Hai

ALTYN TAGH

Chang Tang (Plateau of Tibet)

H I M A L A Y A

NEPAL

Kathmandu

Ganga

Delhi

I N D I A

Deccan

C. Comorin

CEYLON

Colombo

LACCADIVE IS (INDIA)

MALDIVE IS (INDIA)

U N I O N   O F   S O V I E T   S O C I A L I S T   R E P U B L I C S

Srednee Sibirskoye Ploskogor'ye

Lena

Yenisey

Irtysh

Ob'

Zapadno Sibirskaya Nizmennost'

URAL'SKIY KHREBET

TIEN SHAN

Takla Makan

Oz. Issyk-Kul'

Oz. Balkhash

Amu-Dar'ya

Syr-Dar'ya

ARAL'SKOYE MORE

CASPIAN SEA

Moskva

Volga

Don

Dnepr

BOLSHOY KAVKAZ

NOVAYA ZEMLYA

SEVERNAYA ZEMLYA

BARENTSOVO MORE

SVALBARD

ARCTIC CIRCLE

NORWEGIAN SEA

Nordkapp

Onezhskoye Oz.

Ladozhskoye Oz.

BRITISH ISLES

NORTH SEA

BALTIC SEA

ENGLISH CHANNEL

BAY OF BISCAY

E U R O P E

CARPATHIANS

Danube

ADRIATIC SEA

M E D I T E R R A N E A N   S E A

BLACK SEA

Ankara

T U R K E Y

CYPRUS

Nicosia

SYRIA

LEBANON

Beirut

Damascus

ISRAEL

Jerusalem

Amman

JORDAN

Baghdad

I R A Q

Tigris

Euphrates

I R A N

ELBORZ

Tehran

KUHHA-YE ZAGROS

PERSIAN GULF

KUWAIT

NEUTRAL ZONE

BAHRAIN

QATAR

TRUCIAL OMAN

MUSCAT & OMAN

Muscat

G. OF OMAN

ARABIAN SEA

S A U D I   A R A B I A

Riyadh

YEMEN

PROT OF SOUTH ARABIA

G. OF ADEN

C. GUARDAFUI

SOCOTRA (Br.)

RED SEA

Cairo

E G Y P T

Nile

Khartoum

S U D A N

ETHIOPIA

ABYSSINIAN HIGHLANDS

Addis Ababa

SOMALILAND

Djibouti

Mogadiscio

S O M A L I A

KENYA

Nairobi

UGANDA

TANZANIA

Dar es Salaam

MALAGASY REPUBLIC

ÎLES DE COMORE (Fr.)

L I B Y A

Benghazi

Tripoli

TUNISIA

Tunis

ALGERIA

Alger

A R A B I A

HINDU KUSH

AFGHANISTAN

Kabul

PAKISTAN

Islamabad

KASHMIR

JAMMU & KASHMIR

G. OF KUTCH

NORTH SEA

AFRICA

ATLANTIC OCEAN

INDIAN OCEAN

TROPIC OF CANCER

ARCTIC CIRCLE

1500–1650

1650–1763 (Treaty of Paris)

763–1830

1830–end of 19th century

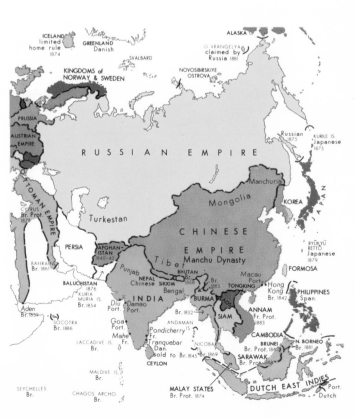

Soils

■	Permanent ice	
▨	Red soils	*Pedalfers (non-lime accumulating soils) in humid, tropical regions, lateritic soils, soils of incomplete leaching*
▨	Laterites	
▨	Yellow soils	
▢	Podsols	*Pedalfers in sub-tropical and humid, temperate regions, podsolic soils, soils of incomplete leaching*
▥	Grey & brown forest soils	
▨	Prairie soils	
▢	Terra Rossa	*Pedocals (lime-accumulating soils) in drier, subtropical regions, soils of impeded leaching*
▤	Grey soils	
▨	Chernozems	*Pedocals in more temperate, less arid regions, soils of impeded leaching*
▨	Brown and chestnut soils	
↓↓	Tundra soils	*Pedocals in polar regions*
⠂⠂	Mountain soils	*Intrazonal soils*
▨	Alluvial soils	
⠂⠂	Sand – mainly dunes	

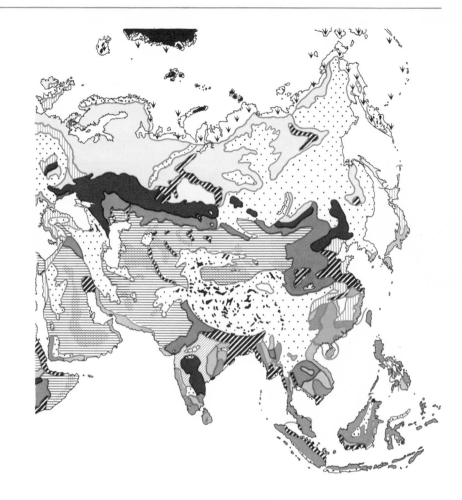

Land use

▢	Unproductive areas
■	Industrial & urban areas
▥	Hunting & gathering; shifting cultivation in tropics
▢	Stock rearing & ranging
▨	Intensive & specialised agriculture
▨	Mixed farming
▨	Forest lands
⌐	Lumbering
↓	Grain production predominant
⊔	Plantation agriculture
Y	Nomadic economies
⠂⠂	Deep sea fishing
⋯	Coastal fishing

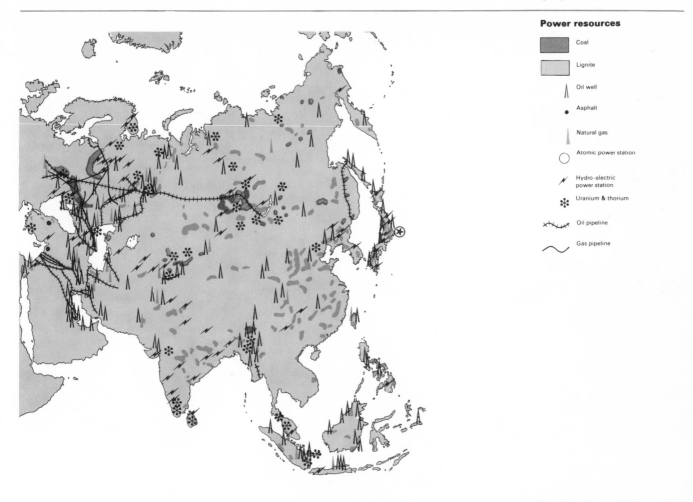

Power resources

	Coal
	Lignite
ʌ	Oil well
•	Asphalt
	Natural gas
○	Atomic power station
⚡	Hydro-electric power station
✳	Uranium & thorium
✕✕✕	Oil pipeline
〜	Gas pipeline

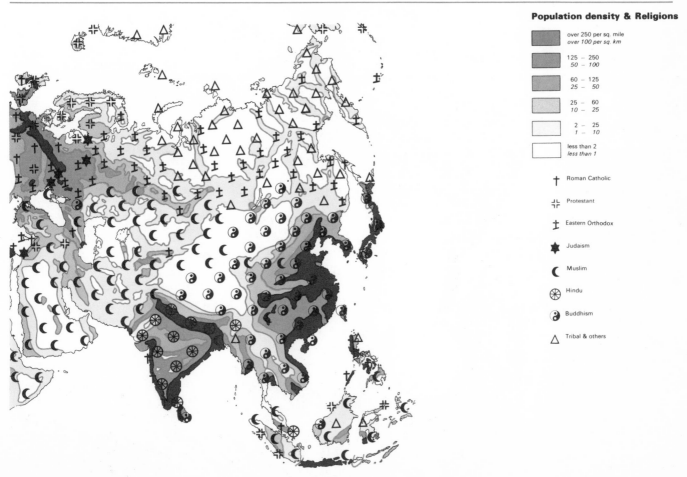

Population density & Religions

	over 250 per sq. mile *over 100 per sq. km*
	125 – 250 *50 – 100*
	60 – 125 *25 – 50*
	25 – 60 *10 – 25*
	2 – 25 *1 – 10*
	less than 2 *less than 1*

✝	Roman Catholic
ⵣ	Protestant
☦	Eastern Orthodox
✡	Judaism
☾	Muslim
☸	Hindu
☯	Buddhism
△	Tribal & others

© Geographical Projects

ARCTIC OCEAN

LOMONOSOV (HARRIS) RIDGE

CHUKCHI SEA

BERING STR

BERING SEA

Aleutian Basin

ALEUTIAN IS.

ATTU

SEVERNAYA ZEMLYA

O. KOMSOMOLETS
VIL'KITSKOGO REVOLYUTSII
O. BOL'SHEVIK

MORE LAPTEVYKH

EAST SIBERIAN SEA

VRANGELYA

ARCTIC CIRCLE

M. Dika
Chelyuskin
Mys Chelyuskin

GORY BYRRANGA
Oz. Taymyr
Pov. Taymyr
Khatanga
Kheta
Nordvik
Tit-Ary
Tiksi

ANADYRSKIY

KHREBET CHERSKOGO

VERKHOYANSKIY KHREBET

KHR. ORULGAN

MOMSKIY KHREBET

KORYAKSKIY KHREBET

KOLYMSKIY

KAMCHATKA

SREDINNYY KHREBET

Norilsk
Dudinka
GORY PUTORANA
Oz. Khantayskoye
Igarka
Turukhansk

Sredne Sibirskaya Nizmennost

Olenëk
Zhigansk

Lena

Yakutsk
Vilyuysk
Vilyuy
Mirnyy

SOVIET SOCIALIST REPUBLICS

OKHOTSKOYE MORE

SEA OF OKHOTSK

SAKHALIN

R.S.F.S.R.

PATOMSKOYE NAGOR'YE
ALDANSKOYE NAGOR'YE
STANOVOY KHREBET

KHREBET DZHUGDZHUR

TATARSKIY PROLIV

KURIL'SKIYE O-VA

KURIL RIDGE

Yeniseysk
Angara
Krasnoyarsk
Kansk
Tayshet
Bratsk
Kirensk
Ust'-Kut
Vitim
Nizhneudinsk
ZAPADNYY SAYAN
VOSTOCHNYY SAYAN
Irkutsk
Baykal
Oz. Baykal
SIKHOTE ALIN

STANOVOYE NAGOR'YE
VITIMSKOYE PLOSKOGOR'YE

YABLONOVYY KHREBET

BORSHCHOVOCHNYY KHREBET

Chita
Nerchinsk
Shilka
Mogocha
Skovorodino
Tyndinskiy
Zeya
Shimanovsk
Belogorsk
Blagoveshchensk
Amur
Komsomol'sk
Khabarovsk
Birobidzhan

Khanka
Vladivostok
Nakhodka

HOKKAIDO
Sapporo
Hakodate
Muroran

HONSHU

TOKYO
Yokohama
Kawasaki
Nagoya
Kyoto
Osaka
Kobe

ABAKAN
Minusinsk
KHR. TANNU OLA
Kyzyl
Malyy Yenisey
Hövsögöl
Ulan-Ude
Petrovsk
Zabaykal'skiy

HANGAYN NURU
HENTEYN NURU
ULAN BATOR
Sühe Bator
Bulagan
Selenge Gol
Orhon Gol

MONGOLIA

Choybalsan
Kerulen

Buyr Nur

M A N C H U R I A

Ha-erh-pin
Ch'i-ch'i-ha-erh

Ch'ang-ch'un
Chi-lin

Fu-shun
Shen-yang
An-shan

NORTH KOREA
PYONG YANG
SOUTH KOREA
SEOUL
Inchon
Taegu
Pusan

YELLOW SEA

SEA OF JAPAN

KYUSHU
Fukuoka
Nagasaki
Kagoshima

SHIKOKU

Hiroshima

PEI-P'ING
Tien-ching
Ching-tao

C H I N A

Inner Mongolia

TA-CH'ING SHAN
HO-LAN SHAN

Ordos
Shih-men
Yang-chü
Chi-nan
Tzepo

NAN SHAN
PEI SHAN

Kao-lan
Cheng-hsien
Hsü-chou

PACIFIC OCEAN

CHINA & KOREA

Towns:

■ over 1,000,000

● over 500,000

◦ over 100,000

· under 100,000

〰 International boundaries

〜 Major railways

✳ International airports

Scale: 1 : 9,700,000

Miles
0 · 50 · 100 · 150 · 200 · 250 · 300

Kilometres
0 · 50 · 100 · 150 · 200 · 250 · 300 · 350 · 400 · 450

Projection: Conical Orthomorphic
Heights in metres

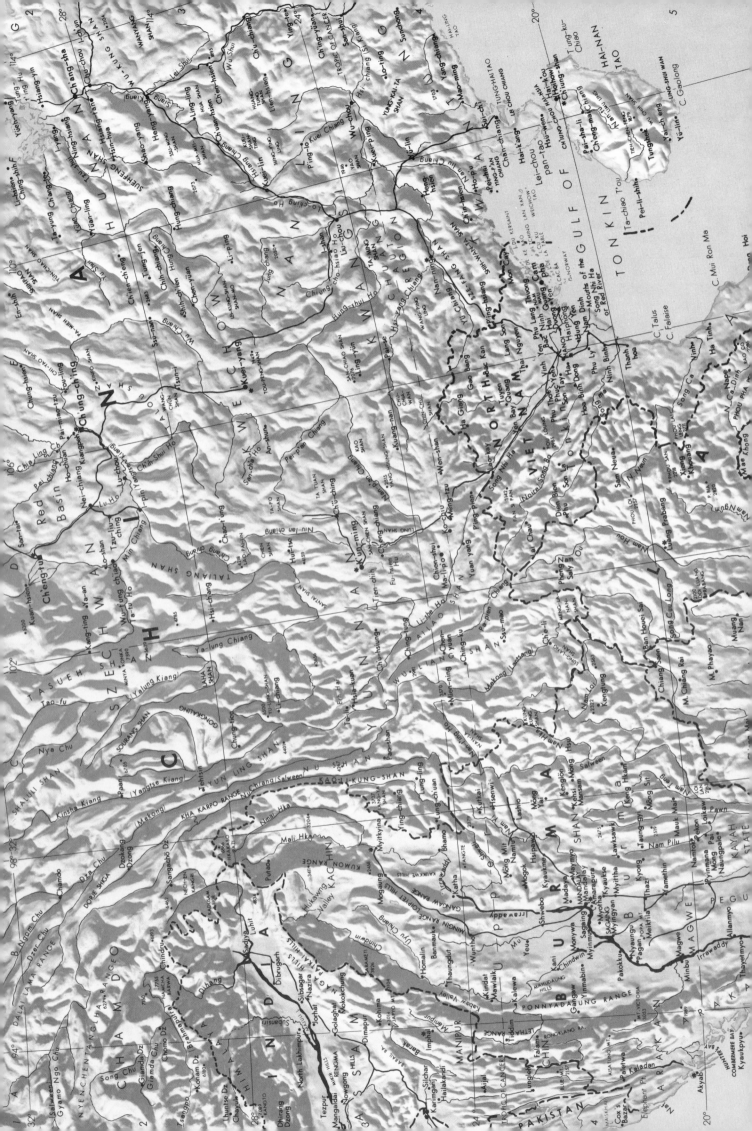

SOUTH EAST ASIA

© Geographical Projects

83

Towns:

■ over 1,000,000
● over 500,000
● over 100,000
• under 100,000

⌇ International boundaries

⌇ Major railways

✳ International airports

○ Ancient sites

Scale: 1 : 7,100,000

Miles

Kilometres

Projection: Conical Orthomorphic
Heights in metres

130° E 140° 20° F 150° G 2

PARECE VELA

ASUNCION

AGRIHAN
PAGAN
ALAMAGAN
GUGUAN

SARIGAN
ANATAHAN
FARALLON DE
MEDINILLA
SAIPAN
TINIAN

ROTA

GUAM
(U.S.A.)

M A R I A N A S (U.S.A.)

P A C I F I C

ILIPPINES

ilogan
AMAR

ban

DINAGAT

ULITHI

YAP

FAIS

GAFERUT

ULUL

MAGUR

TRUK
ISLANDS

SIARGAO
urigao
PUTA IKIS

NGULU
ATOLL

SOROL

FARAULEP

PIGAILOE

LAMOTREK

PULAP

PULUWAT

MINDANAO

Cape San Agustin

onadal

SARANGANI

PALAU IS.

WOLEAI IFALIK

EAURIPIK

C A R O L I N E   I S L A N D S
(U.S.A.)

3

KEP.
TALAUD

SONSOROL IS.

PULO ANNA
MERIR

O C E A N

TOB]

HELEN ISLAND

EQUATOR 0°

Tg. Sopi
MOROTAI

KEP. MAFIA

ado
G. GAMKUNORO
1635

Ternate
ano

HALMAHERA

KEP. ASIA

NINIGO GROUP
PELLELUHU IS.

KANIET IS.

ST. MATTHIAS GROUP
MUSSAU I.
EMIRA

HALMAHERA
SEA

KEP. AJOE

WUVULU I. NINIGO IS.

HERMIT IS.

ADMIRALTY IS.
Lorengau

HORNO IS
RAMBUTYO I.

YSABEL CHANNEL

TABAR I.
GROUP

NEW HANOVER
Kavieng

BATJAN

WAIGEO

SELAT DAMPIER

KWOKA

MANUS I.

PURDY IS.

BISMARCK ARCHIPELAGO

DYAUL

Konos

NEW
IRELAND

LIHIR
GROUP

1054

KEP. OBI

Sorong
Klamono

BIAK

Manokwari P-PA.SCHOUTEN

Bosnek

K. d'Urville

Sukarnapura
(Hollandia)

Aitape

Dagua

SCHOUTEN

BISMARCK   SEA

Namatanai
Rabaul

MANGOLE

BATANTA

Saileen
Sele

Jef Lio Vogelkop
MT.
GWAMONGGA
3100

Sorido Mokmer

JAPEN

Seroei

Maprik
Bainyik

Wewak
Angoram

TERRITORY OF NEW GUINEA
(AUSTR.)

KARKAR I.

VITU IS.

Willaumez
Pena.

Keravat
GazelleMerai

KIMBE
BAY

Kokopo

2300
MT ULAWUN

ULA
SULABESI

MISOOL
SALAWATI

TEL.
BERAOE

Wasian

GEELVINK
BAAI

Barapasi

VAN REES GEBERGTE
Meervlakte

N E W

Sepik

G U I N E A

Bogia

P.A.

CENTRAL Baiyer

Madang

MT.
BANGETA

WHITEMAN
RA.

NEW
BRITAIN

LAUT SERAM
SERAM Wahai

Kokas

Babo

WILHELMINA
TOP
4730

MT. WILHELM

Huon 1107

Talasea

BURU
2114
BINAIJA
3019

Bom-
barai

Fak
Fak

Kaimana
Obome

CARSTENSZ TOPPEN
(16,500)5029
4922
16,250

S N E E U W   G E B.

ORANGE GEB.
WEST

Wabag River

Wapenamanda Mini Chimbu
Tari

Mt.
Hagen Mount

MENDI

Okapa

Lae
Bulolo
Wau

DAMPIER STR.

SOLOMON

AMBON Ambon

Karoefa

NASSAU GEB.

DAAM TOP

IRIAN

Ely Ely

GILUWE

Tage

Morobe

SEA

KEP.
GORONG

Tual

KAI

Dobo

WOKAM
KEP. ARU

El landen
anamerah

Ilagi

Mava

Garaina

TROBRIAND OR
KIRIWINA IS.

KEP. BANDA

KEP.
WATUBELA

BESAR
KAI KETJIL
KEP. KAI

KOBROOR

Rabal

Mappi

TERRITORY

Kikori
Kotari

Aird
Hills

Beara
Ioma
Kumusi

MT.VICTORIA

Kulumadau

GOODENOUGH I.

FERGUSSON I. WOODLARK
DENTRECASTEAUX

KEP PENJU
KEP. LUCIPARA

L A U T   B A N D A

MOLU

TRANGAN

Moeting

OF PAPUA
(AUSTR.) Kerema

Epo
Popondetta
Kokoda Tufi

WARD HUNT STR.

NORMANBY I.

GUNUNGAPI

FREDERIK
HENDRIK
EILAND

Okaba

Gaima
Gesoa GULF

OF PAPUAKairuku

STANLEY

3421

MISIMA I.

ENGINEER GROUP

WETAR KEP. BARAT DAJA

ROMA

DAMAR

JAMDENA
KEP. TANIMBAR

K. Valsch

Merauke

Daru

Laloki

PORT MORESBY

Kila Kila

Baniara
Gehuaa

DEBOYNE IS.

TAGULA I.

LOUISIADE ARCHO.

DILI
PORT.
TIMOR
MOR

KEP. LETI

MO
KEP.
SERMATA

KEP
BABAR

Saumlaki

SELARU

A R A F U R A

Rigo

Abau Boru

Samarai

10°

TIMOR

C. Van Diemen I.

MELVILLE I.

Cobourg
Pena. CROKER I.

WESSEL IS.

C. Wessel

S E A

MULGRAVE I. BANKS I.
THURSDAY I.
PR. OF WALES I.

TORRES STRAIT

C. York

GT. NORTH
EASTERN CHAN.
MURRAY IS.

C O R A L

BATHURST I.

VAN DIEMEN
GULF

C. Arnhem

Cape

Darwin

C. Londonderry
JOSEPH
BONAPARTE
GULF

BEAGLE BAY

Drysdale

FREDERICK HILLS

Arnhem Land

Daly

Katherine

Roper

GULF OF

MARIA I.
LIMMEN
BIGHT

GROOTE
EYLANDT

ALBATROSS
BAY

York

C. Melville

SADDLE
HILL
463
(1473)

C. Flattery

S E A

463

R E E F

A U S T R A L I A

130°

MT. HANN
880(2600)

Wyndham
WESTERN AUSTRALIA

SNORTHERN TERRITORY

Victoria Daly
Waters

SIR EDWARD
PELLEW GROUP

WELLESLEY IS.

140°

C A R P E N T A R I A

Peninsula

Laura

Mitchell

Cooktown

Cairns

G R E A T   B A R R I E R

QUEENSLAND

150° G 5

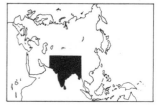

INDIA & PAKISTAN

© Geographical Projects

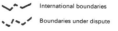

Towns:

- ■ over 1,000,000
- ● over 500,000
- ● over 100,000
- · under 100,000

- International boundaries
- Boundaries under dispute
- Major railways
- ✳ International airports

Scale: 1:11,300,000

Miles
0 100 200 300

Kilometres
0 100 200 300 400

Projection: Conical Orthomorphic
Heights in metres

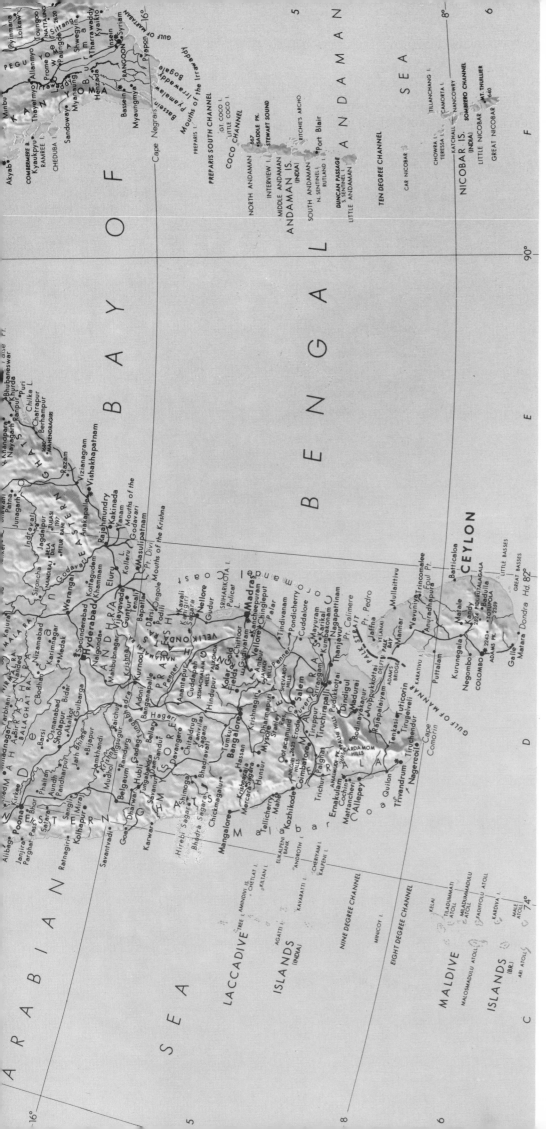

Projection: Conic
Heights in metres

Scale: 1:13,200,000

Miles
0   100   200   300   400

Kilometres
0 100 200 300 400 500 600 700

Towns:
- ■ over 1,000,000
- ● over 500,000
- ● over 100,000
- • under 100,000

- International boundaries
- Boundaries under dispute
- Major railways
- ✱ International airports

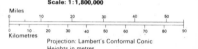

Towns:

● over 500,000

● over 100,000

• under 100,000

〰 International boundaries

〰 Boundaries under dispute

〰 Major railways

✳ International airports

○ Ancient sites

Scale: 1:1,800,000

Miles
0 10   20   30   40   50

Kilometres
0 10 20 30 40 50 60 70 80 90

Projection: Lambert's Conformal Conic
Heights in metres

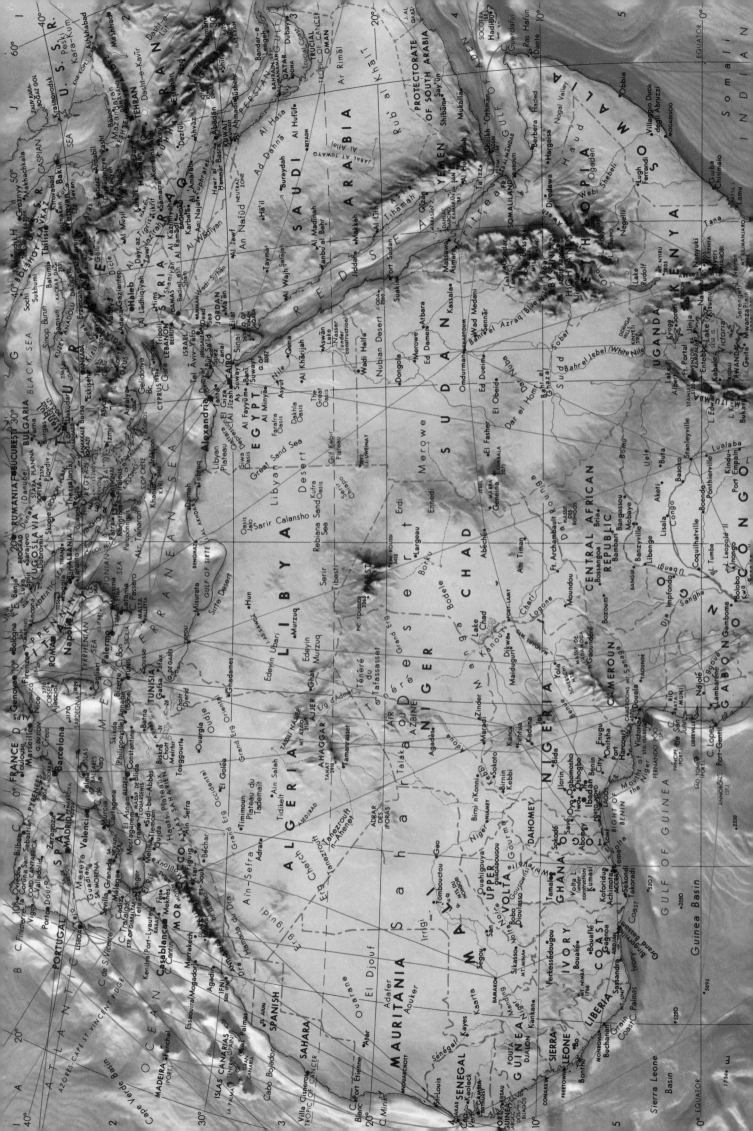

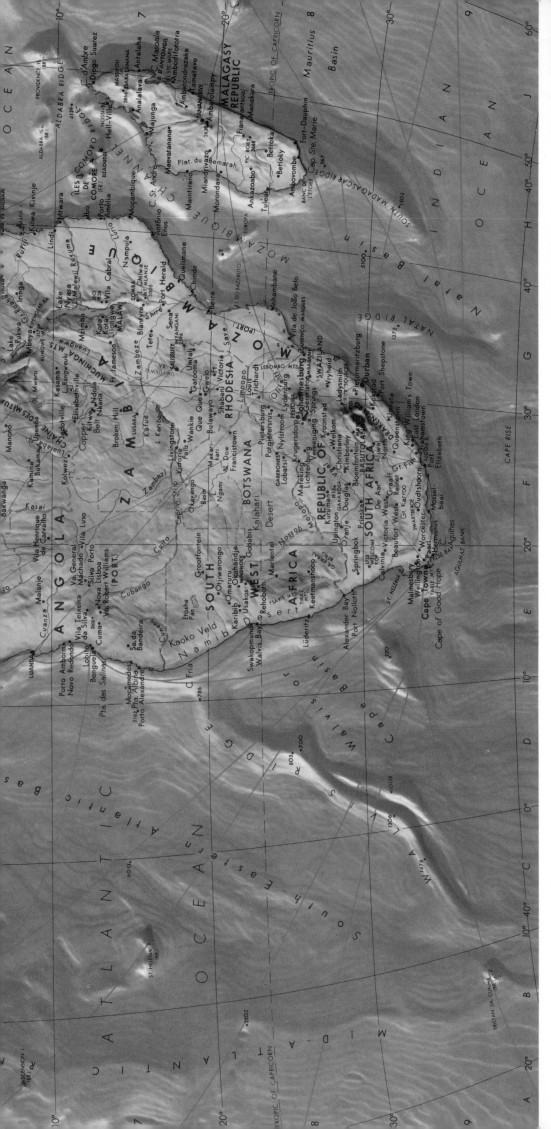

© Geographical Projects

	10,000 feet (3000 metres)
	6000 feet (1800 metres)
	3000 feet (900 metres)
	1500 feet (450 metres)
	1000 feet (300 metres)
	500 feet (150 metres)
	Sea level

Towns:

- ■ over 1,000,000
- ● over 500,000
- ● over 250,000
- • under 250,000

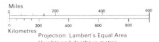

- International boundaries
- Boundaries under dispute
- Major air routes
- Major sea routes

Scale: 1 : 24,300,000

Miles
0   200   400   600

Kilometres
0   200   400   600   800

Projection: Lambert's Equal Area
Heights and depths in metres

January:
Mean monthly temperatures

July:
Mean monthly temperature

	over 30 C		over 86 F
	20 to 30		68 to 86
	10 to 20		50 to 68
	0 to 10		32 to 50
	0 to −10		14 to 32
	below −10		below 14

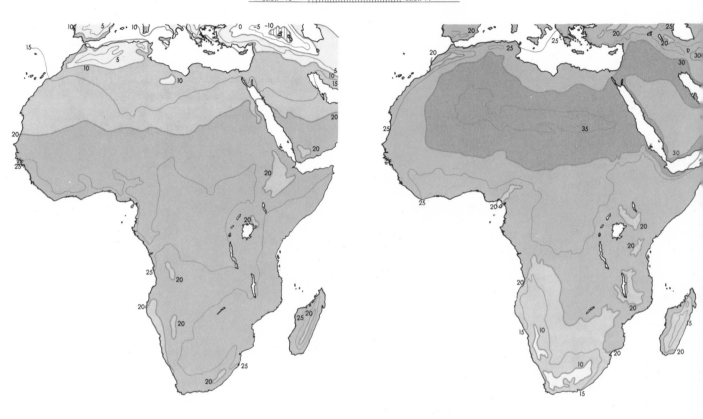

November–April:
Average seasonal rainfall

May–October:
Average seasonal rainfa

	over 200 cms		over 80 inches
	150 to 200		60 to 80
	100 to 150		40 to 60
	75 to 100		30 to 40
	50 to 75		20 to 30
	25 to 50		10 to 20
	12.5 to 25		5 to 10
	less than 12.5		less than 5

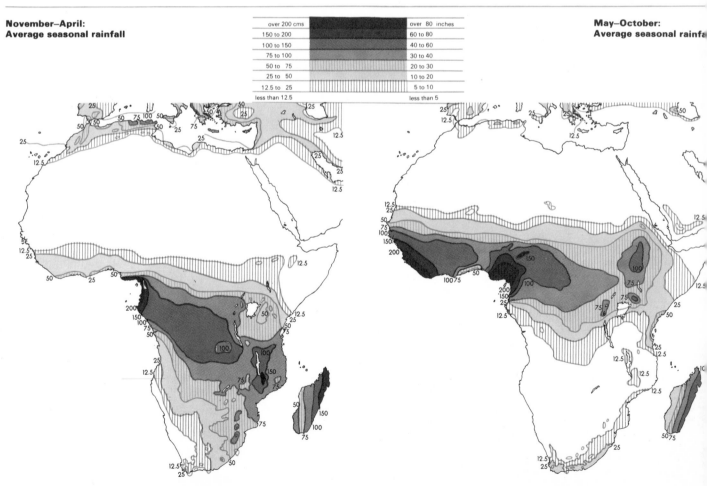

Africa lies mainly within the tropics. Almost everywhere – even in the coolest parts – the sunshine is powerful. Near the equator temperature and humidity are high and constant for most of the year and rainfall is heavy, especially toward the west: the nights are warm and sticky and there is much daytime cloud. The principal rainy areas move north or south of the equator with the seasons (November-April and May-October), so that the wide, tree-dotted grassland and scrub regions nearer the deserts have alternating dry and wet periods. The deserts themselves become intensely hot by day but are relatively cool by night. Mountain areas, such as Ethiopia, have lower temperatures and higher rainfall. In the cooler half of the year frost may occur, notably on the South African tableland, where – as on the Algerian plateau – snow is not uncommon. The shores of Morocco and south-west Africa are generally cooler than the rest of the continent, because of the neighbouring cool ocean currents. South-east Africa is mostly warm and moist, while the 'horn' of Africa (Somalia) is very dry.

erage number of days
r year when frost is unlikely to occur

	more than 60
	more than 90
	more than 120
	more than 180
	more than 240
	occasional frost
	frost free areas

erage number of hours
nshine per year.

	over 4000 hours
	3000 to 4000
	2000 to 3000
	1000 to 2000
	tropical storm paths

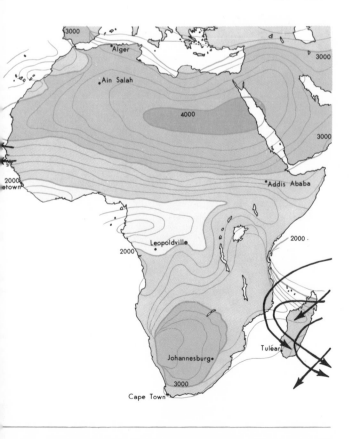

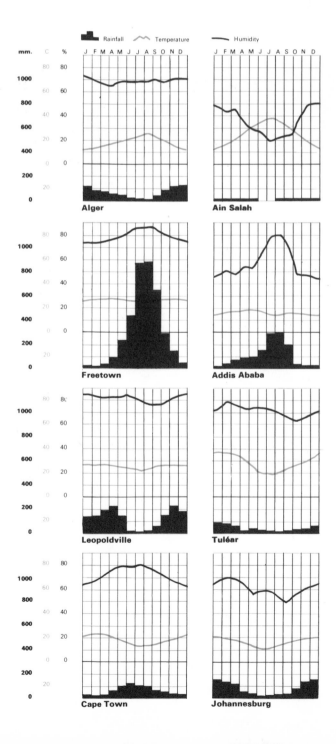

Rainfall Temperature Humidity

Alger   Ain Salah

Freetown   Addis Ababa

Leopoldville   Tuléar

Cape Town   Johannesburg

AFRICA
Political

© Geographical Projects

Projection: Lambert's Equal Area

Scale: 1 : 37,400,000

Miles
0   200   400   600   800   1000   1200

Kilometres
0   200   400   600   800   1000   1200   1400   1600   1800   2000

• Capital cities

C. Finisterre
PORTUGAL
Lisboa
C. de S. Vicente
SPAIN
Madrid
Tajo
ATLANTIC
OCEAN
MADEIRA (PORT.)
C. de la Nao
ISLAS BALEARES
FRANCE
G. DU LION
PYRENEES
ANDORRA
CORSE
MONACO
SARDEGNA
ITALY
SAN MARINO
ADRIATIC SEA
Roma
Tirane
ALBANIA
YUGOSLAVIA
Sofiya
BULGARIA
Danube
GREECE
Athinai
AEGEAN SEA
Pelopón- nisus
KRITI
S. OF MARMARA
Ankara
TURKEY
TORUS DAGLARI
Tuz G.G.
RODHOS
Nicosia
CYPRUS
BLACK SEA
Sinop Burun
ELBRUS 5633
BOLSHOY KAVKAZ
Kura
U.S.S.R.
CASPIAN SEA
BU.AGRIDAGI 5165
Van- Gölü
Daryacheh-ye Rezā'īyeh
RESHTEH-YE ALBORZ
Tehran
KUHHĀ-YE ZAGROS
IRAN

ATLANTIC OCEAN

MEDITERRANEAN SEA

MALTA Valletta
SICILIA
Tunis
C. Bon
Tripoli
Benghazi
G. DE GABES
G. OF SIRTE
Cairo
Suez Canal
Sinai
G. OF SUEZ
Suez
Jerusalem
Dead Sea
Amman
JORDAN
ISRAEL
Damas
Beirūt
LEBANON
SYRIA
Baghdad
Euphrates
IRAQ
Tigris
KUWAIT
Kuwait
NEUTRAL ZONE
BAHRAIN
Al Manāmah
QATAR
Doha
PERSIAN GULF
TRUCIAL OMAN

Rabat
MOROCCO
Alger
Hauts Plateaux
ATLAS SAHARIEN
HAUT ATLAS
Sidi Ifni
IFNI
ISLAS CANARIAS (SPAIN)
El 'Aiun
SPANISH SAHARA
Dra
TROPIC OF CANCER
C. Blanc
MAURITANIA
Nouakchott

ALGERIA
LIBYA
EGYPT
Nile
RED SEA
SAUDI
Riyadh
TROPIC OF CANCER
ARABIA
'ASIR
Rub' al Khāli

AHAGGAR
Sahara Desert
ADRAR DES IFORAS
TIBESTI
AIR OU AZBINE

SENEGAL
Dakar
C. Vert
GAMBIA
Bathurst
PORT. GUINEA
Bissau
GUINEA
Conakry
Freetown
SIERRA LEONE
Monrovia
LIBERIA
C. Palmas

MALI
Bamako
Niger
UPPER VOLTA
Ouagadougou
IVORY COAST
Abidjan
GHANA
Accra
TOGO
Lomé
DAHOMEY
Porto Novo
Niger
Niamey
NIGER
CHAD
Lake Chad
Fort-Lamy
Chari
NIGERIA
Benue
Lagos
JEBEL MARRA
SUDAN
Khartoum
L. Tana
FR. SOMALILAND
Djibouti
ABYSSINIAN
Bel Azraq (Blue Nile)
DAHLAC ARCHIPO.
YEMEN
San'ā
Aden
PROTECTORATE OF SOUTH ARABIA
GULF OF ADEN
C. Guardafui
SOCOTRA (BR.)
Ras Hafun

CENTRAL AFRICAN REPUBLIC
Bangui
CAMEROUN
CAMEROONS MT. 4070
Yaoundé
Sta. Isabel
FERNANDO POO (SP.)
RIO MUNI
Bata
PRINCIPE (PORT.)
Libreville
SÃO TOMÉ (PORT.)
ANNOBÓN (SP.)
GABON
GULF OF GUINEA
Mouths of the Niger

EQUATOR
CONGO
L. Tumba
L. Leopold II
Brazzaville
Leopoldville
CABINDA (ANGOLA)
Congo
Kasai
Luanda
ATLANTIC OCEAN
ASCENSION I. (BR.)
ST. HELENA (BR.)

Congo
Lualaba
L. Mweru
Kwango
ANGOLA (PORT.)
Cubango

CONGO
UGANDA
Kampala
L. Albert 5120
RUWENZORI RA.
L. Edward
L. Kivu
RWANDA
Kigali
Bujumbura
BURUNDI
L. Kyoga
MT. ELGON 4321
KENYA
MT. KENYA 5200
Nairobi
Lake Rudolf
Lake Victoria
MT. KILIMANJARO 5895
Mogadiscio
SOMALIA
INDIAN OCEAN
EQUATOR
AMIRANTE IS. (BR.)

Addis Ababa
HIGHLANDS
ETHIOPIA

TANZANIA
PEMBA I.
ZANZIBAR I.
Dar es Salaam
MAFIA I.
L. Tanganyika
L. Rukwa
RUNGWE MT.
Rufiji
ALDABRA IS. (BR.)
PROVIDENCE IS. (BR.)
FARQUHAR IS. (BR.)

ZAMBIA
Lusaka
L. Kariba
Zambezi
RHODESIA
Salisbury
MT. MLANJE
MOZAMBIQUE (PORT.)
Zambezi
Lake Nyasa
ÎLES DE COMORE (FR.)
Dzaoudzi
C. d'Ambre
I. STE. MARIE
Tananarive

SOUTH WEST AFRICA
Windhoek
Okavango Basin
BOTSWANA
Gaberones
Victoria Falls
Limpopo
MOZAMBIQUE CHANNEL
BASSAS DA INDIA (FR.)
EUROPA (FR.)
MALAGASY REPUBLIC
TROPIC OF CAPRICORN
C. Ste. Marie

TROPIC OF CAPRICORN
Pretoria
Mbabane
SWAZILAND
Lourenço Marques
Vaal
REPUBLIC OF
Maseru
BASUTOLAND
MT. AUX SOURCES 3281
Oranje
SOUTH AFRICA
Gt. Karroo
Oranje
Cape of Good Hope
C. Agulhas

INDIAN OCEAN

TRISTAN DA CUNHA (BR.)
GOUGH I. (BR.)
PRINCE EDWARD IS. (SOUTH AFRICA)
ÎS. CROZET (FR.)

1550–1650

1650–1763 (Treaty of Paris)

1763–1830

1830–1878 (Congress of Berlin)

Soils

▮	Permanent ice	
▩	Red soils	*Pedalfers (non-lime accumulating soils) in humid, tropical regions, lateritic soils, soils of incomplete leaching*
▩	Laterites	
▢	Yellow soils	
▥	Grey & brown forest soils	*Pedalfers in sub-tropical and humid, temperate regions, podsolic soils, soils of incomplete leaching*
▨	Prairie soils	
▤	Terra Rossa	*Pedocals (lime-accumulating soils) in drier, subtropical regions, soils of impeded leaching*
▤	Grey soils	
▮	Chernozems	*Pedocals in more temperate, less arid regions, soils of impeded leaching*
▩	Brown and chestnut soils	
⦙	Mountain soils	*Intrazonal soils*
▨	Alluvial soils	
🌴	Oasis soils	
▢	Sand – mainly dunes	

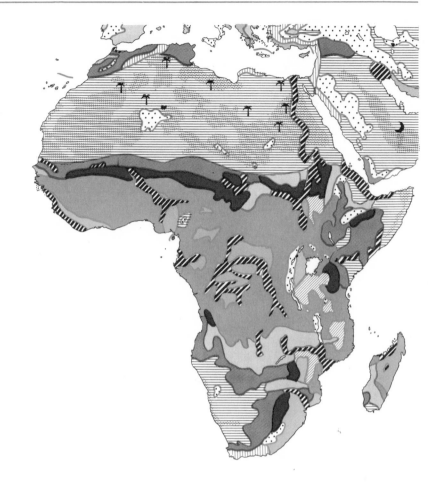

Land use

▢	Unproductive areas
▮	Industrial & urban areas
▥	Hunting, gathering & shifting cultivation
▢	Stock rearing & ranging
▩	Intensive & specialised agriculture
▨	Mixed farming
▢	Forest lands
⌐	Lumbering
⸾	Grain production predominant
Ⴠ	Plantation agriculture
Ⴗ	Nomadic economies
⋯	Deep sea fishing
⋯	Coastal fishing

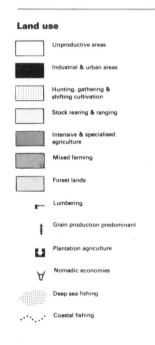

Power resources

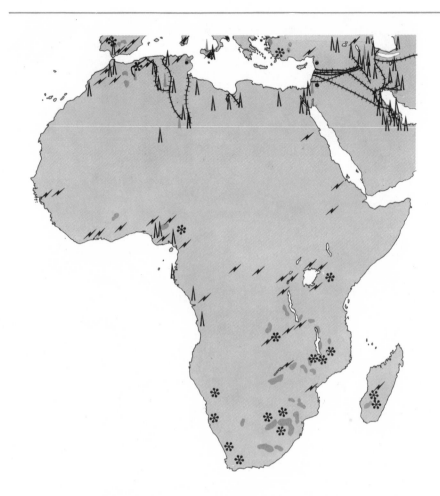

	Coal
	Lignite
\	Oil well
•	Asphalt
	Natural gas
	Hydro-electric power station
☀	Uranium & thorium
	Oil pipeline
~	Gas pipeline

Population density & Religions

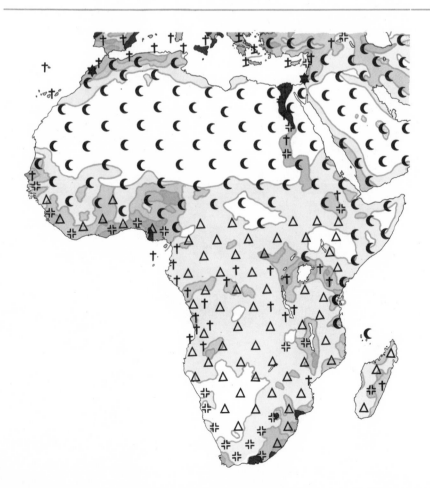

	over 250 per sq. mile / over 100 per sq. km
	125 – 250 / 50 – 100
	60 – 125 / 25 – 50
	25 – 60 / 10 – 25
	2 – 25 / 1 – 10
	less than 2 / less than 1
†	Roman Catholic
⊹	Protestant
‡	Eastern Orthodox
★	Judaism
☾	Muslim
△	Tribal & others

International airports

20°YUGO
SLAVIA
SOFIYA 2376 F
BULGARIA •Burgas
BLACK G SEA
30°
BOL'SHOY KAVKAZ
40°
CASPIAN I
50°
K
U.S.S.R.
Peski
Kara-Kum
60°

Skopje
Plovdiv
Maritsa
Bitola
KRADENIZ BOĞAZI
Zonguldak
Sinop Burun
Sinop
Samsun
Batumi
Leninakan
KIZ
Tbilisi S.
Kirovabad
Oz. Sevan
Baku
40°

Thessaloniki
Istanbul
Üsküdar
KUZEY ANADOLU DAĞLARI
Trabzon
KAÇKAR DAĞI
3931
Erzincan
3197
ARAGATS
4095
Yerevan
KAZ
Nakhichevan
Lenkoran
Mazandaran

Patrai
ATHINAI
Izmit
Adapazari
Sakarya
ÇANAKKALE
Corum
İlgaz
Tokat
Sivas
Kızıl Irmak
MURAT
Erzurum
D.
MT. AĞRI DAĞI
Van Gölü
Khowy
Tabriz
Ardabil
Rasht
RESHTEH-YE ALBORZ
Shahrud
2

SEA OF
MARMARA
Bursa
ANKARA
Kayseri
ERCIYAS D.
Malazgirt
Bitlis
CILO DAĞI
4168
Mahābād
Reza Iyeh
Qazvin DAMAVAND
5664
TEHRAN
Dasht-e-Kavir

Balikesir
Eskişehir
Afyon
Tuz Gölü
3910
Konya Ovasi
Malatya
Diyarbakir
Dicle
Al Qāmishliye
Al Mūsil
Karkūk
Sanandaj
Hamadān
Qom
Birjand

IRAN

Izmir
Gediz
Manisa
Aydin
Burdur
Isparta
TOROS DAĞLARI
Mersin
Adana
İskenderun
Antakya
Haleb SYRIA
Raqqah
Al Hasakah
Tigris
Dayr as Zawr
Euphrates
Tikrit
Sāmarra
Al Kāzimiyah
BAGHDAD
Arāk
Borūjerd
OSHTORĀN KŪH
4070
Esfahān
Yazd
Tabas
Bafq

Antalya
Elmali
Finike
RODHOS
Gelidonya
CYPRUS
NICOSIA
1952
Famagusta
Al Lādhiqiyah
Hamāh
Hims
Ba'albak
Badiet ash Shām
Shamiyāh
Ar Ramādi
Al A'zamiyah
Al Hillah
Karbalā
Al Kūt
Kermānshāh
Dezful
Ahvāz
Khertan
Kavir
Kermān
30°

Akr. Krios
Khania
Iráklion
KRITI
SEA OF CRETE
C. Gata Tripoli
BEIRUT
LEBANON
DAMAS
Dead Sea
AMMAN
An Najaf
Al Amārah
Rāmhormoz
Karūn
Khorramshahr
Abādān
Basra
Kāzerūn
Firūzābād
Shiraz
Fasā
Jahrom
Sa'idābād
4420
KŪH-E ILAZĀRĀN

N E A N   S E A
Shahhat
Darnah
Marj
J. AL AKHDAR
Tubruq
Sidi Barrāni
Alexandria
Al Mansūrah
Rashid
Dumyat
Bûr Sa'id
Port Said
Suez Canal
Tel Aviv-Yāfo
JERUSALEM
ISRAEL
Haifa
Al Mafraq
Wadi Sirhān
Badanah
An Nāsiriyah
Hawr al Hammar
KUWAIT
Al Ahmadī
Al Hasa
Ad Dammām
Dhahrān
PERSIAN GULF
Lār
Bandar-Lengeh
Bandar Abbās
Qeshm
Ra's Qahr
al Hindi
GULF OF OMAN

•Ajedabya
ed Deffa
Libyan Plateau
Matrūh
Shibin al Kawm
Tanta
Al Zaqāzig
Banhā
Al Isma'iliya
Suez
G. OF
SUEZ
Sinai
Al Arayj
Al Jawf
Sakakah
NEUTRAL ZONE
KUWAIT
AL MANĀMAH
BAHRAIN
(BR.)
QATAR
DOHA
Abū Dhabi
Trucial Coast
MUSCAT

•Uqalah
•Gardaba
Oasis
•Jalo
Qattara Depression
EGYPT
CAIRO
Al Gizā
Al Fayyūm
Banī Suwayf
Hulwan
G. OF AQABA
J. KATHĪNAH
2657
J. ASH SHIFA
Al Hismā
•Tabūk
An Nafūd
Ha'il
Buraydah
AL KHUFF
Shaqrāh
RIYADH
Ad Dilam
Ad Dahnā
Al Hufūf
QATAR
Sharjah
Dubayy
Ra's al Khaymah
MUSCAT
TRUCIAL
OMAN
Al Jiwā'
3107
AL AKHDAR

•Siwa
Siwa Oasis
Great Sand Sea
Libyan
Baharīya Oasis
Banī Mazār
Al Minyā
Maaza Plat.
Dayrūt
•Taymā
•Khaybar
Al Madīnah
OMAN

Cyrenaica
Sand Sea of Calansho
Sarīr Calansho
A
Desert
Farafra Oasis
Asyūt
Dishna
Ghurdaqah
•Safājah
Al Wajh
Yanbu' al Bahr
SAUDI
Ar Rimāl

•Tazerbo
•Kufra Oasis
Dakhla Oasis
Al Khārijah
The Great Oasis
Al Balyanā
Qena
Qus
Al Uqsur
J. MASHĀBIH
•Al Qusayr
Rās Banās
•At Tā'if
Makkah
Turābah
TAT TUWAYQ
Al Aflaj
Biyadh
As Sum
OMAN
20°

na Sand Sea
Gilf Kebir Plateau
Sarīr Chalgo
Al Wāhāt al Khārijah
(Kharga Oasis)
Idfu
J. HAMĀTA
1977
Aswan Dam
Aswān
Lake Nasser
(under construction)
J. ASOTERIBA
2217
Rās Hadarba
Ras
Jiddah
SEA
Al Līth
ASIR
Rub'al
Khāli
Al Qa'āmīyāt
J. AL QARA
1129
Salalah
KURIA MURIA
(BR.)

TEDI
HO
Erdi
Depression de Mourdi
Ennedi
Plat. de Basso
Merowe
Dongola
Baiyuda Desert
Berber
Merowe
Atbara
Ed Damer
J. UWEINAT
1892
Wadi Halfa
Nubian Desert
J. ERBA
2218
ODA
2260
Port Sudan
Suakin
Qīzān
Tihāmah
PROTECTORATE OF
SOUTH
Ra's Fartak

KEBKOUR
MOURNE
J. GURGEI
Geneina
JEBEL
MARRA 3071
J. GIMBALA
El Fasher
SUDAN
El Milk
Atbara
Meroë
Shendi
Kassala
Massawa
Keren
DAHLAC ARCHO
Asmara
Adi Ugri
J. FARASAN
J. KAMARAN
(BR.)
3760
SAN'Ā
Al Hudaydah
YEMEN
Habbān
Mukalla
ARABIA
Shibām
Say'ūn
Ra's Qulansīyah
4

•béché
Am Timan
En Nahūd
El Obeid
Omdurman
Khartoum North
KHARTOUM
Wad Medani
Sennār
Gedaref
MELAU
ANCUA
4620
Aduwa
Adigrat
Aksum
Dhamār
Ta'izz
HANISH
3200
Assab
Sheikh 'Othmān
ADEN
GULF OF ADEN
Hadibu
SOCOTRA
(BR.)
ABD AL KURI
(BR.)
THE BROTHERS
(BR.)
C Guardafui

D
W. Ibra
Dar el Homr
Dar Nuba
(White Nile)
Ed Dueim
Kosti
Umm Ruwāba
Asosa
MT. DEINGUERI
Gondar
Sokota
Debra Tabor
L. Tana
1830
GUNA
4331
Debra Markos
Egogi Bad
SOMALILAND
FR.
DJIBOUTI
Ras Khanzira
Berbera
Erigevo
Haded
Ras Hafun
Dante
MONTI CARCAR

Dar
Roungo
Aouk
J. NGAYA
Bahr el Ghazal
Jūr
Sue
White Nile
Bahr el Arab
Bahr el Jebel
Sobat
T. WALLEL
3301
Dembidolo
Sudd
Agaumdir
CHOKE MTS.
BIRHAN
4154
Abbai
Ankober
AHMAR MTS.
Harar
Diredawa
Borama
Hargeisa
Burao
Nogal Valley
Eil
ANDREW SEAMOUNT
1555
DAVID SEAKNOLL
2370

MASSIF DES BONGOS
Bria
Bambari
Bangassou
Mobaye
Banzyville
Zemio
Bondo
Uele
Niangara
Aketi
Buta
Paulis
Watsa
L. Nuong
Gore
ETHIOPIA
Jimma
Sodo
L. Zwai
Maji
Gardula
Gidole
L. Abaya
L. Chamo
Negelli
Adama
Cherchar
Haud
Ogaden
Webi Shebeli
Mudugh
Obbia
I N D I A N

ENTRAL
RICAN REP.
Kotto
Bambari
Bangassou
Mobaye
Bomu
Congo
MT. DEINGUERI
Arua
Nimule
MORUNGOLE
Lotagipi Swamp
L. Stefanie
Lake Rudolf
SOGO HILLS
HUR HILLS
URGOMA MTS.
BATU
4307
Ginir
Lugh Ferrandi
Iscia Baidoa
Villaggio Duca degli Abruzzi
Bardera
S

tville
ira
Boende
Liuaba
Basankusu
Lisala
Mobaye
Banzyville
Tshuapa
Lomami
Lualaba
Kindu-Port Empain
gold II
Banalia
Basoko
Stanleyville
Ponthierville
Buta
Kabalo
RUWENZORI
STANLEY FLS.
L. Edward
L. Kivu
Goma
Giseny
NGALI
Shabunda
Bukavu
RWANDA
Butare
KYOGA
L. Albert
Albert Nile
Mulchison
Falls Dam
Bunia
FT. Portal
UGANDA
Masindi
L. Kyoga
Soroti
Moroto
MT. KULAL
MT. NYIRU
2805
CHERANGANI HILLS
Mbale
MT. ELGON
4321
Kitale
Eldoret
Lorian Swamp
Nanyuki
MT. KENYA
5200
ABERDARE
Nyeri
NAIROBI
CHYULU RAN.
TEITA HILLS
Lamu
Malindi
O C E A N
S o m a l i
B a s i n
5

BURUNDI
BUJUMBURA
Kindu
MT. KARISIMBI
4507
Kabale
Mbarara
Lake
Bukoba
Victoria
1134
Mwanza
KAMPALA
Entebbe
Jinja
Kakamega
Kisumu
Nakuru
Masaka
MT. KILIMANJARO
5895
MERU
Voi
EQUATOR 0°
TANZANIA
L. Eyasi
Serengeti
Plain
Narok
40°
H
50°

RED SEA
JORDAN
IRAQ
SYRIA
TURKEY
GREECE
AEGEAN SEA
SOMALI
KENYA
CONGO

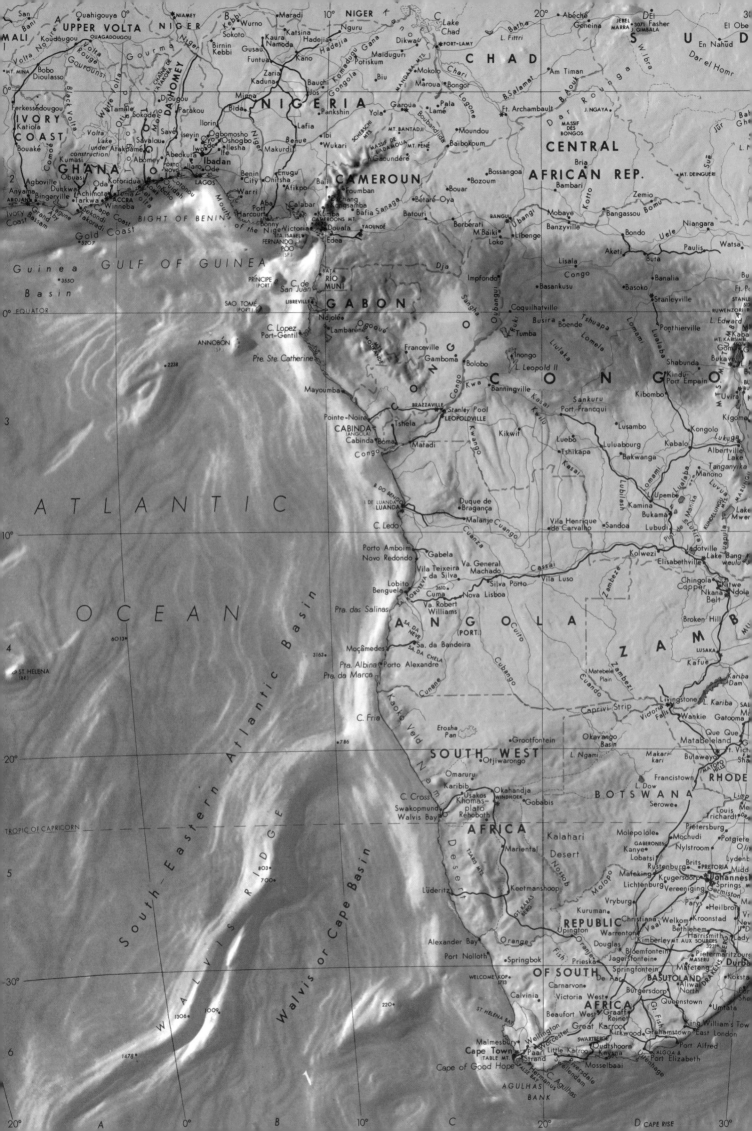

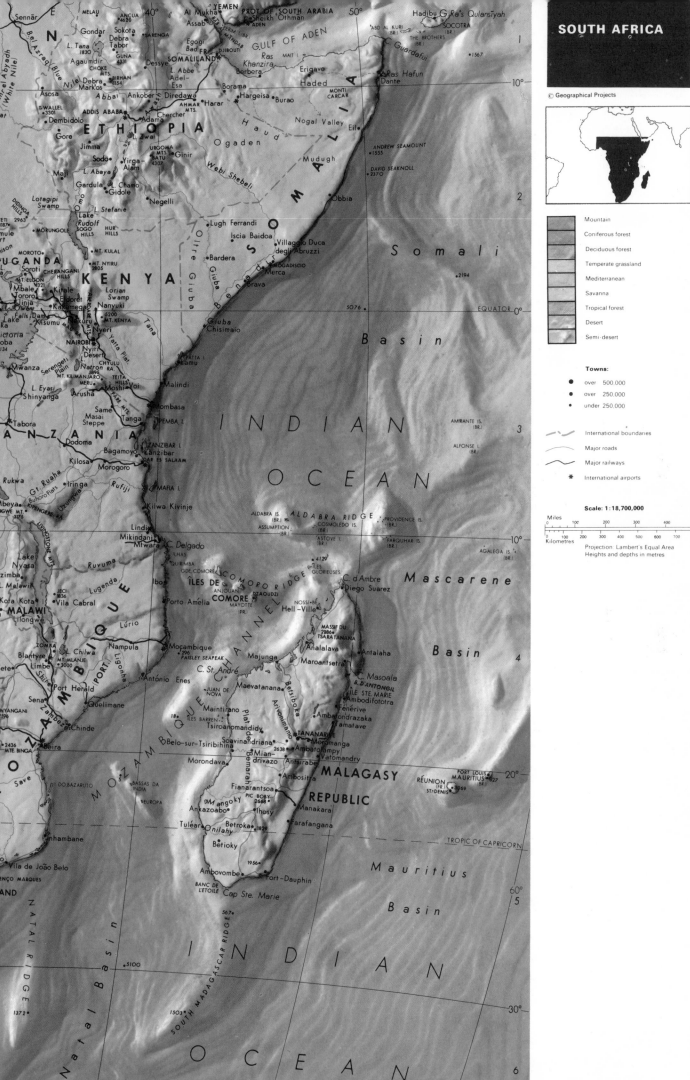

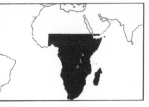
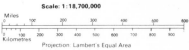

Mountain
Coniferous forest
Deciduous forest
Temperate grassland
Mediterranean
Savanna
Tropical forest
Desert
Semi-desert

Towns:

● over 500,000
● over 250,000
● under 250,000

— — — International boundaries
——— Major roads
~~~ Major railways
✳ International airports

Scale: 1:18,700,000

Miles
0   100   200   300   400   500   600
0 100 200 300 400 500 600 700 800 900
Kilometres

Projection: Lambert's Equal Area
Heights and depths in metres

EAST AFRICA

Projection: Lambert's Equal Area
Heights in metres

Scale: 1 : 9,000,000

Miles

Kilometres

Towns:
- ● over 100,000
- ● under 100,000

〰〰 International boundaries
〰 Major railways
✳ International airports

104

© Geographical Projects

Projection: Lambert's Equal Area
Heights in metres

Scale: 1 : 7,000,000

Miles
0   50   100   150   200

Kilometres
0   50   100   150   200   250   300   350

Towns:
● over 100,000
● under 100,000

⌄⌄ ⌐ International boundaries
〜 Major railways
✷ International airports

TANZANIA
SOUTHERN
Masasi
Rondo Plateau
Makondi Plateau
Lindi
Mikindani
Mtwara
Ras Matunda
Quionga
C. Delgado
Palma
Mocímboa da Praia
Planalto do Mavia
Mueda
Rovuma
B. DE MOCÍMBOA

CABO DELGADO
Mucojo
Macomia
Quissanga
Ilbo
Ancuabe
Porto Amélia
Mecúfi
Lúrio
Montepuez
Balama
Msalu

MOZAMBIQUE (PORT.)
Namapa
Memba
B. DE MEMBA
C. Loguno
B. DE FERNÃO VELOSO
Nacala
MOÇAMBIQUE
Ribáuè
Muecate
Meconta Lumbo
Moçambique
P. Bajona
B. DE CONDÚNCIA
Nampula
Mogincual

ZAMBÉZIA
Nametil
Namaponda
António Enes
Gilé
Moma
Pebane

MOZAMBIQUE CHANNEL

ÎLES DE COMORE (FR.)
GRANDE COMORE
2560
ANJOUAN
1578
MOHÉLI
ÎLES GLORIEUSES
48°
BANC DU GEYSER
DZAOUDZI
MAYOTTE

JUAN DE NOVA
ÎLES BARREN
BASSAS DA INDIA (FR.)
EUROPA (FR.)

C. d'Ambre
Diego Suarez
1475
MGNE. D'AMBRE
NOSSI-BÉ
Hell-Ville
Ambilobe
Vohémar
MASSIF DU
2886
TSARATANANA
2305
Sambava
Analalava
Bealanana
Andapa
Antsohihy
Befandriana
Antalaha
IS. RADAMA
C. Est
Maroantsetra
B. D'ANTONGIL
Mandritsara
C. Masoala
Port-Bergé
Mananara
Majunga
ANKOFA
1300
ÎLE STE. MARIE
Mitsinjo
C. St. André
Marovoay
Ambato-Boéni
Tsaratanana
Ambodifototra
Soalala
Maevatanana
Fénérive
Besalampy
720
L. Alaotra
1445
Morafenobe
1548
Ambatondrazaka
Tamatave
Maintirano
Kiangara
TANANARIVE
Ankazobe
Anjozorobe
Tsiroanomandidy
Ambohidratrimo
★ TANANARIVE
Brickaville
Miarinarivo
Andevoranto
1326
L. Itasy
Arivonimamo
Moramanga
Soavinandriana
Ambatolampy
SIAFAJAVONA
2638
Vatomandry
Belo-sur-Tsiribihina
Miandrivazo
946
Mahanoro
MALAGASY
Betafo
Antsirabe
Marolambo
REPUBLIC
Morondava
Fandriana
Mahabo
Ambatofinandrahana
Ambositra
Nosy-Varika
1868
1405
Ambohimahasoa
Manja
Béroroha
Fianarantsoa
Ifanadiana
Mananjary
Morombe
Ambalavao
2030
1325
PIC BOBY
2658
Fort-Carnot
Manakara
Ankazoaba
Ihosy
1128
Vohipeno
Farafangana
Tuléar
Betroka
1829
Vangaindrano
TROPIC OF CAPRICORN
Onilahy
Midongy du Sud
TROPIC OF CAPRICORN
Betioky
L. Tsimanampetsotsa
MASSE DE LIVAKOANY
Bekily
1188
1916
1956
Ampanihy
Ambovombe
Fort-Dauphin
Pte. Fenambosy
Cap Ste. Marie

INDIAN

OCEAN

Mangoky
MASSIF DU MAKAY
PLATEAU DU BEMARAHA
Manambao
Mahavavy
Ikopa
Betsiboka
MAHAFALY
ONILAHY
MASSIF RUINIFORME DE L'ISALO
Mananara
Mania
ANDRINGITRA
Matsiatra
ANKARATRA
Mangoro

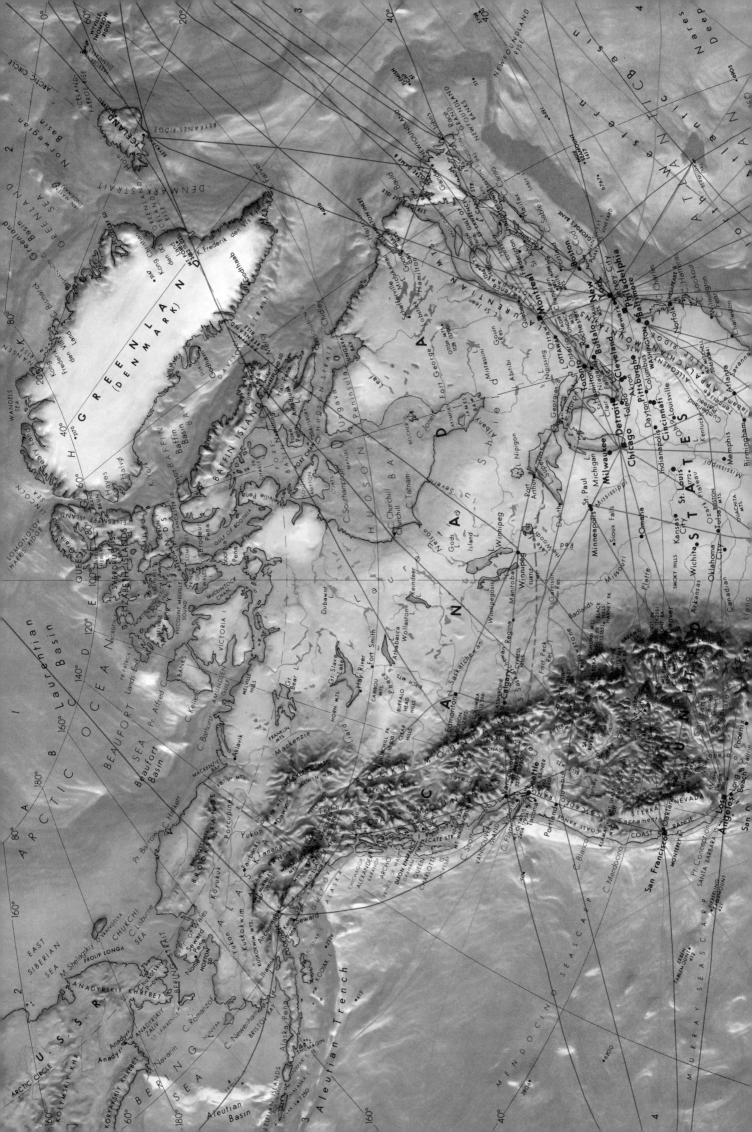

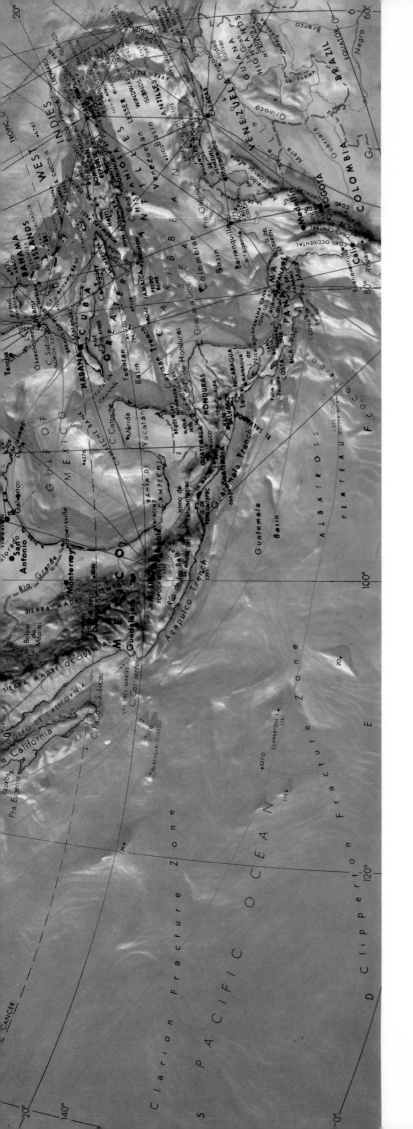

© Geographical Projects

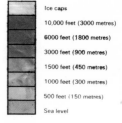

	Ice caps
	10,000 feet (3000 metres)
	6000 feet (1800 metres)
	3000 feet (900 metres)
	1500 feet (450 metres)
	1000 feet (300 metres)
	500 feet (150 metres)
	Sea level

Towns:

■ over 1,000,000

● over 500,000

◐ over 250,000

• under 250,000

 International boundaries

Major air routes

Major sea routes

Scale: 1 : 28,700,000

Miles

Kilometres

Projection: Lambert's Equal Area
Heights and depths in metres

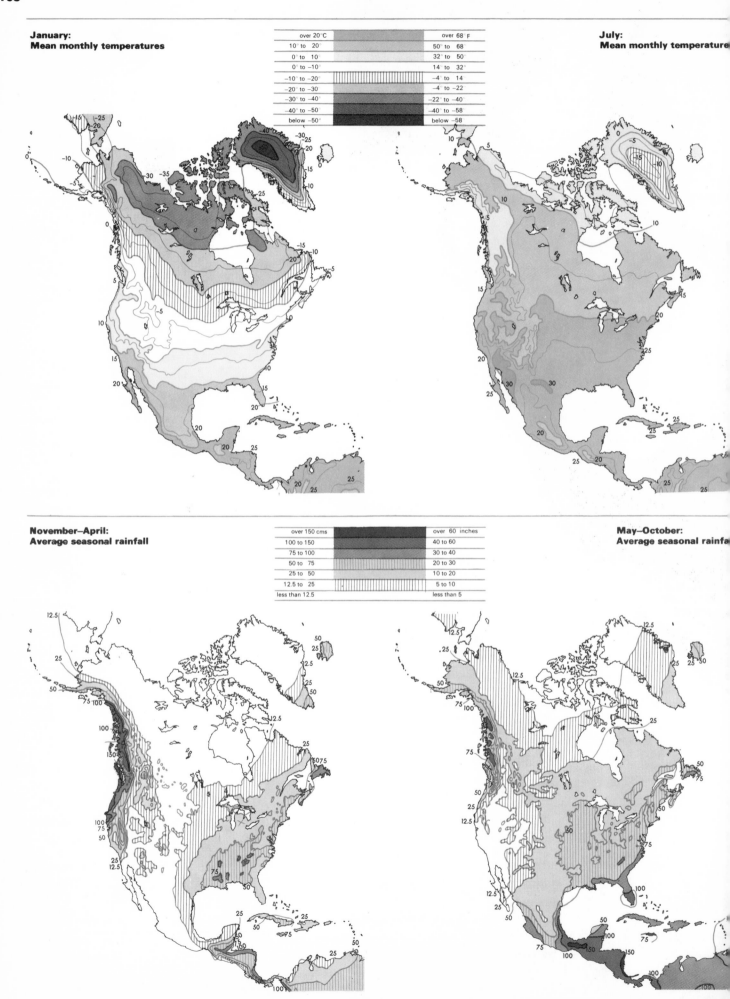

January:
Mean monthly temperatures

	over 20°C		over 68° F
	10° to 20°		50° to 68°
	0° to 10°		32° to 50°
	0° to −10°		14° to 32°
	−10° to −20°		−4° to 14
	−20° to −30		−4° to −22
	−30° to −40°		−22° to −40
	−40° to −50°		−40° to −58
	below −50°		below −58

July:
Mean monthly temperature

November–April:
Average seasonal rainfall

	over 150 cms		over 60 inches
	100 to 150		40 to 60
	75 to 100		30 to 40
	50 to 75		20 to 30
	25 to 50		10 to 20
	12.5 to 25		5 to 10
	less than 12.5		less than 5

May–October:
Average seasonal rainfa

North America stretches from the warm waters of the Gulf of Mexico to the icy Arctic seas and bitter winter cold of the vast Canadian northland. The whole interior of the continent is open to the sweep of air from either extreme—the tropical south or the arctic north. Everywhere winters are cold for the latitude, and much of northern United States and Canada have a lasting cover of snow during the winter. East of the Mississippi, warm air from the south prevails throughout much of the hot and sticky summer, while in winter colder air from the dry west or the snowy north prevails and day-to-day changes in the weather may be very great. The eastern part of the continent has a fairly heavy rainfall, but also much sunshine. Rainfall decreases sharply towards the west; southwards towards Mexico the land is so dry, except at high altitudes, that it is virtually desert. California, and the Pacific coast right up to Alaska, have much milder winters than the interior; in this region rainfall increases steadily from 10 inches (25 cms.) around Los Angeles to over 200 inches (500 cms.) in the mountains of British Columbia.

Average number of days per year when frost is unlikely to occur

less than 60	
more than 60	
more than 90	
more than 120	
more than 180	
more than 240	
occasional frost	
frost free areas	

Average number of hours sunshine per year

over 4000 hours	
3000 to 4000	
2000 to 3000	
1000 to 2000	
less than 1000	
tropical storm paths	

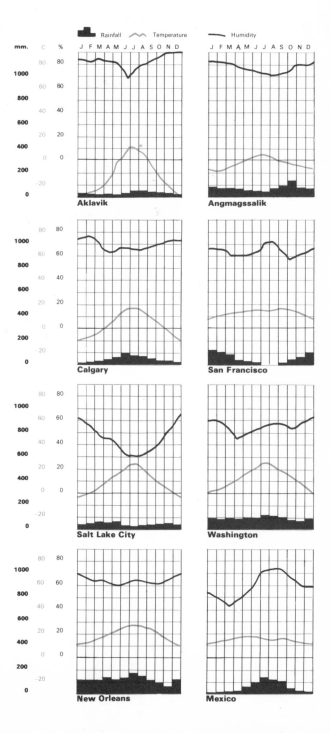

Projection: Lambert's Equal Area

Scale: 1:39,000,000

Miles

Kilometres

● Capital cities

1500–1650

1650–1763 (Treaty of Paris)

63–1830

1830–20th century

Soils

- **Permanent ice**
- **Red soils** / **Yellow soils** — *Pedalfers (non-lime accumulating soils) in humid, tropical regions lateritic soils, soils of incomplete leaching*
- **Podsols** / **Grey & brown forest soils** / **Prairie soils** — *Pedalfers in sub-tropical and humid, temperate regions, podsolic soils, soils of incomplete leaching*
- **Grey soils** — *Pedocals (lime accumulating soils) in drier, subtropical regions, soils of impeded leaching*
- **Chernozems** / **Brown and chestnut soils** — *Pedocals in more temperate, less arid regions, soils of impeded leaching*
- **Tundra soils** — *Pedocals in polar regions*
- **Mountain soils** — *Intrazonal soils*
- **Alluvial soils**
- **Sand – mainly dunes**

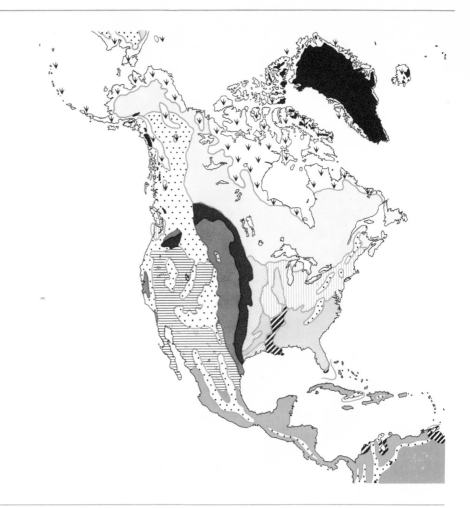

Land use

- **Unproductive areas**
- **Industrial & urban areas**
- **Hunting & gathering; shifting cultivation in tropics**
- **Stock rearing & ranging**
- **Intensive & specialised agriculture**
- **Mixed farming**
- **Forest lands**
- **Lumbering**
- **Grain production predominant**
- **Plantation agriculture**
- **Nomadic economies**
- **Deep sea fishing**
- **Coastal fishing**

Power resources

	Coal
	Lignite
	Oil well
	Asphalt
	Natural gas
	Atomic power station
	Hydro-electric power station
	Uranium & thorium
	Oil pipeline
	Gas pipeline

Population density & Religions

	over 250 per sq. mile / over 100 per sq. km
	125 – 250 / 50 – 100
	60 – 125 / 25 – 50
	25 – 60 / 10 – 25
	2 – 25 / 1 – 10
	less than 2 / less than 1
†	Roman Catholic
	Protestant
	Judaism
△	Tribal & others

© Geographical Projects

Welland Canal

Thousand
Islands

Montreal

200

100

Sea level

100

metres

245·7 ft.

151 ft.

66·5 ft.

20 ft.

Lake Ontario

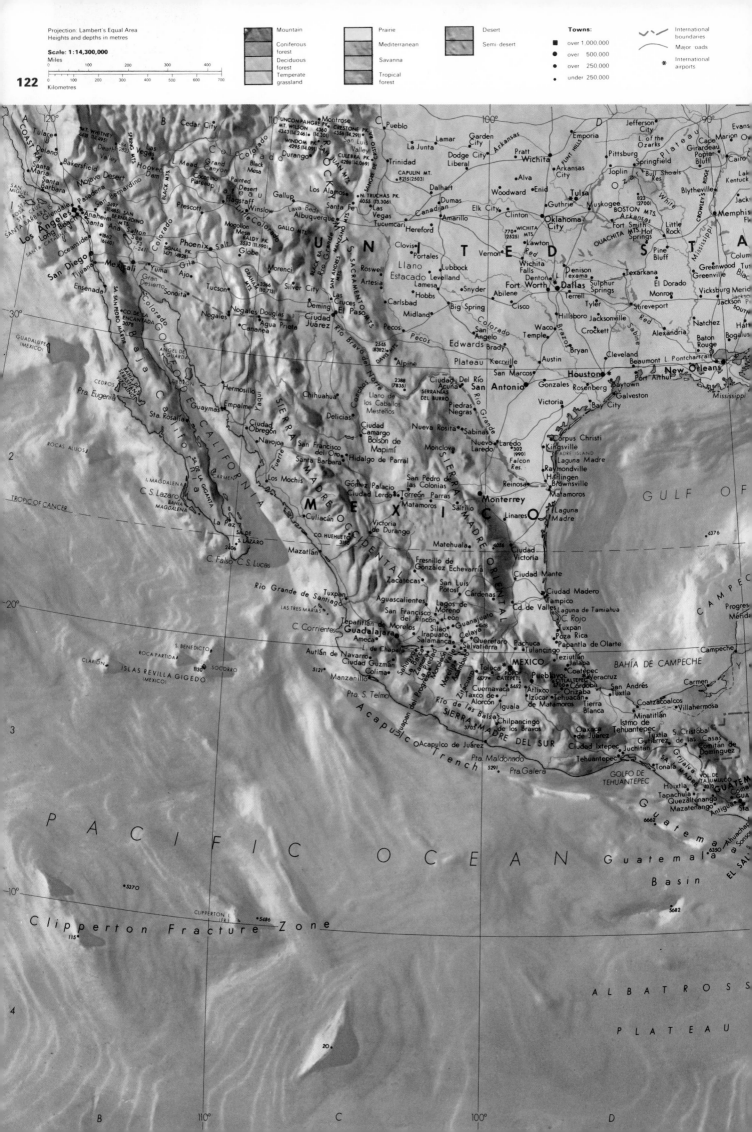

© Geographical Projects

January:
Mean monthly temperatures

over 20 C		over 68 F
10 to 20		50 to 68
0 to 10		32 to 50
below 0		below 32

July:
Mean monthly temperature

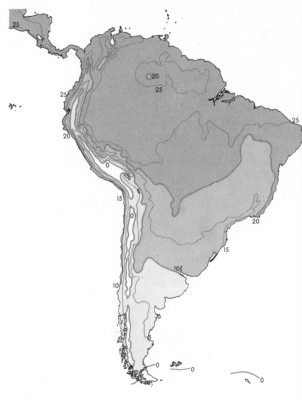

November–April:
Average seasonal rainfall

over 200 cms		over 80 inches
150 to 200		60 to 80
100 to 150		40 to 60
75 to 100		30 to 40
50 to 75		20 to 30
25 to 50		10 to 20
12.5 to 25		5 to 10
less than 12.5		less than 5

May–October:
Average seasonal rainfa

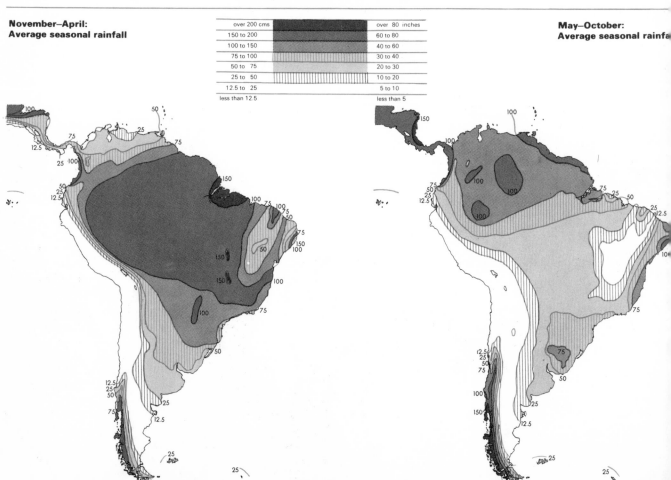

South America lies for the most part within the tropics; the enormous Amazon basin provides the world's largest area of equatorial climate, with uniformly high temperatures, high rainfall over much of the year, high humidity and little wind. Towards the margins of this basin the rainfall gradually becomes more seasonal; in the months when the sun is highest humidity and rainfall are both high, but the 'cooler' season is marked by dry weather and strong sunshine. This general description remains true of the greater part of southern Brazil and the Pampas of Argentina. Much of north-eastern Brazil, however, is seriously deficient in rain. The western and central Andes are also dry and much of the western coastal strip is very dry indeed and relatively cool and cloudy, being influenced by cool ocean currents. By contrast the southern Andes are stormy and very wet as the result of persistent west winds; east of the mountains Patagonia is also windy and cool, but very dry.

**Average number of days
per year when frost is unlikely to occur**

more than 60	
more than 90	
more than 120	
more than 180	
more than 240	
occasional frost	
frost free areas	

**Average number of hours
sunshine per year**

over 4000 hours	
3000 to 4000	
2000 to 3000	
less than 2000	
tropical storm paths	

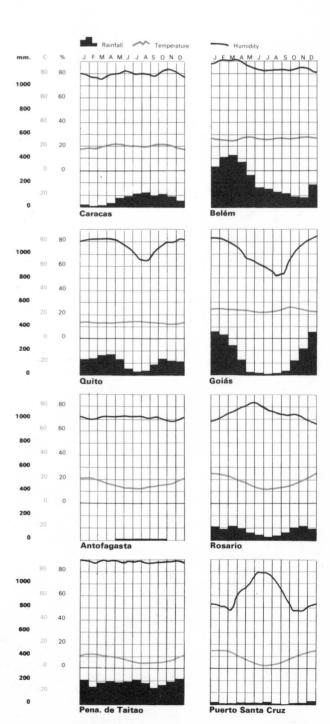

Rainfall   Temperature   Humidity

Caracas

Belém

Quito

Goiás

Antofagasta

Rosario

Pena. de Taitao

Puerto Santa Cruz

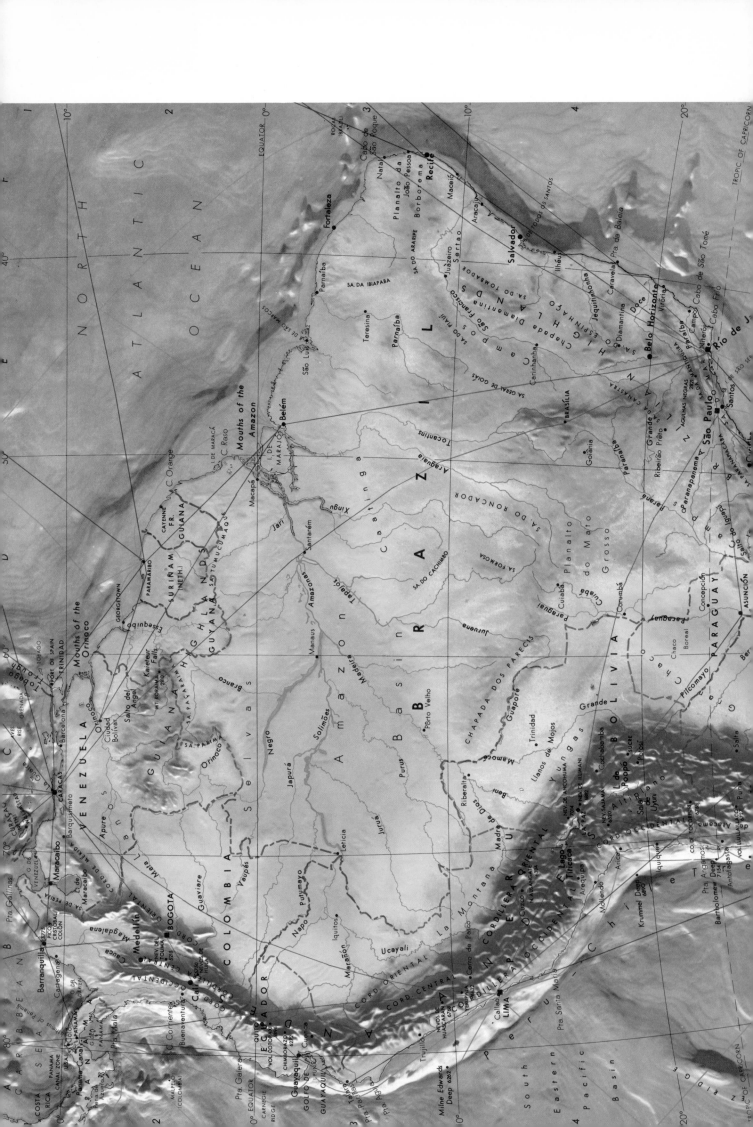

© Geographical Projects

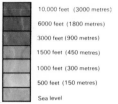

10,000 feet (3000 metres)
6000 feet (1800 metres)
3000 feet (900 metres)
1500 feet (450 metres)
1000 feet (300 metres)
500 feet (150 metres)
Sea level

Towns:

■ over 1,000,000
● over 500,000
● over 250,000
• under 250,000

 International boundaries

Major air routes

Major sea routes

Scale: 1 : 20,300,000

Miles
0 100 200 300 400 500 600

0 100 200 300 400 500 600 700 800 900
Kilometres

Projection: Bipolar Oblique Conic Conformal
Heights and depths in metres

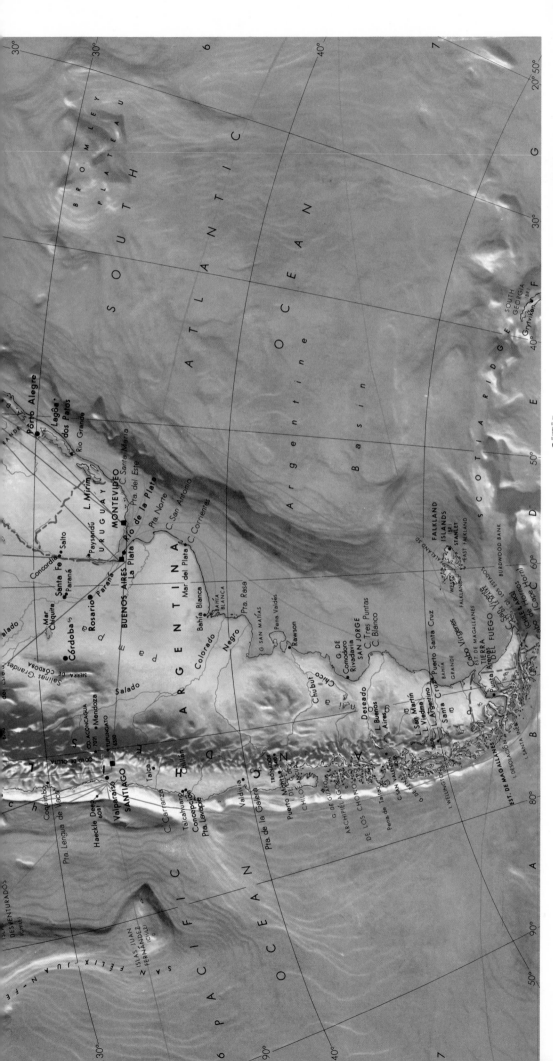

© Geographical Projects

c. 1500–1650

1650–1763 (Treaty of Paris)

1763–1830

1830–20th. century

Projection: Bipolar Oblique Conic Conformal

© Geographical Projects

Scale: 1 : 28,600,000

Miles
0   500   1000   1500   2000   2500   3000   3500   4000   4500

0   1000   2000   3000   4000   5000   6000   7000
Kilometres

• Capital cities

A   80°   B   70°   C   60°   D   50°   E   40°   F   30°

CARIBBEAN SEA

ST. LUCIA
ST. VINCENT
CURAÇAO
(NETH.)   Willemstad   GRENADA   BARBADOS

COSTA
RICA
PANAMA
CANAL ZONE
(U.S.A.)   TOBAGO
Panamá   TRINIDAD
PANAMA   Port of Spain

Caracas

MALPELO
(COLOMBIA)

Bogotá

Orinoco

VENEZUELA   Georgetown   NORTH ATLANTIC

GUYANA   Paramaribo

SURINAM   Cayenne   OCEAN
(NETH.)

FRENCH
GUIANA

COLOMBIA

Magdalena

Guaviare

EQUATOR   Quito   Napo   Putumayo   Negro   Mouths of
the Amazon   EQUATOR

ECUADOR

ROCAS   I. FERNANDO
(BRAZIL)   DE NORONHA

Marañón   Amazonas   B   R

PERU   Purus   Madeira   Tapajós   A   Z   I   L

Tocantins   São Francisco

Lima

Lago
Titicaca   La Paz   BOLIVIA   Brasília

Sucre

Paraguay   Paraná

PARAGUAY   I. DA TRINDADE
(BRAZIL)

TROPIC OF CAPRICORN   Asunción   TROPIC OF CAPRICORN

ISLAS DE LOS
DESVENTURADOS
(CHILE)   Paraná   Uruguay

PACIFIC

Santiago   Montevideo   SOUTH
ISLAS JUAN FERNÁNDEZ   URUGUAY
(CHILE)   Buenos Aires   Río de la Plata

ARGENTINA   ATLANTIC

OCEAN

Colorado

Negro   OCEAN

FALKLAND
ISLANDS
(BR.)
Stanley

TIERRA DEL
FUEGO   SOUTH
GEORGIA
(BR.)
Cabo de Hornos
CHILE & ARG.)   (C. Horn)

A   80°   B   70°   C   60°   D   50°   E   40°   F   30°

© Geographical Projects

Soils

 Permanent ice		
Red soils	*Pedalfers (non-lime accumulating soils) in humid, tropical regions, lateritic soils, soils of incomplete leaching*	
Laterites		
Yellow soils		
Terra Rossa	*Pedocals (lime-accumulating soils) in drier, subtropical regions, soils of impeded leaching*	
Grey soils		
Chernozems	*Pedocals in more temperate, less arid regions, soils of impeded leaching*	
Brown and chestnut soils		
Mountain soils	*Intrazonal soils*	
Alluvial soils		
Sand — mainly dunes		

Land use

Unproductive areas

Industrial & urban areas

Hunting, gathering & shifting cultivation

Stock rearing & ranging

Intensive & specialised agriculture

Mixed farming

Forest lands

Lumbering

Grain production predominant

Plantation agriculture

Deep sea fishing

Coastal fishing

Power resources

	Coal
	Oil well
•	Asphalt
	Natural gas
	Hydro-electric power station
	Uranium & thorium
	Oil pipeline
	Gas pipeline

Population density & Religions

	over 250 per sq. mile *over 100 per sq. km*
	125 – 250 *50 – 100*
	60 – 125 *25 – 50*
	25 – 60 *10 – 25*
	2 – 25 *1 – 10*
	less than 2 *less than 1*
†	Roman Catholic
	Protestant
△	Tribal & others

© Geographical Projects

Mountain
Coniferous forest
Deciduous forest
Temperate grassland
Prairie
Savanna
Tropical forest
Desert
Semi-desert

Towns:

■ over 1,000,000
● over 500,000
● over 250,000
• under 250,000

/ International boundaries
Major roads
Major railways
✳ International airports

Scale: 1:13,900,000

Miles
0   100   200   300   400
0 100 200 300 400 500
Kilometres

Projection: Bipolar Oblique Conic Conformal
Heights and depths in metres

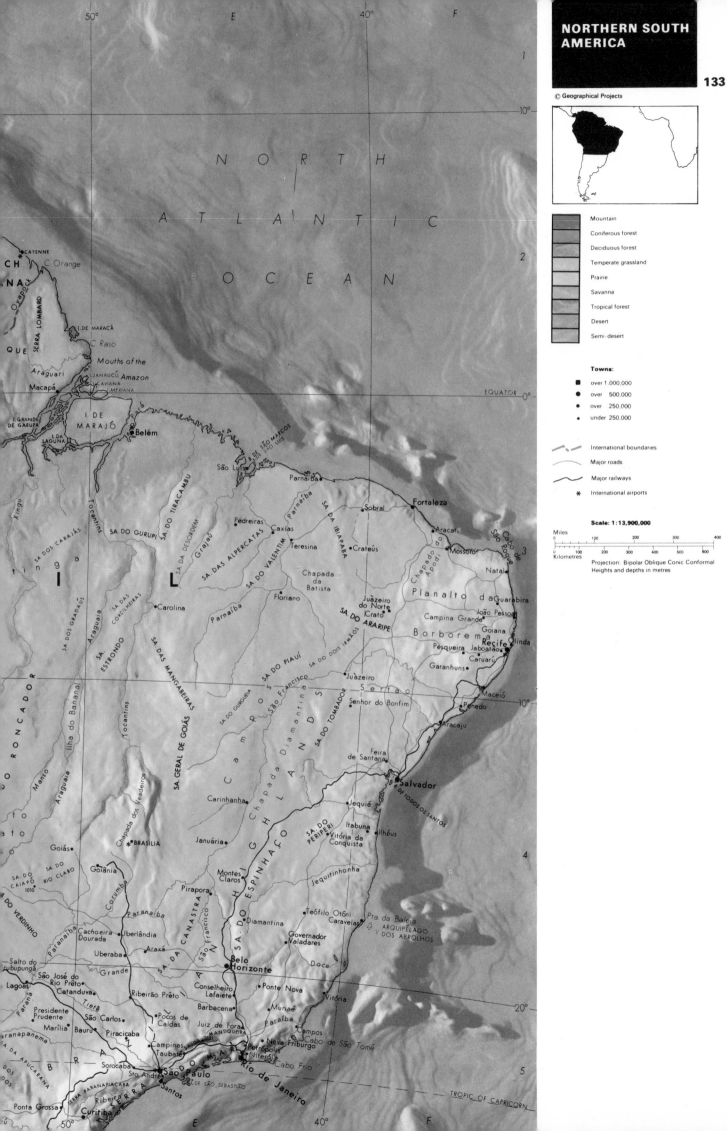

NORTH

ATLANTIC

OCEAN

CAYENNE
C. Orange
CH
NA
QUE
SERRA LOMBARD
I. DE MARACÁ
C. Raso
Araguari
Mouths of the
I. JANAUCÚ
I. CAVIANA
Amazon
Macapá
I. MEXIANA
I. GRANDE DE GARUPÁ
I. DA LAGUNA
I. DE MARAJÓ
Belém
Pará

EQUATOR 0°

Xingu
SA. DOS CARAJÁS
Tocantins
SA. DO GURUPI
SA. DO TIRACAMBU
São Luís
B. DE SÃO MARCOS
B. DE SÃO LUÍS
Parnaíba
tinga
SA. DO GRADAÚS
SA. DAS CONCILHEIRAS
SA. DA DESORDEM
Grajaú
Pedreiras
Caxias
SA. DAS ALPERCATAS
SA. DA IBIAPABA
Parnaíba
Sobral
Fortaleza
Aracati
I
L
Araguaia
SA. ESTRONDO
Carolina
Parnaíba
SA. DO VALENTIM
Teresina
Crateús
Mossoró
Chapado do Apodi
Natal
Chapada da Batista
Juàzeiro do Norte
Crato
SA. DO ARARIPE
Planalto d a
Guarabira
Ilha do Bananal
SA. DAS MANGABEIRAS
SA. DO PIAUÍ
SA. DO GURGUEIA
São Francisco
SA. DO DOIS IRMÃOS
Campina Grande
João Pessoa
RONCADOR
Tocantins
SA. GERAL DE GOIÁS
C A M P O S
Chapada Diamantina
SA. DO TOMBADOR
Juàzeiro
Sertão
Borborema
Recife
Olinda
Goiana
Pesqueira
Jaboatão
Caruarú
Garanhuns
to
Manso
Veadeiros
Senhor do Bonfim
Maceió
Penedo
ato
Araguaia
Carinhanha
Aracaju
Feira de Santana
Chapada dos Veadeiros
BRASÍLIA
Januária
Salvador
B. DE TODOS OS SANTOS
Goiás
Jequié
SA. DO CAIAPÓ
SA. DO RIO CLARO
Goiânia
1010
Montes Claros
SA. DO PERIPERI
Itabuna
Ilhéus
Vitória da Conquista
DO VERDINHO
Corumbá
Piraпora
Jequitinhonha
Paraíba
Paranaíba
Cachoeira Dourada
Uberlândia
Araxá
SA. DA CANASTRA
Diamantina
Teófilo Otôni
Caravelas
Pta. da Baleia
ARQUIPÉLAGO DOS ABROLHOS
Uberaba
Governador Valadares
Salto do Urubupungá
Grande
Belo Horizonte
Doce
Lagoas
São José do Rio Prêto
Catanduva
Conselheiro Lafaiete
Ponte Nova
Vitória
Presidente Prudente
Tietê
São Carlos
Barbacena
Muriaé
Paraíba
Marília
Bauru
Piracicaba
Poços de Caldas
Juiz de Fora
Campos
Cabo de São Tomé
aranapanema
MANTIQUEIRA
Nova Friburgo
SA. DA APUCARANA
Campinas
Taubaté
Petrópolis
Cabo Frio
Sorocaba
Sto. André
São Paulo
Niterói
Rio de Janeiro
Ponta Grossa
SERRA PARANAPIACABA
Santos
I. DE SÃO SEBASTIÃO
Ribeira
Curitiba
BRA
SERRA DO MAR

TROPIC OF CAPRICORN

50°   E   40°   F

1

10°

2

3

10°

4

20°

5

50°   E   40°   F

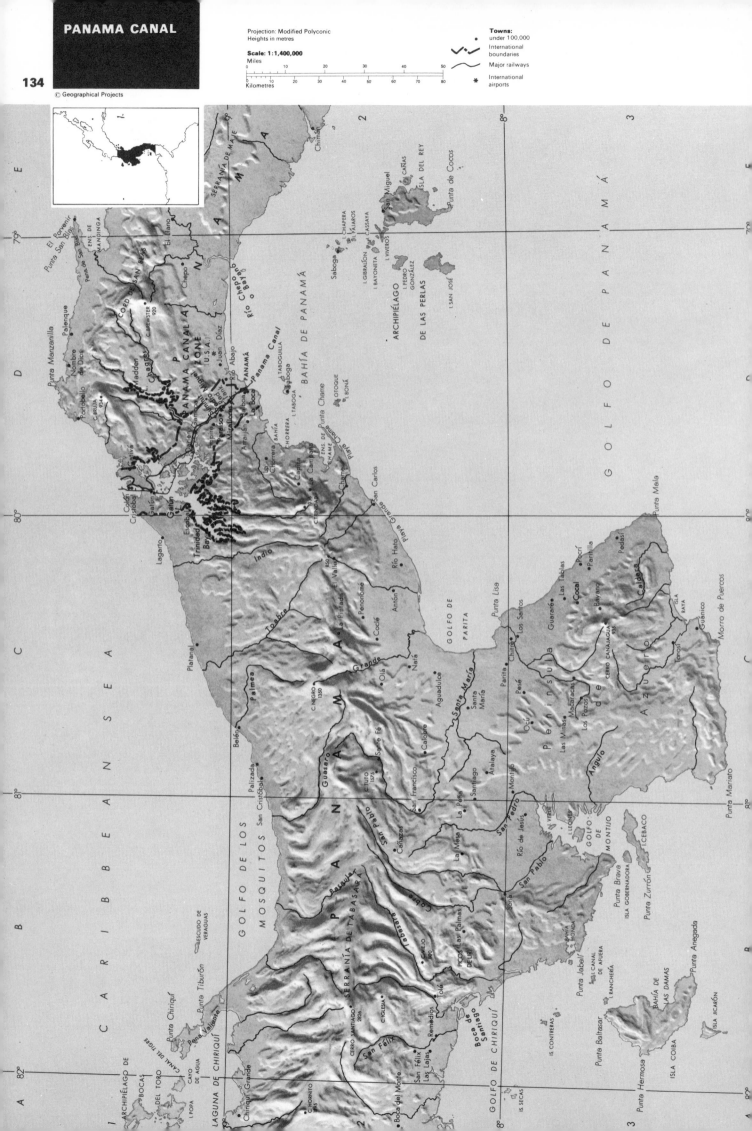

PANAMA CANAL

134

© Geographical Projects

Projection: Modified Polyconic
Heights in metres

Scale: 1:1,400,000

Miles
0   10   20   30   40   50

Kilometres
0   10   20   30   40   50   60   70   80

Towns:
• under 100,000
International boundaries
Major railways
★ International airports

Projection: Bipolar Oblique Conic Conformal
Heights in metres

Scale: 1:13,900,000

Miles
0   100   200   300   400

Kilometres
0   100   200   300   400   500   600   700

Towns:
■ over 1,000,000
● over 500,000
• over 100,000
· under 100,000

〰〰 International boundaries
〰 Major railways
✳ International airports

Projection: Mercator
Heights and depths in metres

Scale: 1:50,700,000 equatorial scale

Miles
0   500   1000   1500

Kilometres
0   500   1000   1500   2000   2500

10,000 feet (3000 metres)
6000 feet (1800 metres)
3000 feet (900 metres)
1500 feet (450 metres)
1000 feet (300 metres)
500 feet (150 metres)
Sea level

International boundaries
Major air routes
Major sea routes

© Geographical Projects

January:
Mean monthly temperatures

over 30 C		over 86 F
20 to 30		68 to 86
10 to 20		50 to 68
below 10		below 50

July:
Mean monthly temperatures

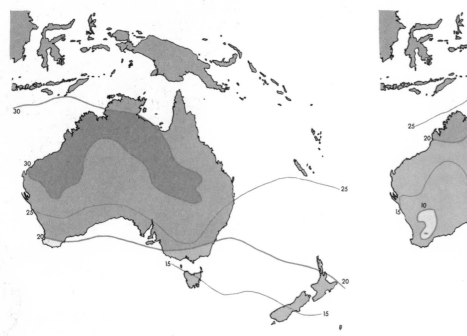

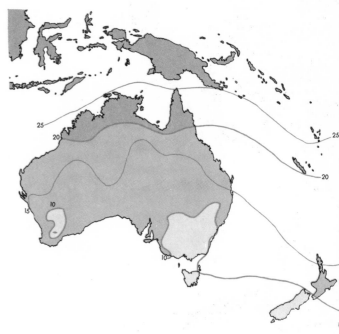

November–April:
Average seasonal rainfall

over 150 cms		over 60 inches
100 to 150		40 to 60
75 to 100		30 to 40
50 to 75		20 to 30
25 to 50		10 to 20
12.5 to 25		5 to 10
less than 12.5		less than 5

May–October:
Average seasonal rainfall

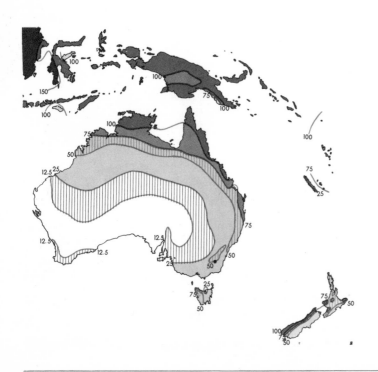

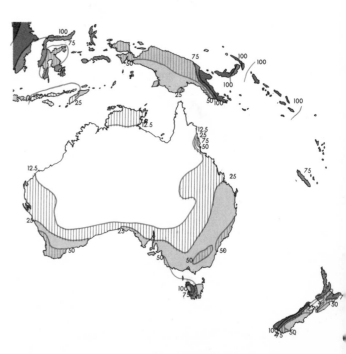

Australasia lies astride the Tropic of Capricorn and, except for Tasmania, does not reach as far south as 40 In the north and north-east is a narrow region having a tropical climate, rainy for a time in the hot summer and largely dry in the still very warm 'cooler' season. The greater part of Australia, however, is generally very dry, with brief and distinctly erratic rains. The south-east and a narrow strip in the south-west are exceptions; in both these areas the weather is more variable and cool moist air from the sea brings welcome rains.

New Zealand, lying mostly farther south, has a more temperate and variable climate, rather like that of England, but with sunnier summers and, in the lowlands, much milder winters.

Average number of days per year when frost is unlikely to occur

more than 90	
more than 120	
more than 180	
more than 240	
occasional frost	
frost free areas	

Average number of hours sunshine per year

over 3000 hours	
2000 to 3000	
less than 2000	
tropical storm paths	←

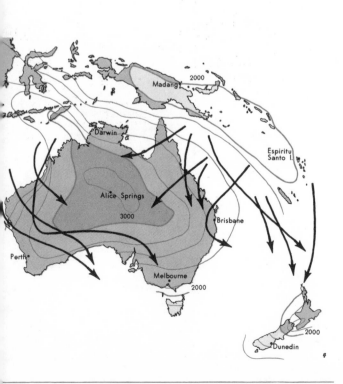

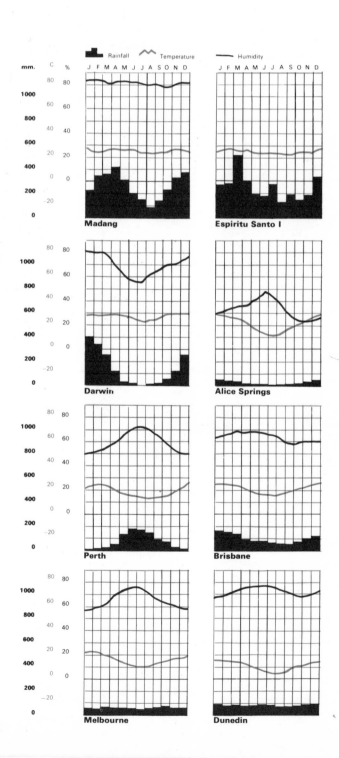

Rainfall   Temperature   Humidity

Madang

Espiritu Santo I

Darwin

Alice Springs

Perth

Brisbane

Melbourne

Dunedin

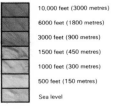

	10,000 feet (3000 metres)
	6000 feet (1800 metres)
	3000 feet (900 metres)
	1500 feet (450 metres)
	1000 feet (300 metres)
	500 feet (150 metres)
	Sea level

Towns:

■ over 1,000,000
● over 500,000
● over 250,000
• under 250,000

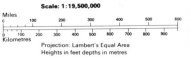

State boundaries

Major air routes

Major sea routes

Scale: 1:19,500,000

Miles
0   100   200   300   400   500   600

Kilometres
0 100 200 300 400 500 600 700 800 900

Projection: Lambert's Equal Area
Heights in feet depths in metres

PACIFIC OCEAN

TARAWA
GILBERT
ISLANDS
(BR.)
EQUATOR 0°

NAURU
(AUSTRALIA)

OCEAN I.
(BR.)

RCK
HIPELAGO
EW
TRELAND

M E L A N E S I A

Planet
Deep
9140m

BOUGAINVILLE I.

CHOISEUL I.

SOLOMON
SANTA ISABEL I.

THE
SLOT
ISLANDS
(BR.)

ELLICE
ISLANDS
(BR.)

NEW GEORGIA
GROUP
MALAITA I.

WOODLARK I.

CASTEAUX IS.

Solomons
Basin

HONIARA
GUADALCANAL

SAN CRISTOBAL I.

SANTA CRUZ IS.
(BR.)

10°

RENNELL RIDGE

LOUISIADE ARCH.

LOUISIADE RIDGE

Santa Cruz
606m

S. Cristobal Tr.

Torres Tr.

Basin

MELANESIAN BORDER PLATEAU

ROTUMA I.

Coral Sea Basin

New Hebrides

BANKS IS.

New Hebrides

North Fiji Basin

VANUA LEVU

C O R A L   SEA

Basin

ESPIRITU SANTO I.

NEW
HEBRIDES
(BR. & FR.)

FIJI
(BR.)

ISH RISE

MALEKULA I.

EFATE

NOU REEF
CAYS

ÎLES CHESTERFIELD
(FR.)

VILA

Nandi
SUVA

VITI LEVU

MARION REEF

New Hebrides Trough

LOYALTY
(FR.) 7660m

20°
180°

SAUMAREZ REEF

BELLONA PLATEAU

NEW
CALEDONIA
(FR.)

CONWAY REEF

HUNTER ISLAND RIDGE

ICORN CHAN.

NOUMEA

MATTHEW
HUNTER

Sandy Cape
FRASER or GT. SANDY I.

WALPOLE

TROPIC OF CAPRICORN

South Fiji Basin

BRISBANE

C. Byron

MIDDLETON CHAN

NORFOLK

KERMADEC IS.
(N.Z.)

LORD HOWE I.
(AUSTRALIA)

NORFOLK I.
(AUSTRALIA)

KERMADEC RIDGE

30°

awke

LORD HOWE RISE

NORFOLK ISLAND RIDGE

Three
Kings
Basin

NORTH CAPE RISE

COLVILLE RIDGE

Galathea
Depth
9994m

mson Deep 5944m

NORFOLK ISLAND TROUGH

Hayre Tr.

Kermadec Trench

C. Maria
van Diemen

North Cape

TASMAN   SEA

Auckland
NORTH
ISLAND

BAY OF
PLENTY

East Cape

40°

C. Farewell Wanganui

L. Taupo

Gisborne

MT. EGMONT

RUAPEHU VOL.
9175

HAWKE BAY
Napier

Nelson

TASMAN B.

NEW
ZEALAND

SOUTH
ISLAND

WELLINGTON
COOK STR.

170°

Christchurch

SOUTHERN ALPS

MT. COOK
12,349

Timaru

CHATHAM RISE

C. Providence

FOVEAUX STRAIT

Dunedin

STEWART I.

Invercargill

CHATHAM IS.
(N.Z.)

NEW ZEALAND

PLATEAU

BOUNTY IS.
(N.Z.)

AUCKLAND IS.
(N.Z.)

ANTIPODES IS.

Soils

■	Permanent ice	
▨	Red soils	*Pedalfers (non-lime accumulating soils) in humid, tropical regions, lateritic soils, soils of incomplete leaching*
▨	Laterites	
▨	Yellow soils	
▥	Grey & brown forest soils	*Pedalfers in sub-tropical and humid, temperate regions, podsolic soils, soils of incomplete leaching*
▤	Terra Rossa	*Pedocals (lime-accumulating soils) in drier, subtropical regions, soils of impeded leaching*
▤	Grey soils	
▨	Chernozems	*Pedocals in more temperate, less arid regions, soils of impeded leaching*
▨	Brown and chestnut soils	
⋰	Mountain soils	*Intrazonal soils*
▨	Alluvial soils	
░	Sand — mainly dunes	

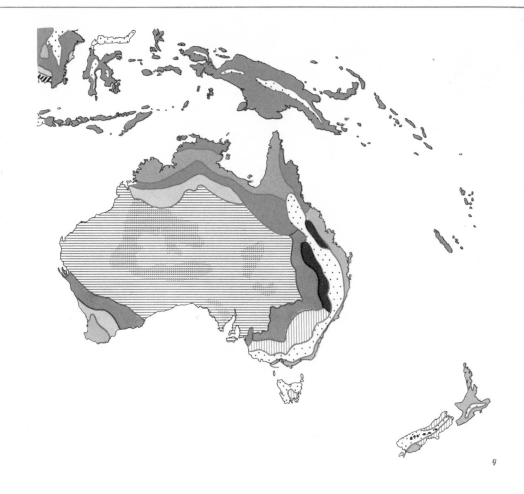

Land use

☐	Unproductive areas
■	Industrial & urban areas
▥	Hunting, gathering & shifting cultivation
▨	Stock rearing & ranging
▨	Intensive & specialised agriculture
▨	Mixed farming
▨	Forest lands
⌐	Lumbering
↓	Grain production predominant
Ⴑ	Plantation agriculture
⋎	Nomadic economies
⋰	Deep sea fishing
⋯	Coastal fishing

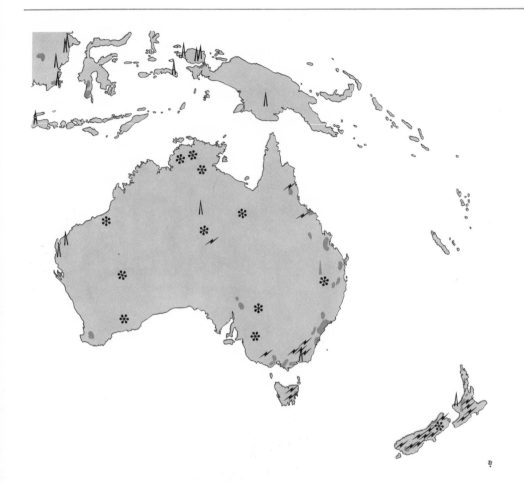

Power resources

▨	Coal
⋀	Oil well
⋀	Natural gas
⚡	Hydro-electric power station
✳	Uranium & thorium

Population density & Religions

■	over 250 per sq. mile *over 100 per sq. km*
	125 – 250 *50 – 100*
	60 – 125 *25 – 50*
	25 – 60 *10 – 25*
	2 – 25 *1 – 10*
	less than 2 *less than 1*

†	Roman Catholic
⊹	Protestant
☾	Muslim
△	Tribal & others

Projection: Lambert's Equal Area

Scale: 1 : 27,000,000
Miles
0   200   400   600   800
0 200 400 600 800 1000 1200 1400 1600
Kilometres

● Capital cities

EQUATOR 0°

PACIFIC OCEAN

Tarawa
GILBERT
ISLANDS
(BR.)

OCEAN I.
(BR.)

NAURU
(AUSTRALIA)

ELLICE I.
ISLANDS (BR.)

SANTA CRUZ IS.
(BR.)

FIJI
(BR.)

Suva

TROPIC OF CAPRICORN

KERMADEC IS.
(N.Z.)

CHATHAM IS.
(N.Z.)

NEW HEBRIDES
(BR. & FR.)

Vila

NEW
ZEALAND

NORTH
ISLAND

Wellington

NORFOLK I.
(AUSTRALIA)

NEW
CALEDONIA
(FR.)

Nouméa

SOUTH
ISLAND

STEWART I.

SOLOMON
ISLANDS
(BR.)

Honiara

SOLOMON
SEA

CORAL
SEA

ÎLES CHESTERFIELD
(FR.)

LORD HOWE I.
(AUSTRALIA)

TASMAN
SEA

BISMARCK
ARCHIPELAGO

TERRITORY OF
NEW GUINEA
(AUSTRALIA)

WESTERN
NEW GUINEA

NEW
GUINEA

TERRITORY
OF PAPUA
(AUSTRALIA)

Port Moresby

GREAT BARRIER REEF

Brisbane

Sydney

LOUISIADE
ARCHO.

ARAFURA
SEA

GULF OF
CARPENTARIA

QUEENSLAND

GREAT DIVIDING RANGE

NEW SOUTH WALES

Barcoo

Darling

Canberra

Lachlan

Murray

VICTORIA

Melbourne

INDONESIA

HALMAHERA

MALUKU
(MOLUCCAS)

SERAM

LAUT BANDA

DILI
(PORT.)

TIMOR
(PORT.)

TIMOR
SEA

Darwin

NORTHERN
TERRITORY

Fitzroy

SOUTH
AUSTRALIA

Lake
Eyre

Adelaide

GREAT AUSTRALIAN BIGHT

BASS STRAIT

TASMANIA

Hobart

CELEBES

BALI
LOMBOK
SUMBAWA
SUMBA

FLORES
LAUT FLORES

INDIAN OCEAN

WESTERN
AUSTRALIA

A U S T R A L I A

Perth

TROPIC OF CAPRICORN

INDIAN
OCEAN

BORNEO
KALIMANTAN

1500–1650

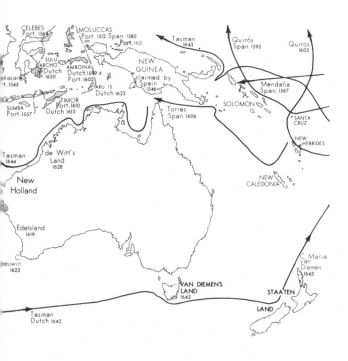

CELEBES
Port. 1564
MOLUCCAS
Port. 1512 Span. 1580
Port. 1621
Tasman 1643
Quirós Span. 1595
Quiros 1605
SULU ARCHO Dutch 1650
AMBOINA Dutch 1599 Port. 1602
NEW GUINEA claimed by Spain 1546
akasar t. 1545
ARU IS. Dutch 1623
Mendaña Span. 1567
SUMBA Port. 1557
TIMOR Port. 1610 Dutch 1613
Torres Span. 1606
SOLOMON IS.
SANTA CRUZ
NEW HEBRIDES
Tasman 1644
de Witt's Land 1628
New Holland
NEW CALEDONIA
Edelsland 1619
C. eeuwin 1622
C. Maria van Diemen 1643
VAN DIEMEN'S LAND 1642
STAATEN LAND
Tasman Dutch 1642

1650–1763 (Treaty of Paris)

CELEBES Dutch 1669 67
MOLUCCAS Dutch 1667
claimed by Holland
NEW GUINEA
AMBOINA Dutch 1650
Dutch 1680
SOLOMON IS.
Makasar Dutch 1667
TANIMBAR Dutch 1672
Port. 1673
TIMOR Dutch 1655
Dutch 1680
Dampier Br. c. 1685
NEW HEBRIDES
Dampier 1699
New Holland
NEW CALEDONIA
VAN DIEMEN'S LAND
STAATEN LAND

63–1830

CELEBES Br. 1810
Dutch 1817
MOLUCCAS Br. 1796-1802, 1810-17 Dutch 1817
1828 claimed by Holland west of 141°E
AMBOINA Br. 1796 Dutch 1817
Dutch 1828
NEW GUINEA
akasar 1812
ch DUTCH EAST INDIES
Port.
SOLOMON IS.
TIMOR Br. 1811-16 Dutch
MELVILLE I. 1824
Bougainville Fr. 1768
WESTERN AUSTRALIA
NEW SOUTH
NEW HEBRIDES
AUSTRALIA 1829
AUSTRALIA
WALES 1824
NEW CALEDONIA
SWAN RIVER COLONY 1829
Brisbane 1825
NEW SOUTH WALES 1778
Sydney 1788
BOTANY BAY
LORD HOWE I. Br. 1788
Kororareka 1825
VAN DIEMEN'S LAND Br. 1805 Colony 1825
NEW ZEALAND Cook 1778
CHATHAM IS. Br. 1791

1830–1878 (Congress of Berlin)

CELEBES
1848 claimed by Holland west of Humboldt Bay
Dutch NEW GUINEA
GERMAN NEW GUINEA 1884
NEW IRELAND German 1884
DUTCH EAST INDIES
Port. 1859
TIMOR
BRITISH NEW GUINEA 1884
NEW BRITAIN German 1884
BOUGAINVILLE German 1899
SOLOMON IS. French missionaries 1845 Br. 1893
Darwin 1839
NORTHERN TERRITORY with South Australia 1863
QUEENSLAND 1859
NEW HEBRIDES Fr./Br. 1887
WESTERN AUSTRALIA
SOUTH AUSTRALIA 1836
NEW SOUTH WALES 1863
NEW CALEDONIA Fr. 1853
IS. LOYAUTE Fr. 1853
NORFOLK I. Br. 1853
LORD HOWE I. Br.
limit of settlement
VICTORIA 1851
TASMANIA renamed 1853
NEW ZEALAND Crown Colony 1840

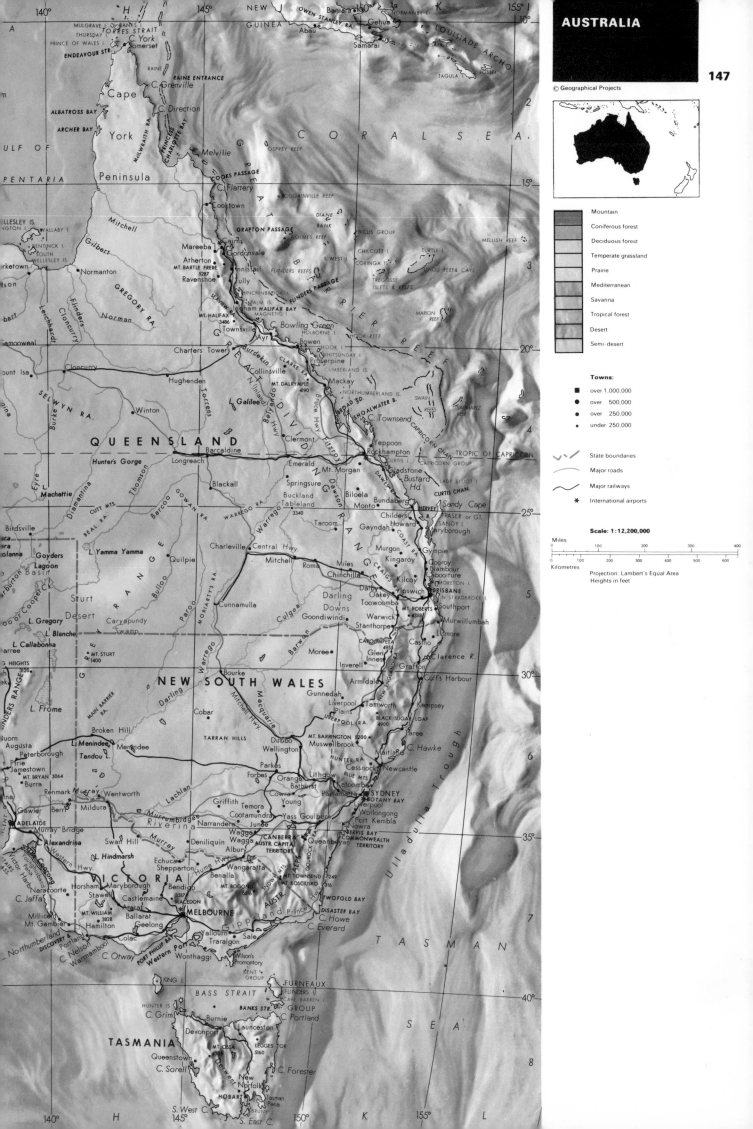

Mountain
Coniferous forest
Deciduous forest
Temperate grassland
Prairie
Mediterranean
Savanna
Tropical forest
Desert
Semi-desert

Towns:

■ over 1,000,000
● over 500,000
● over 250,000
• under 250,000

∨∨ State boundaries

Major roads

Major railways

✱ International airports

Scale: 1:12,200,000

Miles
0   100   200   300   400
0   100   200   300   400   500   600
Kilometres

Projection: Lambert's Equal Area
Heights in feet

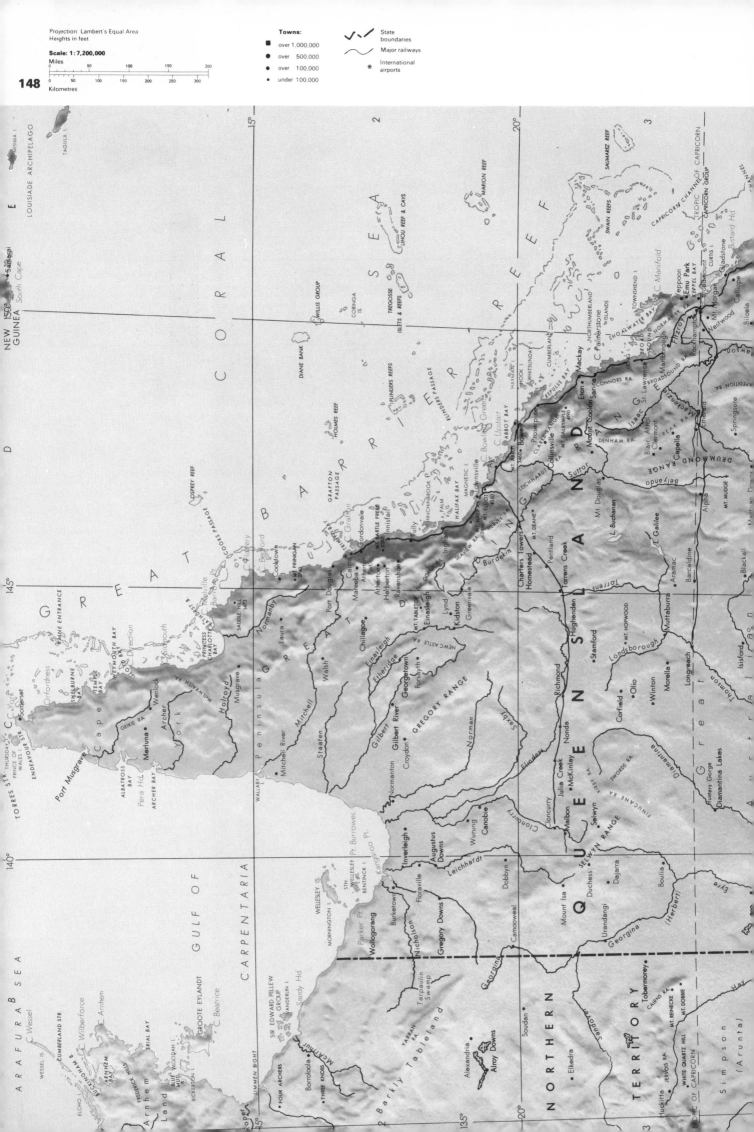

Projection: Lambert's Equal Area
Heights in feet

Scale: 1:7,200,000

Miles
0   50   100   150   200

0   50   100   150   200   250   300
Kilometres

Towns:
■ over 1,000,000
■ over 500,000
● over 100,000
• under 100,000

State boundaries

Major railways

✱ International airports

NEW ZEALAND

	Ice caps
	Mountain
	Coniferous forest
	Deciduous forest
	Temperate grassland
	Prairie

Towns:

● over 250,000

• under 250,000

Major roads

Major railways

＊ International airports

Scale: 1 : 4,000,000

Miles
0 20 40 60 80 100 120

Kilometres
0 20 40 60 80 100 120 140 160 180

Projection: Conic
Heights and depths in feet

PACIFIC OCEAN

CHATHAM RISE

TASMAN SEA

SOUTH ISLAND

STEWART ISLAND

NEW ZEALAND PLATEAU

BOUNTY IS.

MERNOO BANK

CANTERBURY BIGHT

SOUTHERN ALPS

FIORDLAND

OTAGO

CANTERBURY

Christchurch
Dunedin
Invercargill
Greymouth
Hokitika
Oamaru
Timaru
Ashburton
Rangiora
Kaiapoi
Geraldine
Temuka
Milton
Balclutha
Gore
Winton
Mataura
Queenstown
Arrowtown
Alexandra
Cromwell
Ranfurly
Lawrence
Roxburgh
Kaikoura
Runanga
Brunner
Kumara
Ross

Mt Cook
Mt Tasman
Mt Aspiring

Lake Te Anau
Lake Wakatipu
Lake Wanaka
Lake Hawea
Lake Pukaki
Lake Tekapo
Lake Ohau

Waiau R.
Clutha R.
Waitaki R.
Rakaia
Rangitata
Waimakariri

Banks Pena.
Akaroa Harbour
Otago Pena.
Port Chalmers
Green Island
Mosgiel
Nugget Pt.
Long Pt.
South Cape
Southwest Cape
Foveaux Strait
Jackson Hd.
Milford Sound
Doubtful Sound
Dusky Sound
Chalky Inlet
Preservation Inlet
Resolution I.
Secretary I.
Solander I.
Ruapuke Island
Codfish I.
Mutton Bird Islands
Paterson Inlet
Landsborough
National Park
Caples
Hamner
Arthur's Pass
Lewis Pass

WEST AUSTRALIA

152

© Geographical Projects

Projection: Lambert's Equal Area
Height in feet

Scale: 1:7,200,000

Miles
| 50 | 100 | 150 | 200 |

Kilometres
| 100 | 200 | 250 | 350 | 400 |

Towns:
● over 100,000
• under 100,000

〜 Major railways
✳ International airports

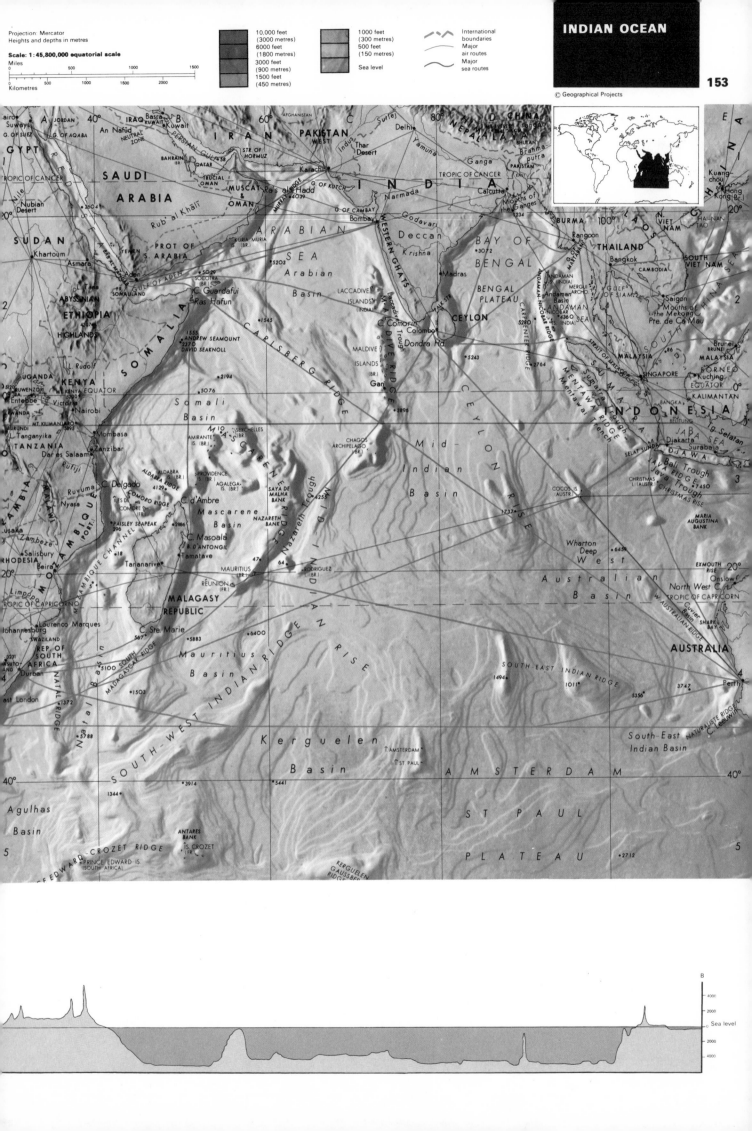

Projection: Mercator
Heights and depths in metres

Scale: 1:45,800,000 equatorial scale

Miles
0   500   1000   1500
0   500   1000   1500   2000
Kilometres

	10,000 feet (3000 metres)
	6000 feet (1800 metres)
	3000 feet (900 metres)
	1500 feet (450 metres)

	1000 feet (300 metres)
	500 feet (150 metres)
	Sea level

International boundaries
Major air routes
Major sea routes

© Geographical Projects

SAUDI ARABIA
IRAQ
IRAN
PAKISTAN WEST
AFGHANISTAN
CHINA
HIMALAYA
NEPAL
BHUTAN
INDIA
Delhi
Ganga
Yamuna
Indus
Thar Desert
Karachi
G. OF KUTCH
Narmada
Krishna
Godavari
Deccan
WESTERN GHATS
Bombay
Madras
Calcutta
Mouths of the Ganges
BURMA
Rangoon
THAILAND
Bangkok
CAMBODIA
SOUTH VIET NAM
Saigon
Mouths of the Mekong
Pte. de Ca Mau
LAOS
N. VIET NAM
HAI-NAN TAO
Kuang-chou
Hong Kong (Br.)

EGYPT
TROPIC OF CANCER
Suways
G. OF SUEZ
G. OF AQABA
JORDAN
NEUTRAL ZONE
KUWAIT
Kuwait
Basra
BAHRAIN (BR)
QATAR
TRUCIAL OMAN
PERSIAN GULF
STR. OF HORMUZ
MUSCAT & OMAN
Ras al Hadd
SUDAN
Khartoum
Nubian Desert
Nile
L. Tana
Asmara
ABYSSINIAN HIGHLANDS
ETHIOPIA
YEMEN
Aden
GULF OF ADEN
PROT OF S. ARABIA
Rub' al Khali
KURIA MURIA IS. (BR.)
SOCOTRA (BR.)
C. Guardafui
Ras Hafun
SOMALILAND
SOMALI

ARABIAN SEA
Arabian Basin
LACCADIVE ISLANDS (INDIA)
TROPIC OF CANCER
EQUATOR

BAY OF BENGAL
BENGAL PLATEAU
ANDAMAN & NICOBAR IS. (INDIA)
ANDAMAN SEA
GULF OF SIAM
MALAYSIA
Kuching
BORNEO
EQUATOR
KALIMANTAN
BANGKA
Bangka
JAVA SEA
SUMATRA
STRAIT OF MALACCA
Singapore
SINGAPORE
INDONESIA
Djakarta
Surabaia
DJAWA
JAVA
BALI
Bali Trough
BRUNEI
MALAYSIA

CEYLON
Colombo
C. Comorin
Dondra Hd.
MALDIVE ISLANDS (BR.)
Gan
Laccadive Trough
MALDIVE RIDGE

SOMALI BASIN
Mombasa
Zanzibar
Dar es Salaam
L. Rudolf
UGANDA
KENYA
Nairobi
L. Victoria
Entebbe
MT. KILIMANJARO
RWANDA
BURUNDI
L. Tanganyika
TANZANIA
RUWENZORI
SEYCHELLES IS. (BR.)
AMIRANTE IS. (BR.)
ALDABRA IS. (BR.)
ALDABRA RIDGE
PROVIDENCE IS. (BR.)
AGALEGA IS. (BR.)
CHAGOS ARCHIPELAGO (BR.)
MASCARENE RIDGE
CARLSBERG RIDGE
ANDREW SEAMOUNT
DAVID SEAKNOLL

Mid-Indian Basin
CEYLON RISE
COCOS IS. (AUSTR.)
CHRISTMAS I. (AUSTR.)
Christmas Rise
MARIA AUGUSTINA BANK

MOZAMBIQUE
ZAMBIA
MALAWI
L. Nyasa
C. Delgado
COMORO RIDGE
ÎLES DE COMORE (FR.)
PAISLEY SEAPEAK
C. d'Ambre
Mascarene Basin
SAYA DE MALHA BANK
NAZARETH BANK
C. Masoala
B. D'ANTONGIL
Tamatave
Tananarive
MAURITIUS (BR.)
RÉUNION (FR.)
RODRIGUEZ (BR.)
MID-INDIAN RIDGE
Mauritius Basin
Madagascar Ridge
SOUTH MADAGASCAR RIDGE
MALAGASY REPUBLIC
C. Ste. Marie
RHODESIA
Salisbury
Beira
Lourenco Marques
SWAZILAND
REP. OF SOUTH AFRICA
Durban
Johannesburg
Limpopo
Zambeze
Ruvuma
Rufiji
Lusaka
East London
NATAL RIDGE
Natal Basin
Agulhas Basin

MID-INDIAN RISE
SOUTH-WEST INDIAN RIDGE
Wharton Deep West
Australian Basin
SOUTH-EAST INDIAN RIDGE
EXMOUTH RISE
Onslow
North West C.
TROPIC OF CAPRICORN
CUVIER
SHARK BAY
AUSTRALIAN RIDGE
AUSTRALIA
Perth
NATURALISTE RIDGE
C. Leeuwin
South-East Indian Basin
Kerguelen Basin
AMSTERDAM
ST PAUL PLATEAU
T. AMSTERDAM
T. ST. PAUL
KERGUELEN GAUSSBERG RIDGE
ANTARES BANK
IS. CROZET (FR.)
CROZET RIDGE
EDWARD
PRINCE EDWARD IS. (SOUTH AFRICA)

2604
2580
5029
5203
5076
2194
1545
1555
2370
10
4039
5243
3072
5280
4360
2764
5441
3896
6459
1737
1494
1011
5356
3742
86
2712
3914
1344
5788
1372
1503
5100
567
5883
6400
47
64
4255
2086
4129
18
296

TROPIC OF CAPRICORN
40°   40°

B
4000
2000
Sea level
2000
4000

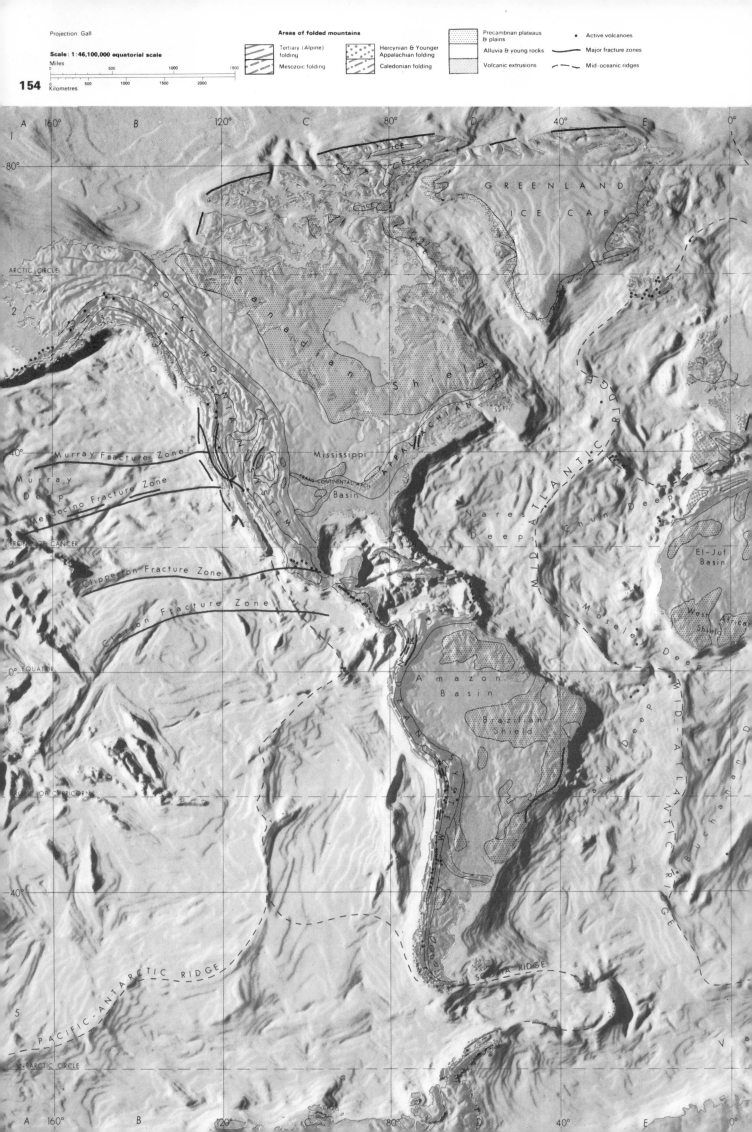

Projection: Gall

Scale: 1:46,100,000 equatorial scale

Miles

0   500   1000   1500

0   500   1000   1500   2000

Kilometres

Areas of folded mountains

Tertiary (Alpine) folding

Mesozoic folding

Hercynian & Younger Appalachian folding

Caledonian folding

Precambrian plateaus & plains

Alluvia & young rocks

Volcanic extrusions

• Active volcanoes

Major fracture zones

Mid-oceanic ridges

A   160°   B   120°   C   80°   D   40°   E   0°

1

-80°

ICE   ICE

G R E E N L A N D

ICE CAP

ARCTIC CIRCLE

2   ROCKY   MOUNTAIN   Canadian   Shield

-40°   Murray Fracture Zone   APPALACHIAN

Murray   Deep   Mississippi   Nares   Deep   Chun   Deep

Mendocino Fracture Zone   TRANS-CONTINENTAL ARCH   Basin   Moseley Deep   MID-ATLANTIC RIDGE

TROPIC OF CANCER   3   El-Juf Basin

Clipperton Fracture Zone   West Africa Shield

Clarion Fracture Zone   Romanche   Deep

4   SYSTEM   MID-ATLANTIC RIDGE

0°   EQUATOR   A m a z o n   B a s i n

ANDES   Brazilian   Shield

TROPIC OF CAPRICORN

-40°

5   PACIFIC-ANTARCTIC   RIDGE   SCOTIA   RIDGE

ANTARCTIC CIRCLE

A   160°   B   120°   C   80°   D   40°   E   0°

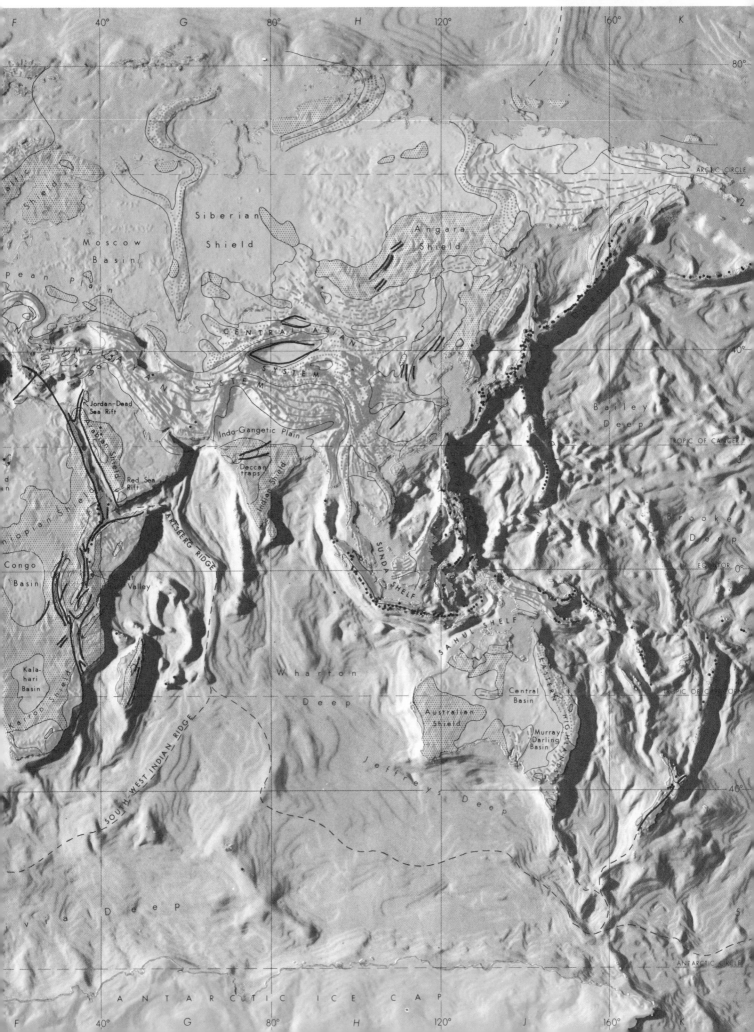

Moscow Basin

Siberian Shield

Angara Shield

Shield

pean Plain

Central Asian System

HIMALAYAN SYSTEM

Jordan-Dead Sea Rift

Arabian Shield

Red Sea Rift

Indo-Gangetic Plain

Deccan traps

Indian Shield

Ethiopian Shield

Congo Basin

Valley

Kala-hari Basin

Kartoo Shield

CARLSBERG RIDGE

SUNDA SHELF

SAHUL SHELF

Wharton Deep

Australian Shield

Central Basin

Murray Darling Basin

EASTERN HIGHLANDS

SOUTH-WEST INDIAN RIDGE

Jeffreys Deep

via Deep

Deep

Bailey Deep

Brooke Deep

ARCTIC CIRCLE

TROPIC OF CANCER

EQUATOR 0°

TROPIC OF CAPRICORN

ANTARCTIC CIRCLE

ANTARCTIC ICE CAP

Scale: 1:197,000,000 equatorial scale

Miles
0   1000   2000   3000   4000   5000   6000

0   1000   2000   3000   4000   5000   6000   7000   8000   9000   10,000
Kilometres

156

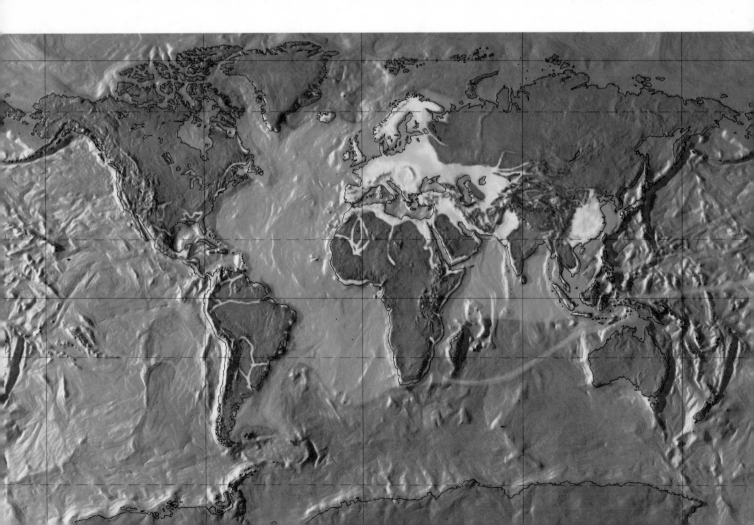

Area known to the Western world in 1700
Area known to the Western world in 1850

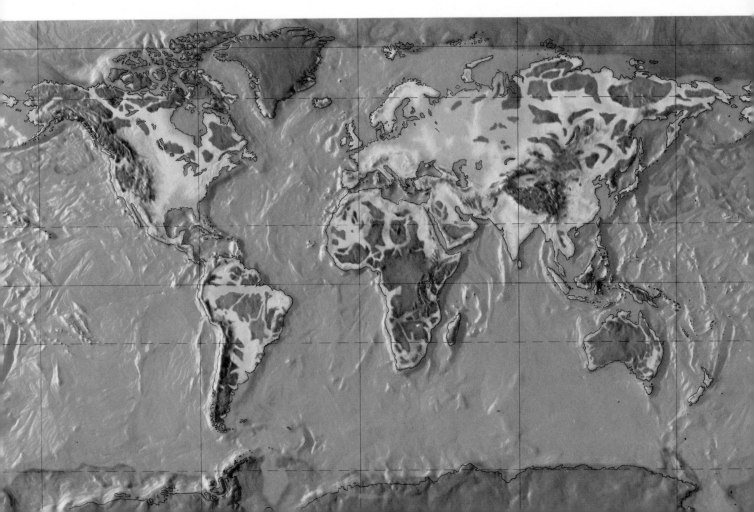

Projection: Gall

158

Scale: 1:46,100,000 equatorial scale

Miles
0   500   1000   1500

Kilometres
0   500   1000   1500   2000

Major civilisations before 1000 B.C.

Major civilisations between 1000 B.C. and the first century A.D.

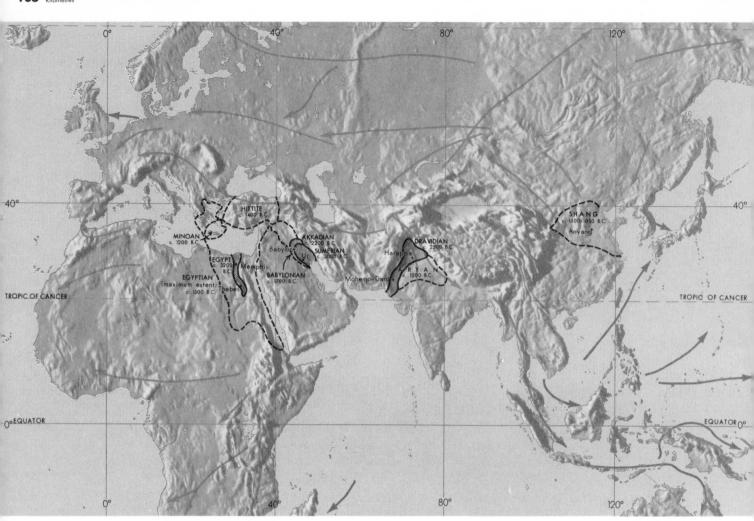

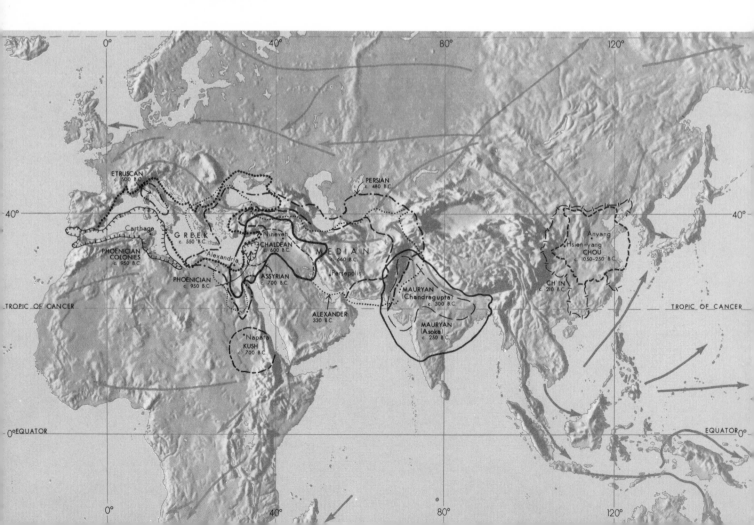

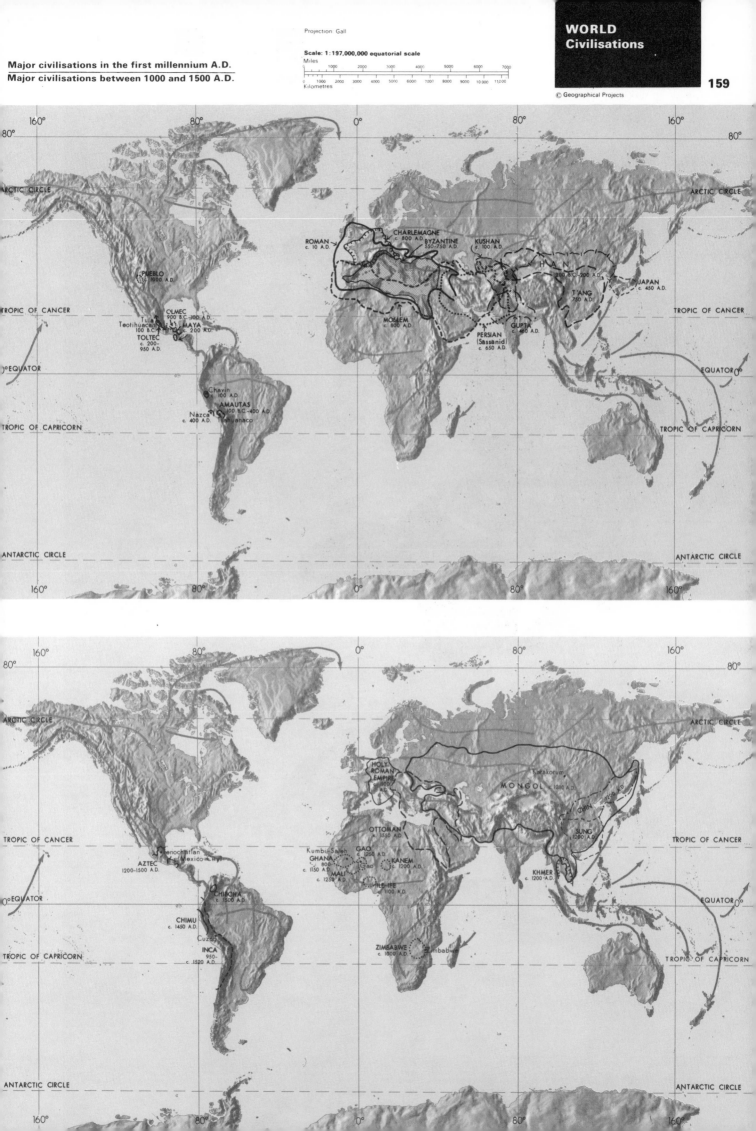

Major civilisations in the first millennium A.D.

Major civilisations between 1000 and 1500 A.D.

Projection Gall

Scale: 1:197,000,000 equatorial scale

Miles

Kilometres

Top map labels:

PUEBLO c. 1000 A.D.

OLMEC 900 B.C.–100 A.D.

Tula
Teotihuacan 100 B.C.

TOLTEC c. 200–950 A.D.

MAYA c. 200 A.D.

Chavin c. 100 A.D.

AMAUTAS 100 B.C.–400 A.D.

Nazca c. 400 A.D. Tiahuanaco

ROMAN c. 10 A.D.

CHARLEMAGNE c. 800 A.D.

BYZANTINE 550–750 A.D.

KUSHAN c. 100 A.D.

HAN 200 B.C.–200 A.D.

T'ANG 750 A.D.

JAPAN c. 450 A.D.

MOSLEM c. 800 A.D.

PERSIAN (Sassanid) c. 650 A.D.

GUPTA c. 460 A.D.

Bottom map labels:

Tenochtitlan (Mexico City)

AZTEC 1200–1500 A.D.

CHIBCHA c. 1500 A.D.

CHIMU c. 1450 A.D.

Cuzco

INCA 950–1520 A.D.

HOLY ROMAN EMPIRE 1100

OTTOMAN 1350 A.D.

Kumbi-Saleh

GHANA 800–1150 A.D.

GAO 1250 A.D.

Gao

MALI c. 1250 A.D.

KANEM c. 1200 A.D.

ILE-IFE 1100 A.D.

ZIMBABWE c. 1800 A.D. Zimbabwe

Karakorum

MONGOL c. 1200 A.D.

CHIN 1200 A.D.

SUNG 1200 A.D.

KHMER 1200 A.D.

© Geographical Projects

Projection: Gall

Scale: 1:156,500,000 equatorial scale

Miles
0   1000   2000   3000   4000   5000

0   1000   2000   3000   4000   5000   6000   7000   8000   9000
Kilometres

less than 2 per sq. mile	125 to 250 per sq. mile
less than 1 per sq. km	*50 to 100 per sq. km*
2 to 25 per sq. mile	over 250 per sq. mile
1 to 10 per sq. km	*over 100 per sq. km*
25 to 60 per sq. mile	**Towns:**
10 to 25 per sq. km	
60 to 125 per sq. mile	over 1,000,000 population
25 to 50 per sq. km	

ARCTIC CIRCLE

TROPIC OF CANCER

EQUATOR 0°

TROPIC OF CAPRICORN

ANTARCTIC CIRCLE

80°   40°   0°   40°

160°   120°   80°   40°   0°   40°   80°   120°   160°

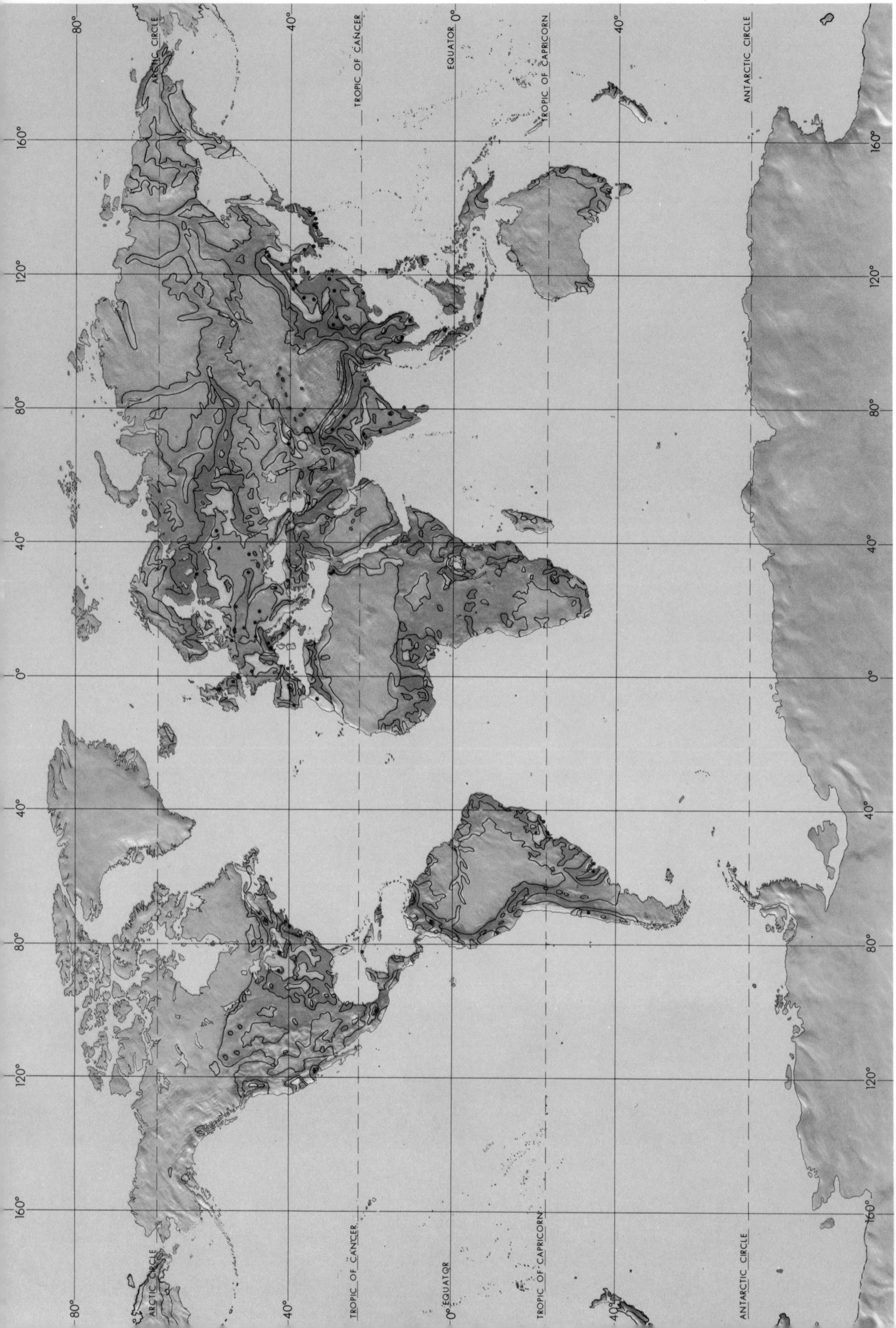

Geographical terms

Bay	**B.**	**Gulf**	**G.**	
Baie	B.	Golfe	G.	
Bahía	B.	Golfo	G.	
Bucht	B.	Körfezi	K.	
Bugt	B.			
Bukten		**Island**	**I.**	
Flói				
Ghubbat		Do		
Guba		Île	Î.	
Khalīj		Ilha	I.	
Kólpos		Isla	I.	
Nada		Isola	I.	
Teluk	Tel.	Jazīra	Jaz.	
Wan		Jima		
Zaliv		Ostrov	O.	
Zatoka		Shima		
		Tao		
Cape	**C.**	Tō		
Ákra	Akr.			
Burnu	Br.	**Islands**	**Is.**	
Cabo	C.	Eilanden	Eil.	
Cap	C.	Gugusan		
Chiao		Guntō		
Head	Hd.	Îles	Îs.	
Kapp	K.	Ilhas	Is.	
Misaki		Islas	Is.	
Mys	M.	Isole	I.	
Piao		Kepulauan	Kep.	
Point	Pt.	Ostrova	O-va	
Pointe	Pte.	Rettō		
Ponta	Pta.			
Punta	Pta.	**Lake**	**L.**	
Ras		Buḥayrah		
Rās		Chott		
Ra's		Danau		
Saki		Daryācheh	D.	
Tandjung	Td.	Embalse	Emb.	
		Étang	É.	
Desert		Gölü	G.	
Dasht		Hawr		
Gobi		Hu		
Hamada		Jezioro	Jez.	
Kum		Ko		
Peski		Köl		
Sha-mo		Kul'		

Lac	**L.**	**Cordillera**	**Cord.**
Lacul	L.	Dağlari	D.
Lago	L.	Gebirge	Geb.
Lagõa	L.	Gory	
Laguna	L.	Khrebet	Khr.
Loch	L.	Massif	
Lough	L.	Melkosopochnik	
Nor		Montagnes	Mgnes.
Nūr		Montes	Mts.
Nuur		Monti	Mti.
Ozero	Oz.	Óri	Ó.
See	S.	Óros	Ó.
Tscho		Planina	Plan.
		Range	Ra.
Mountain	**Mt.**	Sammyaku	Samm.
Ballon		Sanchi	
Beinn		Serra	Sa.
Ben		Serranía	
Cerro	Co.	Shan	
Dāgh	D.	Shan-mo	
Daği	D.	Sierra	Sa.
Gunung	G.	Slieve	Sl.
Horn		Tagh	
Jabal	J.	Ula	
Kūh		Uula	
Mont	M.	Yoma	
Monte	M.		
Montagne	Mgne.	**Peninsula**	**Pena.**
Nevos	Nev.	Hantō	
Peak	Pk.	Khersónisos	
Peña		Pan-tao	
Pico	P.	Presqu'île	
Pik	P.	Poluostrov	Po-v
Piz	P.	Yarimada	Yar.
San			
Tor		**Plain**	
Volcano	Vol.	Nizmennost'	
Yama	Y.	Ténéré	
Mountains	**Mts.**	**Plateau**	**Plat.**
Alin		Planalto	Plan.
Alpen	A.	Plato	
Alpi	A.	Tassili	
Altos		Vozvyshennost'	Vozvysh.
Cerros			

Reservoir	**Res.**	
Dam		
Sagara		
Vodokhranilishche	Vdkhr.	
River	**R.**	
Älv		
Baḥr	B.	
Bü		
Chiang	Ch.	
Chu		
Creek	Cr.	
Dar'ya		
Gol		
Hka		
Ho		
Mae		
Sand dune region		
Edeyin		
Erg		
Ghurd		
Sea		
Laut		
More		
Nada		
Strait	**Str.**	
Baelt		
Bocche		
Gat		
Hai-hsia		
Passage	Pass.	
Proliv		
Selat	Sel.	
Stenón		
Suidō		
Swamp		
Aydar		
Bañados		
Uvaly		
Zalew		

Index

Aisatung Mt., *mountain* 82 A 4
Ai Shan, *mountain* 76 G 4
Aisne, *river* 54 F 3
Aitape 85 F 4
Aitken, Mt., *mountain* 151 B 8
Aitzgorri, Mt., *mt.* 55 C 6
Aix-en-Provence 36 C 2
Aix-la-Chapelle, *see Aachen* 54 H 2
Aix-les-Bains 55 G 5
Aíyina 63 C 5
Aíyina, *island* 63 C 5
Aiyion 63 C 4
Aja 100 C 2
Ajaccio 28 H 5
Ajana 152 A 3
Ajedabya 99 F 2
Ajjer, *mountains* 90 D 3
'Ajlūn 89 B 2
'Ajmah, Jabal al, *mts.* 100 E 3
Ajmer 78 E 3
Ajo 118 E 5
Ajo, Cabo, *cape* 55 C 6
Ajo, Mt., *mountain* 120 D 5
Ajoe, Kep., *island group* 85 E 3
Ak, *river* 63 F 5
Akaishi-san, *mountains* 80 D 4
Akalkot 87 D 4
Akaroa 151 E 6
Akaroa Harb., *harbour* 151 E 6
Akashi 80 C 4
Akato Tagh, *mountains* 86 E 2
Ak-Bulak 65 H 3
Akcha 86 C 2
Akchar, Dunes de l', *sand dunes* 98 B 3
Ak Dağ, *mountain* 62 F 4
Akershus, *county* 51 N 4
Aketi 90 F 5
Akharnaí 62 C 4
Akhdar, J. al, *Libya, mountains* 90 F 2
Akhḑar, J. al., *Muscat & Oman, mountains* 66 D 4
Akhelóös 63 B 4
Akhisar 62 E 4
Akhtopol 62 E 2
Akhtyrka 35 K 3
Akimiski I., *island* 106 F 3
Akita 75 R 6
Akkadian, *civilisation* 158
Ak Kar Chekyl Tagh, *mountains* 86 D 2
Akkeshi-wan, *bay* 80 F 2
'Akko 89 B 2
Akkyr, G., *mountains* 29 N 5
Aklavik 106 D 2
Akmolinsk 66 E 3
Akola 78 E 3
A-k'o-su 86 D 1
Akpatok I., *island* 115 L 2
Akranes 50 B 3
Akron 106 F 3
Akseki 37 F 3
Aksha 75 O 4
Aksum 99 G 4
Aktarsk 65 F 3
Aktí 62 D 3
Aktyubinsk 35 N 3
Akureyri 34 C 2
Akyab 66 F 4
Alabama, *river* 106 F 4
Alabama, *state* 119 K 5
Alabat 81 E 4
Alaejos 52 C 2
Alagón 53 E 2
Alagón, *river* 52 B 3
Alah, *river* 81 F 8
Alahärmä 50 R 3
Al Aḩmadī 78 B 3
Alajuela 123 E 4
Alakurtti 50 U 2
Al'Amādīyah 88 C 2
Alamagan, *island* 85 F 2
Al Amārah 78 B 2
Alameda 52 C 4
Alaminos 81 C 3
Alamo Res., *reservoir* 120 D 5
Alanäs 50 P 3
Aland, *see Ahvenanmaa* 51 Q 4
Alanya 65 C 7
Alaotra, L., *lake* 105 D 3
Alapaha, *river* 121 D 4
Alapayevsk 35 N 3
Al Aqabah 37 G 4
Alarcón, Emb. de, *lake* 52 D 3
Al 'Arīsh 37 G 4
Al Arṭawiyah 88 D 4
Alaşehir 63 F 4
Al Ashmūnayn 100 B 5
Alaska, *state* 106 C 2
Alaska, Gulf of, *gulf* 106 C 3
Alaska Highway 114 C 2
Alaska Pena., *peninsula* 106 C 3
Alaska Ra., *mountains* 18 B 2
Alas, Selat, *strait* 84 C 4
Alatri 60 D 4
Alatyr 35 L 3
Alayor 53 H 3
Alayskiy Khr., *mts.* 66 E 4
Al 'Ayyāt 100 C 3
Al A'ẓamīyah 88 C 3
Alba 60 B 2
Al Bāb 88 B 2
Albacete 36 B 3
Alba de Tormes 52 C 2
Alba Iulia 64 D 3
Albalate del A. 53 E 2
Al Balyanā 99 G 3
Albania 28 J 5
Albany, *Australia* 140 B 5
Albany, *U.S.A., Georgia* 119 L 5
Albany, *U.S.A., New York* 119 N 3
Albany, *U.S.A., Oregon* 120 B 2
Albany, *river* 106 F 3
Albarracín 53 E 2
Albarracín, Sa. de, *mt.* 52 E 2
Albatross B., *bay* 140 E 3
Albatross Plateau, *sea feature* 137 E 2
Albatross Pt., *cape* 150 F 4
Al Batrūn 88 B 3
Al Bayḑā 88 D 7
Albemarle Sd., *sound* 119 M 4
Albenga 60 B 2
Alberche, Embalse del, *lake* 52 C 2
Albères, Mts., *mts.* 55 F 6
Alberga, *river* 140 D 4
Albergaria-a-V. 52 A 2
Alberique 53 E 3
Albert 54 F 2
Albert, *river* 147 G 3
Alberta, *province* 114 F 3
Albert, Lake, *Africa* 90 G 5
Albert, L., *Australia* 149 B 6
Albert Lea 119 J 3
Albert Nile, *river* 99 G 5
Albertville, *Congo* 102 D 3
Albertville, *France* 55 H 5
Albi 36 C 2
Albina, Pta., *cape* 91 E 7
Albir, P. del, *region* 53 E 3
Albocácer 53 E 2
Alboran, I. de, *island* 52 D 5
Alborz, Reshteh-ye, *mts.* 66 D 4
Albox 52 D 4
Albret, Les Pays d', *region* 55 D 5
Albufeira 52 A 4
Albufera, La, *lake* 53 E 3
Albula, *river* 57 E 3
Albuquerque 118 F 4
Alburquerque 52 B 3
Albury 147 J 7
Alcácer do Sal 52 A 3
Alcains 52 B 3
Alcalá de Chivert 53 F 2
Alcalá de H. 52 D 2
Alcalá de los G. 52 C 4
Alcalá la Real 52 D 4
Alcamo 61 D 6
Alcanadre, *river* 53 E 2
Alcanar 53 F 2
Alcanena 52 A 3
Alcañiz 53 E 2
Alcántara 52 B 3
Alcantarilla 53 E 4
Alcaraz 52 D 3
Alcaraz, Sa. de, *mts.* 52 D 3
Alcarria, La, *region* 52 D 2
Alcasovas 52 A 3
Alcaudete 52 C 4
Alcázar de San Juan 52 D 3
Alcazarquivir 36 B 3
Alcester 43 F 2
Alchan, Mt., *mountain* 81 D 3
Alcira 36 B 3
Alcoa 119 L 4
Alcobaça 52 A 3
Alcorisa 53 E 2
Alcoutim 52 B 4
Alcoy 36 B 3
Alcubierre, Sa. de, *mts.* 53 E 2
Alcudia, B. de, *bay* 53 G 3
Aldabra Is., *island group* 91 H 6
Aldabra Ridge, *sea feature* 153 B 3
Aldan 75 P 4
Aldan, *river* 67 H 2
Aldanskoye Nagor'ye, *highlands* 67 H 3
Aldeburgh 39 G 5
Aldeia Nova de S. Bento 52 B 4
Aldermaston 43 F 3
Alderney, *island* 39 E 7
Aldershot 39 F 6
Al Dilinjāt 100 B 2
Aldwick 41 C 4
Aledua, Sa. de., *mts.* 53 E 3
Alegrete 135 C 2
Alegria 81 G 6
Aleksandriya 65 C 4
Aleksandrovsk-Sakhalinskiy 75 R 4
Além Paraíba 135 D 2
Alençon 54 E 3
Alenquer 52 A 3
Aleria 60 B 3
Alès 36 C 2
Alessandria 36 D 2
Ålesund 34 F 2
Aletschhorn, *mountain* 57 C 3
Aleutian Basin, *sea feature* 137 B 1
Aleutian Islands, *island group* 137 B 1
Aleutian Trench, *sea feature* 137 B 1
Alevina, M., *cape* 67 J 3
Alexander 158
Alexander Archo., *island group* 106 D 3
Alexander Bay 91 E 8
Alexander I., *island* 23 R 2
Alexandra 151 C 7
Alexandria, *Australia* 148 B 2
Alexandria, *Egypt* 90 F2
Alexandria, *Rep. of South Africa* 101 E 6
Alexandria, *Rumania* 64 E 4
Alexandria, *U.S.A., Louisiana* 119 J 5
Alexandria, *U.S.A., Virginia* 119 M 4
Alexandrina, L., *lake* 147 G 7
Alexandroúpoulis 62 D 3
Aleysk 74 L 4
Alfabia, Sa. de, *mts.* 53 G 3
Al Fallūjah 88 C 3
Alfambra, *river* 53 E 2
Alfaro 52 E 1
Al Fashn 100 B 4
Al Fayyūm 90 G 3
Alfiós, *river* 63 B 5
Alfonse I., *island* 103 G 3
Alford, *England* 45 J 4
Alford, *Scotland* 46 F 4
Alfred & Marie Ra., *mountains* 146 E 4
Alfreton 45 G 4
Alfriston 41 E 4
Alfta 51 P 4
Algeciras 52 C 4
Algeciras, Bahía de, *bay* 52 C 4
Algemesí 53 E 3
Alger 90 D 2
Alger, B. d', *bay* 53 G 4
Algeria 90 C 3
Alghero 61 B 4
Al Ghurdaqah 99 G 3
Algoa B., *bay* 91 F 9
Algonquin Provincial Park 116 D 2
Alhama de G. 52 D 4
Alhama de M. 53 E 4
Alhama, Sa. de, *mts.* 52 C 4
Alhambra, Sa. de, *mts.* 52 D 3
Alhamilla, Sierra, *mts.* 52 D 4
Al Ḩarīq 88 D 5
Al Hasa, *region* 88 D 4
Al Hasakah 37 H 3
Alhaurin 52 C 4
Al Hillah 78 B 2
Al Hills 88 D 7
Al Hoceima 52 D 5
Alhucemas, Bahia de, *bay* 52 D 5
Al Ḩudaydah 66 D 5
Al Hufūf 78 B 3
Alīābād, Kūh-e, *mt.* 88 E 3
Aliaga 53 E 2
Aliákmon, *river* 62 B 3
'Alī al Gharbī 88 D 3
Alibag 87 C 4
Alibey, *island* 62 E 4
Alí Butús, *mountain* 62 C 3
Alicante 36 B 3
Alicante, B. de, *bay* 53 E 3
Alice Chan., *strait* 81 C 9
Alice, Pta. dell', *cape* 61 F 5
Alice Springs 140 D 4
Alicudi, *island* 61 E 5
Aligarh 78 E 3
Alījūq, Kūh-e, *mountain* 88 E 3
Alimnía, *island* 63 E 5
Ain, *river* 57 A 3
Alingsås 51 O 5
Alipaga 84 C 3
Alipura 86 D 3
Aliquippa 116 D 3
Alisal 120 B 4
Al Ismā'īlīya 99 G 2
Alitus 51 S 6
Aliwal North 91 F 9
Al Jawf, *Jordan* 89 C 4
Al Jawf, *Saudi Arabia* 78 A 3
Aljezur 52 A 4
Al Jīzah, *see El Giza* 90 G 2
Al Jīzah, *province* 100 C 3
Al Jubayl 88 D 4
Aljustrel 52 A 4
Al Kāẓimīyah 88 C 3
Al Khābūrah 88 F 5
Al Khālis 88 C 3
Al Khārijah 90 G 3
Al Khurmah 88 C 5
Alkionídhon Kólpos, *bay* 63 C 4
Alkmaar 34 F 3
Al Kubrā 99 G 2
Al Kūfah 88 C 3
Al Kuntilla 100 F 3
Al Kūt 78 B 2
Al Lādhiqiyah 66 C 4
Allahabad 66 F 4
Allakh-Yun' 75 Q 3
Allanmyo 82 B 5
Allariz 52 B 1
Allegheny, *river* 119 M 3
Allegheny Mts., *mts.* 106 F 4
Allen, Bog of 39 C 5
Allendale Town 45 F 3
Allen, L., *lake* 39 B 4
Allentown 119 M 3
Allepey 79 E 5
Aller, *river* 58 C 2
Allgäuer Alpen, *mts.* 57 F 2
Alliance 118 G 3
Allier, *river* 28 G 4
Alligator L., *lake* 121 E 3
Al Līth 78 B 3
Alloa 47 E 5
Allonby 44 E 3
Allora 149 E 4
Al Luḩayyah 88 C 6
Al Ma'ādī 100 C 3
Alma-Ata 66 E 3
Almada 52 A 3
Almadén 52 C 3
Almadén, Sa. de., *mts.* 52 C 3
Al Madinah 66 C 4
Almadrones 52 D 2
Al Mafraq 37 G 4
Almagro 52 D 3
Al Maḩallah al Kubrá 100 C 2
Al Maḩmūdīyah 100 B 1
Al Mallaḩah, *swamp* 100 E 4
Al Manāmah 66 D 4
Almansa 52 E 3
Al Manşurāh 99 G 2
Al Manzilah 100 C 1
Almanzor, Pico de, *mt.* 52 C 2
Al Marj 99 F 2
Almazán 52 D 2
Almeirim 52 A 3
Almelo 58 B 2
Almenara, *mountain* 52 D 3
Almenara, Sa. de., *mts.* 53 E 4
Almendralejo 52 B 3
Almeria 36 B 3
Almeria, G. de, *gulf* 52 D 4
Al'met'yevsk 65 H 2
Älmhult 51 O 6
Almina, Pta., *cape* 52 C 5
Al Minyā 90 G 3
Al Minyā, *province* 100 B 4
Al Miqdādīyah 88 D 3
Almirós 62 C 4
Almiroú, Kólpos, *bay* 63 D 6
Almodóvar 52 A 4
Almodóvar del Campo 52 C 3
Almond, *river* 47 E 5
Almonte 116 E 2
Al Mubarraz 88 D 4
Al Mudawwara 89 C 5
Almudébar 53 E 1
Al Muharraq 88 E 4
Al Mukhā 78 B 4
Al Mūşil 65 E 7
Aln, *river* 45 G 2
Alnwick 38 F 4
Alor, *island* 67 H 6
Alor, Kep., *island group* 85 D 4
Alora 52 C 4
Alor Star 84 B 3
Aloysius, Mt., *mountain* 146 E 5
Alpercatas, Sa. das, *mts.* 133 E 3
Alpha 148 D 3
Alphen aan de Rijn 56 C 2
Alpi Atesine, *mountains* 59 D 5
Alpine 118 G 5
Alpine-Himalayan System 154 F 2
Alps, *mountains* 25 F 2
Alpstein, *mountain* 57 E 2
Al Qahīrah, *see Cairo* 100 C 2
Al Qāmishliyē 88 C 2
Al Qanṭarah 100 D 2
Al Qaryatayn 88 B 3
Al Qaṭif 88 D 4
Al Qunfudhah 88 C 6
Al Quşayr 99 G 3
Al Ramādī 90 H 2
Alresford 43 F 3
Alroy Downs 148 B 2
Als, *island* 51 N 6
Alsace, *province* 54 H 3
Alsace, Ballon d', *mt.* 54 H 4
Alsásua 52 D 1
Alsásua, *river* 55 C 6
Alsfeld 58 C 3
Al Shā'ib, *mountain* 100 B 3
Alston 45 F 3
Alta 34 H 1
Altaelv, *river* 50 R 1
Alta Gracia 135 B 3
Altamaha, *river* 119 L 5
Altamira, Sa. de, *mts.* 52 C 3
Altamont 120 B 3
Altamura 61 F 4
Altan Bulag 76 D 1
Altay, *mountains* 66 F 3
Altdorf 57 D 3
Altenburg 58 E 3
Altin Köprü 88 C 2
Altiplano, *plateau* 126 C 4
Altissima, L', *mountain* 57 G 3
Altkirch 54 H 4
Altmühl, *river* 59 D 4
Altnaharra 46 D 3
Alto Molócuè 104 D 6
Alton, *England* 43 G 3
Alton, *U.S.A.* 121 B 2
Altona 58 C 2
Altoona 119 M 3
Altos de Cabrejas, *mts.* 52 D 2
Altos de Chinchilla, *mts.* 53 E 3
Altos de Lillo, *mts.* 52 D 3
Altrincham 45 F 4
Altstätten 57 E 2
Alturas 120 B 3
Alturas, Sa. de, *mts.* 52 A 2
Altyn Tagh, *mountains* 66 F 4
Alula 88 E 7
Alunda 51 Q 4
Alung Gangri, *mountain* 86 D 2
Al 'Uqalah 36 E 4
Al Uqsur 37 G 5
Alva 118 H 4
Alvão, Sa. do, *mts.* 52 B 2
Alvdal 34 G 2
Älvdalen 51 O 4
Alvito 52 B 3
Älvkarleby 51 P 4
Älvsborg, *county* 51 O 5
Al Wajh 66 C 4
Alwar 86 D 3
Al Wāsiṭah 100 C 3
Alyaty Pristan' 88 D 2
Al Zaqāziq 99 G 2
Alzette, *river* 56 E 5
Alzey 54 J 3
Amadeus, L., *lake* 140 D 4
Amādīyah 65 E 7
Amadjuak 115 K 2
Amadjuak L., *lake* 106 G 2
Amadora 52 A 3
Amagasaki 67 H 4
Amakusa-nada, *sea* 80 B 4
Amakusa-tō, *island group* 80 B 4
Amål 51 O 5
Amalfi 61 E 4
Amaliás 63 B 5
Amalner 86 D 4
Amami-guntó, *island group* 80 B 5
Amami-Ō-shima, *island* 80 B 5
Amandola 60 D 3
Amantea 61 F 5
Amarante 52 A 2
Amarapura 82 B 4
Amaravati 78 E 3
Amargosa Desert, *desert* 120 C 4
Amargosa Ra., *mountains* 120 C 4
Amarillo 118 G 4
Amaroúsion 62 C 4
Amautas, *civilisation* 159
Amaya, *mountain* 52 C 1
Amazonas, *river* 126 D 3
Amazon Basin, *region* 126 C 3
Amazon, Mouths of the, *river mouths* 126 E 3
Amba Alagi 88 B 7
Amba Farit 88 B 7
Ambala 86 D 3
Ambalavao 105 C 4
Ambarchik 75 T 3
Ambato 132 B 3
Ambato-Boéni 105 C 3
Ambatofinandrahana 105 C 4
Ambatolampy 91 H 7
Ambatondrazaka 91 H 7
Amberg 59 D 4
Ambergris Cay, *reef* 123 E 3
Ambert 55 F 5
Ambilobe 105 D 2
Ambleside 44 E 3
Amblève, *river* 56 D 4
Ambodifototra 91 H 7
Ambohidratrimo 105 C 3
Ambohimahasoa 105 C 4
Ambon 85 D 4
Ambon, *island* 85 D 4
Ambositra 103 F 5
Ambovombe 91 H 8
Ambre, C. d', *cape* 91 H 7
Ambre, Mgne. d', *mt.* 105 D 2
Ambur 87 D 5
Amderma 35 N 1
Ameato, Sa., *mountains* 136 B 1
Ameca 122 C 2
Amedamit, *mountain* 88 B 7
Ameland, *island* 56 D 1
Amelander Gat, *strait* 56 D 1
Amelia I., *island* 121 D 4
Amer, *river* 56 C 3
American Falls 120 D 3
American Falls Res., *reservoir* 120 D 3
Americus 121 C 3
Amer, Pta. del, *cape* 53 G 3
Amersfoort 56 D 2
Amersham 41 C 2
Amery Ice Shelf 23 F 2
Amesbury 43 F 3
Amfíklia 62 C 4
Amfilokhía 62 B 4
Ámfissa 62 C 4
Amherst 83 B 5
Amhurst, Mt., *mountain* 152 D 1
Amiata, M., *mountain* 60 C 3
Amiens 34 F 4
Amindivi Is., *island group* 87 C 5
Amirante Is., *island group* 153 B 3
Amlwch 42 C 1
Amman 29 L 6
Ammanford 39 E 6
Ammarnäs 50 P 3
Ammer, *river* 57 G 2
Ammergeb., *mountains* 57 F 2
Ammerland, *region* 56 G 1
Ammer See, *lake* 59 D 5
Ammi Moussa 53 F 5
Ammouliani, *mountain* 62 C 3
Åmol 88 E 2
Amorgós, *island* 63 D 5
Amoy, *see Hsia-men* 77 F 7
Ampanihy 105 C 5
Amper, *river* 59 D 4
A. Phichai 83 C 5
Amposta 53 E 2
Ampurdán, El, *region* 53 G 1
Amriswil 57 E 2
Amritsar 66 E 4
Amroha 86 D 3
Amrum, *island* 58 C 1
Amsterdam 28 G 3
Amsterdam, Î., *island* 153 C 4
Amsterdam-Rijnkanaal, *canal* 56 C 2
Amsterdam St. Paul Plateau, *sea feature* 153 D 4
Amstetten 59 F 4
Am Timan 90 F 4
Amu-Dar'ya, *river* 66 E 4
Amundsen Gulf, *gulf* 106 D 2
Amundsen Scott, *scientific base* 23 L 1
Amundsen Sea 18 C 5
Amur, *river* 67 H 3
Amurrio 52 D 1
Amvrakikós Kólpos, *bay* 63 B 4
Anacapa Is., *island group* 120 C 5
Anaconda 118 E 2
Anaconda Ra., *mts.* 120 D 2
Anacoora, Mt., *mt.* 149 B 4
Anacortes 120 B 1
Anadia 52 A 2
Anadyr' 67 K 2
Anadyr', *river* 67 K 2
Anadyrskiy Khrebet, *mts.* 106 A 2
Anadyrskiy Zaliv, *bay* 67 L 2

Anadyrskoye Ploskogor'ye, *tableland* 75 U 3
Anáfi 63 D 5
Anafópoulo 63 D 5
'Ānah 88 C 3
Anaheim 118 D 5
Anaimudi Pk., *mountain* 87 D 5
Anakapalle 81 E 4
Anak, Krakatau, *island* 67 G 6
Analalava 91 H 7
Anambar Uula, *mts.* 86 F 2
Anambas, Kep., *island group* 79 H 5
Anamur Br., *cape* 37 G 3
Anand 86 C 4
Anánes 63 D 5
Anantapur 87 D 5
Anas Mts., *mountains* 101 C 3
Anastasia I., *island* 121 D 4
Anatahan, *island* 85 F 2
Añatuya 136 B 1
Ancares, Sa. de Picos de, *mountains* 52 B 1
Ancenis 54 D 4
Anchorage 106 C 2
Anclote Keys, *island grp.* 121 D 4
Ancohuma, Nev. de., *mountain* 126 C 4
Ancona 36 D 2
Ancua, *mountain* 99 G 4
Ancuabe 104 D 6
Ancud, *island* 136 A 3
Ancud, G. de, *gulf* 127 B 7
Åndalsnes 50 M 4
Andalucia, *province* 52 C 4
Andaman Basin, *sea feature* 66 F 5
Andaman Is., *island group* 66 F 5
Andaman-Nicobar Ridge, *sea feature* 153 D 2
Andaman Sea 66 F 5
Andamooka 149 B 5
Andapa 105 D 2
Andean System, *mts.* 154 D 4
Andenne 56 D 4
Andermatt 57 D 3
Andernach 56 F 4
Anderson 116 C 3
Anderson, *river* 114 E 2
Andes 123 F 4
Andes, *mountains* 126 B 3
Andevoranto 105 D 3
Andfj., *fjord* 50 P 1
Andhra Pradesh, *state* 87 D 4
Andía, Sa. de., *mts.* 52 D 1
Andikhasiá Óri, *mts.* 62 B 4
Andikíthira, *island* 63 C 6
Andímolos, *island* 63 D 5
Andipáros, *island* 63 D 5
Andípaxoi, *island* 62 B 4
Andípsara, *island* 63 D 4
Andissa 62 D 4
Andizhan 66 E 3
Andkhui 86 B 2
Andong 76 H 4
Andorra 36 C 2
Andorra, *state* 28 G 4
Andover 39 F 6
Andøy, *island* 50 P 1
Andrew Seamount, *sea feature* 153 B 2
Andria 60 F 4
Andrijevica 62 A 2
Andringitra, *mountains* 105 C 4
Ándros, *Greece, island* 63 D 5
Andros, I., *Bahama Islands, island* 107 G 4
Androscoggin, *river* 117 F 2
Androth, I., *island* 87 C 5
Andújar 52 C 3
Anécho 98 D 5
Anegada Pass., *strait* 107 G 5
Anegada, Punta, *cape* 134 B 3
Aneto, P. de, *mountain* 28 G 4
Angamos, Pta., *cape* 126 B 5
Angara, *river* 66 F 3
Angara Basin, *sea feature* 24 L 1
Angara Shield, *plateau* 155 H 2
Angarsk 75 N 4
Angaston 149 B 5
Angathonísi 63 E 5
Ånge 50 P 4
Angel de la Guarda, *island* 107 E 4
Angelholm 51 O 6
Angels Camp 120 B 4
Ångermanälven, *river* 50 P 3
Angermünde 58 E 2
Angers 34 E 4
Angkor, *ancient site* 83 D 6
Anglem, Mt., *mountain* 151 B 8
Anglesey 42 C 1
Anglesey, I. of, *island* 34 E 3
Angmagssalik 115 O 2
Angmering 41 D 4
Angol 135 A 3
Angola 91 E 7
Angola Swamp, *swamp* 121 E 3
Angoram 85 F 4
Angoulême 36 C 2
Angoumois, *province* 55 E 5
Angren 86 C 1
Ang Thong 83 C 6
Anguila Is., *island group* 121 E 6
Anguilla, *island* 123 G 3
Anguille, C., *cape* 117 J 2
Angul 87 E 4
Angulo, *river* 134 C 3
Angus 46 E 5
Anholt, *island* 51 N 6
An-hsi 66 F 3
Anhwei, *province* 76 F 5
Ánidhros, *island* 63 D 5
Anie, Pic d', *mountain* 36 B 2
Anierin, Sl., *mountain* 48 D 2
Anisiy, M., *cape* 75 Q 2
Aniya, M., *cape* 75 R 5
Anjou, *province* 54 D 4
Anjouan, *island* 103 F 4
Anjozorobe 105 C 3
Anjŭ 75 P 6
An-k'ang 67 G 4
An-kara 37 G 3
Ankaratra, *mountains* 105 C 3
Ankazoabo 91 H 8
Ankazobe 105 C 3
Anklam 58 E 2
Ankober 99 G 5
Ankofa, *mountain* 105 D 3
Anlier, Forêt d', *forest* 56 D 5
Ann, C., *cape* 115 K 4
Annaba 90 D 2
An'Nabk 37 G 4
An Nafūd, *region* 66 D 4
Annagh, *river* 48 D 2
An Najaf 78 B 2
An Nakhl 100 E 3
Annam, *region* 82 E 5
Annan 38 E 4
Annan, *river* 39 E 4
Anna Plains 152 C 1
Annapolis, *Canada* 115 L 4
Annapolis, *U.S.A.* 119 M 4
Annapurna, *mountain* 83 E 3
Ann Arbor 119 L 3
An Nāşirīyah 88 D 3
Annecy 57 B 4
Annecy, Lac d', *lake* 57 B 4
Anne Machin Shan, *mts.* 76 B 4
Annemasse 57 B 3
Anniston 119 K 5
Annobón, *island* 90 D 6
An. Arkhánai 63 D 6
Áno Viánnos 63 D 6
Anóyia 63 D 6
Ansārīye, J. al, *mts.* 88 B 2
Ansbach 59 D 4
An-shan 67 H 3
An-shun 77 D 6
Anso, V. de, *valley* 53 E 1
Anstruther 47 F 5
Antakya 37 G 3
Antalaha 91 J 7
Antalya 37 F 3
Antalya Körfezi, *bay* 29 K 5
Antarctica 19 G 5
Antarctic Ice Cap 154 G 5
Antarctic Pena., *peninsula* 23 R 2
Antares Bank, *sea feature* 153 B 5
An Teallach, *mountain* 46 C 4
Antela, Lac de, *lake* 52 B 1
Antelope I., *island* 120 D 3
Antelope Ra., *mts.* 120 C 4
Antequera 52 C 4
Anti-Atlas, *mountains* 90 C 2
Antibes 55 H 6
Antibes, C. d', *cape* 55 H 6
Anticosti I., *island* 106 G 3
Antifer, C. d', *cape* 54 E 3
Antigua 122 D 3
Antigua, *island* 107 G 5
Antimonan 81 D 5
Antinopolis 100 B 5
Antioch 120 B 4
Antioche, Pertuis d', *strait* 55 D 4
Antipodes, Is., *islands* 141 H 6
Antofagasta 126 B 5
Antoing 56 B 4
Antón 134 C 2
Antongil, B. d', *bay* 91 H 7
António Enes 91 G 7
Antrim 39 C 4
Antrim, *county* 48 E 2
Antrim Mts., *mountains* 34 E 3
Antsirabe 103 F 4
Antsohihy 105 C 2
An-t'u 80 B 2
An-tung 67 H 3
Antwerpen 28 G 3
Antwerpen, *province* 56 C 3
An Uaimh 39 C 5
Anundsjö 50 Q 3
Anuradhaoura 87 D 5
Anvers, *see Antwerpen* 56 C 3
Anvers I., *island* 23 R 2
Anxious Bay 149 A 5
Anyama 98 C 5
An-yang 75 O 6
Anza, *river* 57 D 4
Anzhero-Sudzhensk 75 L 4
Anzio 60 D 4
Ao Ban Don, *bay* 83 C 7
Aogo-shima, *island* 80 D 4
Aoíz 53 E 1
Aomori 67 J 3
Aorangi Mts., *mountains* 150 F 5
Ao Sawi, *bay* 83 C 7
Aosta 60 A 2
Aosta, Valle d', *province* 57 C 4
Aotea Harb., *harbour* 150 F 3
Aouk, B., *river* 99 F 5
Aouker, *region* 90 C 4
Apalachee Bay, *bay* 119 L 5
Apalachicola 119 K 6
Apalachicola Bay, *bay* 121 C 4
Aparri 79 K 4
Apeldoorn 56 D 2
Api, *mountain* 86 D 3
Apo, Mt., *mountain* 81 F 8
Apodi, Chapado do, *region* 133 F 3
Apolda 58 D 3
Apopka, L., *lake* 121 D 4
Apostle Is., *island group* 116 A 2
Appalachian Mountains, *mountains* 106 F 4
Äppelbo 51 O 4
Appennini, *mountains* 28 H 4
Appenzell 57 E 2
Appin 47 C 5
Appleby 45 F 3
Appledore 41 F 3
Appleton 119 K 3
Aprilia 60 D 4
Apsheronskiy Poluostrov, *peninsula* 65 G 6
Apt 55 G 6
Apucarana, Sa. da, *mts.* 133 D 5
Apulyont Gölü, *lake* 62 F 3
Apurauan 81 C 7
Apure, *river* 126 B 2
Apuseni, Munţii, *mts.* 28 J 4
Aqaba, G. of, *gulf* 29 L 6
'Aqabah, W. al, *wadi* 100 F 3
Aquarius Plateau, *plateau* 120 E 4
Aquidauana 132 D 5
Arabatskaya Strelka, *bay* 65 C 5
Arabian Basin, *sea feature* 163 C 2
Arabian Peninsula, *region* 19 F 3
Arabian Sea 153 C 2
Arabian Shield, *sea feature* 155 F 3
Aracaju 126 F 4
Aracati 133 F 3
Aracatuba 135 C 2
Aracena 52 B 4
Aracena, Sa. de, *mts.* 52 B 4
Arad 37 E 2
Arafura Sea 140 D 2
Aragats, *mountain* 37 H 3
Aragón 53 E 1
Aragón, *province* 53 E 2
Aragoncillo, *mountain* 52 D 2
Araguaia, *river* 132 D 4
Araguari, *river* 133 D 2
'Ārah, Ra's al, *cape* 88 C 7
Arak 74 G 6
Arakan, *province* 82 A 4
Arakan Yoma, *mts.* 66 F 4
Araks, *river* 29 M 5
Aralar, Sa. de, *mts.* 52 D 1
Aral'sk 66 E 3
Aral'skoye More, *sea* 66 E 3
Aramac 148 D 3
Aranda de D. 52 D 2
Aran Fawddwy, *mt.* 42 D 2
Aran I., *island* 38 B 4
Aran Islands, *island group* 39 B 5
Aranjuez 52 D 2
Arán, V. de, *valley* 53 F 1
Aranya Prathet 83 D 6
Arapkir 65 D 6
Araraquara 135 D 2
Araras, Sa. das, *mts.* 133 D 4
Ararat 147 H 7
Ararat, Mt., *see Büyük Ağri Daği* 29 M 5
Araripe, Sa. do, *mts.* 126 E 3
Aras, *river* 29 M 5
Arauca 132 C 2
Arauca, *river* 123 F 4
Aravalli Ra., *mountains* 78 E 3
Araxá 133 E 4
Araxes, *see Aras* 65 F 6
Arayj, Al, *region* 88 B 4
Arbatax 61 B 5
Arbay Hēre 75 N 5
Arbil 65 F 7
Arboga 51 P 5
Arbon 57 E 2
Arbroath 38 E 3
Arc, *Provence, river* 55 G 6
Arc, *Savoie, river* 55 H 5
Arcachon 55 D 5
Arc Dome, *mountain* 120 C 4
Archena 52 E 3
Archer, *river* 140 E 3
Archer Bay 147 H 2
Archidona 52 C 4
Arcila, *see Asilah* 52 B 5
Arcis-sur-Aube 54 G 3
Arcos de la F. 52 C 4
Arcos de V. 52 A 2
Arcos, Sa. de, *mt.* 53 E 2
Arctic Bay, *trading post* 114 J 1
Arctic Ocean 18 B 1
Arda 62 D 3
Ardabīl 65 G 6
Ardara 48 C 2
Ard aş Şawwān, *region* 37 G 4
Ard avasar 46 C 4
Ardèche, *river* 55 G 5
Ardee 39 C 5
Ard el Jabban, *region* 89 C 2
Arden, Forest of, *region* 43 F 2
Ardennes, *mountains* 34 F 4
Arderin, *mountain* 49 D 3
Ardestān 88 E 3
Ardgay 46 D 4
Ardglass 48 F 2
Ardila 52 B 3
Ardino 62 D 3
Ardnamurchan, *region* 46 C 5
Ardnamurchan Pt., *cape* 38 C 3
Ardrishaig 47 C 5
Ardrossan 38 D 4
Arena, Pt., *cape* 118 C 4
Arenas de San Pedro 52 C 2
Arenberg, *region* 56 F 2
Arendal 34 G 2
Arequipa 126 B 4
Arévalo 52 C 2
Arévalo, Tierra de, *region* 52 C 2
Arezzo 36 D 2
Arga 52 E 1
Argamasilla de A. 52 D 3
Argao 81 E 7
Argelès-Gazost 55 D 6
Argens, *river* 55 H 6
Argenta 60 C 2
Argentan 54 D 3
Argentera, P., *mountain* 55 H 5
Argentière 57 B 4
Argentina 127 C 6
Argentino, L., *lake* 127 B 7
Argentine Basin, *sea feature* 25 C 7
Argenton-sur-Creuse 55 E 4
Argolikós Kólpos, *bay* 63 C 5
Argonne 54 G 3
Argonne, Forêt d', *forest* 56 D 5
Árgos 63 C 5
Arguello, Pt., *cape* 120 B 5
Argun', *river* 67 G 3
Argyll, *county* 47 C 5
Argyll, *region* 38 D 3
Ariakeno-umi, *bay* 80 B 4
Ariake-wan, *bay* 80 B 5
Ari Atoll, *island* 87 C 6
Arica 126 B 4
Arid, C., *cape* 146 D 6
Ariège, *river* 55 E 6
Arima 123 G 3
Aripuanã, *river* 132 C 3
Arisaig 46 C 5
'Arīsh, W. al, *wadi* 100 E 3
Arivonimamo 103 F 4
Ariza 52 D 2
Arizona, *state* 118 E 5
Arjeplog 50 Q 2
Arjona 52 C 4
Arjonilla 52 C 4
Arkabutla Res., *reservoir* 121 B 3
Arkagala 75 R 3
Arkaig, L., *lake* 46 C 5
Arkansas, *river* 106 E 4
Arkansas, *state* 119 J 4
Arkansas City 122 D 1
Arka Tagh, *mountains* 86 E 2
Arkhangel'sk 29 M 2
Arklow 39 C 5
Árkoi, *island* 63 E 5
Arkoúdhi, *island* 63 B 4
Arlanzón, *river* 52 C 1
Arlberg, *mountains* 57 F 2
Arlbergpass, *pass* 57 F 2
Arles 36 C 2
Arlon 54 G 3
Arly, *river* 57 B 4
Armadale, *Australia* 152 B 4
Armadale, *Scotland* 47 E 6
Armagh 39 C 4
Armagh, *county* 48 E 2
Armagnac, *region* 28 F 4
Armançon, *river* 54 G 4
Armatnhiá, *island* 63 E 6
Armavir 37 H 2
Armenia 132 B 2
Armentières 54 F 2
Armidale 147 K 6
Armstrong 114 F 3
Armutçuk D., *mountain* 63 E 3
Armyanskaya S.S.R., *republic* 65 F 6
Arnedo 52 D 1
Arnes 50 B 2
Arnhem 34 F 3
Arnhem Bay 148 B 1
Arnhem, C., *cape* 140 D 3
Arnhem Land, *region* 140 D 3
Arno, *river* 60 C 3
Arnøy, *island* 50 Q 1
Arnprior 116 E 2
Arnsberg 58 C 3
Arnstadt 58 D 3
Aro, P. de, *mountain* 52 D 1
Aroab 101 C 4
Aroánia Óri, *mountain* 37 E 3
Aroche, Picos de, *mt.* 52 B 3
Arolsen 58 C 3
Aron, *river* 55 F 4
Arona 60 B 2
Aroroy 81 E 5
Arosa 57 E 3
Arosa, Ria de, *inlet* 52 A 1
Arowhana, *mountain* 150 G 4
Arraiján 134 D 2
Arraiolos 52 B 3
Arra Mts., *mountains* 49 C 4
Ar Ramādī 88 C 3
Arran, *island* 38 D 4
Arras 34 F 3
Ar Rawḑah 100 B 5
Arrecife, Pto., *cape* 98 B 3
Arrée, Mt. d', *mt.* 54 C 3
Ar Rihāb, *region* 29 M 6
Ar Rimāl, *region* 29 N 7
Arrochar 47 D 5
Arronches 52 B 3
Arrow, *river* 42 D 2
Arrow, L., *lake* 48 C 2
Arrowsmith, Mt., *mt.* 151 D 6
Arrowtown 151 C 7
Arroyo de la Luz 52 B 3
Arruda dos V. 52 A 3
Arsen'ev 80 C 1
Arta, *Greece* 62 B 4
Arta, *Spain* 53 G 3
Artem 80 C 2
Artemovskiy 35 N 3
Artesa de S. 53 F 2
Artesia 118 G 5
Arthur's Pass, *mt. pass* 151 D 6
Arti 35 N 3
Artigas 135 C 3
Artois, *province* 54 E 2
d'Artois, Collines, *region* 54 F 2
Ar-tsagan Nor, *lake* 76 E 3
Aru, Kep., *island group* 67 H 6
Arua 99 G 5
Aruba, *island* 107 G 5
Arudy 53 E 1
Arun, *river* 41 D 3
Arundel 43 G 4
Arundel Gap, *river gap* 41 C 4
Arunta, *see Simpson Desert* 140 D 4
Aruppukkottai 87 D 5
Arusha 103 E 3
'Arvat Sedom 89 B 4
Arve, *river* 57 B 3
Arvida 115 K 4
Arvidsjaur 50 Q 3
Arvika 51 O 5
Aryan, *civilisation* 158
Arys' 74 J 5
Arzew 53 E 5
Arzew, G. d', *gulf* 53 E 5
Arzúa 52 A 1
Ås 58 E 3
Asahi, *river* 80 C 4
Asahi-d., *mountain* 80 E 2
Asahigawa 67 J 3
Asama y., *mountain* 80 D 3
Asan Man, *bay* 76 H 4
Asansol 79 F 3
Åsarna 50 O 4
Asbest 35 N 3
Ascalon, *ancient site* 89 A 3
Ascension I., *island* 25 E 5
Aschaffenburg 58 C 4
Aschersleben 58 D 3
Ascoli 60 D 3
Ascoli Satriano 60 E 4
Ascot 43 G 3
Åseda 51 P 5
Asedjrad, *mountains* 36 C 5
Asekrem, *mountain* 98 D 3
Åsele 50 P 3
Asenovgrad 63 D 3
Ash 41 G 3
Ash, *river* 41 E 2
Ashbourne 43 F 3
Ashburton, *England* 42 D 4
Ashburton, *New Zealand* 151 D 6
Ashburton, *river* 140 B 4
Ashburton Ra., *mts.* 140 D 3
Ashby de la Zouch 43 F 2
Ashdod 89 A 3
Ashdown Forest, *region* 43 H 3
Asheville 119 L 4
Ashford 39 G 6
Ashfork 120 D 5
Ashikaga 80 D 3
Ashizuri-saki, *cape* 80 C 4
Ashkhabad 66 D 4
Ashland, *U.S.A., Kentucky* 121 D 2
Ashland, *U.S.A., Oregon* 120 B 3
Ashmore Reef, *reef* 146 D 2
Ashmūn 100 B 2
Ashqelon 89 A 3
Ash Sharm, *region* 100 F 5
Ash Sharqāţ 65 E 7
Ash Shihr 88 D 7
Ashtabula 116 D 3
Ashtead 43 G 3
Ashton 120 E 2
Ashton under Lyne 45 F 4
Ashuanipi L., *lake* 115 L 3
'Āsi, *river* 37 G 3
Asia, Kep., *island group* 85 E 3
Asilah 52 B 5
Asinara, Golfo dell', *gulf* 60 B 4
Asino 75 L 4
Asīr 66 D 5
Asi T., *mountain* 62 F 4
Askeaton 49 C 4
Askersund 51 O 5
Askja 50 D 3
'Asl 100 D 3
Asmara 90 G 4
Asopós, *river* 68 C 4
Asosa 99 G 4
Asoteriba, J., *mountain* 99 G 3
Aspinara 36 D 3
Aspiring, Mt., *mountain* 151 C 7
Aspromonte, *mountains* 61 E 5
Assab 66 D 5
Assab B., *bay* 88 F 6
Aş Şaff 100 C 3
Aş Şaḩn, *region* 88 C 3
Assale, L., *lake* 88 C 7
Aş Şāliḩīyah 100 C 2
Assam, *state* 86 F 3
As Samāwah 88 D 3
As Sanţah 100 C 2
Assateague I., *island* 121 F 2
Assen 56 E 2
Assens 51 N 6
Assinara, *island* 60 B 4
As Sinbillāwayn 100 C 2
Assiniboine, *river* 114 H 4
Assiniboine, Mt., *mt.* 106 E 3
As Sirr, *region* 100 E 2
Assis 135 C 2
Assisi 60 D 3
Aş Şummān, *region* 88 D 4
Aş Şummān, *rocky plateau* 88 D 5
Assumption, *island* 103 F 3
As Suwaydā' 88 B 3
As Suwayrah 88 C 3
As Şuways 90 G 3

Berkshire Downs, hills 43 F 3
Berkshire Hills, hills 119 N 3
Berleburg 58 C 3
Berlevåg 50 T 1
Berlin, Germany 66 B 3
Berlin, U.S.A. 117 F 2
Berlin, Mt., mountain 23 O 2
Bermeja, Sa., mountains 52 C 4
Bermejo, river 126 D 5
Bermeo 52 D 1
Bermillo de Sayago 52 B 2
Bermuda, island 25 B 3
Bern 28 G 4
Bernagh, Sl., mountains 39 B 5
Bernay 54 E 3
Bernburg 58 D 3
Berne, see Bern 57 C 3
Berner Alpen, mountains 57 C 3
Berneray, island 38 C 3
Berner Oberland, region 57 C 3
Bernina, mountains 57 E 3
Berninapass, pass 57 F 3
Bernina, Piz., mountain 57 E 3
Bernier B., bay 114 J 1
Bernier I., island 146 B 4
Bernkastel-Kues 58 B 4
Béroroha 105 C 4
Berounka, river 58 E 4
Berre, É. de, lake 55 G 6
Berri 147 H 6
Berrichonne, region 55 E 4
Berringarra 152 B 3
Berrouaghia 53 G 4
Berry, province 55 E 4
Berry Is., island group 119 M 6
Bersted 41 C 4
Berti Hills, mountains 99 F 4
Bertraghboy Bay, bay 48 B 3
Berwick 47 F 6
Berwick-upon-Tweed 38 E 4
Berwyn Mts., mountains 39 E 5
Berzosa, La, region 52 B 2
Besalampy 105 C 3
Besançon 36 C 2
Beskidy Zachodnie, mountains 28 J 4
Bessemer 119 K 5
Bessin, river 54 D 3
Betafo 105 C 3
Betanzos 52 A 1
Betanzos, Ria de, inlet 52 A 1
Bétaré-Oya 98 E 5
Bethal 101 F 4
Bethanie 101 C 4
Bethlehem, Jordan, see Beit Lahm 89 B 3
Bethlehem, Rep. of South Africa 102 D 5
Bethlehem, U.S.A. 117 E 3
Bethulie 101 E 5
Béthune 54 F 2
Béthune, river 54 E 3
Bethesda 42 C 1
Betioky 91 H 8
Betoota 149 C 4
Betpak Dala, steppe 66 E 3
Betroka 91 H 8
Betsiboka, river 103 F 4
Bettembourg 56 E 5
Bettiah 86 E 3
Bettles 114 B 2
Bettws-y-coed 42 D 1
Beult 41 F 3
Beuvron, river 54 E 4
Beverley, Australia 146 C 6
Beverley, England 39 F 5
Bex 57 C 3
Bexhill-on-Sea 43 H 4
Beyçayírî 62 E 3
Bey D., mountain 29 K 5
Beykoz 62 F 3
Beyla 98 C 5
Beyoneisu-retsugan, island 80 D 5
Beypazari 37 F 3
Beyşehir G., lake 28 K 5
Beyt Shean 89 B 2
Bezhetsk 35 K 3
Bezhitsa 35 K 3
Béziers 36 C 2
Bhadaura 86 D 3
Bhadrakh 86 E 4
Bhadra Sagara, lake 87 D 4
Bhadravati 87 D 5
Bhagalpur 79 F 3
Bhamo 66 F 4
Bhandara 86 D 4
Bhanrer Ra., mountains 86 D 4
Bharatpur 86 D 3
Bhatpara 86 E 4
Bhavnagar 78 E 3
Bhawani Patna 87 E 4
Bhima, river 87 D 4
Bhiwani 86 D 3
Bhopal 66 E 4
Bhor 87 C 4
Bhubaneswar 87 E 4
Bhuj 78 D 3
Bhusawal 86 D 4
Bhutan 66 F 4
Bia, P., mountain 79 H 4
Bīābān, region 88 F 4
Biak, island 140 D 2
Biała Podlaska 64 D 2
Białogard 58 F 1
Biały Bór 58 G 2
Białystok 34 H 3
Biao 81 F 8
Biarritz 36 B 2
Biasca 57 D 3
Bibā 100 B 4
Bic 117 G 1
Bicester 43 F 3
Bickerton I., island 146 G 2
Bida 90 D 5
Bidar 87 D 4
Biddeford 117 F 3
Bidean nam Bian, mt. 47 C 5
Bideford 39 D 6
Bideford Bay, bay 39 D 6
Bīdkhān, Kūh-e, mt. 88 F 4
Bi Doup, mountain 79 H 4
Biel 57 C 2
Bielefeld 58 C 2
Bielersee, lake 57 C 2
Biella 60 B 2
Bielsko-Biala 64 C 3
Bien Hoa 83 E 7
Bienville, Lac, lake 115 K 3
Biferno, river 60 E 4
Biga 62 E 3
Big Baldy Mt., mt. 120 E 2
Big Bell 152 B 3
Big Belt Mts., mts. 118 E 2
Big Black, river 121 B 3
Big Black Mt., mt. 121 D 2
Bigbury Bay, bay 42 D 4
Big Cypress Swamp, swamp 121 D 5
Biggar, Canada 114 G 3
Biggar, Scotland 47 E 6
Biggin Hill 41 E 3
Biggleswade 43 G 2
Big Hole, river 120 D 2
Bighorn, river 118 F 2
Bighorn Mts., mts. 106 E 3
Big I., island 115 K 2
Big Lost, river 120 D 3
Bigorre, region 55 D 6
Big Sable Pt., cape 116 B 2
Big Smoky Valley, region 118 D 4
Big Spring 118 G 5
Big Trout L., lake 115 J 3
Big Wood, river 120 D 3
Bihac 60 E 2
Bihar 86 E 3
Bihar, state 86 E 3
Biharamulo 104 B 3
Bihor, mountain 64 D 3
Bijagós, Arqo. dos, island group 90 B 4
Bijapur 87 D 4
Bijār 88 D 2
Bijawar 86 D 3
Bijeljina 64 C 4
Bijelo Polje 62 A 2
Bijnor 86 D 3
Bikaner 78 E 3
Bikin 75 Q 5
Bilaa Pt., cape 81 F 7
Bilaspur 78 F3
Bilauktaung Ra., mts. 79 G 4
Bilbao 28 F 4
Bilbays 100 C 2
Biliran I., island 81 F 6
Bilisht 62 B 3
Bilit 81 C 9
Bill Baileys Bank, sea feature 38 A 1
Billericay 43 H 3
Billings 118 F 2
Billingshurst 41 D 3
Billybillong 152 B 3
Bill Williams, river 120 D 5
Biloela 147 K 4
Bilo Gora, mountain 60 F 2
Biloxi 121 B 4
Bilston 43 E 2
Bilugyun I., island 83 B 5
Bimberi, Mt., mountain 140 E 5
Binaija, mountain 84 D 4
Binalud, Kūh-e, mountain 86 B 2
Binche 54 G 2
Bindura 101 F 2
Binga, Mte., mountain 103 E 4
Bingara 149 E 4
Bingen 58 B 4
Bingerville 90 C 5
Binghamton 117 E 3
Bingkor 81 B 9
Bingley 45 G 4
Binibeca, C., cape 53 H 3
Bintan, P., island 84 B 3
Bint Jubail 89 B 1
Bintulu 79 J 5
Binubusan 81 D 5
Binyamina 89 A 2
Biograd 60 E 3
Bir 87 D 4
Bira, Indonesia 85 E 4
Bira, Jordan 89 B 3
Birac 81 D 3
Birch Mts., mountains 106 E 3
Birchington 41 G 3
Birdsville 147 G 5
Birhan, mountain 90 G 4
Bīrjand 66 D 4
Birkat Muḩayshir, lake 100 C 2
Birkat Qārūn, lake 100 B 3
Birkenfeld 58 B 4
Birkenhead, England 39 E 5
Birkenhead, New Zealand 150 F 3
Birksgate Ra., mts. 146 F 5
Birmingham, England 39 F 5
Birmingham, U.S.A. 106 F 4
Birnin Kebbi 90 D 4
Birni n'Konni 98 D 4
Birobidzhan 75 Q 5
Birr 39 C 5
Bir Rabalou 53 G 4
Birsk 35 M 3
Birstall 45 G 4
Biscarrosse et de Parentis, É. de, lake 55 D 5
Biscay, Bay of, bay 28 F 4
Biscayne B., bay 121 D 5
Bisceglie 60 F 4
Bischofswerda 58 F 3
Biscoe Bay, bay 23 N 2
Biscoe Is., island group 23 R 2
Biševo, island 60 F 3
Bīshah 88 C 6
Bishop 120 C 4
Bishop Auckland 39 F 4
Bishop Rock, rock 39 C 7
Bishops Castle 42 D 2
Bishops Stortford 39 G 6
Bishop's Waltham 41 B 4
Biskra 90 D 2
Bismarck 118 G 2
Bismarck Archipelago, island group 67 J 6
Bismarck, C., cape 106 K 2
Bismarck Ra., mts. 140 E 2
Bismarck Sea 140 E 2
Bissa 53 F 4
Bissau 90 B 4
Bistrita 64 E 3
Bitburg 58 B 4
Bitlis 65 E 6
Bitola 37 E 3
Bitonto 60 F 4
Bitterfeld 58 E 3
Bitterroot, river 120 D 2
Bitterroot Range, mts. 106 E 3
Biu 98 E 4
Biwa Ko, lake 75 Q 6
Biyadh, Al, region 88 D 5
Biysk 75 L 4
Bizerte 90 D 2
Bjelovár 64 C 4
Bjeshkët e Nemuna, mountains 62 A 2
Björklinge 51 P 4
Björna 50 Q 3
Bjørnøya, island 24 L 2
Bjurholm 50 Q 3
Bjuröklubb 50 R 3
Bjursås 51 P 4
Black, U.S.A., Alabama, river 121 C 3
Black, U.S.A., Louisiana, river 121 B 4
Black, U.S.A., Missouri, river 121 B 2
Black, U.S.A., Wisconsin, river 116 A 2
Blackall 147 J 4
Black Bay, bay 116 B 1
Black Belt, region 119 K 5
Blackburn 39 E 5
Blackburn, Mt., mt. 114 C 2
Black Diamond 114 F 3
Blackdown, hill 41 C 3
Blackdown Hills, hills 39 E 6
Blackfoot 120 D 3
Blackfoot, river 120 D 2
Black Hd., cape 48 B 3
Black Hills, mountains 106 E 3
Black Isle, peninsula 46 D 4
Black Mesa, tableland 118 E 4
Blackmoor Vale, valley 43 E 4
Black Mt., mountain 39 E 6
Black Mts., Canada, mountains 117 G 2
Black Mts., England, mountains 39 E 6
Black Mts., U.S.A., mts. 118 E 4
Blackpool 39 E 5
Black Ra., mountains 106 E 4
Black Rock, rock 39 A 4
Black Rock Desert, desert 118 D 3
Black Sea 29 L 4
Blacksod Bay, bay 48 A 2
Black Sugarloaf, mt. 147 K 6
Black Volta, river 98 C 5
Blackwater, England, river 43 H 3
Blackwater, Northern Ireland, river 48 E 2
Blackwater, Rep. of Ireland, Cork, river 39 B 5
Blackwater, Rep. of Ireland, Meath, river 48 E 3
Blackwater Res., reservoir 46 D 5
Blackwood, river 152 B 4
Blaenavon 42 D 3
Blagoevgrad 62 C 2
Blagoveshchensk 75 P 4
Blain 54 D 4
Blair Athol, Australia 148 D 3
Blair Atholl, Scotland 46 E 5
Blairgowrie 38 E 3
Blakeney Pt., spit 38 G 5
Blanc, C., Sp. Sahara, cape 90 B 3
Blanc, C., Tunisia, cape 61 B 6
Blanc, Mt., mountain 28 G 4
Blanca, Bahía, bay 127 C 6
Blanche, L., South Australia, lake 147 G 5
Blanche, L., Western Australia, lake 152 C 2
Blanco, C., Argentina, cape 127 C 7
Blanco, C., Costa Rica, cape 123 E 4
Blanco, C., Spain, cape 53 G 3
Blanco, C., U.S.A., cape 106 D 3
Blandford 43 E 4
Blanes 53 G 2
Blankenberge 56 B 3
Blantyre 91 G 7
Blavet, river 54 C 4
Blaye 55 D 5
Blayney 149 D 5
Bleiburg 59 F 5
Blekinge, county 51 P 6
Blenheim 150 E 5
Bletchley 39 F 6
Bleue 79 G 5
Blida 90 D 2
Blidenhorn, mountain 57 D 3
Blind River 116 C 2
Blitar 84 C 4
Block I., island 117 F 3
Bloemfontein 91 F 8
Blois 54 E 4
Blond, Monts de, mts. 55 E 5
Blönduós 50 C 3
Bloody Foreland, cape 38 B 4
Bloomington, U.S.A., Illinois 119 K 3
Bloomington, U.S.A., Indiana 121 C 2
Blora 84 C 4
Bludenz 57 E 2
Bluebell Hill, hill 41 E 3
Bluefield 119 L 4
Bluefields 123 E 3
Bluegrass Region, region 121 C 2
Blue Mt., India, mt. 82 A 4
Blue Mt., U.S.A., mt. 116 E 3
Blue Mts., Australia, mts. 140 F 5
Blue Mts., New Zealand, mountains 151 C 7
Blue Mts., U.S.A., Maine, mountains 117 F 2
Blue Mts., U.S.A., Oregon, mountains 106 E 3
Blue Mud B., bay 148 B 1
Blue Nile, see Bahr el Azraq 90 G 4
Blue Ridge, mountains 106 F 4
Blue Stack Mts., mts. 39 B 4
Bluff 151 C 8
Bluff Knoll, mountain 152 B 4
Bluff Pt., cape 146 B 5
Blumenau 136 D 1
Blyth 45 G 2
Blyth, river 45 G 2
Blytheville 119 K 4
Bo 90 B 5
Boac 84 D 2
Boal 52 B 1
Boa Vista 132 C 2
Bobbio 60 B 2
Bobia, Sa. de la, mts. 52 B 1
Bobo Dioulasso 90 C 4
Bobolice 58 G 2
Bobon 81 F 5
Bobruysk 35 J 3
Bobr, river 58 F 3
Boby, Pic, mountain 91 H 8
Boca del Monte 134 A 2
Boca de Santiago, bay 134 B 2
Bocage, region 55 D 4
Bocages, region 54 D 4
Bocas del Toro, Archipiélago de, island group 134 A 1
Bocas del Toro 123 E 4
Bonifacio, Bocche di, strait 28 H 5
Bocholt 58 B 3
Bochum 34 F 3
Boddam 46 G 4
Bodele, region 90 E 4
Boden 34 H 2
Bodensee, lake 34 G 4
Boderg, L., lake 48 C 3
Bodhan 87 D 4
Bodiam 41 F 3
Bodinayakanur 87 D 5
Bodmin 39 D 6
Bodmin Moor, moor 39 D 6
Bodø 34 G 1
Bodoquena, Sa. da, mts. 136 C 1
Bodrum 63 E 5
Bodum 50 P 3
Boende 90 F 6
Boeuf, river 121 B 3
Bōfu 80 B 4
Bogale, river mouth 87 F 5
Bogalusa 119 K 5
Bogan, river 149 D 5
Bogdanovich 35 N 3
Bogdo Uula, mountains 66 F 3
Boggeragh Mts., mts. 39 B 5
Bogia 85 F 4
Bognor Regis 39 F 6
Bogo 81 F 6
Bogong, Mt., mountains 147 J 7
Bogor 79 H 6
Bogotá 126 B 2
Bogra 86 E 3
Bogueron, Pto. del, pass 52 C 2
Bohemia, region 59 E 4
Böhmerwald, mountains 28 H 4
Bohol, island 79 K 5
Bohol Strait, strait 81 E 7
Böhönye 60 F 1
Bois Blanc I., island 116 C 2
Bois de Chimay, forest 56 C 4
Boise 118 D 3
Boizenburg 58 D 2
Bojador, Cabo, cape 90 B 3
Bojnūrd 74 H 6
Boké 98 B 4
Bokhara 74 J 6
Boknfjord, fjord 34 F 2
Bolama 98 B 4
Bolangir 87 E 4
Bolarque, Emb. de, lake 52 D 2
Bolbec 54 E 3
Bolesławiec 58 F 3
Bolgrad 64 F 4
Bolinao, C., cape 84 C 2
Bolívar 136 B 2
Bolivia 126 C 4
Boljevac 62 B 2
Bollnäs 51 P 4
Bollon 149 D 4
Bolmen, lake 51 O 6
Bolo 81 E 6
Bolobo 90 E 6
Bologna 28 H 4
Bologoye 35 K 2
Bolovens, Plateau des, plateau 83 E 6
Bolsena, L. di, lake 60 C 3
Bol'sheretsk 75 S 4
Bol'shevik, O., island 75 N 2
Bol'shezemel'skaya Tundra, region 74 H 3
Bol. Balkhan, Khr., mt. 29 N 5
Bol'shoy Kavkaz, mts. 29 M 4
Bol. Kinel', river 65 H 3
Bol. Shantar, O., island 67 H 3
Bolsón de Mapimí, region 107 E 4
Bolsward 56 D 1
Boltaña 53 F 1
Bolt Hd., cape 39 E 6
Bolton, England 39 E 5
Bolton, Philippines 81 F 8
Bolus Hd., cape 49 A 5
Bolvadin 65 B 6
Bolzano 60 C 1
Boma 91 E 6
Bombala 149 D 6
Bombarai, peninsula 85 E 4
Bombarral 52 A 3
Bombay 66 E 5
Bomi Hills, mountains 98 B 5
Bømlafj., fjord 51 L 5
Bomu, river 90 F 5
Bon, C., cape 90 E 2
Boná, I., island 134 D 2
Bonaigarh 86 E 4
Bonaire, island 107 G 5
Bonaire Trench, sea feature 107 G 5
Bonaparte Archipelago, island group 140 C 3
Bonar Bridge 46 D 4
Bonavista Bay, bay 115 M 4
Bondo 102 D 2
Bondoc Pena, peninsula 81 E 5
Bône, see Annaba 90 D 2
Bo'ness 47 E 5
Bone, Teluk, bay 67 H 6
Bonggaw 81 C 9
Bongo I., island 81 F 8
Bongor 98 E 4
Bongos, Massif des, mts. 102 D 2
Bonifacio 60 B 4
Bonin Is., see Ogasawara-Guntō 80 E 6
Bonn 58 B 3
Bonners Ferry 120 C 1
Bonneval 57 C 4
Bonneville 55 H 4
Bonneville Salt Flats, dry lake 120 D 3
Bonnie Rock 152 B 4
Bonny 98 D 5
Bono 61 B 4
Bonthain 67 G 6
Bonthe 90 B 5
Bontoc 77 G 8
Booligal 149 C 5
Boomkensdiep, strait 56 D 1
Boorowa 149 D 5
Boothia, Gulf of, gulf 106 F 2
Boothia Pena., peninsula 106 F 2
Bootle 44 E 4
Bor, Turkey 65 C 7
Bor, U.S.S.R. 65 F 2
Borah Pk., mountain 120 D 2
Borama 99 H 5
Borås 34 G 3
Borāzjān 88 E 4
Borba 52 B 3
Borborema, Planalto da, region 126 F 3
Bordeaux 28 F 4
Bordeaux, Landes de, region 55 D 5
Bordecorex, Sa. de, mountains 52 D 2
Borden I., island 106 E 2
Borden Pena, peninsula 114 J 1
Bordertown 149 C 6
Bordheyri 50 B 3
Bordon Camp 41 C 3
Borehamwood 42 D 2
Boreray, island 38 B 3
Borgå 51 S 4
Borgarnes 50 B 3
Børgefjell, mountains 50 O 3
Borgholm 51 P 6
Borgne, L., lake 121 B 4
Borgo 60 C 1
Borgomanero 57 D 4
Borgosesia 57 D 4
Borgo Val di Taro 60 B 2
Borislav 64 D 3
Borisoglebsk 35 L 3
Borisov 65 B 2
Borja 53 E 2
Borjas Blancas 53 F 2
Borken 56 E 3
Borku, region 90 E 4
Borkum, island 56 E 1
Borlänge 34 G 2
Born, Pays de, region 55 D 5
Borneo, island 67 G 6
Bornes, mountains 52 B 2
Bornholm, island 28 H 3
Bornholmsgattet, strait 51 O 6

Bornos 52 C 4
Borō Horō-Ūla, *mts.* 74 L 5
Boro Uula, *mountains* 76 B 3
Boroughbridge 44 G 3
Borough Green 41 E 3
Borovichi 51 V 5
Borovsk 35 N 2
Borroloola 148 B 2
Borşa 64 E 3
Borshchovochnyy Khr., *mountains* 66 G 3
Bortu Uula, *mountain* 86 E 1
Boru 85 F 5
Borūjerd 78 B 2
Bory Tucholskie, *region* 34 H 3
Borzya 75 O 4
Bosa 61 B 4
Bosanski Novi 60 F 2
Boscastle 42 C 4
Boschplaat, *island* 56 E 1
Boskovice 58 G 4
Bos. Krupa 60 F 2
Bosna-i-Hercegovina, *province* 64 C 4
Bosnek 85 E 4
Bōsō Hantō, *peninsula* 80 E 4
Bosporus, *see Karadeniz Boğazi* 37 F 3
Bosquet 53 F 4
Bossangoa 90 E 5
Boston, *England* 39 F 5
Boston, *U.S.A.* 106 G 3
Boston Mts., *mountains* 106 F 4
Botany Bay, *bay* 147 K 6
Botev, *mountain* 37 F 2
Botevgrad 62 C 2
Bothnia, Gulf of, *gulf* 28 J 2
Bothwell 47 D 6
Botoşani 37 F 2
Botrange, *mountain* 56 E 4
Botswana 91 F 8
Bottesford 43 G 2
Bottrop 58 B 3
Botucatu 135 D 2
Botwood 115 M 4
Bouaflé 90 C 5
Bouaké 90 C 5
Bouar 102 C 2
Bou Arfa 98 C 2
Boubandjida, *region* 98 E 5
Bou Cedraïa 53 G 5
Boufarik 53 G 4
Bougainville, C., *cape* 146 E 2
Bougainville, I., *island* 141 F 2
Bougainville Reef, *reef* 147 J 3
Bougainville Str., *strait* 141 F 2
Bouganeuf 55 E 5
Bougie, *see Bejaïa* 36 C 3
Bou Guezoul 53 G 5
Bouillon 56 D 5
Bouïra 53 G 4
Boulay 54 H 3
Boulder, *Australia* 146 D 6
Boulder, *U.S.A.* 118 F 3
Bouiia 148 B 3
Boulogne s. Mer. 54 E 2
Boumort, Sa. de, *mts.* 53 F 1
Boundary Pk., *mts.* 120 C 4
Bountiful 120 E 3
Bounty Is., *island group* 141 H 6
Bourarhet, Erg, *see Erg Bourarhet* 98 D 3
Bourbonnais, *province* 55 F 4
Bourboule, la 55 F 5
Bourg 55 G 4
Bourges 36 C 2
Bourget, L. du, *lake* 57 A 4
Bourgneuf, B. de, *bay* 54 C 4
Bourgogne, *province* 55 G 4
Bourg-Saint-Maurice 57 B 4
Bourke 147 J 6
Bourne 43 G 2
Bourne End 41 C 2
Bournemouth 39 F 6
Bourtanger Moor, *region* 56 F 2
Bou-Saâda 36 C 3
Boussac 55 F 4
Bouvetøya, *island* 23 C 3
Bovey Tracey 42 D 4
Bovingdon 41 C 2
Bow, *river* 114 F 3
Bowen 147 J 3
Bowland, Forest of, *forest* 39 E 5
Bowling Green 119 K 4
Bowling Green, C., *cape* 147 J 3
Bowman Bay, *bay* 115 K 2
Bowmore 47 B 6
Bowral 149 E 5
Boxtel 56 D 3
Boyle 48 C 3
Boyne, *river* 39 C 5
Bozcaada, *island* 62 E 4
Boz D., *mountains* 37 G 3
Bozdoğan 63 F 5
Bozeman 118 E 2
Bozoum 90 E 5
Bra 60 A 2
Braan, *river* 47 E 5
Brabant, *province* 56 C 4
Brabant I., *island* 23 R 2
Brač, *island* 28 J 4
Bracadale, L., *lake* 46 B 4
Brackley 43 F 2
Bracknell 43 G 3
Bradano, *river* 61 F 4
Bradford 28 F 3
Bradwell 43 H 3
Brady 118 H 5
Brady, Mt., *mountain* 149 B 4
Braemar 46 E 4
Braemar, *region* 38 E 3
Braeriach, *mountain* 46 E 4
Braeside 152 C 2
Braga 52 A 2
Bragado 135 B 3
Braganca 52 B 2
Bragança Paulista 135 D 2
Brahmaputra 66 F 4
Brăila 37 F 2
Braine-l'Alleud 56 C 4
Braintree 43 H 3
Brake 58 C 2
Bramley 41 C 3
Brampton 44 F 3
Bramsche 56 F 2
Bramshill Forest, *region* 41 C 3
Brañas, Las, *region* 52 B 1
Branco, *river* 126 C 2
Brandberg, *mountain* 101 B 3
Brandenburg 34 G 3
Brandes, *region* 55 E 4
Brandfort 101 E 5
Brandon, *Canada* 118 H 2
Brandon, *England* 43 H 2
Brandon Bay, *bay* 49 A 4
Brandon Hd., *cape* 34 D 3
Brandon Mt., *mountain* 39 A 5
Braniewo 64 C 1
Bransfield Str., *strait* 23 R 2
Branston 43 G 1
Brantford 116 D 3
Bras d'Or L., *lake* 117 J 2
Brasília 126 E 4
Braşov 64 E 4
Brassey Ra., *Australia, mountains* 146 D 5
Brassey Ra., *Malaysia, mountains* 84 C 3
Brasstown Bald, *mt.* 119 L 5
Bratislava 36 E 2
Bratsk 66 G 3
Braunau 59 E 4
Braunschweig 34 G 3
Brava 103 F 2
Brava, Punta, *cape* 134 B 3
Brawley 120 D 5
Bray 39 C 5
Bray, Pays de, *region* 54 E 3
Brazil 126 D 3
Brazilian Basin, *sea feature* 25 D 6
Brazilian Highlands, *mts.* 126 E 5
Brazilian Shield, *plateau* 154 D 4
Brazos, *river* 118 H 5
Brazzaville 90 E 6
Brčko 60 G 2
Brdy, *mountains* 34 G 4
Breadalbane, *region* 38 D 3
Breaden, L., *lake* 146 E 5
Breaksea Sound, *inlet* 151 B 7
Bream Bay, *bay* 150 F 2
Brebes 84 B 4
Brechin 38 E 3
Breckland, *region* 39 G 5
Brecknock, *county* 42 D 3
Břeclav 64 C 3
Brecon 39 E 6
Brecon Beacons, *mts.* 39 E 6
Breda 56 C 3
Bredasdorp 101 D 6
Brede, *river* 41 F 4
Bregaglia, Val, *valley* 57 E 3
Bregalnica, *river* 62 C 3
Bregenz 57 E 2
Bregenzer Wald, *wood* 57 E 2
Breidhafjördhur, *bay* 28 D 2
Breil-sur-Roye 60 A 3
Breisgau, *region* 57 C 2
Brembana, V., *valley* 57 E 4
Bremen 28 H 3
Bremerhaven 34 G 3
Bremerton 120 B 2
Brendon Hills, *hills* 42 D 3
Brenne, *region* 55 E 4
Brenner, P., *pass* 36 D 2
Breno 60 C 2
Brenta, *mountains* 57 F 3
Brenta, *river* 60 C 2
Brentwood 39 G 6
Brescia 36 D 2
Breslau, *see Wroclaw* 58 G 3
Bressanone 60 C 1
Bressay, *island* 46 G 1
Bressuire 55 D 4
Brest, *France* 36 B 2
Brest, *U.S.S.R.* 34 H 3
Bretagne, *province* 54 C 3
Breton, C., *cape* 117 J 2
Breton Sd., *inlet* 119 K 6
Brett, C., *cape* 150 F 2
Bretten 59 C 4
Brevik 51 N 5
Brewarrina 149 D 4
Brewster, C., *mountain* 134 D 1
Brežice 60 E 2
Breznik 62 C 2
Brezo, Sa. del, *mts.* 52 C 1
Brezovo 62 D 2
Bria 90 F 5
Briançon 55 H 5
Brianza 57 E 4
Brickaville 105 D 3
Bride, *river* 49 C 4
Bridgend 39 E 6
Bridge of Allan 47 E 5
Bridge Pt., *cape* 121 E 5
Bridgeport 119 N 3
Bridger Pk., *mountain* 120 E 2
Bridgetown, *Australia* 146 C 6
Bridgetown, *Barbados* 123 H 3
Bridgnorth 43 E 3
Bridlington 39 F 4
Bridlington Bay, *bay* 45 H 3
Bridport 42 E 4
Brie, *region* 36 C 2
Brienz 57 D 3
Brienzersee, *lake* 57 D 3
Bridgwater 39 E 6
Bridgwater Bay, *bay* 42 D 3
Briey 56 D 5
Brig 59 B 5
Brigg 45 H 4
Brigham City 118 E 3
Brighouse 45 G 4
Brightlingsea 43 J 3
Brighton 34 E 3
Brightstone Bay, *bay* 41 B 4
Brightstone Forest, *region* 41 B 4
Brignoles 55 H 6
Brihuega 52 D 2
Brilon 58 C 3
Brindisi 36 E 3
Brioude 55 F 5
Brisbane 141 F4
Brisbane, *river* 149 E 4
Bristol, *England* 34 E 3
Bristol, *U.S.A.* 121 D 2
Bristol Bay, *bay* 106 C 3
Bristol Channel, *channel* 34 E 3
Bristol I., *island* 23 A 3
Bristol Lake, *lake* 120 D 5
British Antarctic Territory 23 B 2
British Columbia, *province* 114 E 3
Br. Honduras 107 F 5
British Isles 18 E 2
British Mts., *mountains* 106 D 2
Brits 102 D 5
Britstown 101 D 5
Brittle, L., *lake* 46 B 4
Brive-la-Gaillarde 55 E 5
Briviesca 52 D 1
Brixham 42 D 4
Brno 28 J 4
Broach 86 C 4
Broad Arrow 152 C 4
Broad Bay, *bay* 46 B 3
Broadford 46 C 4
Broad Law, *mountain* 47 E 6
Broadmount 148 E 3
Broad Sd., *inlet* 147 J 4
Broadsound Ra., *mts.* 148 D 3
Broadstairs 43 J 3
Broads, The, *region* 39 G 5
Brochet 114 G 3
Brocken, *mountain* 58 D 3
Brockenhurst 41 A 4
Brockman, Mt., *mt.* 152 B 2
Brockton 117 F 3
Brodeur Pena., *peninsula* 106 F 2
Brodick 47 C 6
Brody 37 F 1
Broken B., *bay* 149 E 5
Broken Hill, *Australia* 140 E 5
Broken Hill, *Zambia* 91 F 7
Bromley 43 H 3
Bromley Plateau, *sea feature* 25 D 6
Bromsgrove 43 E 2
Bromyard 43 E 2
Brønderslev 51 N 5
Brønnøysund 50 O 3
Bronte 61 E 6
Brooke Deep, *sea feature* 155 K 3
Brookings 120 A 3
Brookmans Park 41 D 2
Brooks Range, *mts.* 106 C 2
Broome 140 C 3
Broom, Loch, *lake* 46 C 4
Broome, Mt., *mountain* 146 E 3
Brora 46 E 3
Brora, *river* 47 D 3
Brosna, *river* 39 C 5
Brothers, The, *island group* 99 J 4
Brough 45 F 3
Brough Hd., *cape* 46 E 2
Broughton 44 E 3
Broughty Ferry 47 F5
Browne Ra., *mountains* 152 C 3
Brownhills 43 F 2
Browning 120 D 1
Brown, Mt., *mountain* 149 B 5
Browns Bay 150 F 3
Brownsville 106 F 4
Brown Willy, *mountian* 42 C 4
Browse I., *island* 146 D 2
Broxburn 47 E 6
Broye, *river* 57 B 3
Brozas 52 B 3
Bruay 54 F 2
Bruay-en-Artois 56 A 4
Bruce Hwy. 147 J 4
Bruce, Mt., *mountain* 148 B 4
Bruce Rock 152 B 4
Bruchsal 59 C 4
Bruck, *Austria, Salzburg* 59 E 5
Bruck, *Austria, Burgenland* 59 G 4
Bruck an der Mur 59 F 5
Bruffione, M., *mountain* 57 F 4
Brugg 57 D 2
Brugge 56 B 3
Brunei 67 G 5
Brunei, *state* 67 G 5
Brunflo 50 O 3
Brunner 151 D 6
Brunner, L., *lake* 151 D 6
Brunswick, *Fed. Rep. of Germany, see Braunschweig* 58 D 2
Brunswick, *U.S.A.* 121 D 4
Brunswick B., *bay* 146 D 3
Brunswick, Pena de, *peninsula* 136 A 4
Bruny I., *island* 147 J 8
Brussel 28 G 3
Bruton 43 E 3
Bruxelles, *see Brussel* 56 C 4
Bruya, C., *mountain* 134 D 1
Bryan 119 H 5
Bryan, Mt., *mountain* 140 D 5
Bryansk 35 K 3
Brynamman 42 D 3
Brynmawr 42 D 3
Brzeg 64 C 2
Bü Ağri Daği, *mountain* 37 H 3
Buayan 81 F 8
Bubanza 104 B 3
Bubīyān, J., *island* 88 D 4
Bucaramanga 132 B 2
Bucas Grande I., *island* 81 F 7
Buccaneer Archo., *island group* 140 C 3
Buchach 64 E 3
Buchan, *region* 38 E 3
Buchanan 90 B 5
Buchanan Deep, *sea feature* 155 E 4
Buchanan, L., *lake* 148 D 3
Buchan Deep, *sea feature* 38 F 3
Buchan Ness, *cape* 34 E 3
Bucheggb., *mountains* 57 C 2
Buchloe 57 F 1
Buchs 57 E 2
Buckden 43 G 2
Bückeburg 58 C 2
Buckeye 120 D 5
Buckie 38 E 3
Buckingham 43 G 3
Buckingham, *county* 43 G 3
Buckingham B., *bay* 148 B 1
Buckland Tableland, *plateau* 140 E 4
Bucureşti 28 K 4
Budahīyah, J., *mountains* 100 E 3
Budapest 28 J 4
Budaun 86 D 3
Budd Coast, *region* 23 H 2
Budd, Mt., *mountain* 152 B 3
Bude 39 D 6
Budhareyri 50 E 3
Búdhir 50 E 3
Buenaventura 126 B 2
Buenavista 81 D 5
Buena Vista, B. de, *bay* 121 E 6
Buena Vista L., *lake* 120 C 5
Buenos Aires 127 D 6
Buenos Aires, L., *lake* 127 B 7
Buendia, Emb. de, *lake* 52 D 2
Buer 56 F 3
Buffalo 106 G 3
Buffalo Head Hills, *mts.* 106 E 3
Buffalo, Mt., *mountain* 149 D 6
Buford Res., *reservoir* 121 D 3
Bug, *river* 28 J 3
Buga 132 B 2
Bugala I., *island* 104 C 3
Buganda, *region* 104 B 2
Bugsuk I., *island* 81 B 7
Bagul'ma 35 M 3
Buguruslan 35 M 3
Buḩayrah, *province* 100 B 2
Buḩayrat al Burullus, *lake* 100 B 1
Buḩayrat al Manzilah, *lake* 100 C 1
Buḩayrah al Murrah al Kubrá, Al, *lake* 100 D 2
Buḩayrah al Murrah aş Şughrá, Al, *lake* 100 D 2
Buḩayrat at Timsāh, *lake* 100 D 2
Buḩayrat Idkū, *lake* 100 B 1
Buḩayrat Maryūţ, *lake* 100 A 1
Bühl, *Germany* 54 J 3
Buhl, *U.S.A.* 120 D 3
Buhoro Flats, *region* 103 E 3
Builth Wells 39 E 5
Buin, Piz, *mountain* 57 F 3
Bujalance 52 C 4
Bujumbura 90 F 6
Bukalik Tagh, *mountains* 86 F 2
Bukama 91 F 6
Bukantau, Gy., *mountain* 29 O 4
Bukasa I., *island* 104 C 3
Bukavu 90 F 6
Bukha Mangnai, *mts.* 86 E 2
Bukhara 78 D 2
Bukittinggi 79 H 6
Bukoba 103 E 3
Būl, Kūh-e, *mountain* 29 N 6
Bula 85 E 4
Bulagan 75 N 5
Bulan 81 E 5
Bulawayo 91 F 8
Bulawayo, *district* 101 E 2
Bulayan 76 C 2
Buldan 63 F 4
Buldana 87 D 4
Bulgaria 28 K 4
Bulhar 88 C 7
Buliluyan, C., *cape* 84 C 3
Bullas 52 E 3
Bull Bay, *bay* 121 E 3
Bulle 57 C 3
Buller, *river* 150 E 5
Buller, Mt., *mountain* 140 E 5
Bullfinch 146 C 6
Bull I., *island* 121 E 3
Bulloo, *river* 140 E 4
Bulloo Downs 149 C 4
Bulls 150 F 5
Bull Shoals Res., *reservoir* 119 J 4
Bully Choop Mt., *mt.* 120 B 3
Bulolo 85 F 4
Bulsar 86 C 4
Bulu 81 G 9
Buluan, L., *lake* 81 F 8
Bulude 81 G 9
Bulwer 101 F 5
Bum Bum, P., *island group* 81 C 9
Bü Menderes, *river* 28 K 5
Bumthang 86 F 3
Bunawan 81 F 8
Bunbury 140 B 5
Buncrana 38 C 4
Bundaberg 147 K 4
Bundaleer 149 D 4
Bundoran 48 C 2
Bungay 43 J 2
Bungo-suidō, *strait* 80 B 4
Bunguran Selatan, Kep., *island group* 84 B 3
Bunguran Utara, Kep., *island group* 84 B 3
Bunia 99 G 5
Buñol 53 E 3
Buqayq 88 D 4
Bura 104 D 3
Burakin 152 B 4
Burao 99 H 5
Burauen 81 F 6
Buraydah 99 H 3
Burdeau 53 F 5
Burdekin, *river* 140 E 4
Burdur 37 F 3
Burdwan 66 F 4
Burdwood Bank, *sea feature* 25 B 7
Bureba, La, *region* 52 D 1
Bureinskiy, Khr., *mts.* 67 H 3
Bures 43 H 3
Burford 43 F 3
Būr Fū'ad 100 D 1
Burg 58 D 2
Burgas 37 F 2
Burg auf Fehmarn 58 D 1
Bur Gavo 104 E 3
Burgdorf 57 C 2
Burgenland, *province* 59 G 5
Burgeo 115 M 4
Burgersdorp 102 D 6
Burgess Hill 41 D 4
Burghead 46 E 4
Burgh le Marsh 45 J 4
Burglengenfeld 59 E 4
Burgos 36 B 2
Burgsteinfurt 56 F 2
Burgsvik 51 Q 5
Burhan Buddha Ūla, *mountains* 86 F 2
Burhaniye 62 E 4
Burhanpur 86 D 4
Burias I., *island* 84 D 2
Burica, Pta., *cape* 123 E 4
Burin Pena., *peninsula* 114 M 4
Burke, *river* 147 H 4
Burketown 147 G 3
Burkhala 75 R 3
Burley 120 D 3
Burlingame 120 B 4
Burlington, *U.S.A., Iowa* 119 J 3
Burlington, *U.S.A., N. Carolina* 121 E 2
Burlington, *U.S.A., Vermont* 117 F 2
Burma 66 F 4
Burnett, *river* 141 F 4
Burngup 152 B 4
Burnham 43 H 3
Burnham Beeches 41 C 2
Burnie 147 J 8
Burnley 39 E 5
Burns 120 C 3
Burnt, *river* 120 C 2
Burntisland 47 E 5
Burra 147 G 6
Burray 46 F 3
Burriana 53 E 3
Burrinjuck Res., *reservoir* 149 D 5
Burro, Serrianías del, *mountains* 122 C 2
Burrowes, Pt., *cape* 148 C 2
Burrow Head, *cape* 44 D 3
Burry Inlet, *inlet* 42 C 3
Burry Port 42 C 3
Bursa 37 F 3
Būr Safāga 88 A 4
Būr Sa'īd 99 G 2
Burslem 45 F 4
Būr Tawfīq 100 D 3
Burt L., *lake* 116 C 2
Burton in Kendal 44 F 3
Burton-on-Trent 39 F 5
Burt Plain, *region* 146 F 4
Burtonport 48 C 2
Buru, *island* 67 H 6
Burūk, Wādī al, *wadi* 100 E 2
Burūn, Ra's, *cape* 100 E 1
Burundi 90 F 6
Bururi 104 B 3
Burwash 41 E 4
Burwick 46 F 3
Bury 39 E 5
Burye 88 B 7
Bury St. Edmunds 39 G 5
Busayţah, Al, *region* 88 B 4
Buševa Pl., *mountain* 62 B 3
Būshehr 78 C 3
Bushey 41 D 2
Bushmills 48 E 1
Busira, *river* 102 C 3

Buskerud, *county* 51 M 4
Busra 89 C 2
Busselton 146 C 6
Bussum 56 D 2
Bustān, W. al, *wadi* 100 B 4
Bustard Hd., *cape* 147 K 4
Busto Arsizio 60 B 2
Busuanga I., *island* 81 D 5
Buta 90 F 5
Butare 102 D 3
Bute 47 C 6
Bute, *island* 38 D 4
Butmiye 89 B 2
Butrintit, L.-i-, *lake* 62 B 4
Butser Hill, *hill* 43 F 4
Butte 118 E 2
Buttevant 49 C 4
Butt of Lewis, *cape* 38 C 2
Butuan 85 D 3
Butung, *island* 67 H 6
Buturlinovka 65 E 3
Bützow 58 D 2
Buxton 45 G 4
Buy 35 L 2
Buyr Nūr, *lake* 75 O 5
Büyük Ağri Daği, *mt.* 29 M 5
Büyük Doğanca 62 E 3
Buyuk Kemikli Br., *cape* 62 E 3
Buzachi, P-ov., *peninsula* 74 H 5
Buzançais 55 E 4
Buzău 64 E 4
Buzuluk 35 M 3
Buzzards B., *bay* 117 F 3
Byala 62 D 2
Byam Martin, C., *cape* 115 K 1
Byam Martin I., *island* 114 G 1
Bydgoszcz 34 H 3
Bydgoszcz, *province* 64 C 2
Bydgdeå 50 Q 3
Byers, Mt., *mountain* 116 D 1
Bygland 51 M 5
Bygrave, Mt., *mountain* 149 C 4
Bykhov 64 F 2
Bykleheiane, *mountains* 51 M 5
Bylot I., *island* 106 G 2
Byobitō, *cape* 77 G 7
Byōbu-take, *mountain* 80 E 3
Byrd, *scientific base* 23 O 2
Byron, C., *cape* 141 F 4
Byro Plains, *region* 146 C 5
Byrranga Gory, *mts.* 66 F 2
Byske 50 R 3
Byskeälv, *river* 50 Q 3
Bytom 64 C 2
Bytów 58 G 1
Byumba 104 B 3
Byzantine, *civilisation* 159

Caatinga, *region* 126 D 3
Caballeria, C., *cape* 53 H 2
Cabañas, *mountain* 52 D 4
Cabanatuan City 81 D 4
Cabarruyan I., *island* 81 C 3
Cabeza de Buey 52 C 3
Cabimas 132 B 1
Cabinda, 91 E 6
Cabinda, *state* 91 E 6
Cabinet Mts., *mountains* 118 D 2
Cabo Delgado, *province* 105 A 1
Cabonga, Rés., *reservoir* 115 K 4
Caboolture 147 K 5
Cabot Str., *strait* 106 G 3
Cabras, Sa. de las, *Castilla la Nueva, mountains* 52 D 2
Cabras, Sa. de las, *Murcia, mountains* 53 E 3
Cabreira, *mountain* 52 A 2
Cabrejas, Altos de, *mts.* 52 D 2
Cabrera, *island* 36 C 3
Cabrera, Sa., *Andalucia, mountains* 52 D 4
Cabrera, Sa., *Galicia, mountains* 52 B 1
Cabro del Santo Cristo 52 D 4
Cabugao 81 D 3
Çaburan 81 F 9
Čačak 62 B 2
Cac Ba, I., *island* 82 E 4
Cáceres 52 B 3
Cache Cr., *river* 120 B 4
Cachi, Nos. de, *mountain* 132 C 5
Cachimbo, Sa. do, *mts.* 126 D 3
Cachoeiro de Itapemirim 135 D 2
Cachoeira do Sul 136 C 2
Cactus Ra., *mountains* 120 C 4
Cader Idris, *mountain* 39 E 5
Cadi, Sa. del, *mountains* 53 F 1
Cadig Mts., *mountains* 81 E 4
Cadiz, *Philippines* 81 E 6
Cádiz, *Spain* 28 F 5
Cádiz, B. de, *bay* 52 B 4
Cadiz, Golfo de, *gulf* 52 B 4
Cadiz L., *lake* 120 D 5
Caen 34 E 4
Caerleon 42 E 3
Caernarvon 39 D 5
Caernarvon, *county* 42 C 2
Caernarvon Bay, *bay* 39 D 5
Caerphilly 42 D 3
Caersws 42 D 2
Caesarea, *ancient site* 89 A 2
Caesarea Philippi, *ancient site* 89 B 1
Cagayan 67 H 5
Cagayan, *river* 84 D 2
Cagayan Is., *N. Sulu Sea, island group* 81 D 7
Cagayan Is., *S. Sulu Sea, island group* 81 C 8
Cagliari 28 H 5
Caguas 123 G 3
Caha Mts., *mountains* 39 B 6
Caher 49 D 4
Cahersiveen 49 A 5
Cahore Pt., *cape* 39 C 5
Cahors 55 E 5
Caiapó, Sa. do, *mts.* 133 D 4
Caibarién 121 E 6
Caicos Is., *island group* 123 F 2
Caicos Passage, *strait* 119 N 7
Caillou Bay, *bay* 121 B 4
Caird Coast, *region* 23 A 2
Cairn Gorm, *mountain* 46 E 4
Cairngorm Mts., *mts.* 38 E 3
Cairnryan 48 F 2
Cairns 140 E 3
Cairns Ra., *mountains* 148 B 3
Cairntoul, *mountain* 38 E 3
Cairo, *Egypt* 90 G 2
Cairo, *U.S.A.* 119 K 4
Caistor 45 H 4
Caithness, *county* 46 E 3
Cajamarca 132 B 3
Čakovec 59 G 5
Calabar 102 B 2
Calabozo 123 G 4
Calabria, *province* 61 F 5
Cala, Emb. de, *lake* 52 B 4
Calagua Is., *island group* 81 E 4
Calahorra 52 E 1
Calais 28 G 3
Calalaste, Cord. de, *mountains* 136 B 1
Calama 135 B 2
Calamar 123 F 3
Calamba 81 E 6
Calamian Group, *island group* 79 J 4
Calamocha 53 E 2
Cala Moral, Pta. de, *cape* 52 C 4
Calañas 52 B 4
Calanda 53 E 2
Călānda, *region* 57 E 3
Calapan 79 K 4
Calaraşi 64 E 4
Calar del Mundo, *mts.* 52 D 3
Calasetta 61 B 5
Calasparra 52 E 3
Calatayud 52 E 2
Calatrava, Campo de, *region* 52 D 3
Calauag 81 E 5
Calavà, C., *cape* 61 E 5
Calavite, C., *cape* 81 D 5
Calayan I., *island* 77 G 8
Calbayog 81 F 5
Calbiga 81 F 6
Calcutta 66 F 4
Caldaro 57 G 3
Caldas da Rainha 52 A 3
Caldera, *river* 134 C 3
Caldeirão, Sa. do, *mts.* 52 A 4
Calderina, Sa. de la, *mountains* 52 D 3
Caldew 47 F 7
Caldwell 118 D 3
Caldy I., *island* 39 D 6
Caledon 101 C 6
Caledonian Canal, *canal* 46 D 4
Calexico 120 D 5
Calf of Man, *island* 39 D 4
Calğal Dağ *mountain* 37 G 3
Calgary 106 E 3
Cali 126 B 2
Calicoan I., *island* 81 F 6
Caliente 120 D 4
California, *state* 118 C 4
California, Golfo de, *gulf* 107 E 4
Calimere, Pt., *cape* 87 D 5
Calipatria 120 D 5
Calispell Peak, *mountain* 120 C 1
Callabonna, L., *lake* 147 H 5
Callan 49 D 4
Callander 38 D 3
Callang 81 D 3
Callao 126 B 4
Callington 42 C 4
Calliope 148 E 3
Callosa de E. 52 E 3
Calobre 134 C 2
Calolbon 81 F 5
Calolot 81 E 7
Calshot Spit, *region* 41 B 4
Caltagirone 36 D 3
Caltanissetta 61 E 6
Calvi 60 B 3
Calvia 53 G 3
Calvitero, *mountain* 52 C 2
Calw 59 C 4
Cam, *river* 43 H 2
Camagüey 107 G 4
Camagüey, Archo. de, *island group* 123 F 2
Camarasa, Emb. de, *lake* 53 F 2
Camarat, C., *cape* 55 H 6
Camargues, *region* 55 G 6
Camariñas 52 A 1
Camas 52 B 4
Ca Mau, Pte. de, *cape* 67 G 5
Cambados 52 A 1
Cambay, G. of, *gulf* 66 E 4
Camber 41 F 4
Camberley 41 C 3
Cambodia 67 G 5
Camborne 42 B 4
Cambrai 34 F 3
Cambre 52 A 1
Cambria 120 B 5
Cambrian Mts., *mts.* 34 E 3
Cambridge, *England* 39 G 5
Cambridge, *New Zealand* 150 F 3
Cambridge, *U.S.A.* 117 F 3
Cambridge, *county* 43 H 2
Cambridge Bay 114 G 2
Camden 119 M 4
Camden Haven 149 E 5
Camelford 42 C 4
Cameron Mts., *mts.* 151 B 8
Cameroons Mt., *mt.* 90 D 5
Cameroun 90 E 5
Camiguin I., *Philippines* 81 F 7
Camiguin I., *Philippines, Babuyan Is.* 81 D 2
Caminha 52 A 2
Camino, C. di, *mountain* 57 F 4
Camiri 132 C 5
Camoghe, *mountain* 57 E 3
Camonica, Val, *valley* 57 F 4
Camoniche, Alpi, *mts.* 57 F 4
Camooweal 147 G 3
Camorta I., *island* 87 F 5
Camotes Is., *island group* 81 F 6
Camotes Sea 81 F 6
Campagna, *region* 36 D 2
Campania, *province* 61 E 4
Campanquix, Cerros, *mountains* 132 B 3
Campanario 52 C 3
Campbell 101 D 5
Campbell, C., *cape* 150 F 5
Campbell I., *Burma, island* 83 C 7
Campbell I., *New Zealand, island* 23 L 3
Campbell, Mt., *mountain* 114 D 2
Campbellton 115 L 4
Campbelltown 149 E 5
Campbeltown 38 D 4
Camp de Châlons, *region* 56 C 5
Camp de Villa, *region* 52 C 1
Campeche 122 D 3
Campeche, Bahía de, *bay* 107 F 5
Campeche Bank, *sea feature* 107 F 4
Camperdown 149 C 6
Cam-pha 67 G 4
Campilhas, Barr., *lake* 52 A 4
Campillos 52 C 4
Câmpina 64 E 4
Campiña, La, *region* 52 C 4
Campina Grande 133 F 3
Campinas 133 E 5
Campoalegre 123 F 4
Campobasso 60 E 4
Campo de Cariñena, *reg.* 53 E 2
Campo de Dalías, *region* 52 D 4
Campo Grande 132 D 5
Campo Maior 52 B 3
Campos 126 E 5
Campos, *E. Brazil, reg.* 126 E 4
Campos, *S. Brazil, reg.* 126 D 5
Campos, *Spain, region* 52 C 2
Campos, Tierra de, *reg.* 52 C 1
Campsie Fells, *mountains* 38 D 3
Câmpulung 64 E 4
Câmpulung Moldovenesc 64 E 3
Cam Ranh, B. de, *bay* 83 E 7
Camrose 114 F 3
Canada 106 D 3
Cañada de Gomez 135 B 3
Canadian, *river* 106 E 4
Canadian Shield, *plateau* 154 C 2
Canajagua, Cerro, *mt.* 134 C 3
Çanakkale 62 E 3
Çanakkale Boğazi, *strait* 28 K 5
Canal Beagle, *strait* 136 B 4
Canal Casiquiare, *river* 132 C 2
Canal de Afuera, I., *island* 134 B 3
Cananea 118 E 5
Canarias, Islas, *island grp.* 25 E 3
Cañas, I., *island* 134 E 2
Canastra, Sa. da, *mts.* 126 E 4
Canavese, *region* 57 C 4
Canaway Ra., *mountains* 149 C 4
Cañazas 134 B 2
Canberra 140 E 5
Canche, *river* 56 A 4
Candala 88 D 7
Çandarli Körfezi, *bay* 62 E 4
Candeleda 52 C 2
Candlemas I., *island* 23 A 3
Candon 81 D 3
Canelones 135 C 3
Cañete 53 E 2
Canet, É. de, *lake* 53 G 1
Cangas de Narcea 52 B 1
Caniçado 101 G 4
Canicatti 61 D 6
Canigou, Mt., *mountain* 36 C 2
Canisp, *mountain* 38 D 2
Canjáyar 52 D 4
Çankiri 37 G 3
Canna, *island* 38 C 3
Cannes 36 C 2
Canning Basin, *region* 146 D 3
Cannock 39 E 5
Cannock Chase, *region* 43 F 2
Canobie 148 C 2
Canosa di P. 60 E 4
Canouan 132 C 1
Canso, C., *cape* 106 G 3
Canso, Str. of, *strait* 117 J 2
Cantabria, Sa. de, *mts.* 52 D 1
Cantabrica, Cordillera, *mountains* 28 F 4
Cantal, Massif du, *mts.* 55 F 5
Cantal, Plomb du, *mt.* 55 F 5
Cantalapiedra 52 C 2
Cantanhede 52 A 2
Cantanzaro 61 F 5
Canterbury 39 G 6
Canterbury, *county* 151 D 6
Canterbury Bight, *gulf* 151 E 7
Canterbury Gap, *river gap* 41 G 3
Canterbury Plains, *reg.* 151 D 7
Can Tho 67 G 5
Cantilan 81 F 7
Cantillana 52 C 4
Cantin, C., *cape* 90 C 2
Canton, *see Kuang-chou* 77 E 7
Canton, *U.S.A.* 119 L 3
Cantù 57 E 4
Canvey 41 F 2
Canvey I., *island* 43 H 3
Cap I., *island* 81 D 9
Capcir, *region* 55 F 6
Cape Barren I., *island* 147 J 8
Cape Breton I., *island* 106 G 3
Cape Coast 98 C 5
Cape Cod Bay, *bay* 117 F 3
Cape Dorset, *trading post* 115 K 2
Cape Girardeau 119 K 4
Cape Hope's Advance, *trading post* 115 L 2
Cape I., *island* 121 E 3
C. Johnson Depth, *sea feature* 137 A 2
Capella 148 D 3
Capella, *mountain* 85 F 4
Cape of Good Hope, *province* 101 D 5
Cape Rise, *sea feature* 91 G 9
Capernaum, *ancient site* 89 B 2
Cape Town 90 E 9
Cape Verde Basin, *sea feature* 25 D 3
Cape Verde Is., *island group* 25 D 4
Cape Verde Plateau, *sea feature* 25 D 4
Cape York Peninsula, *peninsula* 140 E 3
Cap-Haïtien 107 G 5
Capira 134 D 2
Capodistria 60 D 2
Capoompeta, *mountain* 147 K 5
Cappoquin 49 D 4
Capraia, *island* 60 B 3
Capri, *island* 36 D 3
Capricorn Chan., *channel* 141 F 4
Capricorn Group, *reefs* 147 K 4
Caprino 60 C 2
Caprivi Strip, *region* 91 F 7
Capua 60 E 4
Capulin Mt., *mountain* 118 G 4
Caquetá, *river* 132 B 3
Carabaya, Cord. de, *mountains* 132 B 4
Caracal 62 D 1
Caracas 126 C 1
Caraghnan Mt., *mountain* 149 D 5
Carajás, Sa. dos, *mts.* 133 D 3
Caramoan Pena., *peninsula* 81 E 4
Caramulo, Sa. do, *mts.* 52 A 2
Caransebeş 64 D 4
Caraquet 117 H 2
Caratasca, Laguna, *lake* 123 E 3
Caravaca 52 E 3
Caravaggio 57 E 4
Caravelas 126 F 4
Carballino 52 A 1
Carballo 52 A 1
Carbonara, C., *cape* 61 B 5
Carboneras, *mountain* 52 C 3
Carcagente 53 E 3
Carcans, Étang de, *lake* 55 D 5
Carcar 81 E 6
Carcar, Monti, *mountain* 99 H 5
Carcassone 36 C 2
Carcross 114 D 2
Cardamon Hills, *mts.* 87 D 5
Cardamones, Chaine des, *mountains* 83 D 6
Cárdenas 122 D 2
Cardiff 28 F 3
Cardigan 39 D 5
Cardigan, *county* 42 C 2
Cardigan Bay, *bay* 39 D 5
Cardoner, *river* 53 F 2
Carei 64 D 3
Carentan 39 F 7
Carey, L., *lake* 140 C 4
Cariaco Trench, *sea feature* 123 G 3
Caribbean Sea 107 F 5
Cariboo Mts., *mountains* 106 D 3
Caribou 114 H 3
Caribou I., *island* 116 C 2
Caribou Mt., *mountain* 120 E 3
Carigara 81 F 6
Cariñena 53 E 2
Carinhanha 126 E 4
Caripito 132 C 1
Carisbrooke 41 B 4
Carleton Mt., *mountain* 117 G 2
Carlingford L., *lake* 48 E 2
Carlisle 34 E 3
Carlit, Pic., *mountain* 55 E 6
Carlow 39 C 5
Carlow, *county* 44 B 5
Carlsbad 118 G 5
Carlsberg Ridge, *sea feature* 153 B 2
Carluke 47 E 6
Carlyle Res., *reservoir* 121 B 2
Carmarthen 39 D 6
Carmarthen, *county* 42 C 3
Carmarthen Bay, *bay* 39 D 6
Carmel, Cape, *cape* 89 A 2
Carmel Hd., *cape* 39 D 5
Carmel, Mt., *mountain* 89 A 2
Carmen, *Colombia* 123 F 4
Carmen, *Mexico* 122 D 3
Carmen, *Philippines* 81 F 7
Carmen, *island* 118 E 6
Carmona 52 C 4
Carnamah 152 B 3
Carnarvon, *Australia* 152 A 2
Carnarvon, *Rep. of S. Africa* 101 D 5
Carnarvon Ra., *Queensland, mountains* 149 D 4
Carnarvon Ra., *W. Australia, mountains* 146 D 5
Carndonagh 48 D 1
Carnedd Llewelyn, *mt.* 42 D 1
Carnegie 152 C 3
Carnegie, L., *lake* 140 C 4
Carnegie Ridge, *sea feature* 25 A 5
Carniche, Alpi, *mts.* 60 D 1
Car Nicobar, *island* 87 F 5
Carno 42 D 2
Carnoustie 47 F 5
Carnsore Pt., *cape* 39 C 5
Carnwath 47 E 6
Carolina 133 E 3
Caroline Islands, *island group* 137 A 2
Caroline-Solomon Ridge, *sea feature* 137 B 2
Caroní, *river* 123 G 4
Carpathians, *mountains* 28 J 4
Carpatii Meridionali, Mti., *mountains* 28 J 4
Carpentaria, Gulf of, *gulf* 140 D 3
Carpenter Ridge, *sea feature* 153 D 2
Carpentras 55 G 5
Carpi 60 C 2
Carra, L., *lake* 48 B 3
Carrantuohill, *mountain* 39 B 6
Carranza, C., *cape* 127 B 6
Carrara, *town* 60 C 2
Carrascoy, Sa. de, *mts.* 53 E 4
Carrbridge 46 E 4
Carriacou, *island* 132 C 1
Carrick, *region* 47 D 6
Carrickfergus 48 F 2
Carrickmacross 48 E 3
Carrick-on-Suir 39 C 5
Carríon 52 C 1
Carrowmore, L., *lake* 48 B 2
Car, Slieve, *mountain* 48 B 2
Carson City 118 D 4
Carson Sink, *region* 118 D 4
Carstairs 47 E 6
Carstensz Toppen, *mt.* 140 D 2
Cartagena, *Colombia* 126 B 1
Cartagena, *Spain* 36 B 3
Cartago 123 F 4
Cartelle 52 A 1
Carterton 150 F 5
Carthage, *ancient site* 61 C 6
Cartier I., *island* 146 D 2
Cartwright 115 M 3
Caruarú 133 F 3
Carúpano 132 C 1
Carvin 56 A 4
Carvoeira, C., *cape* 52 A 3
Caryapundy Swamp, *swamp* 147 H 5
Casablanca 90 C 2
Casa Grande 120 E 5
Casale Monferrato 60 B 2
Casalmaggiore 60 C 2
Casas Ibánez 53 E 3
Casavieja 52 C 2
Cascade 120 C 2
Cascade Dam Res., *res.* 120 C 2
Cascade Range, *mts.* 106 D 3
Cascais 52 A 3
Caserta 36 D 3
Cashel 39 C 5
Cashen 49 C 4
Casilda 135 B 3
Casino 147 K 5
Čáslav 58 F 4
Caso 52 C 1
Caspe 53 E 2
Casper 118 F 3
Caspian Sea 29 N 4
Cassai, *river* 102 D 4
Cassaya, I., *island* 134 D 2
Cassiar Mts., *mountains* 114 D 2
Cassino 60 D 4
Cassley, *river* 47 D 3
Castejón, Montes de, *mountains* 53 E 2
Castellammare del Golfo 61 D 5
Castellammare di Stabia 61 E 4
Castellammare, G. di, *gulf* 61 D 5
Castellane 55 H 6
Castellar 52 D 3
Castellar, El, *region* 53 E 2
Castellón de la Plana 36 C 3
Castellote 53 E 2
Castelltallat, Sa. de, *mountains* 53 F 2
Castelnaudary 55 E 6
Castelo Branco 52 B 3
Castelo de Vide 52 B 3
Castelsarrasin 55 E 5
Castelvetrano 61 D 6
Casterton 149 C 6
Castiglione 53 G 4
Castiglione di Stiviere 57 F 4
Castilla la Nueva, *prov.* 52 C 3
Castilla la Vieja, *prov.* 52 C 2
Castillejos 81 D 4

Castillejo, Sa. de, *mts.* 52 C 3
Castillo, Pampa del, *pampas* 136 B 3
Castlebar 39 B 5
Castlebay 46 A 5
Castleblayney 48 E 2
Castlecliffe 150 F 4
Castlecomer 49 D 4
Castlederg 48 D 2
Castle Douglas 44 E 3
Castleford 45 G 4
Castleisland 49 B 4
Castlemaine 147 H 7
Castlepollard 48 D 3
Castlerea 48 C 3
Castlereagh, *river* 149 D 5
Castle Rock, *mountain* 151 C 7
Castletown 44 D 3
Castletown Bearhaven 49 B 5
Castres 36 C 2
Castries 123 G 3
Castro del Rio 52 C 4
Castrojeriz 52 C 1
Castropol 52 B 1
Castro-Urdiales 52 D 1
Castro Verde 52 A 4
Castrovillari 61 F 5
Catahoula Lake, *lake* 121 A 4
Çatalca 62 F 3
Çatal Daği, *mountain* 62 F 4
Cataluña, *province* 53 F 2
Catamarca 136 B 1
Catanauan 81 E 5
Catanduanes, *island* 81 F 5
Catanduva 133 E 5
Catania 28 H 5
Catania, Golfo di, *gulf* 61 E 6
Catarroja 53 E 3
Catastrophe, C., *cape* 140 D 5
Catbalogan 81 F 6
Cateel 81 G 8
Caterham 41 D 3
Cat I., *island* 107 G 4
Cativá 134 D 1
Catoche, C., *cape* 107 F 4
Catskill Mts., *mountains* 106 G 3
Catterick 44 G 3
Cauca, *river* 126 B 2
Caucasus Mts., *see Bol'shoy Kavkaz* 29 M 4
Caudete 52 E 3
Cau Hai, Lagune de, *lake* 83 E 5
Cauquenes 136 A 2
Caura, *river* 123 G 4
Cauvery, *river* 87 D 5
Caux, *region* 54 E 3
Cávado, *river* 52 A 2
Cavaignac 53 F 4
Cavaillon 55 G 6
Cavan 39 C 5
Cavan, *county* 48 D 3
Caversham 41 C 3
Caviana, I., *island* 133 D 2
Cavite City 81 D 4
Caxias 133 E 3
Caxias do Sul 136 C 1
Caxine, C., *cape* 53 G 4
Cayenne 126 D 2
Cayman Is., *island group* 107 F 5
Cayman Trench, *sea feature* 25 A 4
Cayo de Agua, *island* 134 A 1
Cay Sal Bank, *sea feature* 123 E 2
Cayuga L., *lake* 116 E 3
Cazalla de la S. 52 C 4
Cazaux et de Sanguinet, É. de, *lake* 55 D 5
Cazin 60 E 2
Cea, *river* 52 C 1
Ceanannus Mór 48 E 3
Cebaco, I., *island* 134 B 3
Cebollera, *mountain* 52 D 2
Cebollera, Sa., *mountains* 36 B 2
Cebreros 52 C 2
Cebu 67 H 5
Cebu, *island* 67 H 5
Ceclavín 52 B 3
Cedar City 118 E 4
Cedar Falls 119 J 3
Cedar I., *N. Carolina, island* 121 E 3
Cedar I., *Virginia, island* 121 F 2
Cedar L., *lake* 114 G 3
Cedar Rapids 119 J 3
Cedeira 52 A 1
Cedros, *island* 107 E 4
Ceduna 146 F 6
Cefalù 61 E 5
Cega, *river* 52 C 2
Cegléd 64 C 3
Celanova 52 B 1
Celaya 122 C 2
Celebes, *see Sulawesi* 79 J 6
Celebes Sea 67 H 5
Celje 64 B 3
Celle 58 D 2
Čemerna Plan., *mountains* 62 B 2
Cenis, Mt., *mountain* 60 A 2
Central, *Kenya, region* 104 D 2
Central, *Malawi, region* 104 C 6
Central, *Tanzania, region* 104 C 4
Central, *Zambia, prov.* 101 F 1
Central African Republic 90 E 5
Central Asian System 154 G 2
Central Basin 155 J 4
Central Brahui Ra., *mts.* 86 C 3
Central, Cord., *Bolivia, mountains* 132 C 4
Central, Cordillera, *Colombia, mountains* 126 B 2
Central, Cord., *Dominican Rep., mts.* 123 F 3
Central, Cord., *Peru, mountains* 126 B 3
Central, Cordillera, *Philippines, mountains* 77 G 8
Central Hwy. 147 J 5
Centralia 119 K 4
Central I., *island* 104 D 2
Central Makran Range, *mountains* 86 B 3
Central, Massif, *mts.* 28 G 4
Central Ra., *mountains* 140 E 2
Central Valley 120 B 3
Cerbere, C., *cape* 53 G 1
Cerdaña, La, *region* 53 F 1
Ceret 53 G 1
Cerignola 60 E 4
Cerknica 60 E 2
Cernavoda 64 F 4
Cerrato, Valles de, *valley* 52 C 2
Cerro Pinacate, *mt.* 120 D 6
Cerne Abbas 43 E 4
Cerro de Pasco 126 B 4
Cervati, M., *mountain* 61 E 4
Cervera, *Spain, Cataluña* 53 F 2
Cervera, *Spain, Navarra* 52 E 1
Cervera, C., *cape* 53 E 3
Cervera de P. 52 C 1
Cervera, P. de, *mountain* 52 D 2
Cervione 60 B 3
Cesena 60 D 2
Česká Lípa 58 F 3
České Budějovice 36 D 2
Českezeme, *province* 58 F 4
Českomoravská Vysočina, *mountains* 59 F 4
Český Krumlov 59 F 4
Cess, *river* 98 C 5
Cessnock 147 K 6
Cetinje 64 C 4
Cetraro 61 E 5
Ceuta 36 B 3
Cevedale, M., *mountain* 57 F 3
Cevennes, *mountains* 28 G 4
Ceyhan, *river* 37 G 3
Ceylon, *island* 66 F 5
Ceylon Rise, *sea feature* 153 D 2
Chablais, *region* 57 B 3
Chabounia 53 G 5
Chacabuco 136 B 2
Chacao, G. de, *gulf* 136 A 3
Chachoengsao 83 C 6
Chaco Austral, *region* 127 C 5
Chaco Boreal, *region* 126 D 5
Chaco Central, *region* 132 D 5
Chad 90 E 4
Chad Basin, *region* 155 F 3
Chad, Lake, *lake* 90 E 4
Chagai Hills, *mountains* 66 E 4
Chagos Archipelago, *island group* 66 E 6
Chagres, *river* 134 D 1
Chaiyaphum 83 C 6
Chajarí 135 C 3
Chala Shan, *mountains* 79 G 2
Chaldean, *civilisation* 158
Chaleurs, Baie des, *bay* 117 H 1
Chalfont St. Giles 41 C 2
Chalky Inlet, *inlet* 151 B 8
Challans 55 D 4
Challenger Deep, *sea feature* 155 J 3
Challegner Depth, *sea feature* 137 B 2
Chalmy Varre 50 W 2
Châlons-sur-Marne 54 G 3
Chalon-sur-Saône 55 G 4
Cham 59 E 4
Chamais B., *bay* 101 B 4
Chaman 86 C 3
Chamao, Kh., *mountain* 83 C 6
Chamartin de la Rosa 52 D 2
Chambal, *river* 79 E 3
Chambéry 36 C 2
Chambezi, *river* 104 B 5
Chamdo 66 F 4
Chamdo, *province* 82 A 2
Chame 134 D 2
Chame, Ens. de, *bay* 134 D 2
Chame, Punta, *cape* 134 D 2
Chame, Playa, *peninsula* 134 D 2
Chamo, L., *lake* 90 G 5
Chamonix 55 H 5
Champa 86 E 4
Champagne, *province* 54 G 3
Champagne, *region* 54 E 4
Champagne Charentaise, *region* 55 D 5
Champagnole 57 A 3
Champaign 116 B 3
Champlain, L., *lake* 106 G 3
Champsaur, Mts., *mts.* 55 H 5
Chamusca 52 A 3
Chance I., *island* 83 B 7
Chan-chiang 67 G 4
Chanda 66 E 5
Chandausi 86 D 3
Chandeleur Is., *island group* 121 B 4
Chandeleur Sd., *inlet* 121 B 4
Chandigarh 78 E 2
Chandler's Ford 41 B 4
Ch'ang Ch., *river* 67 G 4
Ch'ang-chih 76 E 4
Ch'ang-ch'un 67 H 3
Chang Ho, *river* 76 E 4
Chang-hua 77 G 7
Ch'ang-li 76 F 4
Chang-p'ai Shan, *mts.* 66 H 4
Ch'ang-p'u 77 F 7
Changsangot, *cape* 76 G 4
Ch'ang-sha 67 G 4
Ch'ang-shan Lieh-tao, *island group* 76 G 4
Ch'ang-shu 76 G 5
Chāng Tāng, *mountains* 76 B 5
Chang Tang, *plateau* 66 F 4
Ch'ang-te 79 J 3
Ch'ang-t'ing 77 F 6
Chang-yeh 75 M 6
Channel Islands, *island group* 28 F 4
Channel Rock, *island* 121 E 6
Chantada 52 B 1
Chanthaburi 79 H 4
Chantonnay 55 D 4
Chanza, *river* 52 B 4
Chanzy 53 E 5
Ch'ao-an 77 F 7
Chao-an Wan, *island* 77 F 7
Ch'ao Hu, *lake* 76 F 5
Chao-t'ung 77 C 6
Chaowula Shan, *mts.* 86 F 2
Chao-yang 77 F 7
Ch'ao-yang-chen 76 H 3
Chapada dos Parecis, *mountains* 126 C 4
Chapala, L., de, *lake* 122 C 2
Chaparral 123 F 4
Chapayevsk 35 M 3
Cap Chat 117 G 1
Chapel-en-le-Frith 45 G 4
Chapera I., *island* 134 D 2
Chaplina, M., *cape* 67 L 2
Chapra 78 F 3
Chaqui 132 C 4
Charchan Darya, *river* 86 E 2
Charcot I., *island* 23 R 2
Chard 39 E 6
Chardzhou 66 E 4
Charente, *river* 55 E 4
Chari, *river* 90 E 4
Charing 43 H 3
Chariton, *river* 121 A 2
Charlbury 43 F 3
Charlemagne, *empire* 159
Charleroi 54 G 2
Charles, C., *cape* 106 G 4
Charles I., *island* 115 K 2
Charles Pk., *mountain* 146 D 6
Charleston, *U.S.A., S. Carolina* 106 G 4
Charleston, *U.S.A., West Virginia* 119 L 4
Charleston Pk., *mountain* 120 D 4
Charlestown, *Rep. of Ireland* 48 C 3
Charleville, *Australia* 147 J 5
Charleville, *France* 54 G 3
Charlotte 119 L 4
Charlotte Amalie 110 G 5
Charlotte Harb., *inlet* 121 D 5
Charlottenberg 51 O 5
Charlottesville 121 E 2
Charlottetown 106 G 3
Charlotte Waters 149 A 4
Charlton 149 C 6
Charnwood Forest, *reg.* 43 F 2
Charolles 55 G 4
Charters Towers 147 J 4
Chartres 54 E 3
Chartreuse, Gde., *mts.* 55 G 5
Chascomas 135 C 3
Chasseral, *mountain* 57 C 2
Chatal Balkan, *mountains* 62 E 2
Châteaubriant 54 D 4
Château-Chinon 54 F 4
Château d'Oex 57 C 3
Châteaudun 54 E 3
Château-Gontier 54 D 4
Châteaulin 54 B 3
Château, Pte. de, *cape* 54 C 3
Châteauroux 55 E 4
Château Salins 54 H 3
Château Thierry 54 F 3
Châteleu, Mt., *mountain* 57 B 3
Châtellerault 55 E 4
Chatham, *Canada, New Brunswick* 115 L 4
Chatham, *Canada, Ontario* 116 C 3
Chatham, *England* 39 G 6
Chatham Is., *island group* 141 J 6
Chatham Rise, *sea feature* 137 B 4
Chatham Str., *strait* 114 D 3
Châtillon 57 C 4
Châtillon-sur-Seine 54 G 4
Chatkal'skiy Khr., *mts.* 86 C 1
Chatrapur 87 E 4
Chattahoochee, *river* 119 K 5
Chattanooga, *river* 119 K 4
Chatteris 43 H 2
Chau Doc 83 D 7
Chaumont 54 G 3
Chaunskaya Guba, *bay* 75 T 3
Chaves 52 B 2
Chavin, *civilisation* 159
Chayatyn, Khr., *mts.* 75 Q 4
Chayul 82 A 2
Cheadle 43 F 2
Cheaha Mt., *mountain* 121 C 3
Cheb 58 E 3
Cheboksary 35 L 3
Chechaouèn 52 C 5
Chech, Erg, *sand dunes* 90 C 3
Cheddar 42 E 3
Cheduba I., *island* 87 F 4
Cheepie 149 C 4
Chehalis 120 B 2
Cheju 76 H 5
Cheju Do, *island* 75 P 6
Cheju Haehyŏp, *strait* 76 H 5
Chekiang, *province* 76 F 6
Chela, Sa. da, *mountains* 102 C 4
Che-lang-piao, *cape* 77 F 7
Chelan, L., *lake* 120 B 1
Ch'e-li 77 C 7
Chéliff, *river* 28 G 5
Chelkar 74 H 5
Chellala 53 G 5
Chełm 64 D 2
Chelmer, *river* 41 E 2
Chełmno 64 C 2
Chelmsford 39 G 6
Cheltenham 39 E 6
Chelva 53 E 3
Chelyabinsk 29 O 3
Chelyuskin 75 N 2
Chelyuskin, Mys, *cape* 66 G 2
Chemba 101 G 2
Chemnitz, *see Karl-Marx-Stadt* 58 E 3
Chenab, *river* 86 D 2
Chen-chiang 79 J 2
Ch'eng-chiang 79 H 3
Ch'eng-hai 77 F 7
Cheng-hsien 67 G 4
Ch'eng-mai 77 D 8
Chengshan Tow, *cape* 79 K 2
Ch'eng-te 76 F 3
Cheng-ting 76 E 4
Ch'eng-tu 66 G 4
Chen-hai 76 G 6
Chen-hsi 75 M 5
Ch'en-hsien 67 G 4
Chen-yüan, *China, Kweichow* 76 D 6
Chen-yuan, *China, Yunnan* 77 C 7
Chepo 134 D 1
Chepstow 42 E 3
Cher, *river* 54 E 4
Cherangani Hills, *mts.* 99 G 5
Cherbourg 34 E 4
Cherchel 98 D 2
Chercher, *region* 99 H 5
Cherdyn 35 N 2
Cheremkhovo 66 G 3
Cherepovets 35 K 2
Cheriyam I., *island* 87 C 5
Cherkassy 37 F 2
Cherkessk 65 E 5
Chernigov 35 J 3
Chernigovka 80 C 1
Chernikovsk 35 N 3
Cherni Vrŭkh, *mountain* 62 C 2
Chernovtsy 37 F 2
Chernyakhovsk 64 D 1
Chernysheva, Kryazh, *mountains* 29 O 1
Cherokee 119 H 3
Cherokee Pt., *cape* 121 E 5
Cherokees, L. O'The, *lake* 119 H 4
Cherrabun 152 D 1
Cherry Creek Mt., *mt.* 120 D 3
Cherskogo, Khrebet, *mountains* 67 H 2
Chertsey 43 G 3
Cherven Brya 62 D 2
Cherwell, *river* 43 F 3
Chesapeake B., *bay* 106 G 4
Chesham 43 G 2
Cheshire, *county* 45 F 4
Cheshire Plain, *region* 45 F 4
Cheshskaya Guba, *bay* 35 L 1
Cheshunt 43 G 3
Chesil Beach, *beach* 42 E 4
Cheste 53 E 3
Chester 39 E 5
Chesterfield 39 F 5
Chesterfield, Îles, *reefs* 141 F 3
Chesterfield Inlet 114 H 2
Chester le Street 45 G 3
Chetlat I., *island* 87 C 5
Chetumal 123 E 3
Cheviot Hills, *mountains* 34 E 3
Cheviot Ra., *mountains* 149 C 4
Cheviot, The, *mountain* 38 E 4
Cheyenne 118 G 3
Cheyenne, *river* 118 G 3
Chhindwara 86 D 4
Chhuikhadan 86 D 4
Chia-hsing 76 G 5
Chia-ling Chiang, *river* 76 D 5
Chia-mu-ssu 75 Q 5
Chi-an, *China, Kiangsi* 77 E 6
Chi-an, *China, Liaoning* 76 H 3
Chiang-ling 77 E 5
Chiang Mai 66 F 5
Chiang Saen 82 C 4
Chiang-tu 79 J 2
Chiao-chou Wan, *bay* 76 G 4
Chiao-hsien 76 F 4
Chiao-tso 76 E 4
Chiari 57 E 4
Chiasso 57 E 4
Chiavari 60 B 2
Chiavenna 57 E 3
Chia Wang 76 F 5
Chiba 67 J 4
Chibcha, *civilisation* 159
Chibuto 101 G 4
Chicago 106 F 3
Chichagof I., *island* 106 D 3
Chichester 39 F 6
Chichester Harb., *harbour* 41 C 4
Ch'i-ch'i-ha-erh 67 H 3
Chickamauga L., *lake* 121 C 3
Chickmagalur 87 D 5
Chiclana de la F. 52 B 4
Chiclayo 132 B 3
Chico, *Argentina, river* 127 C 7
Chico, *S. Argentina, river* 136 B 3
Chico, *Philippines, river* 81 D 3
Chico, *U.S.A.* 120 B 4
Chicoa 104 C 6
Chicoutimi 115 K 4
Chidley, C., *cape* 106 G 2
Chieh-shih Wan, *bay* 77 F 7
Chiem See, *lake* 59 E 5
Chienchang 76 F 3
Ch'ien-ch'eng 77 D 6
Chien-ou 79 J 3
Chien-p'ing 76 F 3
Chien Shan, *mountains* 77 C 6
Chien-shih 77 F 7
Chien-shui 77 C 7
Chien-yang 77 F 6
Chierh Shan 75 L 5
Chieti 60 E 3
Chifre, Sa. do, *mountains* 135 D 1
Chih-chiang 77 D 6
Ch'ih-feng 75 O 5
Chihli, Gulf of, *see Po 'Hai* 76 F 4
Ch'ih-Shui Ho, *river* 82 D 2
Chihuahua 122 C 2
Chikwawa 101 G 2
Chilas 86 D 2
Chilcott I., *island* 147 K 3
Childers 147 K 5
Chile 127 B 6
Chilham 43 H 3
Ch'i-lien Shan, *mountains* 76 B 4
Chi-lin 67 H 3
Chilka Lake, *lake* 66 F 5
Chillagoe 148 C 2
Chillán 127 B 6
Chillicothe 121 D 2
Chiloé, I. de, *island* 127 B 7
Chilpancingo de los Bravos 122 D 3
Chilterns, *hills* 34 E 3
Chi-lung 79 K 3
Chilwa, L., *lake* 91 G 7
Chimán 134 E 2
Chiman Tagh, *mountains* 86 E 2
Chimay 56 C 4
Chimbay 74 H 5
Chimborazo, *mountains* 126 B 3
Chimbu 85 F 4
Chimkent 74 J 5
Chimmo Pt., *cape* 77 F 7
Chimtarga, *mountain* 86 C 2
Chimu, *civilisation* 159
Chin, *civilisation* 159
Ch'in, *civilisation* 158
Chin, *province* 82 A 4
China 66 F 4
China Lake 120 C 5
Chi-nan 67 G 4
Chinandega 123 E 3
Chin-chiang 67 G 4
Chin Chiang, *river* 77 E 6
Chinchilla 147 K 5
Chinchilla, Altos de, *mountains* 53 E 3
Chinchilla de Monte Aragón 52 E 3
Chinchón 52 D 2
Chin-chou 75 P 5
Chin-Chou Wan, *bay* 76 G 4
Chin-chu Shan, *mountains* 77 D 7
Chincoteague Bay, *bay* 121 F 2
Chinde 91 G 7
Chin-do, *island* 76 H 5
Chindru 86 F 3
Chindwin, *river* 79 G 3
Ch'ing Chiang, *river* 77 E 5
Ch'ing Hai, *lake* 66 G 4
Ching Ho, *river* 76 D 4
Ching-hsing 76 G 2
Ching-ku 79 H 3
Chingleput 87 D 5
Chingola 102 D 4
Ching-po Hu, *lake* 76 H 3
Ch'ing-p'u 76 G 5
Ching Shan, *mountains* 76 E 5
Ching-shih 77 E 6
Ch'ing-tao 67 H 4
Ching-tung 77 C 7
Ch'ing-yang 76 D 4
Ch'ing-yüan, *China, Hopeh* 76 F 4
Ch'ing-yüan, *China, Kwantung* 77 E 7
Ch'ing-yü Hu, *lake* 76 C 4
Ch'in-hsien 77 D 7
Chin-hua 79 J 3
Ch'in-huang-tao 75 O 6
Chi-ning, *China, Inner Mongolia* 76 E 3
Chi-ning, *China, Shantung* 76 F 4
Chinju 76 H 4
Chinkang 81 E 8
Chink Kaplankyr, *mts.* 29 O 5
Chin-ling Shan, *mountains* 66 G 4
Chin-men Chiang, *bay* 77 F 7
Chin-men Tao, *island* 77 F 7
Chinon 54 E 4
Chinsah 104 C 5
Chioggia 60 D 2
Chipoka 104 C 6
Chippenham 39 E 6
Chippewa, *river* 116 A 2
Chipping Norton 43 F 3
Chipping Ongar 41 E 2
Chipping Sodbury 43 E 3
Chirchik 86 C 1
Chirk 42 D 2
Chiriquí, Golfo de, *gulf* 123 E 4
Chiriquí Grande 134 A 2
Chiriquí, Laguna de, *lagoon* 134 A 1
Chiriquí, Punta, *cape* 134 B 1
Chirripó, *mountain* 107 F 5
Chiromo 101 G 2
Chirpan 62 D 2
Chisamba 104 B 6
Chisamula I., *island* 104 C 6

Cornwall, *county* 42 B 4
Cornwall, Cape, *cape* 42 B 4
Cornwallis I., *island* 114 H 1
Coro 132 C 1
Corocoro, Isla, *island* 132 C 2
Coroico 135 B 1
Coromandel Coast, *reg.* 78 F 4
Coromandel Pena., *peninsula* 150 F 3
Coromandel Ra., *mts.* 150 F 3
Coronado 120 C 5
Coronation Gulf, *gulf* 114 F 2
Coronation I., *island* 23 S 2
Coronel 135 A 3
Coronel Pringles 136 B 2
Coronel Suárez 136 B 2
Co Roong, *mountains* 82 E 5
Corpus Christi 119 H 6
Corral de A. 52 D 3
Correnti, C. I. de, *cape* 61 E 6
Corrib, L., *lake* 39 B 5
Corrientes 127 D 5
Corrientes, C., *Argentina cape* 127 D 6
Corrientes, C., *Colombia, cape* 126 B 2
Corrientes, C., *Cuba, cape* 123 E 2
Corrientes, C., Mexico, *cape* 107 E 4
Corrigin 146 C 6
Corringham 41 E 2
Corse, *island* 28 H 4
Corse, C., *cape* 36 D 2
Corsewall Pt., *cape* 39 D 4
Corsica, *see* Corse 60 B 3
Corte 60 B 3
Cortegana 52 B 4
Cortez Mts., *mountains* 118 D 3
Cortona 60 C 3
Coruche 52 A 3
Çoruh, *river* 37 H 3
Çorum 37 G 3
Corumbá 126 D 4
Corumbá, *river* 133 D 4
Corvallis 120 B 2
Corwen 42 D 2
Cosenza 61 F 5
Cosmoledo Is., *island group* 103 F 3
Cosne 54 F 4
Costa de Mosquitos, *reg.* 123 E 3
Costa Rica 107 F 5
Costigan Mts., *mts.* 117 G 2
Cotabato 81 F 8
Cotagaita 135 B 2
Cote Blanche B., *bay* 121 B 4
Côte d'Azur, *region* 28 G 4
Côte d'Or, *region* 55 G 4
Côte, la, *region* 57 B 3
Coteau, The, *region* 118 F 1
Cotentin, *region* 54 D 3
Côtes de Meuse, *region* 54 G 3
Côtes Lorraines, *region* 56 D 5
Cotonou 98 D 5
Cotopaxi, Vol., *mountain* 126 B 3
Cotswolds, *hills* 39 E 6
Cottage Grove 120 B 3
Cottbus 34 G 3
Cottiennes, Alpes, *mts.* 60 A 2
Cottonwood 120 E 5
Coulommiers 54 F 3
Coulsdon 41 D 3
Council Bluffs 119 H 3
Coupar Angus 47 E 5
Couronne, C., *cape* 55 G 6
Courtenay 118 B 2
Coutances 54 D 3
Covarrubias, Sa. de, *mts.* 52 D 1
Cove I., *island* 116 D 2
Coventry 28 F 3
Covilhão 52 B 2
Covington 121 C 2
Cowal, L., *lake* 149 D 5
Cowall, *region* 38 D 3
Cowan, L., *lake* 140 C 5
Cow Cr., *river* 120 C 2
Cowdenbeath 47 E 5
Cowell 149 B 5
Cowen, Mt., *mountain* 120 E 2
Cowes 39 F 6
Cowley 41 B 2
Cowlitz, *river* 120 B 2
Cowra 147 J 6
Cox's Bazar 79 G 3
Cozie, Alpi, *mountains* 55 H 5
Cozumel, I. de, *island* 123 E 2
Crab Cr., *river* 120 C 2
Crab Orchard L., *lake* 121 B 2
Cradock 101 E 6
Craigellachie 46 E 4
Craighouse 47 C 6
Craigs Ra., *mountains* 140 F 4
Crailsheim 59 D 4
Craiova 37 E 2
Cranborne Chase, *region* 43 E 4
Cranbrook, *Canada* 114 F 4
Cranbrook, *England* 43 B 2
Craneligh 43 G 3
Cranwell 45 H 4
Crary Mts., *mountains* 23 P 2
Crater L., *lake* 120 B 3
Crateús 133 E 3
Crati, *river* 61 F 5
Crato, *Brazil* 133 F 3
Crato, *Spain* 52 B 3
Craven Arms 42 E 2
Crawford Pt., *cape* 81 C 6
Crawley 43 G 3
Crazy Mts., *mountains* 106 E 3
Creag Meagaidh, *mts.* 46 D 5
Crediton 42 D 4
Cree, *river* 39 D 4
Cree L., *lake* 114 G 3
Creil 54 F 3
Crema 60 B 2
Cremona 60 B 2
Cres 60 E 2
Cres, *island* 36 D 2
Crescent L., *lake* 121 D 4
Crest 55 G 5
Crestone Pk., *mountain* 118 F 4
Crêt de la Neige, *mt.* 55 G 4
Crete, Sea of 28 K 5
Creus, C., *cape* 36 C 2
Creuse, *river* 55 F 4
Crevillente 52 E 3
Crewe 39 E 5
Crewkerne 42 E 4
Crianlarich 47 D 5
Criccieth 42 C 2
Cricklade 43 F 3
Crieff 38 E 3
Criffell, *mountain* 44 E 3
Crimmitschau 58 E 3
Cristóbal Colón, Pico, *mountain* 126 B 1
Crna, *river* 62 B 3
Crna Gora, *mountains* 62 B 2
Crna Gora, *province* 62 A 2
Crni Drim, *river* 62 B 3
Croce, C. S., *cape* 61 E 6
Crocker Range, *mountain* 84 C 3
Crockett 119 H 5
Croisette, C., *cape* 55 G 6
Croker I., *island* 146 F 2
Cromarty 46 D 4
Cromarty Firth, *firth* 46 D 4
Cromer 39 G 5
Cromwell 151 C 7
Crook 44 G 3
Crooked, *river* 120 B 2
Crooked I., *island* 119 N 7
Crooked I. Pass., *strait* 119 N 7
Crosby 44 E 4
Cross, C., *cape* 102 C 5
Cross Fell, *mountain* 39 E 4
Cross L., *lake* 114 H 3
Crossley, M., *mountain* 151 E 6
Cross Sd., *inlet* 114 D 3
Crotone 61 F 5
Crouch, *river* 43 H 3
Crowborough 41 E 3
Crowle 45 H 4
Crowley's Ridge, *hills* 119 J 4
Crow's Nest 149 E 4
Crowsnest Pass, *pass* 118 E 2
Croydon, *Australia* 148 C 2
Croydon, *England* 28 F 3
Crozet, Is., *island group* 153 B 5
Crozier C., *cape* 23 L 2
Cruden Bay, *bay* 46 G 4
Crumlin 48 E 2
Cruz Alta 135 C 2
Cruz, C., *cape* 123 F 3
Cruz del Eje 135 B 3
Cruzeiro 135 D 2
Cruziero do Sul 132 B 3
Crymmych Arms 42 C 3
Crystal B., *bay* 121 D 4
Csongrád 64 D 3
Csurgó 60 F 1
Cua Cung Hau, *river mouth* 83 E 7
Cua Dinh An, *river mouth* 83 E 7
Cuamba 104 D 6
Cuando, *river* 102 D 4
Cuando-Cubango, *prov.* 101 C 2
Cuangar 101 C 2
Cuango, *river* 102 C 3
Cuanza, *river* 91 E 6
Cua Soirap, *river mouth* 83 E 7
Cua Tranh De, *river mouth* 83 E 7
Cuba 52 B 3
Cuba, *island* 107 F 4
Cubango, *river* 91 E 7
Cucalon, Sa. de, *mts.* 53 E 2
Cuchilla Grande, *mts.* 136 C 2
Cuckfield 43 G 3
Cuckmere, *river* 41 E 4
Cúcuta 123 F 4
Cuddalore 87 D 5
Cuddapah 87 D 5
Cue 152 B 3
Cuéllar 52 C 2
Cuenca, *Ecuador* 126 B 3
Cuenca, *Spain* 52 D 2
Cuenca, Serranía de, *mountains* 28 F 5
Cuernavaca 122 D 3
Cuerta del Pozo, Emb. de, *lake* 52 D 2
Cuffley 41 D 2
Cuiabá 126 D 4
Cuiabá, *river* 126 D 4
Cuilcagh, *mountain* 48 D 2
Cuillin Hills, *hills* 46 B 4
Cuillin Sd., *inlet* 38 C 3
Cuito, *river* 91 E 7
Cu Lao Re, *island group* 83 E 6
Cul Beag, *mountain* 46 C 3
Culcairn 149 D 6
Culebra Pk., *mountain* 118 F 4
Culebra, Sa. de la, *mt.* 52 B 2
Culemborg 56 D 3
Culgoa, *river* 140 E 4
Culiacán 118 F 7
Culion 81 C 6
Culion I., *island* 81 C 6
Cullarin Ra., *mountains* 149 D 5
Cullen 46 F 4
Cullera 53 E 3
Cullera, C., *cape* 53 E 3
Cul Mor, *mountain* 46 C 3
Culter Fell, *mountain* 47 E 6
Culter Hill, *mountain* 44 E 2
Culvain, *mountain* 38 D 3
Culver Pt., *cape* 146 D 6
Cuma 91 E 7
Cumalî 62 E 3
Cumaná 132 C 1
Cumberland 121 E 2
Cumberland, *county* 44 E 3
Cumberland, *river* 119 K 4
Cumberland House 114 G 3
Cumberland I., *island* 121 D 4
Cumberland Is., *island group* 147 J 4
Cumberland, L., *lake* 119 K 4
Cumberland Mts., *mts.* 121 C 2
Cumberland Pena., *peninsula* 106 G 2
Cumberland Plateau, *plateau* 106 F 4
Cumberland Sd., *inlet* 106 G 2
Cumberland Str., *strait* 148 B 1
Cumbre Alta, *mountain* 52 C 3
Cummins 149 B 5
Cumnock 47 D 6
Cunderdin 152 B 4
Cunene, *river* 91 E 7
Cuneo 60 A 2
Cunillera, I., *island* 53 F 3
Cunnamulla 147 J 5
Cunningham, *region* 38 D 4
Cunningsburgh 46 G 1
Cupar 38 E 3
Ćuprija 62 B 2
Curaçao, *island* 107 G 5
Curacautin 136 A 2
Curicó 136 A 2
Curitiba 126 E 5
Currane, L., *lake* 49 A 5
Curraun Pena., *peninsula* 48 B 3
Current I., *island* 121 E 5
Currituck Sd., *inlet* 121 F 2
Currockbilly, Mt., *mt.* 149 E 6
Curtis 52 A 1
Curtis Chan., *channel* 147 K 4
Curtis I., *island* 147 K 4
Curupira, Sa., *mountains* 132 C 2
Curuzú Cuatiá 136 C 1
Curvelo 135 D 1
Cushcamcarragh, *mt.* 48 B 3
Cushendall 48 E 1
Cushendun 48 E 1
Cuttack 66 F 4
Cutt Mts., *mountains* 147 H 4
Cuvier Basin, *sea feature* 153 E 4
Cuvier, Cape, *cape* 152 A 2
Cuvier I., *island* 150 F 3
Cuxhaven 58 C 2
Cu Xu, I., *island* 82 E 4
Cuyapo 81 D 4
Cuyo East Pass., *channel* 81 D 6
Cuyo Is., *island group* 81 D 6
Cuyo West Pass., *chan.* 81 D 6
Cuzco 126 B 4
Cwmbran 42 D 3
Cyclades, *see Kikládhes* 63 D 5
Cynwyl Elfed 42 C 3
Cyprus, *island* 29 L5
Cypress Hills, *mountains* 106 E 3
Cyrenaica, *region* 98 F 3
Czaplinek 58 G 2
Czarnków 58 G 2
Czechoslovakia 28 H 4
Czestochowa 34 H 3
Człopa 58 G 2

Daam Top, *mountain* 140 D 2
Dab'a 89 C 3
Dabasan Nuur, *lake* 86 F 2
Dabat 88 B 7
Dablineau 53 F 5
Dabola 98 B 4
Dacca 66 F 4
Dacca, *state* 86 F 3
Da Dung, *river* 83 E 7
Daet 67 H 5
Dafdaf, J., *mountain* 100 G 4
Dagenham 43 H 3
Dagua 85 F 4
Dagupan City 81 D 3
Dahab 100 F 4
Dahanu 86 C 4
Dahlac Archo., *island group* 90 H 4
Dahme 58 E 3
Dahomey 90 D 4
Dahra, *region* 28 G 5
Dā'il 89 C 2
Daio-zaki, *cape* 80 D 4
Daimiel 52 D 3
Daito Is., *island group* 67 H 4
Dajarra 148 B 3
Dakar 90 B 4
Dakhla Oasis 90 F 3
Dakovica 62 B 2
Dal, *river* 28 J 2
Dalaba 98 B 4
Dalai Lama Ra., *mts.* 79 G 2
Dalai Nor, *lake* 75 O 5
Dalanganem Is., *island group* 81 D 6
Dalat 79 H 4
Dalbeattie 47 E 7
Dalby, *Australia* 147 K 5
Dalby, *Sweden* 51 O 4
Dale 51 L 4
Dalhart 118 G 4
Dalhousie, C., *cape* 114 E 1
Daliao 81 F 8
Dalkeith 47 E 6
Dalkey 48 E 3
Dallas 107 F 4
Dallol Bosso, *river* 98 D 4
Dalmally 47 D 5
Dalmatia, *region* 28 H 4
Dalmellington 47 D 6
Daloa 98 C 5
Dalry 47 D 6
Dalrymple, Mt., *mt.* 147 J 4
Dalton, *England* 44 E 3
Dalton, *U.S.A.* 121 C 3
Daltonganj 86 E 3
Dalupiri I., *island* 81 D 2
Dalwallinu 152 B 4
Dalwhinnie 46 D 5
Daly, *river* 140 D 3
Daly Waters 146 F 3
Damanhûr 37 F 4
Damao 66 E 5
Damar, *island* 85 D 4
Damas 29 L 6
Damas, Bahía de las, *bay* 134 B 3
Damāvand 88 E 2
Dāmāvānd, *mountain* 29 N 5
Dāmghān 88 E 2
Damietta, *see Dumyāt* 100 C 1
Damoh 86 D 4
Dampier Archo., *island group* 140 B 4
Dampier Land, *region* 140 C 3
Dampier, Sel., *strait* 140 D 2
Dampier Str., *strait* 140 E 2
Dan, *river* 121 E 2
Dānā 89 B 4
Da Nang, *see Tourane* 84 B 2
Danau Poso, *lake* 84 D 4
Danau Toba, *lake* 79 G 5
Danau Towuti, *lake* 84 D 4
Danbury 41 F 2
Danby L. 120 D 5
Dandenong 149 D 6
Dangrek, Chaine des, *mountains* 83 D 6
Dankhar 86 D 2
Dannemora 51 P 4
Dannenberg 58 D 2
Dannevirke 150 G 5
Dansalan 81 F 7
Dante 90 J 4
Danube, *see Donau, Duna, Dunărea and Dunay* 28 K 4
Danville, *U.S.A., Illinois* 119 K 3
Danville, *U.S.A., Virginia* 119 M 4
Daoud 36 C 3
Daphnae, *ancient site* 100 D 2
Dapiak, Mt., *mountain* 81 E 7
Dapitan 81 E 7
Daqahlīyah, *province* 100 C 2
Dārāb 88 E 4
Daraçya Yar., *peninsula* 63 F 5
Daraga 81 E 6
Dārah, J., *mountain* 100 D 5
Dārān 88 E 3
Daravica, *mountain* 62 B 2
Darbhanga 79 F 3
Dardanelles, *see Çanakkale Boğazi* 65 A 6
Dar el Homr., *region* 90 F 4
Darent, *river* 41 E 3
Dar es Salaam 91 G 6
Dargaville 150 E 2
Darien 134 D 1
Darién, G. del, *gulf* 107 G 5
Darjeeling 66 F 4
Darling, *river* 140 E 5
Darling Downs, *region* 140 E 4
Darling Ra., *mountains* 140 B 5
Darlington 39 F 4
Darmstadt 58 C 4
Darnah 90 F 2
Darnétal 54 E 3
Darnick 149 C 5
Darnley Bay, *bay* 114 E 2
Dar Nuba, *region* 90 F 4
Daroca 53 E 2
Darran Mts., *mountains* 151 C 7
Dar Rounga, *mountains* 90 F 5
Darsi 87 D 5
Dart, C., *cape* 23 O 2
Dart, *river* 42 D 4
Dartford 43 H 3
Dartmoor, *moor* 34 E 3
Dartmouth, *Canada* 115 L 4
Dartmouth, *England* 39 E 6
Dartmouth, L., *lake* 149 D 4
Dartry Mts., *mountains* 48 C 2
Dartuch, C., *cape* 53 G 3
Daru 67 J 6
Darvel Bay, *bay* 81 C 9
Darwen 45 F 4
Darwin 140 D 3
Darwin, Cord., *mts.* 136 A 3
Darwin, Mt., *Chile, mt.* 136 B 4
Darwin, Mt., *Rhodesia, mountain* 101 F 2
Daryācheh-ye Namak, *see Namak* 29 N 5
Daryācheh-ye Rezā'īyeh, *see Rezā'īyeh* 29 M 5
Daryācheh-ye Sistān, *see Sistān* 78 D 2
Dasht, *river* 86 B 3
Dasht-e-Kavīr, *desert* 66 D 4
Dasht-e-Lūt, *desert* 66 D 4
Dasht-e-Margo, *desert* 78 D 2
Dasht-e-Naomid, *desert* 86 B 2
Daspalla 87 E 4
Daspur 86 E 4
Datchet 41 C 3
Datha 86 C 4
Datia 86 D 3
Datu, Tg., *cape* 67 G 5
Daugavpils 35 J 3
Daulat Yar 78 D 2
Daun 56 E 4
Dauphin 114 G 3
Dauphiné, *province* 55 G 5
Dauphin L., *lake* 115 H 3
Dava 46 E 4
Davangere 87 D 5
Davao 67 H 5
Davao Gulf, *gulf* 79 K 5
Davenport 119 J 3
Daventry 43 F 2
David 123 E 4
David-Gorodok 64 E 2
David Seaknoll, *sea feature* 103 G 2
Davis 120 B 4
Davis, *scientific base* 23 F 2
Davis Inlet 115 L 3
Davis I., *island* 83 C 7
Davis, Mt., *mountain* 121 E 2
Davis Mts., *mountains* 118 G 5
Davis Strait, *strait* 106 H 2
Davlekanovo 35 M 3
Davos 60 B 1
Davos-Dorf 57 E 3
Davos-Platz 57 E 3
Davyhurst 152 C 4
Dawa, *river* 104 E 1
Dawes Ra., *mountains* 147 K 4
Dawḥat Sawqarah, *bay* 88 F 6
Dawlish 42 D 4
Dawna Range, *mountains* 83 B 5
Dawson 106 D 2
Dawson, *river* 140 E 4
Dawson Creek 114 E 3
Daylesford 149 C 6
Dayr az Zawr 90 H 2
Dayr Mawās 100 B 5
Dayrūt 99 G 3
Dayton 106 F 4
Daytona Beach 119 L 6
Dax 55 D 6
De Aar 91 F 9
Dead, *river* 49 C 4
Dead Mts., *mountains* 120 D 5
Dead Sea, *inland sea* 29 L 6
Deal 43 J 3
Deane, Mt., *mountain* 148 D 3
Dean, Forest of, *forest* 39 E 6
Deán Funes 136 B 2
Dearborn 119 L 3
Dease Str., *strait* 114 G 2
Death Valley, *valley* 106 E 4
Deauville 54 E 3
Debenham 43 J 2
Débo, L., *lake* 98 C 4
Deborah, Mt., *mountain* 114 C 2
Deboyne Is., *islands* 85 G 5
Debra Birhan 88 B 8
Debra Mark'os 99 G 4
Debra Tabor 99 G 4
Debrecen 37 E 2
Decatur, *U.S.A., Alabama* 119 K 5
Decatur, *U.S.A., Illinois* 119 K 4
Deccan, *plateau* 66 E 5
Deccan traps, *lava beds* 155 G 3
Decelles, L., *lake* 116 D 2
Deception I., *island* 23 R2
Děčín 58 F 3
Deddington 43 F 3
Dedza 104 C 6
Dee, *Scotland, Aberdeen, river* 38 E 3
Dee, *Scotland, Kirkcudbright, river* 47 D 7
Dee, *Wales, river* 39 E 5
Deel, *Rep. of Ireland, Limerick, river* 49 C 4
Deel, *Rep. of Ireland, Mayo, river* 48 B 2
Deep Bay 104 C 5
Deep Creek Ra., *mt.* 120 D 4
Deering, Mt., *mountain* 146 E 5
Deer Lake 115 M 4
Deer Lodge 120 D 2
Deer Park 120 C 2
Deffa, ed., *region* 37 E 4
Deggendorf 59 E 4
De Grey 152 B 2
De Grey, *river* 140 B 4
Dehra Dun 78 E 2
Deingueri, Mt., *mountain* 99 F 5
Dej 64 D 3
Deja, *mountain* 63 B 3
Dek I., *island* 88 B 7
Delano 118 D 4
Delano Pk., *mountain* 120 D 4
Delaware, *river* 117 E 3
Delaware, *state* 119 M 4
Delaware B., *bay* 119 M 4
Delčevo 62 C 3
De Lemmer 56 D 2
Delémont 57 C 2
Delet Teili, *channel* 51 Q 4
Delft 56 C 2
Delft I., *island* 87 D 5
Delfzijl 56 E 1
Delgado, C., *cape* 103 F 4
Delhi 66 E 4
Delicias 118 F 6
Deli Jovan, *mountain* 62 C 1
Delisle I., *island* 83 C 7
Delitzsch 58 E 3
Della Maiella, M., *mts.* 60 E 3
Delle 57 B 2
Dellys 98 D 2
Delmenhorst 58 C 2
Delnice 60 E 2
De-Longa, O-va., *island group* 67 J 2
Delphi, *ancient site* 63 C 4

Front Ra., *mountains* 106 E 3
Frosinone 60 D 4
Frøya, *island* 50 M 3
Frunze 66 E 3
Frutingen 57 C 3
Frýdlant 58 F 3
Fu-chin 75 Q 5
Fu-chou, *China, Fukien* 77 F 6
Fu-chou, *China, Liaoning* 76 G 4
Fu-chow 67 G 4
Fuerte, *river* 118 F 6
Fuerteventura, *island* 98 B 3
Fuga I., *island* 77 G 8
Fu-hsien Hu, *lake* 77 C 7
Fujinomiya 80 D 4
Fuji-san, *mountain* 80 D 4
Fujisawa 80 D 4
Fukien, *province* 77 F 6
Fukuchiyama 80 C 4
Fukue-shima, *island* 80 B 4
Fukui 80 D 3
Fukuoka 67 H 4
Fukushima 75 R 6
Fukuyama 80 C 4
Fu-la-erh-chi 76 G 2
Fulda 58 C 3
Fumay 56 C 5
Fu-min-chen 76 G 5
Fumo, M., *mountain* 57 F 3
Funabashi 80 E 4
Funchal 90 B 2
Fundão 52 B 2
Fundusfeiler, *mountain* 57 F 2
Fuente Álamo 53 E 4
Fuente de Cantos 52 B 3
Fuenteovejuna 52 C 3
Fuensanta, Emb. de la, *lake* 52 D 3
Fuentesaúco 52 C 2
Fuentes de A. 52 C 4
Fu-niu Shan 76 E 5
Funtua 90 D 4
Fundy, B. of, *bay* 106 G 3
Furancungo 104 C 6
Furkapass, *pass* 57 D 3
Furneaux Group, *island group* 140 E 5
Furness 44 E 3
Fürstenwalde 58 F 2
Fürth, *east Bayern* 59 E 4
Fürth, *west Bayern* 59 D 4
Fury & Hecla Str., *strait* 114 J 2
Fuse 80 C 4
Fu-shun 67 H 3
Füssen 57 F 2
Fuwah 100 B 1
Fu-yu 75 P 5
Fylde, *region* 44 F 4
Fyn, *island* 28 H 3
Fyne, Loch, *lake* 38 D 3

Gabarones 101 E 4
Gabas 53 E 1
Gabela 102 C 4
Gabès 98 E 2
Gabès, G. de, *gulf* 90 E 2
Gable End Foreland, *cape* 150 H 4
Gabon 90 E 6
Gabrovo 62 D 2
Gacko 60 G 3
Gadag 87 D 5
Gádor, Sa. de, *mountains* 52 D 4
Gadsden 119 K 5
Gaerwen 42 C 1
Gaeta 60 D 4
Gaeta, G. di, *gulf* 36 D 3
Gaferut, *island* 85 F 3
Gafsa 90 D 2
Gagnoa 90 C 5
Gaíba, L., *lake* 135 C 1
Gaïdhouronisi, *island* 63 D 6
Gaillac 55 E 6
Gaillimh, *see Galway* 48 B 3
Gailtaler Alpen, *mts.* 59 E 5
Gaima 85 F 4
Gainesville, *U.S.A., Florida* 121 D 4
Gainesville, *U.S.A., Georgia* 121 D 3
Gainsborough 54 D 1
Gairdner, L., *lake* 140 D 5
Gairloch 46 C 4
Gairn, *river* 46 E 4
Gakarosa, *mountain* 91 F 8
Gala G., *lake* 62 E 3
Galana, *river* 104 D 3
Galapágos, Islas, *island group* 137 E 2
Galashiels 47 F 6
Galathea Depth, *Kermadec Trench, sea feature* 141 J 5
Galathea Depth, *Philippine Trench, sea feature* 67 H 5
Galati 37 F 2
Galdhøpiggen, *mountains* 28 H 2
Galera, Pta. de la, *cape* 127 B 7
Galera, Pta., *Ecuador, cape* 126 A 2
Galera, Pta., *Mexico, cape* 122 D 3
Galera Pt., *cape* 123 G 3
Galesburg 116 A 3
Galey, *river* 49 B 4
Galicia 52 B 1
Galilee, *region* 89 B 2
Galilee, L., *lake* 147 J 4
Galilee, Sea of, *see Lake Tiberias* 89 B 2
Galimyy 75 S 3
Galite, *island* 61 B 6
Gallabat 88 B 7
Gallarate 57 D 4
Galle 66 F 5
Gállego, *river* 53 E 1
Galley Hd., *cape* 49 C 5
Galley Hill, *hill* 41 D 2
Galliate 57 D 4
Gallina K., *mountain* 57 E 2
Gallinas, Pta., *cape* 126 B 1
Gaillion, Sl., *mountains* 48 E 2
Gallipoli, *Italy* 61 F 4
Gallipoli, *Turkey, see Gellbolu* 62 E 3
Gällivare 34 H 1
Gallocanta, L. de, *lake* 53 E 2
Gallo Mts., *mountains* 118 F 5
Galloway, *region* 39 D 4
Galloway, Mull of, *cape* 39 D 4
Galty Mts. 39 B 5
Galtymore, *mountain* 49 C 4
Gallup 118 F 4
Galveias 52 B 3
Galveston 106 F 4
Galvez 135 B 3
Galway 39 B 5
Galway Bay, *bay* 39 B 5
Gambia 90 B 4
Gambia, *river* 98 B 4
Gambier Is., *island group* 146 G 7
Gamboa 134 D 1
Gamboma 90 E 6
Gamkunoro, G., *mountain* 85 D 3
Gamova, Mys., *cape* 80 B 2
Gamu-Gofa, *province* 104 D 1
Gamph, Sl., *mountains* 48 C 2
Gamvik 50 T 1
Gan 153 C 2
Gand 54 F 2
Gander 106 H 3
Gandesa 53 F 2
Gandía 52 E 3
Ganga, *river* 66 F 4
Gangaw 82 B 4
Gangaw Range, *mountains* 82 B 3
Ganges, Mouths of the, *river mouth* 66 F 4
Gangotri, *mountain* 86 D 3
Gangtok 66 F 4
Gannat 55 F 4
Gannet I., *island* 150 F 3
Gannet Pk., *mountain* 106 E 3
Gantheaume Bay, *bay* 152 A 3
Gao 90 C 4
Gao-Bang 79 H 3
Gaolong, C., *cape* 79 H 4
Gap 55 H 5
Garaina 85 F 4
Gara, L., *lake* 48 C 3
Garanbi, *cape* 67 H 4
Garanhuns 133 F 3
Gārboṣh, Kūh-e, *mt.* 88 E 3
Gard, *river* 55 G 6
Garda, L. di, *lake* 36 D 2
Gardaba, *region* 99 F 3
Gardelegen 58 D 2
Garden City 118 G 4
Gardiner's Ra., *mts.* 146 F 4
Gardo 88 D 8
Gardno, J., *lake* 58 G 1
Gardula 99 G 5
Garelochhead 47 D 5
Garet el Djenoun, *mt.* 98 D 3
Garfield Mt., *mountain* 120 D 2
Gargano, M., *mountain* 28 H 5
Garissa 104 D 3
Garmisch 59 D 5
Garmisch-Partenkirchen 57 G 2
Garmsel, *region* 86 B 3
Gardner Inlet, *inlet* 23 S 2
Gargaliánoi 63 B 5
Garo Hills, *mountains* 86 F 3
Garonne, *river* 28 F 4
Garoua 98 E 5
Garrigues, *mountains* 55 F 6
Garrison Res., *reservoir* 106 E 3
Garrocha, Sa. la, *mts.* 53 E 2
Garron Point, *cape* 48 F 1
Garrovillas 52 B 3
Garry L., *lake* 114 G 2
Gartempe, *river* 55 E 4
Garth 42 D 2
Gartok 78 F 2
Gartz 58 F 2
Garvagh 48 E 2
Garve 46 O 4
Gary 119 K 3
Garzón 123 F 4
Gascogne, *province* 55 D 5
Gascoyne, *river* 140 B 4
Gascogne, G. de, *gulf* 28 F 4
Gascoyne Junction 152 B 3
Gascoyne, Mt., *mountain* 152 B 2
Gasherbrum, *mountain* 86 D 2
Gashuun Gobi, *desert* 86 F 1
Gashuun Nuur, *lake* 75 N 5
Gasparilla, *island* 121 D 5
Gaspé 117 H 1
Gaspé, C., *cape* 115 L 4
Gaspé Pena, *peninsula* 106 G 3
Gas san, *mountain* 80 E 3
Gastonia 121 D 3
Gastoúni 63 B 5
Gata 52 B 2
Gata, C., *cape* 37 G 3
Gata, C. de, *cape* 36 B 3
Gata, Sa. de, *mountains* 52 B 2
Gatchina 51 U 5
Gatehouse of Fleet 47 D 7
Gateshead 39 F 4
Gateshead I., *island* 114 G 1
Gâtinals, *region* 54 F 3
Gattinara 57 D 4
Gâtine, *region* 54 E 4
Gâtine, Hauteurs de, *region* 55 D 4
Gatooma 91 F 7
Gatún 134 D 1
Gatún L., *lake* 134 D 1
Gatwick 41 D 3
Gaud-i-Zirreh, *seasonal lake* 86 B 3
Gauja, *river* 51 S 5
Gauhati 79 G 3
Gaular 51 L 4
Gavdhopoúla, *island* 63 C 6
Gávdhos, *island* 63 D 6
Gave de Pau, *river* 55 D 6
Gävle 34 H 2
Gävleborg, *province* 51 P 4
Gävle bukten, *bay* 51 P 4
Gâvur Dağlari, *mountain* 65 C 7
Gawilgarh Hills, *mts.* 86 D 4
Gawler 147 G 6
Gawler Ras., *mountains* 140 D 5
Gåxsjö 50 P 3
Gaya 66 F 4
Gayndah 149 E 4
Gayvoron 64 F 3
Gaza, *province* 101 G 4
Gazelle Pena., *peninsula* 85 G 4
Gaziantep 37 G 3
Gdańsk 28 J 3
Gdańsk, *province* 64 C 1
Gdańska, Zatoka, *bay* 34 H 3
Gdynia 64 C 1
Gearhart Mt., *mountain* 120 B 3
Geba 98 B 4
Gedaref 99 G 4
Gedera 89 A 3
Gedser 58 D 1
Gediz 28 K 5
Geel 56 C 3
Geelong 140 E 5
Geelvink Baai, *bay* 140 D 2
Geelvink Channel, *channel* 140 B 4
Gefara 28 H 6
Gehua 85 G 5
Geikie Ra., *mountains* 148 C 1
Geita 90 G 6
Geldern 58 B 3
Gelderland, *province* 56 E 2
Gelibolu 63 E 3
Gelidonya Br., *cape* 37 F 3
Gelsenkirchen 36 C 1
Gembloux 56 C 4
Gemeh 81 G 9
Gemlik K., *bay* 62 F 3
Gemona 60 D 1
Geneina 90 F 4
Gen. Alvear 135 B 3
Generalisimo, Emb. del, *lake* 53 E 3
Gen. Luna 81 G 7
Gen. MacArthur 81 F 6
General Toshevo 62 F 2
Generoso, M., *mountain* 57 E 4
Geneva, *see Genève* 57 B 3
Geneva, L., *see Léman* 57 B 3
Genève 36 C 2
Genève, *province* 57 B 3
Genil, *river* 52 C 4
Genk 56 D 4
Gennargentu, Monti del, *mountain* 61 B 5
Genoa, *see Genova* 60 B 2
Genova 28 H 4
Genova, G. di, *gulf* 36 D 2
Gent 36 C 1
Genthin 58 E 2
Geographe Bay, *bay* 152 B 4
Geographe Chan., *channel* 140 B 4
George 101 D 6
George Bay, *bay* 117 J 2
George Bligh Bank, *sea feature* 28 E 2
George Bryan Coast, *region* 23 R 2
George, L., *Australia, lake* 149 D 6
George, L., *Uganda, lake* 104 B 3
George, L., *U.S.A., lake* 121 D 4
George River 115 L 3
George's Bank, *sea feature* 106 G 3
George V Land, *region* 23 K 2
George VI Sound, *inlet* 23 R 2
Georgetown, *Australia* 148 C 2
Georgetown, *Cayman Is.* 123 E 3
Georgetown, *Guyana* 126 D 2
George Town 66 F 5
Georgia 119 L 5
Georgian B., *bay* 106 F 3
Georgia Str., *strait* 114 E 4
Georgina, *river* 140 D 4
Georgiyevsk 37 H 2
Gera 58 E 3
Geraardsbergen 56 B 4
Geral, Sa., *mountains* 126 D 5
Geral de Goiás, Sa., *mts.* 126 E 4
Geraldine 151 D 7
Geraldton 146 B 5
Gérgal 52 D 4
Gerlachovsky Štít, *mt.* 64 D 3
Germany 28 H 3
Germencik 63 E 5
Germiston 91 F 8
Gerona 36 C 3
Gerrards Cross 41 C 2
Gera, *river* 52 F 1
Gesoa 85 F 4
Getafe 52 D 2
Getz Ice Shelf 23 O 2
Geureudong, G., *mt.* 84 A 3
Gévaudan, *region* 55 F 5
Gevelsberg 56 F 3
Gex 55 H 4
Geyser, Banc du, *island* 105 C 2
Ghadames 90 D 2
Ghaghra, *river* 86 E 3
Gha'īb, W. al., *wadi* 100 F 4
Ghamr 89 B 4
Ghana 90 C 5
Ghanīm, *region* 88 E 6
Ghānim, Jaz., *island* 100 E 5
Gharandal 89 B 4
Gharbīyah, *province* 100 B 1
Ghardaïa 98 D 2
Ghardimaou 61 B 6
Gharib, J., *mountain* 100 D 4
Gharw, Jaz., *island* 100 A 1
Ghat 90 E 3
Ghayl Bā Wazīr 88 D 7
Ghazal, Bahr el, *river* 99 F 5
Ghaziabad 86 D 3
Ghazipur 86 E 3
Ghaz Köl, *lake* 86 F 2
Ghazni 78 D 2
Ghazzah 37 G 4
Ghazzah Strip, *district* 100 F 1
Ghent, *see Gent* 56 B 3
Ghor, El, *region* 89 B 3
Ghor, El, *Jordan valley, region* 89 B 3
Ghubbat al Būş, *bay* 100 D 3
Ghub. al Jamsah, *bay* 100 E 5
Ghubbat al Qāmar, *bay* 78 C 4
Ghub. az Zayt, *bay* 100 E 5
Ghurd Abū Muharrik, *sand dunes* 100 A 4
Ghurd al Dēw, *sand dunes* 100 A 2
Ghurd al Ḥalīf, *sand dunes* 100 A 2
Ghurd al Ḥunayshāt, *sand dunes* 100 A 2
Ghurd al Ḥunayshāt al Wasṭānī, *sand dunes* 100 A 2
Ghurd al Kalb, *sand dunes* 100 A 3
Ghurd al Mashrūkah, *sand dunes* 100 A 2
Ghurd al Qaṭṭanīyāh, *sand dunes* 100 B 2
Ghurd ar Rammāk, *sand dunes* 100 A 3
Ghurd at Tafāsīkh, *sand dunes* 100 A 3
Ghurian 86 B 2
Ghuwaybbah, W., *wadi* 100 D 3
Ghuwayrib, J., *mountain* 100 D 4
Gia Dinh 83 E 7
Giamda Chu, *river* 82 A 2
Giamda Dz 86 F 3
Giant's Causeway, *rocks* 48 E 1
Gibbet Hill, *hill* 41 C 3
Gibbs I., *island* 23 S 2
Gibeon 101 C 4
Gibraleón 52 B 4
Gibralíon, I., *island* 134 D 2
Gibraltar 28 F 5
Gibraltar, Campo de, *cape* 52 C 4
Gibraltar Point, *cape* 42 H 1
Gibraltar, Strait of, *strait* 28 F 5
Gibson Desert, *desert* 140 C 4
Gichigene Īn Nurū, *mts.* 75 M 5
Gidole 99 G 5
Gien 54 F 4
Giens, Presqu'île de, *peninsula* 55 H 6
Giessen 58 C 3
Gifford 47 F 6
Gifhorn 58 D 2
Gifu 67 H 4
Giganta, Sa. de la, *mts.* 122 B 2
Gigha I., *island* 38 D 4
Giglio, *island* 60 C 3
Gijón 36 B 2
Gila, *river* 106 E 4
Gila Bend 120 D 5
Gilbert, *river* 140 E 3
Gilbert Islands, *island group* 137 B 2
Gilbert River 148 C 2
Gilé 104 D 7
Gilead, *region* 89 B 2
Gilf Kebir Plateau, *plateau* 90 F 3
Gilgit 78 E 2
Gilkicker Pt., *cape* 41 B 4
Gilles, L., *lake* 146 G 6
Gillingham 43 H 3
Gill, L., *lake* 48 C 2
Gilroy 120 B 4
Giluwe, Mt., *mountain* 85 F 4
Gimbala, J., *mountain* 90 F 4
Gimli 114 H 3
Gimone, *river* 55 E 6
Gingin 152 B 4
Gin Gin 149 E 3
Ginir 103 F 2
Ginzo de Limia 52 B 1
Giona, *mountain* 63 C 4
Gippsland, *region* 140 E 5
Girardot 132 B 2
Giresun 37 G 3
Girdle Ness, *cape* 38 E 3
Girishk 86 B 3
Gironde, *estuary* 55 D 5
Girvan 38 D 4
Gisborne 150 H 4
Gisenyi 102 D 3
Gisors 54 E 3
Gissarskiy Khr., *mts.* 86 C 2
Gistral, Sa. del, *mountains* 52 B 1
Giuba 91 H 6
Giurgeni 64 E 4
Giurgiu 37 F 2
Givet 54 G 2
Giza Pyramids, *ancient site* 100 C 3
Gizhiga 24 C 2
Gizhiginskaya Guba, *gulf* 75 S 3
Gji i Durrësit, *gulf* 62 A 3
Gji i Lalzës, *gulf* 62 A 3
Gjirokastër 62 B 3
Gjoa Haven, *trading post* 114 H 2
Gjol i Nartës, *lake* 62 A 3
Gjøvik 51 N 4
Gjuhëzës, K. i, *cape* 62 A 3
Glace Bay 115 M 4
Glacier Pk., *mountain* 120 B 1
Gladbeck 58 B 3
Gladstone, *Australia, Queensland* 147 K 4
Gladstone, *Australia, South Australia* 149 B 5
Glamis 47 E 5
Glamoč 60 F 2
Glamorgan, *county* 42 D 3
Glan 87 F 9
Glarner Alpen, *mountains* 57 D 3
Glärnisch, *mountain* 57 E 2
Glarus 57 E 2
Glarus, *canton* 57 E 3
Glasgow 28 F 3
Glas Maol, *mountain* 38 E 3
Glass, L., *lake* 46 D 4
Glastonbury 42 E 3
Glauchau 58 E 3
Glazov 35 M 2
Glen Affric, *valley* 46 D 4
Glen App, *valley* 47 D 6
Glenarm 48 F 2
Glen Cannich, *valley* 46 D 4
Glen Clova, *valley* 46 E 5
Glencoe 101 F 5
Glen Coe, *valley* 46 C 5
Glen Carron, *valley* 46 C 4
Glendale, *U.S.A., Arizona* 120 D 5
Glendale, *U.S.A., California* 118 D 5
Gleneagles 47 E 5
Glenelg 149 B 5
Glenelg, *river* 149 C 6
Glen Florry 152 B 2
Glengariff 49 B 5
Glen Garry, *valley* 46 C 4
Glen Innes 147 K 5
Glenluce 47 D 7
Glen Lyon, *valley* 47 D 5
Glen More, *valley* 46 D 4
Glenmorgan 149 D 4
Glen Moriston, *valley* 46 D 4
Glenns Ferry 120 D 3
Gleno, M., *mountain* 57 F 3
Glen Roy, *valley* 46 D 5
Glen Shee, *valley* 46 E 5
Glen Spean, *valley* 46 D 5
Glenties 48 C 2
Glittertind, *mountain* 50 M 4
Gliwice 34 H 3
Globe 118 E 5
Głogów 64 C 2
Glomma, *river* 28 H 2
Glorieuses, Îles, *island group* 103 F 4
Glossop 45 G 4
Gloucester, *England* 39 E 6
Gloucester, *U.S.A.* 117 F 3
Gloucester, *county* 43 E 3
Gloversville 117 E 3
Glyde, *river* 48 E 3
Glyme, *river* 41 B 2
Glyndebourne 41 E 4
Gmünd, *Austria* 59 E 5
Gmünd, *Czechoslovakia* 59 F 4
Gmunden 59 E 5
Gnarp 50 P 4
Gniezno 64 C 2
Goa 66 E 5
Goat Fell, *mountain* 38 D 4
Goat Mt., *mountain* 120 D 1
Gobabis 91 E 8
Gobernadora, Isla, *island group* 134 B 3
Gobi, *desert* 66 G 3
Goch 56 E 3
Go Cong 83 E 7
Godalming 43 G 3
Godavari, *river* 66 E 5
Godavari, Mouths of the, *river mouths* 87 E 4
Godech 62 C 2
Godhavn 106 H 2
Godhra 86 C 4
Godmanchester 43 G 2
Gods L., *lake* 106 F 3
Godthaab 106 H 2
Goëland, Lac au, *lake* 116 E 1
Goeree, *island* 56 B 3
Goeree-Overflakkee, *polder* 54 G 2
Goes 56 B 3
Gogebic Ra., *mountains* 116 B 2
Gogunda 86 C 3
Göhren 58 E 1
Goiana, *river* 133 F 3
Goiânia 126 E 4
Goiás 133 D 4
Goil, L., *lake* 47 D 5
Goitso Tala, *region* 76 C 3

Gökbel D., *mountain* 63 F 5
Gök Tepe, *mountain* 63 F 5
Gol 34 G 2
Golada 52 B 1
Golaghat 82 A 3
Gold Coast, *region* 98 C 5
Golden Bay, *bay* 150 E 5
Goldendale 120 B 2
Goldfield 120 C 4
Golden Gate, *strait* 118 C 4
Golden Ridge 152 C 4
Golden Vale, *region* 39 B 5
Goldsboro 121 E 3
Golija, *province* 62 B 2
Golpāyegān 88 E 3
Golspie 46 E 4
Golūl Dāgh, *mountains* 29 O 5
Goma 102 D 3
Gomel' 37 F 1
Gomera, *island* 98 B 3
Gómez Palacio 118 G 6
Goms, *region* 57 D 3
Gonave, I. de la, *island* 123 F 3
Gonbad-e Kāvūs 88 F 2
Gonda 86 E 3
Gondar 90 G 4
Gondomar 52 A 1
Gönen 62 E 3
Gönen, *river* 62 E 3
Gongkaling, *mountain* 77 C 6
Gongola, *river* 98 E 4
Gōno, *river* 80 C 4
Gonzales 118 H 6
Goodenough I., *island* 85 G 4
Gooding 120 D 3
Goodrich Bank, *sea feature* 146 F 2
Good Hope, Cape of, *cape* 91 E 9
Goodwin Sands, *sea feature* 43 J 3
Goole 39 F 5
Goomalling 146 C 6
Goondiwindi 147 K 5
Goongarrie 152 C 4
Goose Bay 106 G 3
Goose L., *lake* 120 B 3
Göppingen 59 C 4
Góra 58 G 3
Goradetski, Mys, *cape* 50 X 2
Gorakhpur 78 F 3
Gorbea, Pa. de, *mts.* 55 C 6
Gorda, Punta, *cape* 120 A 3
Gördes 62 F 4
Gordonvale 147 J 3
Gore, *Ethiopia* 99 G 5
Gore, *New Zealand* 151 C 8
Gorebridge 47 E 6
Görenez D., *mountain* 62 E 4
Gorey 49 E 4
Gorgān 88 E 2
Gorge Ra., The, *mts.* 148 D 2
Gorgona, I., *island* 132 B 2
Gori 37 H 3
Gorinchem 56 C 3
Goring 41 B 2
Goring Gap, *river gap* 43 F 3
Gorizia 60 D 2
Gorjanci, *mountains* 60 E 2
Gor'kiy 29 M 3
Gor'kovskoye Vdkhr., *reservoir* 35 L 3
Gorleston 43 J 2
Gorlija, *mountain* 64 D 4
Görlitz 34 G 3
Gorlovka 29 L 4
Gorna Oryakhovitsa 62 D 2
Gorodenka 64 E 3
Gorodok 75 N 4
Goroka 85 F 4
Gorong, Kep, *island grp.* 85 E 4
Gorongosa, Serra de, *mountains* 101 G 2
Gorontalo 84 D 3
Gort 49 C 3
Gorumna I., *island* 48 B 3
Gory Baysuntau, *mountain* 86 C 2
Gory Byrranga, *mountain* 24 F 2
Goryn', *river* 64 E 2
Görzke 58 E 2
Gorzów Wlkp. 64 B 2
Gosainthan, *mountain* 86 E 3
Goslar 58 D 3
Gospić 64 B 4
Gosport 43 F 4
Gossau 57 E 2
Göta, *river* 34 G 2
Göta Kanal, *canal* 34 G 2
Göteborg 28 H 3
Göteborg och Bohus, *county* 51 N 5
Gotha 58 D 3
Gotland, *island* 28 J 3
Gotland, *county* 51 Q 5
Gotō-rettō, *island group* 80 B 4
Gotse Delchev 62 C 3
Gotska Sandön, *island* 51 Q 5
Göttingen 58 C 3
Gottwaldov 64 C 3
Gouda 56 C 2
Gough I., *island* 25 E 7
Gouin Res., *reservoir* 106 G 3
Goulburn 140 E 5
Goulburn, *river* 149 D 6
Goulburn Is., *island grp.* 146 F 2
Goundam 98 C 4
Gourara, *region* 98 C 3
Gouraya 53 F 4
Gourdon 55 E 5
Gourma, *region* 90 D 4
Gournay-en-Bray 54 E 3
Gourock 47 D 6
Gourock Ra., *mountains* 140 E 5
Gourounsi, *region* 90 C 4
Governador Valadares 133 E 4
Gowan Ra., *mountains* 147 H 4
Gower, *peninsula* 39 D 6
Gowna, L., *lake* 48 D 3
Gowrie, Carse of, *region* 46 E 5
Goya 135 C 2
Goyder's Lagoon, *seasonal lake* 147 G 5
Gozo, *island* 28 H 5
Goz Regeb 88 B 6
Graaff Reinet 91 F 9
Graboúsa, *island* 63 C 6
Grabs 57 E 2
Gračac 60 E 2
Gracanica 60 G 2
Grace, Lake, *seasonal lake* 152 B 4
Gracias a Dios, C., *cape* 107 F 5
Gradaús, Sa. dos, *mts.* 133 D 3
Gradeška Pl., *mountains* 62 C 3
Grafton 147 K 5
Grafton, C., *cape* 148 D 2
Grafton Passage, *channel* 147 J 3
Graham I., *island* 106 D 3
Graham Land, *district* 23 S 2
Graham Mts., *mountains* 118 E 5
Grahamstown 91 F 9
Graie, Alpi, *mountains* 60 A 2
Grain Coast, *region* 90 B 5
Grajaú, *river* 133 E 3
Gralheira, Sa., *mountains* 52 A 2
Gramat, Causse de, *limestone region* 55 E 5
Grampian Mts., *mountains* 28 F 3
Grampians, *mountains* 149 C 6
Grámvoúsa, *island* 63 C 6
Granada, *Nicaragua* 123 E 3
Granada, *Spain* 36 B 3
Gran Altiplanicie Central, *plateau* 136 B 3
Granby 117 F 2
Gran Canaria, *island* 90 B 3
Gran Chaco, *region* 126 C 5
Grand, *river* 116 C 3
Grand Bahama, *island* 107 G 4
Grande, Bahiá, *bay* 127 C 8
Grand Bassam 90 C 5
Grand Canal, *see Yun Ho* 76 F 5
Gd. Cañon du Verdon, *gorge* 55 H 6
Grand Canyon 120 D 4
Grand Canyon, *gorge* 106 E 4
Grand Cays, *reefs* 121 E 5
Gd. Combin, *mountain* 57 C 4
Grande, *Bolivia, river* 126 C 4
Grande, *Brazil, river* 133 D 4
Grande, *Panama, river* 134 C 2
Grande Brière, *region* 54 C 4
Gde. Comore, *island* 103 F 4
Gd. Coulee Dam, *dam* 118 D 2
Gd. Coulee Equalising Res., *reservoir* 120 C 2
Grande de Garupa, I., *island* 133 D 3
Gde. Miquelon, *island* 115 M 4
Grande Prairie 114 F 3
Grand Erg, *sand dunes* 90 E 4
Grand Erg Occidental, *sand dunes* 90 C 3
Grand Erg Oriental, *sand dunes* 90 D 3
Grande Ronde, *river* 120 C 2
Gde. Rousse, *mountains* 57 B 4
Gran Desierto, *desert* 122 B 1
Grandes Landes, *region* 55 D 5
Grand Falls 115 M 4
Grand Falls, *falls* 115 L 3
Grandfather Mt., *mt.* 121 D 2
Grand Forks 118 H 2
Grand Island 118 H 3
Grand I., *island* 116 B 2
Grand Isle, *island* 121 B 4
Grand Junction 118 F 4
Grand Lac, *see Tonle Sap* 83 D 6
Grand Lake, *Canada, New Brunswick, lake* 117 G 2
Grand L., *Canada, Newfoundland, lake* 115 M 4
Grand L., *U.S.A., Louisiana, lake* 121 B 4
Grand L., *U.S.A., Ohio, lake* 121 C 1
Grand-Lieu, L. de, *lake* 54 D 4
Grand Manan I., *island* 117 G 2
Grand'Mère 117 F 2
Grand Newfoundland Banks, *sea feature* 106 H 3
Grandola 52 A 3
Grandola, Sa., *mountains* 52 A 4
Grand Rapids, *Canada* 114 H 3
Grand Rapids, *U.S.A., Michigan* 119 K 3
Grand Rapids, *U.S.A., Minnesota* 119 J 2
Gd. St. Bernard P., *pass* 57 C 4
Grand Turk, *island* 123 F 2
Grand Union Canal, *canal* 41 C 2
Grane 50 O 3
Grangemouth 47 E 5
Grangeville 120 C 2
Graninge 50 P 3
Granite Pk., *mountain* 118 F 2
Granite Ra., *mountains* 120 C 3
Granja de T. 52 C 3
Gränna 51 O 5
Granollers 53 G 2
Gran Paradiso, *mountain* 57 C 4
Gran Sabana, la, *region* 132 C 2
Gran Sasso d'Italia, *mt.* 60 D 3
Grant Duff Ra., *mts.* 146 D 5
Grantham 39 F 5
Grant Land, *region* 106 F 1
Gran Tournalin, *mt.* 57 C 4
Grant, Mt., *U.S.A., Clan Alpine Mts., mountain* 120 C 4
Grant Mt., *U.S.A., Wassuk Ra., mountain* 120 C 4
Granton 47 E 6
Grantown 46 E 4
Grant Ra., *mountains* 120 D 4
Grants Pass 118 Q 3
Granville 54 D 3
Grasmere 44 E 3
Gras, Lac de, *lake* 114 F 2
Grasse 55 H 6
Grass Patch 152 C 4
Grass Valley 120 B 4
Grassy Knob, *mountain* 121 D 2
Grästorp 51 O 5
Graubünden, *canton* 57 E 3
Grave, Pte. de, *cape* 36 B 2
's-Gravenhage 28 G 3
Gravelines 54 F 2
Gravesend 39 G 6
Gray 54 G 4
Grays Harb., *harbour* 120 A 2
Grays Thurrock 41 E 3
Graz 36 D 2
Greaca, Lacul, *lake* 62 E 1
Gt. Abaco, *island* 107 G 4
Gr. Arber, *mountain* 59 E 4
Great Australian Basin, *region* 149 C 3
Great Australian Bight, *bay* 140 C 5
Gt. Baddow 41 E 2
Gt. Bahama Bank, *sea feature* 107 G 4
Great Barrier Island, *island* 150 F 3
Great Barrier Reef, *reefs* 85 F 5
Great Basin, *region* 106 E 3
Great Basses, *island grp.* 87 D 6
Gt. Bear L., *lake* 106 E 2
Great Bend 118 H 4
Gt. Bernera, *island* 38 C 2
Gt. Bitter Lake, *see Al Buḥayrah al Murrah al Kubrá* 100 D 2
Gt. Blasket I., *island* 49 A 4
Great Bushman Land, *region* 101 C 5
Gt. Chart 41 F 3
Gt. Coco I., *island* 87 F 5
Gt. Cumbrae, *island* 47 D 6
Great Dividing Range, *mountains* 141 E 4
Great Driffield 45 H 4
Great Dunmow 43 H 3
Greater Antilles, *island group* 107 F 4
Greater Khingan Range, *see Ta-hsing-an-ling Shan-mo* 76 G 2
Greater London 41 D 2
Greater Sunda Islands, *island group* 66 G 5
Gt. Exhibition Bay, *bay* 150 E 2
Great Exuma, *island* 119 M 7
Great Falls 118 E 2
Gt. Fish, *river* 91 F 9
Gt. Fisher Bank, *sea feature* 34 F 3
Gt. Gable, *mountain* 44 E 3
Gt. Gandak, *river* 86 E 3
Great Glen, The, *valley* 38 D 3
Gt. Guana Cay, *reef* 121 E 5
Great Guana Cay, *Great Abaco, reef* 121 E 5
Gt. Inagua, *island* 107 G 4
Great Isaac I., *island* 121 E 5
Gt. Karas Berg, *mountains* 91 E 8
Gt. Karroo, *region* 91 F 9
Gt. Kei, *river* 101 E 6
Great Malvern 43 E 2
Great Nicobar, *island* 87 F 6
Gt. N.E. Channel, *channel* 140 E 2
Gt. Northern Hwy. 146 C 5
Great Oasis, The, *region* 90 F 3
Gt. Ormes Hd., *cape* 39 E 5
Great Rann of Kutch, *flood area* 66 E 4
Great Rift Valley, *rift* 155 F 4
Gt. Ruaha, *river* 91 G 6
Great Sale Cay, *reef* 121 E 5
Gt. Salt Lake, *lake* 106 E 3
Great Salt Lake Desert, *desert* 118 E 3
Great Sand Hills, *mts.* 118 F 1
Great Sand Sea, *dune area* 90 F 3
Gt. Sand Sea of Calansho, *dune area* 99 F 3
Great Sandy Desert, *desert* 140 C 4
Gt. Sandy I., *see Fraser I.* 141 F 4
Gt. Slave Lake, *lake* 106 E 2
Gt. Smoky Mts., *mts.* 119 L 4
Great Sole Bank, *sea feature* 39 B 7
Great South Bay, *bay* 117 F 3
Gt. Stour, *river* 41 F 3
Gt. Swinton Is., *island group* 83 C 7
Great Valley, *region* 119 L 4
Great Victoria Desert, *desert* 140 C 4
Gt. Wakering 41 F 2
Great Whale River 115 K 3
Great Whernside, *mt.* 39 F 4
Great Yarmouth 39 G 5
Gredos, Sa. de, *mts.* 28 F 5
Greece 28 J 5
Greek, *civilisation* 158
Greeley 118 G 3
Green, *river* 118 F 3
Green Bay 116 B 2
Green Bay, *bay* 119 K 2
Green Bluff, *cape* 149 E 5
Green Hd., *cape* 152 A 4
Green Island 151 D 7
Green Island Bay, *bay* 81 C 6
Greenland 106 H 2
Greenland Basin, *sea feature* 24 M 2
Greenland Ice Cap 154 D 2
Greenland-Iceland Rise, *sea feature* 24 N 2
Greenland Sea 24 M 2
Greenlaw 47 F 6
Green Lowther, *mt.* 38 E 4
Greenly I., *island* 146 F 6
Green Mts., *mountains* 119 N 3
Greenock 38 D 4
Greensboro 119 M 4
Greenstone Pt., *cape* 46 C 4
Green Swamp, *swamp* 121 E 3
Greenvale 148 D 2
Greenville, *U.S.A., Mississippi* 119 J 5
Greenville, *U.S.A., N. Carolina* 121 E 3
Greenville, *U.S.A., S. Carolina* 119 L 5
Greenwich 43 H 3
Greenwood 119 J 5
Gregory Downs 148 B 2
Gregory, L., *S. Australia, lake* 147 G 5
Gregory L., *W. Australia, lake* 146 E 4
Gregory Ra., *mountains* 140 E 3
Greifswald 58 E 1
Greiz 58 E 3
Gremikha 50 X 2
Grenå 51 N 6
Grenada, *island* 107 G 5
Grenada Res., *reservoir* 121 B 3
Grenadines, The, *island group* 123 G 3
Grenchen 57 C 2
Grenen, *cape* 28 H 3
Grenoble 55 G 5
Grenville, C., *cape* 147 H 2
Gresik 84 C 4
Gretna Green 47 E 6
Grevelingen, *estuary* 56 B 3
Grevenå 62 B 3
Grevesmühlen 58 D 2
Grey, *river* 151 D 6
Greymouth 151 D 6
Grey Range, *mountains* 140 E 4
Grey's Plains, *region* 140 B 4
Greytown, *New Zealand* 150 F 5
Greytown, *Rep. of S. Africa* 101 F 5
Griba, *mountains* 62 A 3
Gribb Seamount, *sea feature* 23 G 2
Griekwastad 101 D 5
Griffin 121 C 3
Griffith 147 J 6
Grigna, *mountain* 57 E 4
Grigoriopol' 64 F 3
Grijalva, *river* 122 D 3
Grim, C., *cape* 140 E 6
Grimma 58 E 3
Grimsby 39 F 5
Grimselpass, *pass* 57 D 3
Grimshaw 114 F 3
Grimstad 51 M 5
Grindelwald 57 D 3
Gris Nez, C., *cape* 54 E 2
Grivola, *mountain* 57 C 4
Grmeč Plan., *mountains* 64 C 4
Grobina 51 R 6
Grodno 36 E 1
Grodzisk 58 G 2
Groenlo 56 E 2
Grombalia 61 C 6
Groningen 34 F 3
Groningen, *province* 56 E 1
Groninger Wad, *channel* 56 E 1
Gronau 58 B 2
Groote Eylandt, *island* 140 D 3
Grootfontein 91 E 7
Gr. Arber, *mountain* 64 B 3
Grossenhain 58 E 3
Grosseto 60 C 3
Grossglockner, *mountain* 28 H 4
Grottes de Hans, *grotto* 56 D 4
Groznyy 29 M 4
Grudovo 62 E 2
Grudziadz 36 E 1
Grundsunda 50 Q 3
Gruyères 57 C 3
Gruzinskaya S.S.R., *republic* 74 G 5
Gryfice 58 F 2
Gryfino 64 B 2
Grytviken 23 A 3
Guacanayabo, G. de, *gulf* 123 F 2
Guadalerzas, Las, *region* 52 D 3
Guadalajara, *Mexico* 107 E 4
Guadalajara, *Spain* 52 D 2
Guadalcanal 52 C 3
Guadalcanal I., *island* 140 F 2
Guadalmellato, Emb. de, *lake* 52 C 3
Guadalupe, *Philippines* 81 E 6
Guadalupe, *U.S.A.* 120 B 5
Guadalupe, *island* 107 E 4
Guadalupe, Sao. de, *mts.* 36 B 3
Guadalquivir, *river* 28 F 5
Gúdar, Sa. de, *mountains* 53 E 2
Guadarrama, Sa. de, *mts.* 28 F 5
Guadeloupe, *island* 107 G 5
Guadeloupe Pass., *channel* 123 G 3
Guadiana, *river* 28 F 5
Guadiana, B. de, *bay* 121 C 6
Gudiana Menor, *river* 52 D 4
Guadix 52 D 4
Guafo, G. de, *gulf* 127 B 7
Guainía, *river* 132 C 2
Guaíra, Salto do, *falls* 136 C 1
Guajaba, C., *cape* 121 E 6
Guajará Mirim 132 C 4
Guajira, Pena. de, *peninsula* 123 F 3
Gualeguay 136 C 2
Gualeguaychu 135 C 3
Guam, *island* 67 J 5
Guanahacabibes, Pena. de, *peninsula* 121 C 6
Guanajuato 122 C 2
Guanare 123 G 4
Guánico 134 C 3
Guantánamo 123 F 2
Guaporé, *river* 126 C 4
Guaqui 132 C 4
Guarabira 133 F 3
Guaranda 132 B 3
Guararé 134 C 3
Guara, Sa. de, *mountains* 52 E 1
Guaratinguetá 135 D 2
Guarda 52 B 2
Guardafui, C., *cape* 90 J 4
Guardunha, Sa. do., *mts.* 52 B 2
Guasaro, *river* 134 C 2
Guastalla 60 C 2
Guatemala 107 F 5
Guatemala, *state* 107 F 5
Guatemala Basin, *sea feature* 107 F 5
Guatemala Trench, *sea feature* 107 F 5
Guaviare, *river* 126 B 2
Guaxupé 135 D 2
Guayaquil 126 A 3
Guayaquil, Golfo de, *gulf* 126 A 3
Guaymas 122 B 2
Guba Buorkhaya, *gulf* 75 P 2
Gubakha 35 N 2
Guban, *region* 78 B 4
Gubat 81 F 5
Gubbio 60 D 3
Gubin 64 B 2
Gudbrandsdalen, *valley* 34 G 2
Gudiyatam 87 D 5
Gudur 87 D 5
Guebwiller 54 H 4
Guelma 98 D 2
Guelph 116 D 3
Guéret 55 E 4
Guernica 52 D 1
Guernsey, *island* 54 C 3
Guest I., *island* 23 N 2
Guguan, *island* 85 F 2
Gugusan Banggai, *island group* 84 D 4
Gugusan Spermonde, *island group* 84 C 4
Guiana Highlands, *mts.* 126 C 2
Guichen B., *bay* 149 B 6
Guiers, L. de, *lake* 98 B 4
Guildford, *Australia* 152 B 4
Guildford, *England* 39 F 6
Guilianova 60 D 3
Guimarães 52 A 2
Guimaras I., *island* 81 E 6
Guinchos Cay, *reef* 121 E 6
Guinea 90 B 4
Guinea Basin, *sea feature* 90 C 5
Guinea, Gulf of, *sea* 90 C 5
Güines 121 D 6
Guingamp 54 C 3
Guisborough 44 G 3
Guise 54 F 3
Guiuan 81 F 6
Gujarat, *state* 86 C 4
Gujranwala 78 E 2
Gujrat 86 D 2
Gulbarga 87 D 4
Gulf Basin, *region* 140 C 3
Gulfport 121 B 4
Gulu 104 C 2
Gummersbach 54 H 2
Guna 86 D 3
Guna, *mountain* 99 G 4
Gun Cay, *reef* 121 E 5
Gundagai 149 D 6
Güney 63 F 4
Gunnedah 147 K 6
Gunnerus Bank, *sea feature* 23 D 3
Guntersville L., *lake* 121 C 3
Guntur 78 F 4
Gunungapi, *island* 85 D 4
Günzburg 59 D 4
Gupta, *civlisation* 159
Gura, El, *region* 100 F 1
Gurdaspur 86 D 2
Gurgaon 86 D 3
Gurgei, J., *mountain* 99 F 4
Gurgueia, Sa. de, *mts.* 133 E 4
Gurla Mandhata, *mountain* 86 D 3
Gürün 65 D 6
Gurupi, Sa. do, *mountain* 133 E 3
Guru Sikhar, *mountain* 86 C 3
Gur'yev 35 M 4
Gust Adolf 51 O 4
Gusau 98 D 4
Gusi 81 B 8
Gusmar 62 A 3
Gustine 120 B 4
Güstrow 58 E 2
Gütersloh 58 C 3

Guthrie 122 D 1
Guyana 126 D 2
Guyenne, *province* 55 E 5
Gwadar 86 B 3
Gwalior 66 E 4
Gwamongga, Mt., *mt.* 85 E 4
Gwanda 101 F 3
Gweebarra Bay, *bay* 39 B 4
Gwelo 91 F 7
Gwelo, *province* 101 F 2
Gwent, *region* 39 E 6
Gwydir, *river* 149 D 4
Gyāla Peri, *mountain* 86 F 3
Gyamo Ngo Chu, *river* 86 F 3
Gyangtse Dz 79 F 3
Gympie 147 K 5
Gyöngyös 64 D 3
Györ 36 E 2
Gyula 64 D 3

Haapsalu 51 R 5
Ha'arava, *valley* 89 B 4
Haarlem 56 C 2
Habana 107 F 4
Ḥabbān 99 H 4
Habbānīyah 88 C 3
Habesor, *river* 100 F 1
Hachijo-jima, *island* 80 D 4
Hachinohe 75 R 5
Hachiōji 80 D 4
Hachirō-gata, *bay* 80 D 2
Hackås 50 O 4
Hada Mts., *mountains* 86 C 3
Hadarba, Râs, *cape* 99 G 3
Hadd, Ra's al, *cape* 66 D 4
Haddenham 41 C 2
Haddington 38 E 4
Haded, *region* 90 H 4
Hadejia 98 E 4
Hadejia, *river* 98 E 4
Hadera 89 A 2
Hadera, *river* 89 B 2
Haderslev 51 N 6
Hādī, Jebel el, *mountains* 89 C 4
Hadibu 90 J 4
Ḥadīd, J., *mountain* 100 B 2
Hadimkoy 62 F 3
Hadley Bay, *gulf* 114 G 1
Ha Dong 79 H 3
Hadsel 50 P 2
Hadsund 51 N 6
Haeckle Deep, *sea feature* 127 B 6
Haeju 76 H 4
Ha-erh-pin 67 H 3
Hafnarfjördhur 50 B 3
Hafun, Ras, *cape* 90 J 4
Hagari, *river* 87 D 5
Hagen 58 B 3
Hagerstown 119 M 4
Häggenås 50 O 3
Hagi 80 B 4
Ha Giang 82 D 4
Haggs Hd., *cape* 39 B 5
Hague, C. de la, *cape* 54 D 3
Haguenau 54 H 3
Hai 89 B 4
Hai Duong 82 E 4
Haifa 37 G 4
Haig 152 D 4
Hai-k'ang 77 E 7
Haikau Wan, *bay* 77 G 7
Hai-k'ou 66 G 5
Ḥā'il 90 H 3
Hailakandi 82 A 3
Hailey 120 D 3
Hai-ling Tao, *island* 77 E 7
Hailsham 43 H 4
Hai-lun 76 H 2
Hai-lung 76 H 3
Hailuoto, *island* 50 S 3
Hai-men-chen 79 K 3
Hai-nan Tao, *island* 67 G 5
Hainaut, *province* 56 B 4
Hainaut, *region* 56 B 4
Haines 114 D 3
Haines Junction 114 D 2
Haiphong 67 G 4
Hai-t'an Tao, *island* 77 F 6
Haiti, *state* 107 G 5
Ḥajā'id, Wādī al, *wadi* 100 E 2
Ḥajar al Gharbī, Al, *reg.* 88 F 5
Ḥajar ash Sharqī, Al, *reg.* 88 F 5
Hajdúböszörmény 64 D 3
Hajdunánás 64 D 3
Hajdúszoboszló 64 D 3
Hajiki-saki, *cape* 80 D 3
Hajo-do, *island* 76 H 5
Hakansson, Mts., *mts.* 104 A 5
Hakelhuincul, Altiplanicie de, *plateau* 136 B 3
Hakkâri 88 C 2
Hakken-san, *mountain* 80 C 4
Hakkoda-yama, *mountain* 80 E 2
Hakodate 67 J 3
Hakos Mts., *mountains* 101 C 3
Haku-san, *mountains* 80 D 3
Halab 88 D 2
Halabja 65 F 7
Halaib 88 B 5
Halberstadt 58 D 3
Halcon, Mt., *mountain* 81 D 5
Halden 51 N 5
Hale, Mt., *mountain* 146 C 5
Haleb 29 L 5
Halesworth 43 J 2
Haliburton Highlands, *mountains* 115 K 4
Halicarnassus 63 E 5
Halifax, *Canada* 106 G 3
Halifax, *England* 39 F 5
Halifax Bay, *bay* 147 J 3
Halifax, Mt., *mountain* 147 J 3
Halkett, C., *cape* 106 C 2
Halkirk 46 E 3
Hall 59 C 4
Halland, *province* 51 O 6
Halle, *Belgium* 56 C 4
Halle, *Fed. Rep. of Germany* 28 H 3
Hallein 59 E 5
Hallen 50 O 3
Hallett, C., *cape* 23 L 2
Halley Bay, *scientific base* 23 A 2
Hallingdalselv, *river* 51 M 4
Hällnäs 50 Q 3
Hall Pena, *peninsula* 106 G 2
Hallsberg 51 P 5
Halls Creek 146 E 3
Hallwilersee, *lake* 57 D 2
Halmahera, *island* 67 H 5
Halmahera Sea 85 D 5
Halmstad 34 G 3
Halsa 50 M 3
Hälsingborg 34 G 3
Halstead 43 H 3
Halstow Marshes, *marsh* 41 F 3
Haltenbanken, *sea feature* 34 G 2
Haltern 56 F 3
Haltwhistle 45 F 3
Halwān, see *Hulwān* 100 C 3
Hamad, El, *region* 29 L 6
Hamada de Tinrhert, *desert* 36 C 4
Hamada du Dra, *desert* 90 C 3
Hamada du Guir, *desert* 98 C 2
Hamada el Haricha, *desert* 98 C 3
Ḥamādah al Ḥamrā', Al, *region* 98 E 3
Hamadān 66 D 4
Hamada Tounassine, *desert* 28 F 6
Hamāh 66 C 4
Hamamatsu, *region* 67 H 4
Hamana-ko, *lake* 80 D 4
Hamar 51 N 4
Hamarøy 50 P 2
Ḥamāṭa, J., *mountains* 88 B 5
Hamble, *river* 41 B 4
Hambledon 41 B 4
Hambleton Hills, *mts.* 45 G 3
Hamborn 56 E 3
Hamburg 28 H 3
Häme, *county* 50 S 4
Hämeenlinna 51 S 4
Hamelin Pool 152 A 3
Hamelin Pool, *gulf* 152 A 3
Hameln 58 C 2
Hamersley Ra., *mts.* 140 B 4
Hamhung 75 P 5
Ha-mi 75 M 5
Hamilton, *Australia* 147 H 7
Hamilton, *Bermuda* 123 G 1
Hamilton, *Canada* 106 G 3
Hamilton, *New Zealand* 150 F 3
Hamilton, *Scotland* 38 D 4
Hamilton, *U.S.A., Montana* 120 D 2
Hamilton, *U.S.A., Ohio* 119 L 4
Hamilton, *river* 106 G 3
Hamilton Inlet, *inlet* 106 H 3
Hamina 51 T 4
Hamirpur 86 D 3
Hamm 36 C 1
Hammam bou Hadjar 53 E 5
Hammamet 61 C 6
Hammami, *region* 98 B 3
Hammerdal 50 P 3
Hammerfest 50 R 1
Hammond 119 K 3
Hampden 151 D 7
Hampden Park 41 E 4
Hampshire, *county* 43 F 3
Hampshire Downs, *hills* 41 B 3
Hampstead 41 D 2
Hampton Tableland, *plateau* 146 E 6
Hamra 51 P 4
Hamrånge 51 P 4
Hamrīn, Jabal, *mountains* 88 C 2
Ham Street 43 H 3
Hāmūn-e Jaz Mūrīān, *lake* 88 F 4
Hamun-i Mashkel, *seasonal lake* 86 B 3
Han, *civilisation* 159
Hanam Plateau, *plateau* 102 C 5
Hanang, *mountain* 104 C 4
Hanau 58 C 3
Han Chiang, *river* 79 H 2
Handcross 41 D 3
Handeni 104 D 4
Hanford 120 C 4
Hangang, *river* 76 H 4
Hangayn Nurū, *mts.* 66 F 3
Hang-chou Wan, *bay* 79 K 2
Hang-chow 67 H 4
Hanish, J., *island* 99 H 4
Haniyah, Al, *region* 88 D 4
Hanko 34 H 2
Han-k'ou 77 E 5
Hanley 39 E 5
Hanmer 151 E 6
Hann, Mt., *mountain* 147 E 3
Hann Ra., *mountains* 147 F 4
Hannibal 119 J 4
Hannover 28 H 3
Hann Uula, *mountains* 76 D 3
Hanöbukten 34 G 3
Hanoi 67 G 4
Hanover 116 D 2
Han-tan 75 O 6
Han-yang 77 E 5
Hao Binh 82 D 4
Haogoundou, L., *lake* 98 C 4
Hao-pi-chi 76 E 4
Hao-wang Chiao, *bay* 77 F 7
Haparanda 50 S 3
Hapur 86 D 3
Hara Nariin Uula, *mts.* 76 D 3
Harana, Sa., *mountain* 52 D 4
Hara Nuur, *lake* 76 B 4
Harappa, *ancient site* 158
Harar 103 F 2
Harar, *province* 104 E 1
Hara Usa Nūr, *lake* 75 M 5
Harb, J., *lake* 100 G 5
Harbin, see *Ha-erh-pin* 76 H 2
Harboi Hills, *mountains* 86 C 3
Harburg 58 C 2
Harcuvar Mts., *mountains* 120 D 5
Hardangerfj., *fjord* 28 G 2
Harderwijk 56 D 2
Hardey, *river* 152 B 2
Hardt, *mountains* 58 B 4
Hardwar 86 D 3
Hardy 53 F 5
Harfleur 54 E 3
Hargeisa 90 H 5
Hari, *river* 84 B 4
Haringvliet, *estuary* 56 C 3
Harīrūd, *river* 78 D 2
Harlech 39 D 5
Harleston 43 J 2
Harlingen, *Netherlands* 56 D 1
Harlingen, *U.S.A.* 118 H 6
Harlinger Land, *province* 56 F 1
Harlow 43 H 3
Harmerhill 42 E 2
Harney Basin, *region* 106 D 3
Harney Pk., *mountain* 106 E 3
Härnösand 34 H 2
Haro 52 D 1
Harpenden 41 D 2
Harper, Mt., *mountain* 114 C 2
Ḥarrat al 'Uwayrid, *lava beds* 29 L 6
Ḥarrat Khaybar, *lava beds* 88 B 4
Harray, L. of, *lake* 46 E 2
Harricanaw, *river* 119 M 1
Harris, *island* 38 C 3
Harris Mts., *mountains* 151 C 7
Harris, Sd. of, *inlet* 38 C 3
Harrisburg 119 M 3
Harrismith 102 D 5
Harrison, C., *cape* 115 M 3
Harrison Bay, *bay* 114 B 1
Harrogate 39 F 5
Harrow 43 G 3
Hartfeld, *region* 59 D 4
Hart Fell, *mountain* 47 E 6
Hartford 119 N 3
Hartland 42 C 4
Hartland Pt., *cape* 39 D 6
Hartlepool 44 G 3
Hartley 101 F 2
Harts Ra., *mountains* 146 F 4
Haruj al Aswad, J., *mts.* 98 E 3
Harvey 146 C 6
Harwell 41 B 2
Harwich 28 G 3
Harwich Harbour, *harbour* 41 G 2
Harz, *mountains* 28 H 3
Hasa, Al, *region* 29 N 6
Hasa, W. el, *wadi* 89 B 3
Hase, *river* 58 B 2
Håsjö 50 P 3
Haslemere 43 G 3
Haslingden 45 F 4
Hassan 87 D 5
Hasselt 56 D 4
Hassenmatt, *mountain* 57 C 2
Hässleholm 51 O 6
Hassocks 41 D 4
Hastings, *England* 39 G 6
Hastings, *New Zealand* 150 G 4
Hastings Ra., *mountains* 140 E 5
Hatfield 43 G 3
Hatherleigh 42 C 4
Hathras 86 D 3
Ha Tien 83 D 7
Ha Tinh 77 D 8
Hatteras, C., *cape* 106 G 4
Hattiesburg 119 K 5
Hattras Pass., *channel* 83 B 6
Haud, *region* 90 H 5
Haugesund 34 F 2
Hauhungaroa Ra., *mts.* 150 F 4
Haukivesi, *lake* 50 T 4
Hauraki Gulf, *gulf* 150 F 3
Hauroko, L., *lake* 151 B 7
Hausruck, *mountains* 59 E 4
Haut Atlas, *mountains* 90 C 2
Haut-Congo, *province* 104 A 2
Haute Joux, *region* 57 B 3
Hauteluce 57 B 4
Hautes Fagnes, *region* 56 D 4
Hauts Plateaux, *mts.* 90 C 2
Havant 43 G 4
Havasu Lake, *lake* 120 D 5
Havel, *river* 58 E 2
Havelberg 58 E 2
Havelock I., *island* 83 A 7
Havelock North 150 G 4
Haverfordwest 39 D 6
Haverhill, *England* 43 H 2
Haverhill, *U.S.A.* 117 F 3
Havero 50 P 4
Havre 118 F 2
Havre Aubert 115 L 4
Havre Tr., *sea feature* 141 H 5
Havsa 62 E 3
Hawaii, *state* 137 C 2
Hawaiian Islands, *island group* 137 C 2
Hawaiian Ridge, *sea feature* 137 C 2
Hawarden 42 D 1
Hawashīyah, Wādī, *wadi* 100 D 4
Hawea, Lake, *lake* 151 C 7
Hawera 150 F 4
Hawes 45 F 3
Hawes Water, *lake* 44 F 3
Hawick 38 E 4
Hawk Chan., *channel* 121 D 5
Hawke Bay, *bay* 150 G 4
Hawke, C., *cape* 141 F 5
Hawker 149 B 5
Hawkes Bay, *county* 150 G 4
Hawkesbury 117 E 2
Hawkesbury R., *river* 149 E 5
Hawkhurst 41 F 3
Hawksbill Cay, *reef* 121 E 5
Hawr al Ḥammar, *lake* 29 M 6
Ḥawṭah, Al, *region* 88 D 5
Hawthorne 120 C 4
Hay 149 C 5
Hay, *Australia, river* 146 G 4
Hay, *Canada, river* 114 F 3
Hayes Halvø, *region* 106 G 2
Hayes, Mt., *mountain* 114 C 2
Hayling I., *island* 43 G 4
Hayman I., *island* 148 D 3
Hay-on-Wye 42 D 2
Hayrabolu 62 E 3
Hayrabolu, *river* 62 E 3
Hay River 106 E 2
Haywards Heath 43 G 4
Hazarajat, *region* 86 B 2
Hazaribagh 86 E 4
Hazaribagh Ra., *mountains* 86 E 4
Hazār Masjed, Kūh-e, *mt.* 86 B 2
Hazebrouck 54 F 2
Hazeva 89 B 4
Hazīm, Al, *region* 100 F 3
Hazleton 114 E 3
Hazuur 101 C 4
Headcorn 41 F 3
Headley 41 C 3
Headlong Pk., *mountain* 151 C 7
Heads, The, *cape* 120 A 3
Healdsburg 120 B 4
Healesville 149 D 6
Heanor 45 G 4
Heard I., *island* 19 G 5
Hearst 116 C 1
Heath End 41 B 3
Heathfield 41 E 4
Heath Pt., *cape* 115 L 4
Heathrow 41 D 3
Hebrides, *island group* 78 B 4
Hebrides, Sea of the 38 C 3
Hebron, *Canada* 115 L 3
Hebron, *Jordan* 89 B 3
Heby 51 P 5
Hecate Str., *strait* 106 D 3
Heceta Hd., *cape* 120 A 2
Hector, *mountain* 150 F 5
Hede 50 O 4
Hedemora 51 P 4
Hedmark, *region* 34 G 2
Heerenveen 56 D 2
Heerlen 56 D 4
Heidan, *river* 89 B 3
Heidelberg, *Germany* 59 C 4
Heidelberg, *Rep. of S. Africa* 101 F 4
Heidenheim 59 D 4
Heilbron 102 D 5
Heilbronn 59 C 4
Heiligenhafen 58 D 1
Heilungkiang, *province* 76 H 2
Heing-hua Wan, *bay* 77 F 6
Heinze Bay, *bay* 83 B 6
Heinze Is., *island group* 83 B 6
Heitō 79 K 3
Hekuru-jima, *island* 80 D 3
Helena 106 E 3
Helen Island, *island* 85 E 3
Helensburgh 47 D 5
Helensville 150 F 3
Helgeland, *region* 34 G 2
Helgoland, *island* 34 F 3
Heliopolis, see *Miṣr al Jadīdah* 100 C 2
Hellín 52 E 3
Hell-Ville 91 H 7
Hellweg, *province* 56 F 3
Helmand, *river* 66 E 4
Helmond 56 D 3
Helmsdale 46 E 3
Helmsdale, *river* 46 E 3
Helmsley 44 G 3
Helmstedt 58 D 2
Helpman 56 E 1
Helsingør 34 G 3
Helsinki 28 K 2
Helston 42 B 4
Helvellyn, *mountain* 39 E 4
Helvick Hd., *cape* 39 C 5
Hemel Hempstead 43 G 3
Hemet, H., *mountain* 100 F 2
Hen & Chickens Is., *island group* 150 F 2
Henderson, *U.S.A., Kentucky* 121 C 2
Henderson, *U.S.A., Nevada* 120 D 4
Henderson, *U.S.A., N. Carolina* 121 E 2
Hendon 43 G 3
Henfield 41 D 4
Hengelo 56 E 2
Heng-hsien 79 H 3
Heng Shan, *mountains* 79 J 2
Heng-yang 67 G 4
Hénin-Lietard 56 A 4
Henley on Thames 43 G 3
Henlopen, C., *cape* 121 F 2
Hennebont 54 C 4
Henri d'Orleans Mts., *mountains* 86 E 2
Henrietta Maria, C., *cape* 115 J 3
Henry, C., *cape* 119 M 4
Henshaw Lake, *lake* 120 C 5
Henteyn Nurū, *mountains* 66 G 3
Henzada 66 F 5
Héradhsflói, *bay* 50 E 3
Herat 66 E 4
Hérault, *river* 55 F 6
Herbert, see *Georgina* 148 B 3
Herberton 148 D 2
Hercegnovi 60 G 3
Heredia 123 E 4
Hereford, *England* 39 E 5
Hereford, *U.S.A.* 118 G 5
Hereford, *county* 42 E 2
Herencia 52 D 3
Hérens, Val d', *valley* 57 C 3
Herentals 56 C 3
Herford 58 C 2
Héricourt 57 B 2
Herisau 57 E 2
Herm, *island* 39 E 7
Herma Ness, *cape* 38 F 1
Hermanus 91 E 9
Hermit Is., *island group* 85 F 4
Hermon, Mt., see *J. esh Sheikh* 89 B 1
Hermosa, Punta, *cape* 134 B 3
Hermosillo 122 B 2
Herne 58 B 3
Herne Bay 43 J 3
Herning 51 M 6
Heron, L., *lake* 151 D 6
Herowābād 88 D 2
Herrera 52 C 4
Herrera, *mountain* 53 E 2
Herrera del Duque 52 C 3
Herrera de P. 52 C 1
Hers, *river* 53 F 1
Herschel 101 E 5
Hersfeld 58 C 3
Herstmonceux 41 E 4
Hertford 39 F 6
Hertford, *county* 43 G 3
's-Hertogenbosch 56 D 3
Hervas 52 C 2
Herve, *region* 56 D 4
Hervey B., *bay* 147 K 5
Hervey Ra., *mountains* 148 D 2
Herzberg 58 E 3
Herzliya 89 A 2
Hesbaye, *region* 56 D 4
Hessen, *länder* 58 C 3
Hesteyri 50 B 2
Heston & Isleworth 41 D 3
Hetton-le-Hole 45 G 3
Hève, C. de la, *cape* 54 E 3
Hever 41 E 3
Hexham 39 E 4
Heysham 44 F 3
Heywood 45 F 4
Ḥibāk, Al, *region* 88 E 6
Hibata, *region* 88 C 6
Hibernia Reef, *reef* 146 D 2
Hickory 121 D 3
Hidaka samm., *mountains* 80 E 2
Hidalgo de Parral 122 C 2
Hiddensee, *island* 58 E 1
Hierro, *island* 98 B 3
High Desert, *desert* 120 B 3
Highdown Hill, *hill* 41 D 4
High Point 121 E 3
High Prairie 114 F 3
High River 114 F 3
High Wycombe 39 F 6
Higuera la Real 52 B 3
Hiiumaa, *island* 28 J 2
Hij, B. el, *lake* 89 C 1
Híjar 53 E 2
Hijaz 29 L 6
Ḥijāz, Al, *province* 88 B 4
Ḥijāz, Al, *region* 88 C 6
Hikone 80 D 4
Hikurangi 150 F 2
Hikurangi, *mountain* 150 H 3
Hilāl, J., *mountain* 100 E 2
Hildesheim 58 C 2
Hilgard Deep, *sea feature* 137 C 3
Hillerød 51 O 6
Hillsboro 118 H 5
Hilton Head I., *island* 121 D 3
Hilversum 56 D 2
Himalaya, *mountains* 66 F 4
Himalchuli, *mountain* 86 E 3
Himeji 67 H 4
Himmelbg., *mountain* 51 N 6
Ḥims 37 G 3
Himugaan 81 E 6
Hinatuan 81 G 7
Hinchinbrook I., *island* 147 J 3
Hinckley 43 F 2
Hindhead 41 C 3
Hindmarsh, L., *lake* 147 H 7
Hindol 87 E 4
Hindu Kush, *mountains* 66 E 4
Hindupur 87 D 5
Hinganghat 87 D 4
Hinnøy, *island* 34 G 1
Hinojosa del Duque 52 C 3
Ḥiqf, Al, *region* 88 F 5
Hirabit D., *mountain* 29 M 5
Hirado-sh., *island* 80 B 4
Hirakimata, *mountain* 150 F 3
Hirakud Res., *reservoir* 78 F 3

Ingalls, Mt., *mountain* 120 B 4
Ingatestone 41 E 2
Ingham 147 J 3
Ingleborough, *mountain* 39 E 4
Inglewood 150 F 4
Inglewood Forest, *region* 44 E 3
Ingolstadt 59 D 4
Ingrid Cristensen Coast, *region* 23 F 2
Inhaca, Pena., *peninsula* 101 G 4
Inhambane 91 G 8
Inhambane, *province* 101 G 3
Inharrime 101 G 4
I-ning 66 F 3
Inírida, *river* 132 C 2
Inishark, *island* 48 A 3
Inishbofin, *island* 39 A 5
Inishcrone 48 G 1
Inisheer, *island* 49 B 3
Inishkea, *island* 48 A 2
Inishmaan, *island* 48 B 3
Inishmore, *island* 48 B 3
Inishmurray, *island* 48 C 2
Inishowen, *region* 48 D 1
Inishowen Hd., *cape* 48 E 1
Inishtrahull, *island* 48 D 1
Inishtrahull Sd., *inlet* 38 C 4
Inishturk, *island* 39 A 5
Injune 149 D 4
Inkermann 53 F 5
Inland Kaikoura Ra., *mountains* 151 E 6
Inn, *river* 28 H 4
Innerleithen 47 E 6
Inner Mongolia, *region* 66 G 3
Inner Mongolian Aut. Region, *province* 76 C 3
Inner Sd., *inlet* 38 D 3
Innherad, *region* 34 G 2
Innisfail 147 J 3
Innsbruck 36 D 2
Inn Tal, *valley* 57 F 2
Inny, *river* 48 D 3
Inongo 90 E 6
Inowrocław 64 C 2
Inscription, Cape, *cape* 152 A 3
Insein 83 B 5
Interlaken 57 C 3
International Falls 114 H 4
Interview I., *island* 87 F 5
Inubō-saki, *cape* 80 E 4
Inveraray 47 C 5
Inverbervie 46 F 5
Invercargill 141 G 6
Inverell 147 K 5
Invergordon 46 D 4
Inverleigh 148 C 2
Inverness 38 D 3
Inverness, *county* 46 D 4
Inverurie 38 E 3
Investigator Chan., *channel* 83 B 6
Investigator Group, *island group* 146 F 6
Investigator Shoal, *sea feature* 67 G 5
Investigator Str., *strait* 140 D 5
Inyangani, *mountain* 91 G 7
Inyo Mts., *mountains* 118 D 4
Ioánnina 37 E 3
Ioanninon, L., *lake* 62 B 4
Ioma 85 F 4
Iona, *island* 38 C 3
Ionian Sea 28 J 5
Iónioi Nísoi, *island group* 28 J 5
Iony, O., *island* 75 R 4
Íos, *island* 63 D 5
Iowa, *state* 119 H 3
Ipil 81 E 8
I-pin 79 H 3
Ípiros, *region* 62 B 4
Ipoh 66 G 5
Ipsala 62 E 3
Ipswich, *Australia* 147 K 5
Ipswich, *England* 34 F 3
Iquique 126 B 5
Iquitos 126 B 3
Iráklia, *island* 63 D 5
Iráklion 37 F 3
Iran 66 D 4
Iran Geb., *mountains* 79 J 5
Irapuato 122 C 2
Iraq 66 D 4
Iraylovgrad 62 E 3
Irbid 89 B 2
Ireland, Republic of 39 B 5
Irharhar, *river* 98 D 3
Irharharene, *region* 98 D 3
Irī D., *mountain* 88 D 2
Iriga 81 E 5
Iringa 91 G 6
Iriomote-jima, *island* 77 G 7
Iriri, *river* 133 D 3
Irish Sea 28 F 3
Irkutsk 66 G 3
Iroise, *bay* 54 B 3
Ironbridge 43 E 2
Iron Canyon Res., *reservoir* 120 B 3
Iron Gate, *gorge* 37 E 2
Iron Knob 149 B 5
Iron Mountain 116 B 2
Iron Mts., *mountains* 39 C 4
Ironton 121 D 2
Ironwood 119 J 2
Irō-saki, *cape* 80 D 4
Irosin 79 K 4
Irrawaddy, *river* 66 F 4
Irrawaddy, Mouths of the, *river mouths* 66 F 5
Irrigi, *region* 90 C 4
Irta, Sa. de, *mountains* 53 F 2
Irthing, *river* 45 F 3
Irtysh, *river* 66 E 3
Irumu 104 B 2
Irún 52 E 1
Irvine 47 D 6
Irvine, *river* 47 D 6
Irvinestown 48 D 2
Isaac, *river* 140 E 4
Isabelia, Cord., *mts.* 123 E 3
Isabella Res., *reservoir* 120 C 5
Ísafjardhardjúp, *gulf* 50 B 2
Ísafjördhur 34 C 1
Isā, Ra's, *cape* 88 C 6
Isar, *river* 59 D 5
Ischia, *island* 36 D 3
Iscia Baidoa 99 H 5
Ise 80 D 4
Ise Fj., *fjord* 51 N 6
Iselin Bank, *sea feature* 23 M 2
Iseo 57 F 4
Iseo, L. d', *lake* 60 C 2
Isère, *river* 55 G 5
Iserlohn 58 B 3
Isernia 60 E 4
Iseyin 102 B 2
Isezaki 80 D 3
I-shan 82 E 3
Ishigaki-shima, *island* 77 G 7
Ishikari, *river* 80 E 2
Ishikari-wan, *bay* 80 E 2
Ishim 74 J 4
Ishim, *river* 74 J 4
Ishimbay 65 H 3
Ishimskaya Step', *steppe* 66 E 3
Ishinomaki 80 E 3
Ishinomaki wan, *bay* 80 E 3
Ishizuchi-zan, *mountain* 80 C 4
Isipingo Beach 101 F 5
Isis, *see Thames* 41 A 2
Isisford 148 C 3
Iskandil Br., *cape* 63 E 5
İskenderun 37 G 3
İskenderun Körfezi 65 C 7
Iskŭr, *river* 62 D 2
Isla, *river* 46 E 5
Islamabad 66 E 4
Island Lagoon, *lake* 146 G 6
Island L., *lake* 106 F 3
Island Magee, *region* 48 F 2
Island Park Res., *reservoir* 120 E 2
Island Pt., *cape* 152 B 4
Islands, Bay of, *bay* 150 F 2
Islay 44 B 2
Islay, *island* 38 C 4
Isle, *river* 55 E 5
I. of Grain, *region* 41 F 3
I. of Harty, *region* 41 F 3
I. of Oxney, *region* 41 F 3
I. of Thanet, *region* 39 G 6
Isle Verte 117 G 2
Islip 41 B 2
Isoka 104 C 5
Isosyöte, *mountain* 50 T 3
Iso-wan, *bay* 80 D 4
Isparta 37 F 3
Isperikh 62 E 2
Israel 66 C 4
Israelite Bay, *bay* 146 D 6
Isser 53 G 4
Issoire 55 F 5
Issoudun 55 E 4
Issyk-Kul', Oz., *lake* 66 E 3
İstanbul 28 K 5
Istiaía 62 C 4
Istra, *peninsula* 28 H 4
Istranca Dağlari, *mts.* 28 K 5
Itabuna 133 F 4
Itajaí 136 D 1
Itajubá 135 D 2
Italy 28 H 4
Itambé, P. de, *mountain* 135 D 1
Itapetininga 135 D 2
Itapeva 135 D 2
Itaqui 135 C 2
Itasy, L., *lake* 105 C 3
Itbayat I., *island* 81 D 1
Itchen 43 F 4
Itchen, *river* 43 F 4
Itéa 62 C 4
Ithaca 116 E 3
Itháki, *island* 63 B 4
Ithrīyat, Jebel, *mountains* 89 C 3
Iton, *river* 54 E 3
Iṭṣā 100 B 3
Itu, *Brazil* 135 D 2
I-tu, *China* 76 F 4
Ituri, *river* 104 A 2
Iturup, O., *island* 75 R 5
Ityāy al Bārūd 100 B 2
Itzehoe 58 C 2
Iul'tin 75 V 3
Ivakoany, Massif de l', *mountains* 105 C 4
Ivalo, *river* 50 S 2
Ivanhoe 149 C 5
Ivano-Frankovsk 37 F 2
Ivanovo 29 M 3
Ivdel' 66 D 2
Ivi, C., *cape* 53 F 4
Ivigtut 115 N 2
Ivory Coast 90 C 5
Ivory Coast, *region* 90 C 5
Ivrea 60 A 2
Ivybridge 42 D 4
Iwaki san, *mountain* 80 E 2
Iwakuni 80 C 4
Iwanai 80 E 2
Iwate y., *mountain* 48 D 3
Iwo 90 D 5
Iwo Jima, *island* 67 J 4
Ixworth 43 H 2
I-yang 79 J 3
Iyo-nada, *bay* 80 C 4
Izabal, L. de, *lake* 122 E 3
Izegem 56 B 4
Izhevsk 29 N 3
Izhma, *river* 29 N 2
Izmail 64 F 4
İzmir 28 K 5
İzmir Boz Sira Dağlari, *mountains* 63 E 4
İzmir Körfezi, *bay* 63 E 4
İzmit 37 F 3
İzmit Körfezi, *bay* 62 F 3
İznik G., *lake* 37 F 3
Izra' 89 C 2
Izúcar de Matamoros 122 D 3
Izu Hantō, *peninsula* 80 D 4
Izumo 80 C 4
Izu shichi tō, *island* 80 D 4

Jabal Bārez, Kūh-e, *mt.* 88 F 4
Jabalí, Punta, *cape* 134 B 5
Jabalpur 66 E 4
Jablanica, *mountain* 62 B 3
Jablonec 58 F 3
Jaboatão 133 F 3
Jaboticabal 135 D 2
Jabrīn, *region* 29 N 7
Jaca 53 E 1
Jáchymov 58 E 3
Jacks Mt., *mountain* 116 E 3
Jackson, *U.S.A., California* 120 B 4
Jackson, *U.S.A., Michigan* 116 C 3
Jackson, *U.S.A., Mississippi* 119 J 5
Jackson, *U.S.A., Tennessee* 119 K 4
Jackson, C., *cape* 150 F 5
Jackson Hd., *cape* 151 C 6
Jackson Prairie, *region* 106 F 4
Jacksonville, *U.S.A., Florida* 106 F 4
Jacksonville, *U.S.A., Illinois* 121 B 2
Jacksonville, *U.S.A., Texas* 119 H 5
Jacmel 123 F 3
Jacobabad 78 D 3
Jacques Cartier, Mt., *mt.* 117 H 1
Jaddat al Juwayfah, *region* 88 D 5
Jade B., *bay* 58 C 2
Jadotville 91 F 7
Jadraque 52 D 2
Jaeggeyarre, *mountain* 50 Q 1
Jaén 36 B 3
Jaffa, *see Tel Avīv-Yāfo* 89 A 2
Jaffa, C., *cape* 147 G 7
Jaffna 78 F 5
Jāfūrah, Al, *region* 88 E 5
Jagdalpur 87 E 4
Jagersfontein 102 D 5
Jahrom 78 C 3
Jaipur 66 E 4
Jajce 60 F 2
Jakupica, *mountain* 62 B 3
Jaladah, Al, *region* 88 D 6
Jalālah al Baḥrīyah, Jabal, *mountain* 100 C 3
Jalālat al Qiblīyah, Jabal al, *mountain* 100 D 4
Ja'lan, *region* 88 F 5
Jalapa 122 D 3
Jaldessa 88 C 8
Jalgaon 86 D 4
Jallas, Pais del, *region* 52 A 1
Jalna 87 D 4
Jalpaiguri 86 E 3
Jamaica 107 G 5
Jamaica Chan., *channel* 123 F 3
Jamalpur 86 E 3
Jambongan, *island* 81 B 8
Jamdena, *island* 85 E 4
James, *U.S.A., S. Dakota, river* 118 H 2
James, *U.S.A., Virginia, river* 119 M 4
James Bay, *bay* 106 F 3
James Ra., *mountains* 146 F 4
James Ross I., *island* 23 S 2
James Ross Str., *strait* 114 H 2
Jamestown, *Australia* 147 G 6
Jamestown, *U.S.A., New York* 119 M 3
Jamestown, *U.S.A., N. Dakota* 118 H 2
Jamkhandi 87 D 4
Jammu 66 E 4
Jammu & Kashmir 66 E 4
Jamnagar 66 E 4
Jamshedpur 66 F 4
Jämtland, *county* 50 O 3
Janaucú, I., *island* 133 D 2
Janda, L. de la, *lake* 52 C 4
Jandowae 149 E 4
Jane Pk., *mountain* 151 C 7
Janesville 116 B 3
Janjira 87 C 4
Jan Kemp 101 E 4
Jan Mayen, *island* 28 E 1
Jao-p'ing 77 F 7
Jaora 86 D 4
Januária 133 E 4
Japan 67 H 4
Japan, Sea of 67 H 3
Japan Trench, *sea feature* 67 J 4
Japen, *island* 85 E 4
Japurá, *river* 126 C 3
Japyo Mt., *mountain* 86 F 3
Jara, La, *region* 52 C 3
Jaraiz 52 C 2
Jarandilla 52 C 2
Jarash 89 B 2
Jardines de la Reina, *island group* 123 F 2
Jari, *river* 126 D 3
Jaro 81 E 6
Jaroměř 58 F 3
Jaroslaw 64 D 2
Jarrow 45 G 3
Jashpurnagar 86 E 4
Jāsk 78 C 3
Jason Pena., *peninsula* 23 S 2
Jasper 114 F 3
Jastrebac, *mountain* 62 B 2
Jastrebarsko 60 E 2
Jastrowie 58 G 2
Jászberény 64 C 3
Jath 87 D 4
Játiva 52 E 3
Jaú 135 D 2
Jaunpass, *pass* 57 C 3
Jaunpur 78 F 3
Java, *see Djawa* 144 A 2
Javadi Hills, *mountains* 87 D 5
Javalambre, *mountain* 53 E 2
Javalon, *mountain* 53 E 2
Java Ridge, *sea feature* 153 E 3
Java Sea 67 G 6
Java Trough, *sea feature* 153 E 3
Jávea 53 F 3
Javor 64 C 4
Jawhar, *mountain* 87 C 4
Jawneegavia 152 B 2
Jazīrah, Al, *region* 29 M 5
Jebba 52 C 5
Jebel, B. el, *river* 94 F 5
Jech Doab, *interfluve* 86 C 3
Jeci, *mountain* 91 G 7
Jedburgh 47 F 6
Jefferson City 119 J 4
Jefferson, Mt., *U.S.A., Nevada, mountain* 120 C 4
Jefferson, Mt., *U.S.A., Oregon, mountain* 120 B 2
Jeffreys Deep, *sea feature* 155 H 4
Jef Lio 85 E 4
Jelenia Góra 58 F 3
Jena 58 D 3
Jenin 89 B 2
Jequié 133 E 4
Jequitinhonha, *river* 126 E 4
Jeremie 123 F 3
Jerez de la Frontera 52 B 4
Jerez de los Caballeros 52 B 3
Jericho 89 B 3
Jerilderie 149 D 6
Jerome, *U.S.A., Arizona* 120 D 5
Jerome, *U.S.A., Idaho* 120 D 3
Jersey, *island* 39 E 7
Jersey City 106 G 3
Jerusalem, *Israel* 29 L 6
Jerusalem, *Jordan* 89 B 3
Jervis Bay, *bay* 147 K 7
Jervois Ra., *mountains* 146 G 4
Jeseníky, *mountain* 58 G 3
Jessamine Creek Res., *reservoir* 121 D 2
Jesselton 67 G 5
Jezzīn 89 B 1
Jhang Maghiana 78 E 2
Jhansi 78 E 3
Jhelum 86 C 2
Jhelum, *river* 86 C 2
Jibhalanta 66 F 3
Jicarón, Isla, *island* 134 B 3
Jičín 58 F 3
Jidd, Al, *region* 88 C 5
Jiddah 66 C 4
Jiddat al Ḥarāsīs, *region* 88 F 6
Jiddī, Jabal al, *mountain* 100 E 2
Jihlava 36 D 2
Jijiga 88 C 8
Jijona 52 E 3
Jilayjīlīh, Jaz., *island* 100 G 5
Jilh, Al, *mountain* 88 C 4
Jiloca, *river* 53 E 2
Jimma 90 G 5
Jim Woodruff Res., *reservoir* 121 C 4
Jindřichův Hradec 59 F 4
Jinja 90 G 5
Jirgalanta 66 F 3
Jitarning 152 B 4
Jiu, *river* 62 C 2
Jiwā', Al, *region* 78 C 3
Jizera, *river* 58 F 3
Joanna Res., *reservoir* 121 B 2
João Pessoa 126 F 3
Jódar 52 D 4
Jodhpur 78 E 3
Joensuu 50 T 4
Jogjakarta 67 G 6
Johannesburg 90 F 8
John Day, *river* 120 B 2
John H. Kerr Res., *reservoir* 121 E 2
Johnson City 121 D 2
Johnstone 47 D 6
John o'Groats 46 E 3
Johore Bahru 67 G 5
Joigny 54 F 4
Joinville 136 D 1
Joinville I., *island* 23 S 2
Jokkmokk 34 H 2
Jökulsá á Fjöllum, *river* 50 D 3
Joliet 119 K 3
Jolo 79 K 5
Jolo I., *island* 81 D 9
Joma, *mountain* 86 F 2
Jones Bank, *sea feature* 39 B 7
Jonesboro 121 B 3
Jones, C., *cape* 106 G 3
Jones Mts., *mountains* 23 Q 2
Jönköping 34 G 3
Jönköping, *county* 51 O 5
Jonquière 117 F 1
Jonzac 55 D 5
Joplin 119 J 4
Jordan 29 L 6
Jordan, *river* 37 G 4
Jordan-Dead Sea Rift, *rift* 155 F 3
Jorhat 79 G 3
Jos 90 D 5
Jose Pañganiban 81 E 4
Joseph Bonaparte Gulf, *gulf* 140 C 3
Joseph, L., *lake* 115 L 3
Jostedalsbre, *snowfield* 34 F 2
Jotunheimen, *mountains* 28 H 2
Joulters Cays, *reefs* 121 E 5
Joure 56 D 2
Joux, Lac de, *lake* 57 B 3
Joyces Country, *region* 48 B 3
Juan de Fuca Str., *strait* 114 E 4
Juan de Nova, *island* 103 F 4
Juan Díaz 134 D 1
Juan Fernández, Is., *island group* 137 E 3
Juárez, Sierra de, *mts.* 120 D 6
Juàzeiro 126 E 3
Juàzeiro do Norte 133 F 3
Juba 99 G 5
Jubilee L., *lake* 146 E 5
Júcar, *river* 53 E 3
Juchitán 122 D 3
Judaea, *region* 89 A 3
Judenburg 59 F 5
Judio, *mountain* 52 C 3
Jufrah, Wādī al, *wadi* 100 C 2
Jui-an 77 G 6
Juist 58 B 2
Juiz de Fora 133 E 5
Ju-kao 76 G 5
Juliaca 132 B 4
Julia Creek 148 C 3
Julianehaab 115 N 2
Jülich 54 H 2
Julierpass, *pass* 57 E 3
Julijske A., *mountains* 59 E 5
Jullundur 78 E 2
Jumat Qa'ara, *region* 88 C 3
Jumna, *see Yamuna* 86 D 3
Jumilla 52 E 3
Junagadh 86 C 4
Junagarh 87 E 4
Junaynah, Ra's al, *mt.* 100 E 3
Junaynat al 'Aṭash, *mt.* 100 C 4
Junction City 119 H 4
Jundah 148 C 3
Jundiaí 135 D 2
Juneau 106 D 3
Junee 147 J 6
Jung Chang, *river* 77 D 6
Jungfrau, *mountain* 28 G 4
Junín 136 B 2
Junnah, Jabal, *mountain* 100 F 4
Junsele 50 P 3
Junto, Mte., *mountain* 52 A 3
Juojärvi, *lake* 50 T 4
Jūr, *river* 99 F 5
Jura, *island* 38 D 4
Jura, *mountains* 28 G 4
Jura, Sound of, *inlet* 38 D 4
Juruá, *river* 126 C 3
Juruena, *river* 126 D 4
Ju Shui, *river* 77 F 6
Jüterbog 58 E 3
Juticalpa 123 E 3
Juwaya 89 B 1
Juzur Jūbāl, *island* 100 E 5
Jyekundo 76 B 5
Jylland, *region* 28 H 3
Jyväskylä 50 S 4
Južna Morava, *river* 62 B 2

K2, *mountain* 66 E 4
Kaaing Veld, *region* 101 D 5
Kaapplato, *plateau* 101 D 5
Kaarta, *region* 90 C 4
Kabajana, *island* 84 D 4
Kabale 90 F 6
Kabalo 91 F 6
Kabambare 104 A 4
Kabasalan 81 E 8
Kabatov, Mys, *cape* 50 V 3
Kabaw Valley, *valley* 82 B 4
Kabinakagami L., *lake* 116 C 1
Kabīr Kūh, *mountains* 29 M 6
Kabongo 104 A 4
Kabul 66 E 4
Kabul, *river* 86 C 2
Kabwe, L., *lake* 104 A 5
Kachin, *province* 82 B 3
Kaçkar Daği, *mountains* 29 M 5
Kadijica, *mountain* 62 C 3
Kadiköy 62 F 3
Kadina 147 G 6
Kadirga Br., *cape* 63 F 5
Kadiyevka 35 K 4
Kaduna 90 D 4
Kadusam, *mountain* 77 B 6
Kadzherom 35 N 2
Kaédi 98 B 4
Kaesŏng 76 H 4
Kafirévs, Akr., *cape* 63 D 4

Kafr ad Dawwār 100 B 1
Kafr al Zayyāt 100 B 2
Kafr ash Shaykh 100 B 1
Kafue 101 F 1
Kafue, *river* 91 F 7
Kagera, *river* 104 B 3
Kagi 77 G 7
Kagoshima 67 H 4
Kagoshima-wan, *bay* 80 B 5
Kagul 64 F 4
Kaḩalīyah, J., *mountain* 100 D 3
Kahama 104 C 3
Kahan 86 C 3
Kaharoa, *mountain* 150 G 4
Kaiapoi 151 E 6
Kaibab Plateau, *plateau* 120 D 4
Kai Besar, *island* 85 E 4
Kaieteur Falls, *falls* 126 D 2
K'ai-feng 67 G 4
Kai, Kep., *island group* 67 H 6
Kai Ketjil, *island* 85 E 4
Kaikohe 150 E 2
Kaikoura 151 E 6
Kaikoura Pena., *peninsula* 151 E 6
Kailās Range, *mountains* 66 F 4
K'ai Lu 75 P 5
Kaimai Ra., *mountains* 150 F 3
Kaimakchalan, *mountain* 63 B 3
Kaimana 85 E 4
Kaimanawa Mts., *mts.* 150 F 4
Kaimur Ra., *mountains* 78 F 3
Kainan 80 C 4
Kainchal, *mountain* 62 D 3
Kaingaroa Plains, *region* 150 G 4
Kaipara Flats, *region* 150 F 3
Kaipara Harb., *harbour* 150 F 3
Kaiparowits Plateau, *plateau* 120 E 4
Kai-p'ing 76 G 3
Kairouan 98 E 2
Kairuku 85 F 4
Kaiserslautern 59 B 4
Kaitaia 150 E 2
Kaitangata 151 C 8
Kajaani 50 T 3
Kajan, *river* 84 C 3
Kajo Kaji 104 B 2
Kakamega 99 G 5
Kakanui Mts., *mountains* 151 D 7
Kakhovskoye Vdkhr., *reservoir* 35 K 4
Kakinada 78 F 4
Kakuryu-tan, *cape* 76 H 4
Kalabakan 81 B 9
Kalach-na-Donu 37 H 2
Kaladan, *river* 82 A 4
Kalahari Basin, *region* 155 F 4
Kalahari Desert, *desert* 91 F 8
Kalajoki, *river* 50 S 3
Kalámai 37 E 3
Kalamazoo 119 K 3
Kalambáka 62 B 4
Kálamos, *island* 63 B 4
Kalannie 152 B 4
Kalaotoa, *island* 84 D 4
Kalarash 64 F 3
Kälarne 50 P 4
Kalat 86 C 3
Kalat, *province* 86 B 3
Kalávrita 62 C 4
Kaldi Dağ, *mountain* 37 G 3
Kale, *river* 47 F 6
Kalehe 104 B 3
Kalewa 82 B 4
Kalgoorlie 140 C 5
Kaliakra, N., *cape* 28 K 4
Kalimantan, *province* 79 J 6
Kálimnos, *island* 63 E 5
Kalinin 29 L 3
Kaliningrad 28 J 3
Kalinkovichi 64 F 2
Kalispell 118 E 2
Kalisz 34 H 3
Kalix älv, *river* 50 R 2
Kalkberge 58 E 2
Kalk Plateau, *plateau* 101 C 4
Kallakoopah, *river* 149 B 4
Kallavesi, *lake* 50 T 4
Kallídhromon Óri, *mts.* 63 C 4
Kallonís K., *bay* 62 E 4
Kallsjön, *lake* 50 O 3
Kalmar 34 H 3
Kalmar, *county* 51 P 5
Kalmarsund, *strait* 51 P 6
Kalocsa 60 G 1
Kalomo 101 E 2
Kalpeni I., *island* 87 C 5
Kalta Alakan Tagh, *mts.* 86 E 2
Kaluga 35 K 3
Kalundborg 51 N 6
Kalvarija 64 D 1
Kal'ya 35 N 2
Kalyan 78 E 4
Kalyazin 65 D 2
Kama, *river* 24 J 3
Kamaishi 80 E 3
Kamakura 80 D 4
Kamarān, J., *island* 90 H 4
Kambo Ho, *mountain* 76 H 3
Kamchatka, *peninsula* 67 K 3
Kamchatskiy P-ov, *peninsula* 75 T 4
Kamchiya, *river* 62 E 2
Kamenets-Podol'skiy 35 J 4
Kamenjak, Rt., *cape* 36 D 2
Kamen'-na-Obi 74 L 4
Kamennyy, M., *cape* 75 S 2
Kamensk-Shakhtinskiy 37 H 2
Kamensk-Ural'skiy 35 N 3
Kamet, *mountain* 86 D 3
Kamienna Góra 58 G 3
Kamień Pomorski 58 F 2
Kamieskroon 101 C 5
Kamja, *mountain* 63 B 3
Kamloops 114 E 3
Kamnik 59 F 5
Kamo 80 D 3
Kampala 90 G 5
Kampalili, Mt., *mountain* 81 G 8
Kampar, *river* 84 B 3
Kampen 56 D 2
Kamphaeng Phet 83 C 5
Kampolombo, L., *lake* 104 B 5
Kampot 67 G 5
Kamptee 86 D 4
Kamskoye Vdkhr., *reservoir* 66 D 2
Kamvoúnia Óri, *mts.* 62 B 4
Kamyshin 35 L 3
Kanab 120 D 4
Kanab Cr., *river* 120 D 4
Kanash 65 F 2
Kanastraíon, Ákr., *cape* 62 C 4
Kanawha, *river* 121 D 2
Kanazawa 67 H 4
Kanchanaburi 83 C 6
Kancheepuram 87 D 5
Kanchenjunga *mountain* 79 F 3
Kan Chiang, *river* 77 F 6
Kan-chou Ho, *river* 76 B 4
Kandahar 66 E 4
Kandalaksha 24 K 2
Kandalakshskaya Guba, *gulf* 35 K 1
Kandersteg 57 C 3
Kandy 66 F 5
Kane Basin, *sea feature* 24 P 2
Kanem, *civilisation* 159
Kangān 88 E 4
Kangaroo I., *island* 140 D 5
Kangaroo Pt., *cape* 148 B 2
Kangāvar 88 D 3
Kangean, Kep., *island group* 84 C 4
Kangnŭng 80 B 3
Kang-ting 77 C 5
Kangto, *mountain* 82 A 3
Kan-hsien 79 J 3
Kani 82 B 4
Kaniapiskau L., *lake* 115 K 3
Kaniere, L., *lake* 151 D 6
Kaniet Is., *island group* 85 F 4
Kanigiri sagari, *reservoir* 86 D 5
Kanin Nos, Mys, *cape* 28 M 1
Kanin, P-ov., *peninsula* 66 D 2
Kanjiža 64 D 3
Kankakee 116 B 3
Kankan 90 C 4
Kanker 78 F 3
Kano 90 D 4
Kanouri, *region* 90 E 4
Kanoya 90 B 5
Kanpur 66 F 4
Kansas, *state* 118 H 4
Kansas City, *U.S.A., Kansas* 119 J 4
Kansas City, *U.S.A., Missouri* 106 F 4
Kansk 75 M 4
Kansu, *province* 76 C 4
Kan-ting 79 H 2
Kanto san., *mountain* 80 D 3
Kanturk 49 C 4
Kanye 102 D 5
Kaoko Veld, *region* 91 E 7
Kaolack 90 B 4
Kao-lan 66 G 4
Kao-li-kung-shan, *mts.* 77 B 6
Kao Shan, *mountains* 77 D 7
Kao-yu 76 F 5
Kao-yu Hu, *lake* 76 F 5
Kapagere 85 F 4
Kapidaği Yar., *peninsula* 62 E 3
Kapiti I., *island* 150 F 5
Kaplice 59 F 4
Kapoeta 104 C 1
Kapos, *river* 60 F 1
Kaposvar 60 F 1
Kapsukas 64 D 1
Kapuas, *river* 79 J 5
Kapuas Hulu, Peg., *mt.* 84 C 3
Kapunda 149 B 5
Kapuskasing 119 L 2
Kapuskasing, *river* 116 C 1
Kaputar, *mountain* 149 E 5
Kapydzhik, G., *mountain* 88 D 2
Kara-Bogaz Gol, Zaliv, *bay* 29 N 5
Kara Br., *western Turkey, cape* 63 E 4
Kara Br., *southern Turkey, cape* 63 E 5
Karabük 37 G 3
Kara Burun Köl, *lake* 86 E 2
Karacaköy 62 F 3
Karacasu 63 F 5
Karachi 66 E 4
Karadeniz Boğazi, *strait* 28 K 5
Karaganda 29 Q 4
Karagayn Uula, *mts.* 76 B 3
Karaginskiy, O., *island* 67 K 3
Karaginskiy Zaliv, *bay* 75 T 4
Karaj 88 E 2
Karak 88 B 3
Kara Kash Darya, *river* 86 D 2
Karakelong, P., *island* 81 G 9
Karakoram Ra., *mts.* 66 E 4
Karakorum, *ancient site* 159
Karaköse 65 E 6
Karakul', Oz., *lake* 86 C 2
Kara-Kum, Peski, *region* 74 H 6
Karaman 37 G 3
Karamea Bight, *bay* 150 D 5
Karand 65 F 7
Karasjok 50 S 1
Karasuk 74 K 4
Kara Tau 74 K 5
Karatau, Khr., *mountains* 29 P 4
Karativu I., *island* 87 D 5
Karatsu 80 B 4
Kara Uzun Tali, *mts.* 86 E 1
Karávi, *island* 63 C 5
Karawanken, *mountains* 59 F 5
Karbalā' 37 H 4
Kårböle 50 O 4
Karcag 64 D 3
Kardhítsa 62 B 4
Kardiva I., *island* 87 C 6
Karelo Finnskaya S.S.R., *republic* 35 K 2
Karet, *region* 98 C 3
Kargopol' 35 K 2
Kariba Dam, *dam* 101 F 2
Kariba, L., *lake* 91 F 7
Karibib 91 E 8
Karikal 87 D 5
Karikari, C., *cape* 150 E 2
Karimata, Kep., *island group* 84 B 4
Karimata, Selat, *strait* 67 G 6
Karimganj 82 A 3
Karimnagar 87 D 4
Karimundjawa, Kep., *island group* 84 C 4
Karin 88 D 7
Karincali Daği, *mountains* 63 F 5
Karinca Tep., *mountain* 63 F 4
Karisimbi, Mt., *mountain* 99 F 6
Karkaralinsk 74 K 5
Karkar I., *island* 140 E 2
Karkas, Kūh-e, *mountain* 88 E 3
Karkheh, *river* 88 D 3
Karkinitskiy Zaliv, *bay* 37 G 2
Karkūk 65 F 7
Karla Marksa, Pik, *mt.* 86 C 2
Karlek, *mountain* 62 D 3
Karlik Tagh, *mountains* 86 F 1
Karl-Marx-Stadt 29 H 3
Karlobag 60 E 2
Karlovac 60 E 2
Karlovo 62 D 2
Karlovy Vary 58 E 3
Karlshamn 51 O 6
Karlskrona 34 G 3
Karlsøy 50 Q 1
Karlsruhe 34 G 4
Karlstad 34 G 2
Karnafuli Res., *reservoir* 86 F 4
Karnal 78 E 3
Karnobat 62 E 2
Kärnten, *province* 59 E 5
Karoefa 85 E 4
Karonga 104 C 5
Karora 88 B 6
Karow 58 E 2
Kárpathos, *island* 28 K 5
Kárpathos Strait, *strait* 63 E 6
Karpaty, *mountains* 36 E 2
Karpensión 62 B 4
Karpinsk 35 N 2
Karragullen 152 B 4
Karratsfj., *fjord* 115 M 1
Karree Berge, *mountains* 101 D 5
Karroo Shield, *plateau* 155 F 4
Kars 65 E 6
Karshi 74 J 6
Karşiyaka 63 E 4
Karskiye Vorota, *strait* 35 N 1
Karskoye More, *sea* 66 E 2
Kartal 62 F 3
Kartaly 35 N 3
Kártsino, Akr., *cape* 62 D 4
Kārūn, *river* 88 D 3
Karunki 50 S 2
Karviná 64 C 3
Karwar 87 D 5
Kasai, *river* 90 E 6
Kasama 91 G 7
Kasane 101 E 2
Kasanga 104 B 5
Kasar, Ras, *cape* 88 B 6
Kasba L., *lake* 114 G 2
Kasempa 104 A 6
Kasenga 104 B 5
Kāshān 88 E 3
Kashgar, *see Su-fu* 86 D 2
Kashiwazaki 80 D 3
Kashkūl, Al, *region* 100 E 2
Kāshmar 86 B 2
Kashmir, Vale of, *valley* 86 D 2
Kashum Tsho, *lake* 86 E 2
Kaskaskia, *river* 121 B 2
Kaskinen 50 R 4
Kas Kong, *island* 83 D 7
Kasongo 104 A 4
Kásos, *island* 63 E 6
Kásos Str., *strait* 63 E 6
Kaspiysk 37 H 2
Kas Rong 83 D 7
Kas Rong Sam Lem, *island* 83 D 7
Kassala 90 G 4
Kassándra, *peninsula* 62 C 3
Kassel 34 G 3
Kasserine 98 D 2
Kastélli 63 C 6
Kastéllion 63 D 6
Kastoria 62 B 3
Kastorías, L., *lake* 62 B 3
Kastós, *island* 63 B 4
Kástron 62 D 4
Kasulu 104 B 4
Kasumiga-ura, *lake* 80 E 3
Katahdin, Mt., *mountain* 117 G 2
Katanga-Oriental, *prov.* 104 A 5
Katanning 146 C 6
Katchall, *island* 87 F 6
Katha 82 B 3
Katherine 146 F 2
Kathiawar, *peninsula* 66 E 4
Kathīb al Makhāzin, *reg.* 100 D 2
Kathīb as Sabakh, *region* 100 E 2
Kathleen L., *lake* 116 C 2
Kathleen Valley 152 C 3
Kathrabba 89 B 3
Kati 98 C 4
Katihar 86 E 3
Katiola 98 C 5
Katmandu 66 F 4
Katoomba 147 K 6
Katowice 28 J 3
Katrīnah, J., *mountain* 90 G 3
Katrine, L., *lake* 47 D 5
Katrineholm 51 P 5
Katsina 98 D 4
Katta-Kurgan 86 C 2
Kattasang Hills, *mts.* 86 C 2
Kattaviá 63 E 6
Kattegat, *channel* 28 H 3
Kaufbeuren 57 F 2
Kaukkwe Hills, *mts.* 82 B 3
Kauliranta 50 R 2
Kaunas 34 H 3
Kaupstadhur 50 C 3
Kaura Namoda 98 D 4
Kautokeino 50 R 2
Kavadarci 62 G 3
Kavali 87 D 5
Kavålla 62 D 3
Kavaratti I., *island* 87 C 5
Kavarna 62 F 2
Kavieng 85 G 4
Kavīr, *region* 29 N 6
Kavirondo Gulf, *gulf* 104 C 3
Kawagoe 80 D 4
Kawambwa 104 B 5
Kawardha 86 D 4
Kawartha Lakes, *lakes* 116 D 2
Kawasaki 67 H 4
Kawau I., *island* 150 F 3
Kaweka Ra., *mountains* 150 G 4
Kawerau 150 G 4
Kawhia Harb., *harbour* 150 F 4
Kawi, J., *mountain* 88 F 5
Kawimbi 104 B 5
Kawio, Kep., *island group* 85 D 3
Kawkareik 83 C 5
Kawm Ḩamādah 100 B 2
Kawthoolei, *state* 82 B 5
Kayah State, *state* 82 B 5
Kayes 90 B 4
Kayseri 37 G 3
Kazakhskiy Melkosopochnik, *mts.* 66 E 3
Kazakhskiy Zaliv, *bay* 65 H 5
Kazakhstanskaya S.S.R., *republic* 35 M 4
Kazalinsk 74 J 5
Kazan' 29 N 3
Kazan, *river* 114 H 2
Kazandzhik 88 F 2
Kazanlŭk 62 D 2
Kazan Rettō, *island group* 67 J 4
Kazatin 64 F 3
Kazbek, *mountain* 29 M 4
Kaz Daği, *mountain* 62 E 4
Kāzerūn 78 C 3
Kazi Magomed 88 D 1
Kéa 63 D 5
Kéa, *island* 63 D 5
Keady 48 E 2
Kearney 118 H 3
Ke Bao, I. de, *island* 82 E 4
Kebbi, *river* 90 D 4
Kebnekaise, *mountain* 28 J 1
Kebock Hd., *cape* 46 B 3
Kecskemét 37 E 2
Kediri 79 J 6
Keele Pk., *mountain* 114 D 2
Keeper Hill, *hill* 49 C 4
Keetmanshoop 91 E 8
Keewatin 114 H 4
Keewatin, *region* 114 H 2
Kefali, K., *cape* 62 A 4
Kefallinía, *island* 37 E 3
Kefar Ata 89 B 2
Kefar Sava 89 A 2
Keflavík 50 B 3
Ke Ga, Pt. de, *cape* 83 E 7
Kegueur Tedi, *mountain* 99 E 3
Kehl 54 H 3
Kehsi Mansam 82 B 4
Keighley 45 G 4
Keitele, *lake* 50 S 3
Keith 38 E 3
Kelai, *island* 87 C 6
Kelheim 59 D 4
Kélibia 36 D 3
Kelifskiy Uzboy, *region* 29 O 5
Kelkit, *river* 29 L 5
Kellerberrin 146 C 6
Kellet, C., *cape* 106 D 2
Kellogg 120 C 2
Kells, *see Ceanannus Mór* 48 E 3
Kells Ra., *mountains* 47 D 6
Kelowna 114 F 4
Kelso, *Scotland* 47 F 6
Kelso, *U.S.A.* 120 B 2
Kelvedon 43 H 3
Kem' 50 V 3
Kemah 65 D 6
Kemaliye 65 D 6
Kemerovo 29 R 3
Kemi 50 S 3
Kemijärvi 50 T 2
Kemijärvi, *lake* 50 T 2
Kemijoki, *river* 28 K 1
Kempenland, *region* 56 C 3
Kemp Land, *region* 23 E 2
Kempsey 147 K 6
Kempt, L., *lake* 117 E 2
Kempten 57 F 2
Kemsing 41 E 3
Ken, *river* 47 D 6
Kenadsa 98 C 2
Kenai Pena., *peninsula* 106 C 3
Kendal 39 E 4
Kendall, Mt., *mountain* 150 E 5
Kendari 79 K 6
Kënet'-e-Karavastas, *lake* 62 A 3
Keng Hkam 77 B 7
Kenglön 77 B 7
Kengtung 79 G 3
Kenhardt 101 D 5
Kenilworth 43 F 2
Keningau 81 B 9
Kenitra 90 C 2
Kenko Shan, *mountains* 76 B 5
Kenmare 49 B 5
Kenmare R., *estuary* 39 B 6
Kenmore 47 E 5
Kennebec, *river* 117 G 2
Kennedy, C., *cape* 107 F 4
Kennedy Ra., *mountains* 152 B 2
Kennet, *river* 39 F 6
Kennet, Vale of, *valley* 41 B 3
Kennewick 120 C 2
Kenogami, *river* 116 C 1
Kenora 119 J 2
Kenosha 116 B 3
Kent 120 B 2
Kent, *county* 43 H 3
Kentau 74 J 5
Kent Group, *island group* 147 J 7
Kent Pena., *peninsula* 114 G 2
Kentucky, *river* 121 D 2
Kentucky, *state* 119 K 4
Kentucky, L., *lake* 106 F 4
Kent, Vale of, *valley* 43 H 3
Kenya 90 G 5
Kenya, Mt., *mountain* 90 G 6
Keppel Bay, *bay* 148 E 3
Kepulauan Kawio, *island group* 81 F 9
Kepulauan Mentawai, *island group* 66 F 6
Kerala, *province* 87 D 5
Kerang 149 C 6
Keravat 85 G 4
Kerch' 37 G 2
Kerchenskiy Proliv, *strait* 37 G 2
Kerdhíllion, *mountain* 62 C 3
Kerema 85 F 4
Keren 88 B 6
Keretéa 63 C 5
Keret', Oz., *lake* 50 V 3
Kerets, Mys, *cape* 50 X 3
Kerguelen Basin, *sea feature* 153 C 4
Kerguelen-Gaussberg Ridge, *sea feature* 153 C 5
Kerguelen, Is., *island group* 153 C 5
Kericho 104 C 3
Kerintji, G., *mountain* 79 H 6
Kerio, *river* 104 D 2
Keriya Darya, *river* 86 D 2
Kerkenna, Is., *island group* 98 E 2
Kerki 86 B 2
Kerkinítis, L., *lake* 62 C 3
Kérkira, *island* 28 J 5
Kerkour Nourene, *mts.* 99 F 4
Kermadec Is., *island group* 137 C 3
Kermadec Ridge, *sea feature* 137 B 3
Kermadec Tr., *sea feature* 137 B 3
Kermān 66 D 4
Kerman, *desert* 88 F 4
Kermānshāh 66 D 4
Kerme Körfezi, *bay* 63 E 5
Kern, *river* 120 C 5
Kerrville, *river* 118 H 5
Kerry, *county* 49 B 4
Kerry Head, *cape* 49 B 4
Kersaint, I. du, *island* 77 D 7
Kerulen, *river* 67 G 3
Keşan 62 E 3
Kesch, Piz, *mountain* 57 E 3
Kesten'ga 50 U 3
Keswick 39 E 4
Keta 98 D 5
Ketchikan 114 D 3
Ketmen', Khr., *mountain* 86 D 1
Ketrzyn 51 R 6
Kettering 39 F 5
Kettle River Ra., *mts.* 120 C 1
Kettlestone Bay, *bay* 115 K 2
Keweenaw Bay, *bay* 116 B 2
Keweenaw Pena., *peninsula* 114 J 4
Keweenaw Pt., *cape* 116 B 2
Key, L., *lake* 48 C 2
Key Largo, *island* 121 D 5
Key West 119 L 7
Khabab 89 C 1
Khabarovsk 67 H 3
Khaipur, *state* 86 C 3
Khairagarh 86 D 4
Khairpur 86 C 3
Kha Karpo Range, *mts.* 77 B 6
Khalajestan 88 D 2
Khalīj Abū Qīr, *bay* 100 B 1
Khalīj al 'Abab, *bay* 100 A 2
Khalīj al Maşīrah, *bay* 78 C 4
Khalīj aţ Ţīnah, *bay* 100 D 1
Khalīj 'Aynūna, *bay* 100 G 4
Khalik Tau, *mountains* 86 D 1
Khálki, *island* 63 E 5
Khalkidhikí, *region* 36 E 3
Khalkís 62 C 4
Khamar-Daman, Khr., *mountains* 66 G 3
Khamilí, *island* 63 E 6

Kowloon 79 J 3
Köyceğiz Gölü, *lake* 63 F 5
Koyp, G., *mountain* 29 O 2
Koyukuk, *river* 106 C 2
Kozáni 62 B 3
Kozhikode 78 E 4
Kozhva 35 N 2
Kozlovets 62 D 2
Kożuchów 58 F 3
Kōzu-sh., *island* 80 D 4
Kra, Isthmus of, *isthmus* 79 G 5
Krabi 84 A 3
Kragerø 51 N 5
Kragujevac 37 E 2
Krakatoa, see *Anak Krakatau* 79 H 6
Kraków 28 J 3
Kraków, *province* 64 D 2
Králíky 58 G 3
Kralovice, West *Czechoslovakia* 58 E 4
Královice, Central *Czechoslovakia* 58 F 4
Kramatorsk 37 G 2
Kramis, C., *cape* 53 F 4
Kranj 60 E 1
Krapina 59 F 5
Krasnoarmeyskoye 75 U 3
Krasnodar 29 L 4
Krasnokamsk 35 M 2
Krasnoslobodsk 65 F 4
Krasnotur'insk 35 N 2
Krasnoufimsk 35 N 3
Krasnovishersk 35 N 2
Krasnovodsk 66 D 3
Krasnovodskiy Zaliv, *bay* 88 E 2
Krasnoyarsk 66 F 3
Krasnyy Chikoy 76 D 1
Kratie 67 G 5
Krefeld 58 B 3
Kremenchug 37 G 2
Kremenets 64 E 2
Krems 59 F 4
Krestovyy Pereval, *pass* 37 H 2
Kretinga 51 R 6
Kreuzlingen 57 E 2
Kreuznach 58 B 4
Kriens 57 D 2
Krimml 59 E 5
Kriós, Akr., *cape* 63 C 6
Krishna, *river* 66 E 5
Krishna, Mouths of the, *river mouths* 87 D 5
Krishnagiri 87 D 5
Krishnanagar 86 E 4
Krishnaraja Sagara, *reservoir* 87 D 5
Kristel 53 E 5
Kristiansand 34 F 2
Kristianstad 51 O 6
Kristianstad, *county* 51 O 6
Kristiansund 50 M 3
Kristiinankaupunki 50 R 4
Kristinehamn 34 G 2
Kríti, *island* 28 K 5
Kritsá 63 D 6
Krivoy Rog 29 L 4
Križevci 59 G 5
Krk 60 E 2
Krk, *island* 60 E 2
Krka 60 E 2
Krkonose, *mountains* 58 F 3
Krnov 64 C 2
Kroměříž 59 G 4
Kronoberg, *county* 51 O 6
Kronotskiy P-ov., *peninsula* 75 T 4
Kronprinsesse Märtha Kyst, *region* 23 B 2
Kronprins Olav Kyst, *region* 23 E 2
Kronshtadt 35 J 2
Kroonstad 91 F 8
Kropotkin 37 H 2
Krosno 58 F 2
Krotoszyn 58 G 3
Krottenkopf, *mountain* 57 G 2
Kroussónas 63 D 6
Krrab, *mountain* 62 A 2
Krrabë, *mountains* 62 A 3
Kruger National Park 101 F 4
Krugersdorp 91 F 8
Krujë 62 A 3
Krummel Deep, *sea feature* 126 B 4
Krumovgrad 62 D 3
Krung Thep, see *Bangkok* 83 C 6
Kruševac 62 B 2
Krušovo 62 B 3
Kryazh Chernysheva, *mountains* 35 N 1
Kryazh Polousnyy, *mts.* 67 H 2
Krym, *peninsula* 29 L 4
Krymskiye Gory, *mts.* 28 L 4
Krzyż 58 G 2
Ksar el Boukhari 36 C 3
Ksar-es-Souk 90 C 2
Ksour Essaf 98 E 2
Ksour, Mts. des, *mts.* 98 D 2
Ksours, Mts. des, *mts.* 28 G 6
Kuala Lumpur 66 G 5
Kuala Penyu 81 A 9
Kuala Trengganu 84 B 3
Kuamut 81 B 9
Ku-an 76 F 4
Kuang-chou 67 G 4
Kuang-hua 76 E 5
Kuang-nan 79 H 3
Kuan-hsien 79 H 2
Kuantan 67 G 5
Kuba 37 J 3
Kuban', *river* 29 L 4
Kubor, Mt., *mountain* 85 F 4
Kubrat 62 E 2
K'u-ch'e 66 F 3
Kuchen Sp., *mountain* 57 F 2
Kuching 67 G 5
Kuchino-sh., *island* 80 B 5
Küçük Menderes, *river* 63 E 4
Kudat 79 J 5
Kudus 79 J 6
Küdzüpchi Sands, *region* 76 D 3
Kuei Chiang, *river* 77 E 7
Kuei-lin 79 J 3
Kuei-p'ing 79 H 3
Kuei-shan-ting, *mountain* 77 E 6
Kuei-sui 79 J 1
Kuei-yang 67 G 4
Kufra Oasis, *region* 90 F 3
Kufstein 59 E 5
Kuhanbokano, *mountain* 86 E 3
Kuhhā-ye Zagros, *mts.* 66 D 4
Kūhrān, Kūh-e, *mountain* 88 F 4
Kuiling Shan, *mountains* 77 E 6
Kuiseb, *seasonal river* 101 B 3
Kuju zan, *mountain* 80 B 4
Kukālār, Kūh-e, *mountain* 29 N 6
Kukës 62 B 2
Kulal, Mt., *mountain* 99 G 5
Kulaly, O., *island* 65 G 5
Kuldiga 51 R 6
Kulgera 146 F 5
Kulmbach 58 D 3
Kulon, Ug., *cape* 84 B 4
Kul'sary 35 M 4
Kulumadau 85 G 4
Kulundinskaya Step', *steppe* 66 E 3
Kulyab 86 C 2
Kuma, *river* 37 H 2
Kumagaya 80 D 3
Kumamoto 80 B 4
Kumanovo 62 B 2
Kumara 151 D 6
Kumasi 90 C 5
Kumba 98 D 5
Kumbakonam 87 D 5
Kumbetsu-yama, *mts.* 80 E 2
Kumbi-Saleh, *civilisation* 159
Kum Darya, *river* 86 E 1
Kumon Ra., *mountains* 79 G 3
Kunashir, *island* 75 R 5
Kundelungu Mts., *mts.* 102 D 3
Kungälv 51 N 5
Kung-chu-ling 76 H 3
Kungey Alatau, Khr., *mts.* 86 D 1
Kung-lung Shan, *mts.* 77 B 7
K'ung-ming 82 D 3
Kungsbacka 51 O 5
Kungur 35 N 3
Kungwe, C., *cape* 104 B 4
Kun Lun Plains, *region* 86 D 2
Kun-lun Shan, *mountains* 66 F 4
K'un-ming 66 G 4
Kunsan 76 H 4
Kuntsevo 35 K 3
Kuolayarvi 50 T 2
Kuo-lo Shan, *mountains* 76 C 5
Kuopio 34 J 2
Kuopio, *county* 50 T 3
Kupa, *river* 60 E 2
Kupang 67 H 6
Kura, *river* 29 N 5
Kurashiki 80 C 4
Kurayoshi 80 C 4
Kŭrdzhali 62 D 3
Kure 75 Q 6
Kureyka, *river* 75 L 3
Kurgan 66 E 3
Kurgan-Tyube 86 C 2
Kuria Muria Bay, *bay* 88 F 6
Kuria Muria Is., *island group* 66 D 5
Kuril Ridge, *sea features* 137 B 1
Kuril'sk 75 R 5
Kuril'skiye O-va., *island group* 67 J 3
Kuril Trench, *sea feature* 137 B 1
Kurnool 78 E 4
Kurri Kurri 149 E 5
Kursk 35 K 3
Kurskiy Zaliv, *bay* 34 H 3
Kurtoğlu Br., *cape* 63 F 5
Kuruk Tagh, *mountains* 66 F 3
Kuruman 91 F 8
Kurume 80 B 4
Kurunegala 87 D 6
Kusfors 50 Q 3
Kush, *civilisation* 158
Kushan, *civilisation* 159
Kushikino 80 B 5
Kushiro 67 J 3
Kushk 86 B 2
Kushka 86 B 2
Kuskokwim, *river* 106 C 2
Kuskokwim Mts., *mts.* 106 C 2
Kustanay 35 N 3
Kütahya 65 B 6
Kutai, *river* 79 J 6
Kutaisi 37 H 2
Kutaradja 66 F 5
Kutch, Great Rann of, see *Great Rann of Kutch* 66 E 4
Kutch, G. of, *gulf* 66 E 4
Kutch, Little Rann of, see *Little Rann of Kutch* 86 C 4
Kutcharo-ko, *lake* 80 F 2
Kutina 60 F 2
Kutkai 77 B 7
Kutná Hora 58 F 4
Kutno 64 C 2
Kuvandyk 65 J 3
Kuwait 29 N 6
Kuwait, *state* 29 M 6
Kuybyshev, Central *R.S.F.S.R.* 74 K 4
Kuybyshev, West *R.S.F.S.R.* 74 H 4
Kuybyshevskoye Vdkhr., *reservoir* 66 D 3
Kuytun, G., *mountain* 66 F 3
Kuyucak 63 F 5
Kuzey Anadolu Dağlari, *mountains* 29 L 5
Kuznetsk 35 L 3
Kuznetskiy Alatau, *mts.* 29 S 3
Kvaenangen, *island* 50 R 1
Kvaløy, *island* 50 Q 1
Kvarken, O., *island* 50 R 3
Kvarner, *channel* 60 E 2
Kvarnerič, *channel* 60 E 2
Kvikkjokk 50 P 2
Kwa, *river* 91 E 6
Kwangju 67 H 4
Kwango, *river* 91 E 6
Kwangsi, *province* 77 D 7
Kwantung, *province* 77 D 7
Kwasyō Tō, *island* 77 G 7
Kweichow, *province* 77 C 6
Kwidzyn 51 Q 7
Kwilu, *river* 90 E 6
Kwobrup 152 B 4
Kwoka, *mountain* 85 E 4
Kyaikto 83 B 5
Kyakhta 75 N 4
Kyaring Tso, *lake* 86 E 3
Kyaukme 82 B 4
Kyaukpyu 79 G 4
Kyaukse 82 B 4
Kyebang-san, *mountain* 80 B 3
Kyle, *region* 38 D 4
Kyleakin 46 C 4
Kyle of Lochalsh 46 C 4
Kyll, *river* 56 E 4
Kymi, *county* 51 T 4
Kymi, *river* 51 S 4
Kyoga, L., *lake* 90 G 5
Kyong 82 B 4
Kyōto 67 H 4
Kyra 76 E 2
Kyrenia 37 G 3
Kyrön joki, *river* 50 R 4
Kyūshū, *island* 67 H 4
Kyūshū-Palau Ridge, *sea feature* 137 A 2
Kyūshū sanchi, *mountains* 80 B 4
Kyustendil 62 C 2
Kyzyl 75 M 4
Kyzyl-Kiya 86 C 1
Kyzyl-Kum, Peski, *desert* 74 J 5
Kzyl-Orda 74 J 5
La Almunia 53 E 2
Labadie Bank, *sea feature* 39 B 6
La Banda 136 B 1
La Bañeza 52 C 1
La Barca 122 C 2
Labason 81 E 8
Labé 98 B 4
Labe, *river* 34 G 3
Labian, Tg., *cape* 81 C 9
Labin 60 E 2
La Blanquilla, Isla, *island* 132 C 1
Labo 81 E 4
La Boca 134 D 1
Labrador, *region* 115 L 3
Labuagan 81 D 3
Labuan, *island* 79 J 5
Labuk, *river* 81 B 9
Labuk Bay, *bay* 81 B 8
Labytnangi 66 E 2
La Campana 134 D 2
Lacanau, Étang de, *lake* 55 D 5
La Cañiza 52 A 1
La Carolina 52 D 3
Laccadive Islands, *island group* 153 C 2
Laccadive Trough, *sea feature* 153 C 2
La Ceiba 123 E 3
Lacepede Bay, *bay* 149 B 6
la Chambre 57 B 4
La Châtre 55 E 4
La Chaux-de-Fonds 57 B 2
Lachish, *ancient site* 89 A 3
Lachlan, *river* 140 E 5
La Chorrera 134 D 2
la Ciotat 55 G 6
La Columna, P., *mt.* 132 B 2
Laconi 61 B 5
La Coruña 36 A 2
la Costa I., *island* 121 D 5
La Crosse 119 J 3
Ladakh Ra., *mountain* 78 E 2
Ladder Hills, *mountains* 46 E 4
Ladismith 101 D 6
La Dôle, *mountain* 57 B 3
Ladozhsko-Ozerskiy Kanal, *canal* 51 U 4
Ladozhskoye Ozero, *lake* 28 K 2
Ladybrand 101 E 5
Lady Elliot I., *island* 147 K 4
Ladysmith 91 F 8
Lae 85 F 4
Laem Pracham Hiang, *cape* 83 C 7
Laem Riu, *cape* 83 C 7
Laerdalsöyri 51 M 4
Laesø, *island* 51 N 5
La Estrada 52 A 1
Lafayette, U.S.A., *Indiana* 119 K 3
Lafayette, U.S.A., *Louisiana* 119 J 5
La Fère 56 B 5
la Ferté-Bernard 54 E 3
la Ferté-Macé 54 D 3
Lafia 102 B 2
La Flèche 54 D 4
Lagan, *river* 48 E 2
Lagan, Pte., *cape* 83 E 7
Lagarto 134 C 1
Lågen, *river* 28 H 2
Lage, Ria de, *inlet* 52 A 1
Laggan, L., *lake* 46 D 5
Laghouat 98 D 2
Lagit, K. i, *cape* 62 A 3
Lagoa 52 A 4
Lagonegro 61 E 4
Lagonoy Gulf, *gulf* 81 E 5
Lagos, *Nigeria* 90 D 5
Lagos, *Portugal* 52 A 4
Lagos de Moreno 122 C 2
La Goulette 61 C 6
La Grande 118 D 2
La Grange, *Australia* 152 C 1
La Grange, *U.S.A.* 121 C 3
La Guaira 126 C 1
La Guardia 52 A 2
Laguna 136 D 1
Laguna Beach 120 C 5
Laguna, I. da, *island* 133 D 3
Lagune Aby, *lake* 102 A 2
Lahad Datu 79 J 5
Laha Shan, *mountains* 77 C 6
Laḥej 88 C 7
Lāhījān 88 E 2
Lahn, *river* 58 C 3
Laholm 51 O 6
Lahore 66 E 4
Lahore, *state* 86 C 3
Lahti 34 J 2
Lai Chau 77 C 7
Laigle 54 E 3
Lai-Lo 81 D 2
Laingsburg 101 D 6
Lainio älv, *river* 50 R 2
Lairg 46 D 3
Lais 81 F 8
Lajes 135 C 2
La Junta 118 G 4
Lak Bissigh, *river* 104 E 2
Lak Dera, *river* 104 D 2
Lake, *province* 104 C 3
Lake Charles 119 J 5
Lake District, *region* 39 E 4
Lake Eyre Basin, *region* 140 D 4
Lake Harbour, *trading post* 115 L 2
Lake King 152 B 4
Lake Ra., *mountains* 120 C 3
Lake River 115 J 3
Lakeview 120 B 3
Lake Worth Inlet, *strait* 121 D 5
Lakonikós Kólpos, *bay* 63 C 5
Laksefjord, *fjord* 50 S 1
Lakselv 34 J 1
Lala 81 E 8
La Laguna 98 B 3
Lalín 52 A 1
La Línea de la Concepción 52 C 4
La-lin Ho, *river* 80 A 1
La Loche 114 G 3
Laloki 85 F 4
La Louvière 56 C 4
La Maddalena 60 B 4
Lamag 81 B 9
La Malbaie 117 F 2
Lamar 118 G 4
La Martre, Lac, *lake* 114 F 2
Lambaréné 90 E 6
Lambay I., *island* 48 E 3
Lambert, C., *cape* 152 B 2
Lambert Glacier 23 F 2
Lambeth 41 D 3
Lambton, C., *cape* 114 E 1
Lambourn 43 F 3
Lambourn, *river* 41 B 3
Lambourn Downs 41 A 2
Lam Chi, *river* 82 D 5
Lamé 98 E 5
Lamego 52 B 2
Lamesa 118 G 5
La Mesa, *Panama* 134 B 2
La Mesa, *U.S.A.* 120 C 5
Lamía 62 C 4
Lamigan Pt., *cape* 81 G 8
Lamitan 79 K 5
Lamlash 47 C 6
Lammermuir Hills, *hills* 38 E 4
La Mola, *mountain* 53 F 3
Lamon Bay, *bay* 81 D 4
Lamotrek 85 F 3
Lampeter 42 C 2
Lampi, *island* 79 G 4
Lamu 90 H 6
Lanao, L., *lake* 81 F 8
Lanark 38 E 4
Lanark, *county* 47 D 6
Lanas 81 B 9
Lancashire, *county* 45 F 4
Lancaster 39 E 4
Lancaster Sd., *inlet* 106 F 2
Lanchow, see *Kao-lan* 76 C 4
Lancing 41 D 4
Landau, *Germany, Bayern* 59 E 4
Landau, *Germany, Rheinland-Pfalz* 59 C 4
Landeck 57 F 2
Lander, *river* 146 F 4
Landerneau 54 B 3
Landes, *region* 28 F 4
Landfall I., *island* 83 A 6
Landquart, *river* 57 E 3
Landsberg, *river* 59 D 4
Landsborough 151 C 6
Lands End, *Canada, cape* 106 D 2
Land's End, *England, cape* 28 F 3
Landshut 59 E 4
Landskrona 51 O 6
Langa de D. 52 D 2
Langadhás 62 C 3
Lange Berg, *mountain* 101 C 5
Langeland, *island* 51 N 6
Langenthal 57 C 2
Langensalza 58 D 3
Langeoog, *island* 58 B 2
Langhateuk, Phu Kh., *mt.* 84 A 3
Langholm 44 E 2
Langjökull, *snowfield* 50 C 3
Langkawi, P., *island* 84 A 3
Langkon 81 B 8
Langnau 57 C 3
Langney Pt., *cape* 41 E 4
Langøy, *island* 50 O 2
Langres 54 G 4
Langres, Plateau de, *plateau* 36 C 2
Lang Shan, see *Hara Narin Uula* 76 D 3
Lang Son 77 D 7
Languedoc, *province* 55 F 6
Lang-ya Shan, *mountain* 77 B 6
Lanín, Vol., *mountain* 136 A 2
Lanjaron 52 D 4
Lannemezan, *region* 55 E 6
Lannion 54 C 3
Lansing 119 L 3
Lansdowne House 115 J 3
L'Anse au Loup 115 M 3
Lanškroun 58 G 4
Lanterne, *river* 57 B 2
Lantsang, see *Mekong* 82 C 4
Lanuza 81 G 7
Lanzarote, *island* 98 B 3
Laoag 67 H 5
Laoang 81 F 5
Laodicea, *ancient site* 63 F 5
Laois 49 D 4
Lao-kay 66 G 4
Lao-ling Shan-mo, *mts.* 80 B 2
Laon 54 F 3
Lao-pai-lin, *mountain* 77 C 6
La Orchila, I., *island* 123 G 3
La Oroya 132 B 4
Laos 67 G 5
Lao-t'ien-shan Shui-tao, *strait* 76 G 4
Laoy 81 F 7
Lao-yao 79 J 2
Lao-yeh-Ling Shan-mo, *mountains* 76 H 3
Lapalisse 55 F 4
Lapa, Sa. da, *mountains* 52 B 2
La Paz, *Argentina* 135 C 3
La Paz, *Bolivia* 126 C 4
La Paz, *Mexico* 122 B 2
La Palma 52 B 4
La Palma, *island* 90 B 3
Lapalme, É. de, *lake* 53 G 1
La Panza Ra., *mountains* 120 B 5
La Peña 134 B 2
La Perouse Str., *strait* 67 J 3
La Piedad 122 C 2
La Pintada 134 C 2
La Plata 127 D 6
La Pola de Gordón 52 C 1
Lappajärvi, *lake* 50 R 3
Lappeenranta 51 T 4
Lappi, *county* 50 S 2
Lappland, *region* 28 J 1
Lâpseki 62 E 3
Laptevykh, More, *sea* 24 E 2
La Puebla 53 G 3
La Puebla de C. 52 C 4
La Puebla de M. 52 C 3
La Punta, *cape* 52 F 2
L'Aquila 36 D 2
Lār 78 C 3
Larache 52 B 5
La Rambla 52 C 4
Laramie 118 F 3
Laramie Ra., *mountains* 106 E 3
Larantuka 84 D 4
Larbert 47 E 5
Lärbro 51 Q 5
Laredo, *Spain* 52 D 1
Laredo, *U.S.A.* 118 H 6
Laren 56 D 2
la Réole 55 D 5
Largeau 90 E 4
Largentière 55 G 5
Largs 47 D 6
Larino 60 E 4
La Rioja 136 B 1
Lárisa 37 E 3
Lark, *river* 43 H 2
Larnaca 37 G 3
Larne 39 D 4
Larne, L., *lake* 48 F 2
La Roche-en-Ardenne 56 D 4
La Rochelle 34 E 4
La Roche-sur-Yon 55 D 4
La Roda 52 D 3
La Romana 123 G 3
La Ronge 114 G 3
La Ronge, Lac, *lake* 114 G 3
Larouco, Sa. do, *mts.* 52 B 2
Larrey Pt., *cape* 146 C 3
Lars Christensen Coast, *region* 23 F 2
Larsen Ice Shelf 23 R 2
Larvik 34 G 2
Larzac, *region* 55 F 6
Las Cruces 118 F 5
La Serena 136 A 1
La Serra, *mountain* 57 D 4
Las Flores 136 C 2
Lashio 79 G 3

Main Barrier Ra., *mts.* 140 E 5
Mainburg 59 D 4
Main Channel, *strait* 116 D 2
Maine, *France, province* 54 D 3
Maine, *U.S.A., state* 119 N 2
Maine, *river* 49 B 4
Mainit 81 F 7
Mainit, L. *lake* 81 F 7
Mainland, *Orkney, island* 38 E 2
Mainland, *Shetland, island* 38 F 1
Mainpat, *mountain* 86 E 4
Mainpuri 86 D 3
Maintirano 91 H 7
Mainz 58 C 4
Maiquetía 132 C 1
Maira, *river* 60 A 2
Maire, Est. de le, *strait* 127 C 8
Mainsí, C., *cape* 123 F 2
Maiskhal I., *island* 82 A 4
Maisome I., *island* 104 C 3
Maison Carrée 53 G 4
Mait I., *island* 103 F 1
Maitland 147 K 6
Maitland, L., *seasonal lake* 152 C 3
Maitland Ra., *mountains* 81 B 9
Maíz, Is. del, *island group* 123 E 3
Maizuru 80 C 4
Maja, P., *island* 84 B 4
Maje, Serranía de, *mts.* 134 E 1
Maji 103 E 2
Majorca, *see Mallorca* 53 G 3
Majuli I., *interfluve* 86 F 3
Majunga 91 H 7
Majunga, *province* 105 C 3
Makalu, *mountain* 86 E 3
Makarikari, *swamp* 91 F 8
Makarov 75 R 5
Makarska 60 F 3
Makasar 67 G 6
Makasar, Sel., *strait* 67 G 6
Makatini Flats, *region* 101 G 4
Makedhonia, *province* 62 B 3
Makedonija, *province* 62 B 3
Makeyevka 29 L 4
Makhachkala 37 H 2
Makhtesh Hagadol, *desert* 89 A 4
Makhtesh Haqatan, *desert* 89 B 3
Makhtesh Ramon, *desert* 89 A 4
Makinsk 74 K 4
Makkah 66 C 4
Makkaur 50 U 1
Makó 64 D 3
Makondi Plateau, *plateau* 105 A 1
Makorako, *mountain* 150 G 4
Makrá, *island* 63 D 5
Makrai 86 D 4
Makran, *region* 66 E 4
Makran Coast Range, *see Talat-i Band* 86 B 3
Makrónisos, *island* 63 D 5
Makteir, *region* 98 B 3
Maku 65 F 6
Makunga Mts., *mts.* 104 B 5
Makurazaki 80 B 5
Makurdi 98 D 5
Malå 50 Q 3
Malabar Coast, *region* 87 D 5
Malacca 66 G 5
Malacca, Str. of, *strait* 66 F 5
Malacky 59 G 4
Malad 87 C 4
Malad City 120 D 3
Maladeta, *mountain* 53 F 1
Málaga, *Colombia* 123 F 4
Málaga, *Spain* 28 F 5
Málaga, M. de, *mountains* 52 C 4
Malagarasi 104 B 4
Malagasy Republic 91 H 8
Malagón 52 D 3
Malaita I., *island* 141 G 2
Malakand 86 C 2
Malakoff 53 F 4
Malang 67 G 6
Malanje 91 E 6
Mala, Pta., *cape* 126 B 2
Mälaren, *lake* 28 J 2
Malartic 116 D 1
Malatya 37 G 3
Malawi 91 G 7
Malawi, L., *see Lake Nyasa* 91 G 7
Malaya, *province* 84 B 3
Malaybalay 81 F 7
Malāyer 88 D 3
Malay Pena., *peninsula* 66 G 5
Malaysia 66 G 5
Malazgirt 37 H 3
Malbon 148 C 3
Malbork 64 C 2
Malchin 58 E 2
Malcolm 152 C 3
Maldegem 56 B 3
Malditos, Montes, *mts.* 53 F 1
Maldive Islands, *island group* 153 C 2
Maldive Ridge, *sea feature* 153 C 2
Maldon 43 H 3
Maldonado 136 C 2
Maldonado, Pta., *cape* 122 D 3
Maléa, Akr., *cape* 37 E 3
Male Atoll, *reef* 87 C 6
Malegaon 78 E 3
Malekula, *island* 141 G 3
Malen'ga 50 W 3
Malgomaj, *lake* 50 P 3
Malhão, Sa. do, *mts.* 52 A 4
Malheur Lake, *lake* 120 C 3
Mali, *civilisation* 159
Mali, *state* 90 C 4
Mali Hka, *river* 82 B 3
Malik Naro, *mountain* 86 B 3
Målilla 51 P 5
Malimba, Mts., *mts.* 104 B 4
Malindang, Mt., *mt.* 81 E 7
Malindi 90 H 6
Maling, G., *mountain* 84 D 3
Malin Hd., *cape* 28 F 3
Malin More 48 C 2
Ma-li-p'o 77 C 7
Malita 81 F 8
Malitbog 81 F 6
Malkapur 86 D 4
Malkara 62 E 3
Malkhanskiy, Khrebet, *mountains* 76 D 1
Malko Tŭrnovo 62 E 3
Mallaig 38 D 3
Mallani, *region* 86 C 3
Mallawī 100 B 5
Mallorca, *island* 28 G 5
Mallow 39 B 5
Malmberget 50 Q 2
Malmédy 56 E 4
Malmesbury 91 E 9
Malmköping 51 P 5
Malmö 28 H 3
Malmöhus, *county* 51 O 6
Malmyzh 65 G 2
Malombe, L., *lake* 104 C 6
Malosmadulu Atoll, *reef* 87 C 6
Maloti Mts., *mountains* 101 F 5
Malozoemel'skaya Tundra, *region* 29 N 1
Malpartida de C. 52 B 3
Malpelo 137 E 2
Målselv 50 Q 1
Malta, *island* 28 H 5
Malta Chan., *channel* 28 H 5
Maltahöhe 101 C 4
Malton 45 H 3
Maluku, *island group* 67 H 6
Maluku, Laut, *sea* 67 H 6
Malung 51 O 4
Malvern Hills, *hills* 43 E 2
Malwy Taung Hills, *mountains* 83 C 6
Malyy Kavkaz, *mts.* 37 H 3
Malyy Yenisey, *river* 75 M 4
Mamaia 64 F 4
Mamanovo 64 C 1
Mamarr Mitla, *region* 100 D 2
Mambasa 104 B 2
Mamberamo, *river* 84 E 4
Mambone 101 G 3
Mamburao 81 D 5
Mamers 54 E 3
Mamonovo 51 Q 6
Mamoré, *river* 126 C 4
Mamou 98 B 4
Mampodre, *mountain* 52 C 1
Mam Soul, *mountain* 46 C 4
Man 98 C 5
Manacor 36 C 3
Manado 67 H 5
Managua 107 F 5
Managua, L. de, *lake* 123 E 3
Manakara 91 H 8
Manambao, *river* 105 C 3
Manambolo, *river* 105 C 3
Mananara 105 D 3
Mananara, *river* 105 C 4
Mananjary 105 D 4
Mānasarowar L., *lake* 78 F 2
Manaslu, *mountain* 86 E 3
Manaus 126 C 3
Manawatu, *river* 150 F 5
Manawatu Gorge, *gorge* 150 F 5
Mancha, La, *region* 36 B 3
Mancha Real 52 D 4
Manchester, *England* 28 F 3
Manchester, *U.S.A.* 119 N 3
Manchouli 75 O 5
Manchuria, *region* 67 H 3
Manda 104 C 5
Mandal 34 F 2
Mandalay 66 F 4
Mandalay, *province* 82 B 4
Mandalya Körfezi, *gulf* 63 E 5
Mandan 114 G 4
Mandaon 81 E 5
Mandar, Teluk, *bay* 84 C 4
Mandara Mts., *mts.* 90 E 4
Mandasor 86 D 3
Mandav Hills, *mountains* 86 C 4
Mandih 81 E 7
Manding, *region* 90 C 4
Mandinga, Ens. de, *bay* 134 D 1
Mandla 86 D 4
Mandra, *river* 62 E 2
Mandritsara 105 D 2
Mandurah 152 B 4
Manduria 61 F 4
Manfredonia, Golfo di, *gulf* 60 F 4
Manga, *region* 90 E 4
Mangabeiras, Sa. das, *mountains* 133 E 4
Mangakino 150 F 4
Mangaldai 82 A 3
Mangalia 62 F 2
Mangalore 66 E 5
Mangaweka, *mountain* 150 G 4
Mangerton Mt., *mt.* 49 B 5
Mangoky, *river* 105 F 5
Mangole, *island* 85 D 4
Mangoro, *river* 105 D 3
Mangrol 86 C 4
Mangsahan 83 D 6
Mangualde 52 B 2
Mangueni, Hamada, *plateau* 98 E 3
Mangyshlak ,P-ov, *peninsula* 29 N 4
Manhica 101 G 3
Maní, *region* 63 C 5
Maniamba 104 C 6
Manica e Sofala, *province* 101 G 2
Manicouagan, *river* 117 G 1
Maniema, *province* 104 A 4
Manifold, C., *cape* 148 E 3
Manika, Plat. de la, *plateau* 102 D 4
Manila 67 H 5
Manila Bay, *bay* 81 D 4
Manindjau, D., *lake* 84 B 4
Manipur, *province* 82 A 3
Manipur, *river* 82 A 3
Manirang, *mountain* 86 D 3
Manisa 37 F 3
Man, I. of, *island* 28 F 3
Manitoba, *province* 114 H 3
Manitoba, L., *lake* 106 F 3
Manitou, I., *island* 116 B 2
Manitoulin I., *island* 115 J 4
Manitowoc 116 B 2
Maniwaki 116 E 2
Manizales 132 B 2
Manja 105 C 4
Manjacaze 101 G 4
Manjimup 146 C 6
Manlleu 53 G 2
Manly 149 E 5
Manmad 86 D 4
Mannar 87 D 5
Mannar, G. of, *gulf* 66 E 5
Mannheim 28 H 4
Mannin Bay, *bay* 48 A 3
Manningtree 43 J 3
Mannu 61 B 5
Manokwari 67 H 6
Manono 91 F 6
Manorhamilton 48 C 2
Manosque 55 G 6
Mano-w., *bay* 80 D 3
Manresa 36 C 3
Mansel I., *island* 106 F 2
Mansfield, *Australia* 149 D 6
Mansfield, *England* 39 F 5
Mansfield, *U.S.A.* 119 L 3
Manso, *river* 133 D 4
Manta 132 A 3
Mantalingajan, Mt., *mountain* 81 B 7
Mantanzas 121 D 6
Mantap San 76 H 3
Manteca 120 B 4
Mantes-Gassicourt 54 E 3
Manti 120 E 4
Mantiqueira, Sa. da, *mountains* 126 E 5
Mantova 60 C 2
Mantuan Downs 148 D 3
Manuan Lake, *lake* 117 F 1
Manucan 81 E 7
Manukau Harb., *harbour* 150 F 3
Manulla 48 B 3
Manus I., *island* 85 F 4
Manyara, L., *lake* 104 C 3
Manyas Gölü, *lake* 62 E 3
Manych-Gudilo, Ozero, *lake* 37 H 2
Manychskaya Vpadina, *region* 37 H 2
Manyoni 104 C 4
Manzanares 52 D 3
Manzanilla, Punta, *cape* 134 D 1
Manzanillo, *Cuba* 123 F 2
Manzanillo, *Mexico* 122 C 3
Manzano Mts., *mountains* 118 F 5
Manzil 89 C 3
Manzilah, Qanā al, *canal* 100 C 1
Manzini 102 E 5
Mao-mao Shan, *mts.* 76 C 4
Mao-ming 77 E 7
Maouin Pena., *peninsula* 28 H 5
Mapia, Kep., *island group* 85 E 3
Maple Creek 114 G 4
Mappi 85 E 4
Maprik 85 F 4
Mapuera, *river* 132 D 3
Maqla, J. al, *mountain* 100 G 4
Maqueda 52 C 2
Mar del Plata 127 D 6
Mar, Sa. do, *mountains* 126 E 5
Maracá, I. de, *island* 126 D 2
Maracaibo 126 B 1
Maracaibo, L. de, *lake* 126 B 2
Maracajú, Sa. de, *mts.* 132 D 5
Maracay 132 C 1
Maradi 90 D 4
Marāgheh 65 F 7
Marahuaca, Co., *mt.* 123 G 4
Marajó, I. de, *island* 126 E 3
Marand 65 F 6
Marandellas 101 F 2
Maranoa, *river* 149 D 4
Marañón, *river* 126 B 3
Marão, *mountain* 52 B 2
Marapi, G., *mountain* 84 B 4
Maraş 37 G 3
Marau Pt., *cape* 150 H 4
Marbella 52 C 4
Marble Bar 146 C 4
Marble Canyon, *gorge* 120 E 4
Marburg 58 C 3
Marca, Pta. da, *cape* 102 C 4
Marçal D., *mountains* 63 E 5
Marcali 60 F 1
March 43 H 2
Marchant Hill, *mountain* 149 B 5
Marche, *France, province* 55 E 4
Marche, *Italy, province* 60 D 3
Marchena 52 C 4
Marche-en-Famenne 56 D 4
Marche, Plateau de la, *plateau* 55 E 4
Mar Chica, *lake* 52 D 5
Mar Chiquita, *lake* 127 C 6
Marco Polo Ra., *see Bukalik Tagh* 86 F 2
Marcus I., *island* 67 J 4
Marcus-Necker Rise, *sea feature* 137 B 2
Marcy, Mt., *mountain* 117 F 2
Mardan 78 E 2
Mardie 152 B 2
Mardin 37 H 3
Maree, Loch, *lake* 38 D 3
Mareeba 147 J 3
Marengo 53 G 4
Marennes 55 D 5
Maresfield 41 E 4
Marettimo, *island* 61 D 6
Margam 42 D 3
Margaret, *river* 146 E 3
Margarita, I. de, *island* 123 G 3
Margate 39 G 6
Margosatubig 81 E 8
Marguerite, Mts. de la, *mountains* 55 F 5
Marguerite Bay, *bay* 23 R 2
Margungu, *mountain* 102 D 3
Maria Augustina Bank, *sea feature* 153 E 3
María Elena 132 C 5
Maria I., *island* 146 G 2
Marianao 123 E 2
Marianas, *island group* 137 B 2
Marianas Ridge, *sea feature* 137 B 2
Marianas Tr., *sea feature* 137 B 2
Mariánské Lázně 58 E 4
Marias, *river* 120 D 1
Maria, Sa. de, *mountains* 52 D 4
Marias Pass, *pass* 120 D 1
Mariato, Punta, *cape* 134 C 3
Maria van Diemen, C ., *cape* 141 H 5
Maribo 58 D 1
Maribor 64 B 3
Maridi 104 B 1
Marie Byrd Land, *district* 23 P 1
Mariefred 51 P 5
Marie Galante, *island* 123 G 3
Mariental 91 E 8
Mariestad 51 O 5
Marietta 121 C 3
Mariinsk 75 L 4
Marília 133 D 5
Marimas, Las, *region* 36 B 3
Marin 52 A 1
Marinduque I., *island* 81 D 5
Marinha Grande 52 A3
Marion, *U.S.A., Illinois* 119 K 4
Marion, *U.S.A., Indiana* 116 C 3
Marion, *U.S.A., Ohio* 116 C 3
Marion I., *island* 23 D 3
Marion, L., *lake* 119 L5
Marion Reef, *reef* 141 F 3
Maritimes, Alpes, *mts.* 55 H 5
Maritsa 62 D 2
Maritsa, *river* 28 K 4
Marittime, Alpi, *mts.* 28 G 4
Mark, *river* 56 C 3
Markaryd 51 O 6
Marken, *island* 56 D 2
Markerwaard, *polder* 56 D 2
Market Deeping 43 G 2
Market Drayton 43 E 2
Market Harborough 43 G 2
Market Rasen 45 H 4
Market Weighton 45 H 4
Marlborough, *Australia* 148 D 3
Marlborough, *England* 43 F 3
Marlborough, *county* 150 E 5
Marlborough Downs, *hills* 43 F 3
Marlin 119 H 5
Marlow 43 G 3
Marmande 55 E 5
Marmara, *island* 62 E 3
Marmara Gölü, *lake* 63 E 4
Marmara, Sea of, 28 K 5
Marmaris 63 F 5
Mar Menor, *lake* 53 E 4
Marmolada, *mountain* 59 D 5
Marmoleja 52 C 3
Marne, *river* 54 G 3
Maroantsetra 103 F 4
Marolambo 105 D 4
Maroonah 152 B 2
Maroua 98 E 4
Marovoay 105 C 3
Marquesas, *island group* 137 D 3
Marquesas Keys, *island group* 121 D 5
Marquette 119 K 2
Marquina 52 D 1
Marra, Jebel, *mountains* 90 F 4
Marrakech 90 C 2
Marree 147 G 5
Marroquí, Pta., *cape* 52 C 4
Marrupa 104 D 6
Marsabit 104 D 2
Marsala 36 D 3
Marsá Thalmah, *bay* 100 D 3
Marsdiep, *strait* 56 C 1
Marseille 28 G 4
Marseilles, *see Marseille* 55 G 6
Marsh I., *island* 121 B 4
Marshall Islands, *island group* 137 B 2
Martaban 83 B 5
Martaban, G. of, *gulf* 66 F 5
Martes, *mountain* 53 E 3
Martha's Vineyard, *island* 106 G 3
Martigny-Ville 57 C 3
Martina 61 F 4
Martinborough 150 F 5
Martinique, *island* 107 G 5
Martinique Pass., *strait* 123 G 3
Martin L., *lake* 121 C 3
Martinsville 121 E 2
Martin Vaz, *island* 25 D 5
Marton 150 F 5
Martorell 53 F 2
Martos 52 D 4
Marvine, Mt., *mountain* 120 E 4
Mary 86 B 2
Maryborough, *Australia, Queensland* 147 K 5
Maryborough, *Australia, Victoria* 147 H 7
Maryborough, *Rep. of Ireland, see Port Laoise* 49 D 3
Maryland, *state* 119 M 4
Maryport 44 E 3
Marysville 120 B 4
Marvejols 55 F 5
Maşabb Dumyat, *cape* 100 C 1
Maşabb Rashīd, *cape* 100 B 1
Masada, *ancient site* 89 B 3
Masai Steppe, *steppe* 90 G 6
Masaka 103 E 3
Masan 75 P 6
Masansane B., *bay* 101 G 2
Masasi 104 D 5
Masaya 123 E 3
Masbate 67 H 5
Masbate, *island* 81 E 6
Mascara 36 C 3
Mascarene Basin, *sea feature* 153 B 3
Mascarene Ridge, *sea feature* 153 B 3
Maseru 91 F 8
Mashābih, J., *island* 99 G 3
Masham 44 G 3
Mashhad 66 D 4
Mashonaland, *region* 102 E 4
Masindi 99 G 5
Maşīrah, J., *island* 66 D 4
Masirah Chan., *channel* 88 F 5
Masisi 104 B 3
Masjed Soleymān 88 D 3
Mask, L., *lake* 39 B 5
Masoala, C., *cape* 91 J 7
Massa 60 C 2
Massachusetts, *state* 117 F 3
Massachusetts Bay, *bay* 117 F 3
Massanutten Mt., *mt.* 121 E 2
Massawa 90 G 4
Massena 117 E 2
Massif Central, *mts.* 36 C 2
Massif de l'Oisans, *mts.* 55 H 5
Massif de L'Ouarsenis, *mountains* 36 C 3
Massif des Maures, *mts.* 55 H 6
Massif du Diois, *mts.* 55 G 5
Massif du Makay, *mts.* 105 C 4
Massif du Tsaratanana, *mountains* 78 B 7
Massinga 101 G 3
Masterton 150 F 5
Mástikho, Akr., *cape* 63 D 4
Masuda 80 B 4
Masulipatnam 66 F 5
Mata, Sa. de, *mountains* 132 C 2
Matabeleland, *region* 102 D 4
Matabele Plain, *region* 102 D 4
Matadi 91 E 6
Matagalls, *mountain* 53 G 2
Matagalpa 123 E 3
Matagorda I., *island* 119 H 6
Mataimoana, *mountain* 150 F 4
Matakana I., *island* 150 G 3
Matale 87 D 6
Matama 88 B 7
Matamata 150 F 3
Matamoros, *Central Mexico* 122 C 2
Matamoros, *East Mexico* 122 D 2
Matandu, *river* 104 D 5
Matane 117 G 1
Matanzas 106 F 4
Matanzas Inlet, *inlet* 121 D 4
Matapedia, *river* 117 G 1
Matapozuelos 52 C 2
Matara 87 D 6
Mataram 79 J 6
Matarani 135 A 1
Matārimah, Ra's, *cape* 100 D 3
Mataró 53 G 2
Matatiele 101 F 5
Mataura 151 C 8
Matehuala 122 C 2
Mateke Hills, *mountains* 101 F 3
Matera 61 F 4
Matese, *mountain* 60 E 4
Mátészalka 64 D 3
Mateur 61 B 6
Mathry 42 B 3
Mathura 78 E 3
Mati 81 G 8
Matifou, C., *cape* 53 G 4
Matjan, Kep., *island group* 84 D 4
Matlock 45 G 4
Matochkin Shar, Proliv, *strait* 66 D 2
Mato Grosso, Planalto do, *plateau* 126 D 4
Matope 104 C 6
Matopo Hills, *mountains* 102 D 5
Matozinhos 52 A 2
Maţraḩ 88 F 5
Matrūh 99 F 2
Matsang Tsangpo, *river* 86 E 3

Newcastle, *N. Ireland* **48** F 2
Newcastle, *Rep. of Ireland* **48** E 3
Newcastle, *Rep. of South Africa* **102** D 5
New Castle **116** D 3
Newcastle Emlyn **42** C 2
Newcastle Ra., *mountains* **148** C 2
Newcastle-under-Lyme **39** E 5
Newcastle West **39** B 5
New Deer **46** F 4
Newdegate **152** B 4
New Eng. Ra., *mountains* **140** F 5
Newenham, C., *cape* **106** B 3
New Forest, *forest* **39** F 6
Newfoundland, *island* **106** H 3
Newfoundland, *province* **115** L 3
Newfoundland Rise, *sea feature* **25** C 2
New Georgia Group, *island group* **140** F 2
New Galloway **47** D 6
New Glasgow **115** L 4
New Guinea, *island* **67** H 6
New Guinea, Territory of **140** E 2
New Hampshire, *state* **119** N 3
New Hanover, *island* **85** G 4
Newhaven **39** G 6
New Haven **119** N 3
New Hebrides, *island group* **141** G 3
New Hebrides Basin, *sea feature* **141** G 3
New Hebrides Trough, *sea feature* **141** G 3
New Ireland, *island* **141** F 2
New Jersey, *state* **119** N 3
Newland Ra., *mountains* **152** C 3
New Liskeard **116** D 2
New London **119** N 3
Newman **120** B 4
Newmarket, *England* **39** G 5
Newmarket, *Rep. of Ireland* **49** B 4
New Mexico, *state* **118** F 5
New Norfolk **147** J 8
New Orleans **107** F 4
New Pitsligo **46** F 4
New Plymouth **150** F 4
Newport, *England, Isle of Wight* **39** F 6
Newport, *England, Shropshire* **43** E 2
Newport, *Rep. of Ireland* **48** B 3
Newport, *Scotland* **47** F 5
Newport, *U.S.A., Kentucky* **121** C 2
Newport, *U.S.A., Oregon* **120** A 2
Newport, *U.S.A., Washington* **120** C 1
Newport, *Wales* **39** E 6
Newport Beach **120** C 5
Newport News **119** M 4
Newport Pagnell **43** G 2
New Providence, *state* **119** M 6
New Quay **42** C 2
Newquay **39** D 6
New Radnor **42** D 2
New Richmond **117** H 1
New Romney **43** H 4
New Ross **39** C 5
Newry **39** C 4
New South Wales, *state* **140** E 5
Newton Abbot **42** D 4
Newton Aycliffe **44** G 3
Newtongrange **47** E 6
Newtonmore **46** D 4
Newtown **39** E 5
Newton Stewart **39** D 4
Newtownards **39** D 4
Newtown Bay, *bay* **41** B 4
Newtown Butler **48** D 2
Newtown Hamilton **48** E 2
Newtown Stewart **48** D 2
New Westminster **118** C 2
New York **106** G 3
New York, *state* **119** M 3
New Zealand **141** H 6
New Zealand Plateau, *sea feature* **137** B 4
Neyrīz **88** E 4
Neyshābūr **86** B 2
Nezhin **35** J 3
Ngamatea Swamp, *swamp* **150** G 4
Ngami, L., *lake* **91** F 8
Nganglaring Tso, *lake* **86** E 3
n'Gaoundéré **90** E 5
Ngaruawahia **150** F 3
Ngaya, J., *mountain* **102** D 2
Ngok Linh, *mountain* **79** H 4
Ngom Chu, *river* **76** B 5
Ngong **104** D 3
Ngorongoro Crater, *mt.* **104** C 3
Ngozi **104** B 3
Ngulu Atoll, *reef* **85** E 3
Ngundju, Tg., *cape* **84** D 5
Nguru **98** E 4
Nhamarroi **104** D 6
Nha Trang **67** G 5
Nhill **149** C 6
Niagara **152** C 3
Niagara, *river* **116** D 3
Niagara Falls **119** M 3
Niagara Falls, *falls* **106** G 3
Niamey **90** D 4
Niangara **102** D 2
Nias **66** F 5
Niassa, *province* **104** C 6
Nicaragua **107** F 5
Nicaragua, L. de, *lake* **107** F 5
Nicastro **61** F 5
Nice **28** G 4
Nichicun, L., *lake* **115** K 3
Nicobar Is., *island group* **66** F 5
Nicosia, *Cyprus* **29** L 5
Nicosia, *Italy* **61** E 6
Nicholas Chan., *channel* **119** L 7
Nicholson, *river* **140** D 3
Nickol Bay, *bay* **152** B 2
Nicotera **61** E 5
Nicoya, G. de, *gulf* **123** E 4
Nicoya, Pena. de, *peninsula* **107** F 5
Nidd, *river* **45** F 3
Nied, *river* **56** E 5
Nieder Österreich, *prov.* **59** F 4
Niedere Tauern, *mts.* **36** D 2
Niedersachsen, *länder* **58** C 2
Nienburg **58** C 2
Niesen, *mountain* **57** C 3
Niete Mts., *mountains* **98** C 5
Nieuwpoort **56** A 3
Nigel **101** F 4
Niger, *river* **90** C 4
Niger, *state* **90** D 4
Nigeria **90** D 5
Niger, Mouths of the, *river mouths* **90** D 5
Nighthawk L., *lake* **116** D 1
Nigríta **62** C 3
Niigata **67** H 4
Niihama **80** C 4
Nii-jima, *island* **80** D 4
Nijmegen **36** C 1
Nikel' **50** T 1
Nikko **80** D 3
Nikolayev **29** K 4
Nikolayevsk **67** J 3
Nikolayevskiy **35** L 3
Nikopol' **37** G 2
Nikšić **64** C 4
Nile, *river* **90** G 3
Niles **120** B 4
Nilgiri **86** E 4
Nilgiri Hills, *mountains* **66** E 5
Nimba, Mt., *mountain* **90** C 5
Nîmes **36** C 2
Nimule **99** G 5
Nine Degree Channel, *channel* **87** C 5
Ninety Mile Beach, *beach* **150** E 2
Nineveh, *ancient site* **158**
Ninh Binh **82** D 4
Ning-hsiang **77** E 6
Ningsia Hui Aut. Region, *province* **76** D 4
Ning-te **77** F 6
Ning Ting Shan **79** G 2
Ning-tu **77** F 6
Ning-wu **76** E 4
Ninigo Group, *island group* **140** E 2
Ninigo Is., *island group* **85** F 4
Ninove **56** C 4
Nioro **98** C 4
Niort **55** D 4
Nipigon **115** J 4
Nipigon Bay, *bay* **116** B 1
Nipigon, L., *lake* **106** F 3
Nipissing, L., *lake* **106** G 3
Nirmal Ra., *mountains* **87** D 4
Niš **37** E 2
Nisa, *Poland* **64** C 2
Nisa, *Portugal* **52** B 3
Nisa, *river* **58** G 3
Nishinomiya **80** C 4
Nísiros, *island* **63** E 5
Nísoi Iouniá, *island group* **63** E 6
Nísoi Oinoúsai, *island group* **63** B 5
Nith, *river* **38** E 4
Nitchequon **115** K 3
Niterói **126** E 5
Nitra **64** C 3
Nith, *river* **47** E 6
Nithsdale, *valley* **47** E 6
Niu-lan Chiang, *river* **82** D 3
Niut, G., *mountain* **84** C 3
Nivelles **56** C 4
Nivernais, Côtes du, *reg.* **54** F 4
Nizamabad **87** D 4
Nizana **89** A 4
Nizh. Tunguska, *river* **19** H 2
Nizh. Tura **35** N 2
Nizhneudinsk **75** M 4
Nizh. Kuyto, Oz., *lake* **50** U 3
Nizhniye Sergi **74** H 4
Nizhniy Tagil **74** H 4
Nizke Tatry **28** J 4
Njombe **104** C 5
Njurunda **50** P 4
Njutånger **51** P 4
Nkana **91** F 7
Nkata Bay **104** C 5
n'Kongsamba **102** C 2
Nmai Hka, *river* **82** C 3
Nobeoka **80** B 4
Noce, *river* **57** G 3
Nockatunga **149** C 4
Noeux-les-Mines **56** A 4
Nogales, *Mexico* **122** B 1
Nogales, *U.S.A.* **118** E 5
Nogal Valley, *valley* **90** H 5
Nogara **60** C 2
Nogayskaya Step', *steppe* **37** H 2
Nogent-le-Rotrou **54** E 3
Nogent-sur-Seine **54** F 3
Noginsk **35** K 3
Nogueira, *mountain* **52** B 2
Noguera, La, *region* **53** F 2
Noires, Montagnes, *mts.* **54** C 3
Noire, *see Song Bo* **82** D 4
Noirmont, *mountain* **57** B 3
Noirmoutier, Île de, *island* **55** C 4
Nojima-saki, *cape* **80** D 4
Nokke Suidō, *channel* **80** F 2
Nolinsk **35** M 3
Nombre de Dios **134** D 1
Nome **106** B 2
Nomo Saki, *cape* **80** B 4
Nonda **148** C 3
Nong Khai **83** D 5
Nongoma **101** F 4
Nonning, Mt., *mountain* **149** B 5
Nonoc I., *island* **81** F 7
Nonthaburi **83** C 6
Nontron **55** E 5
Noonkanbah **152** C 1
Noord Brabant, *province* **56** C 3
Noord Holland, *province* **56** C 2
Noordoostpolder, *polder* **56** D 2
Noordwijk aan Zee **56** C 2
Noordzeekanaal, *canal* **56** C 2
Nora **51** P 5
Noranda **116** D 1
Norcia **60** D 3
Norcott, Mt., *mountain* **152** C 4
Nd. Beveland, *island* **56** B 3
Norddal **50** M 4
Norden **56** F 1
Nordenshel'da, Arkh., *island group* **75** M 2
Norderney **58** B 2
N. Finnskoga **51** O 4
Nordfj., *fjord* **34** F 2
Nordfjordeid **50** M 4
Nordfold **50** P 2
Nordhausen **58** D 3
Nordhorn **56** F 2
Nordkapp, *cape* **28** K 1
Nord-Katanga, *province* **104** A 4
Nord-Kivu, province **104** B 3
Nordland *county* **50** O 2
Nördlingen **59** D 4
Nordmaling **50** Q 3
Nordmør, *region* **34** F 2
Nordrhein-Westfalen, *länder* **58** B 3
Nordstrand, *island* **58** C 1
Nord-Trøndelag, *county* **50** N 3
Nordvik **66** G 2
Nore **51** M 4
Nore, *river* **39** C 5
Norfeo, C., *cape* **53** G 1
Norfolk, *U.S.A., Nebraska* **118** H 3
Norfolk, *U.S.A., Virginia* **106** G 4
Norfolk, *county* **43** H 2
Norfolk Edge, *hills* **43** H 2
Norfolk I., *island* **141** G 4
Norfolk Island Trough, *sea feature* **141** G 4
Norfolk Island Ridge, *sea feature* **141** G 5
Norfolk Res., *reservoir* **121** A 2
Norikura d., *mountain* **80** D 3
Noril'sk **66** F 2
Norman, *river* **140** E 3
Normanby, *river* **148** C 2
Normanby I., *island* **85** G 5
Normanby Ra., *mts.* **148** E 3
Normandie, *province* **54** D 3
Normanton **147** H 3
Norman Wells **114** E 2
Nornalup **152** B 4
N. Ny **51** O 4
Norrbotten, *county* **50** P 2
Norresundby **51** N 5
Norrfjärden **50** S 3
Norrfors **50** Q 3
Norris L., *lake* **121** C 2
Norristown **117** E 3
Norrköping **34** H 2
Norrtälje **51** Q 5
Norseman **146** D 6
Norsjö **50** Q 3
Norte, Pta., *cape* **127** D 6
Norte, Sa. do, *mountains* **132** D 4
Northallerton **39** F 4
Northam **146** C 6
Northampton, *Australia* **146** B 5
Northampton, *England* **39** F 5
Northampton, *U.S.A., Mass.* **117** F 3
Northampton, *county* **43** G 2
North Andaman, *island* **87** F 5
North Atlantic Ocean **25** C 5
North Battleford **114** G 3
North Bay **115** K 4
North Bend **120** A 3
North Berwick **47** F 5
N. Bimini, *island* **121** E 5
North Cape, *see Nordkapp* **50** S 1
North, C., *cape* **115** L 4
North Cape, *New Zealand* **141** H 5
North Cape Rise, *sea feature* **141** H 5
North Carolina, *state* **119** L 4
N. Cat Cay, *island* **121** E 5
North Channel, *British Isles, channel* **38** D 4
North Channel, *Canada, channel* **116** C 2
Northcliffe **152** B 4
North Dakota, *state* **118** G 2
N. Dorset Downs, *hills* **43** E 4
North Downs, *hills* **38** F 6
North-Eastern Atlantic Basin, *sea feature* **25** D 2
N.E. Providence Chan., *channel* **119** M 6
Northeim **58** C 3
N. Emine, *cape* **28** K 4
Northern, *Kenya, region* **104** D 2
Northern, *Malawi, reg.* **104** C 5
Northern, *Tanzania, reg.* **104** C 3
Northern, *Uganda, reg.* **104** B 2
Northern, *Zambia, prov.* **104** B 5
Northern Ireland **39** C 4
Northern Territory, *state* **140** D 3
N. Esk, *river* **38** E 3
North European Plain, *region* **18** F 2
Northey I., *island* **41** F 2
North Fiji Basin, *sea feature* **137** B 3
N. Foreland, *cape* **39** G 6
North Frisian Is., *island group* **34** G 3
N. (Inland) Hwy. **147** J 4
North I., *Australia, island* **146** F 2
North I., *Kenya, island* **104** D 1
North Island, *New Zealand, island* **141** H 5
North I., *U.S.A., island* **121** E 3
North Islet **81** D 7
North Korea **67** H 3
North Lakhimpur **82** B 3
Northleach **43** F 3
North Little Rock **121** A 3
North Magnetic Pole 1960 **106** E 2
N. Manitou I., *island* **116** B 2
North Minch, *channel* **38** D 2
North Palisade, *mt.* **118** D 4
North Platte **118** G 3
North Platte, *river* **118** G 3
North Pt., *Canada, cape* **117** H 2
North Pt., *U.S.A., cape* **116** C 2
N. Rat. I. Ridge, *sea feat.* **137** C 1
N. Rona, *island* **34** E 2
N. Ronaldsay, *island* **38** E 2
N. Santiam, *river* **120** B 2
N. Saskatchewan, *river* **106** E 3
North Sea **28** G 3
N. Sentinel, *island* **87** F 5
North Shields **45** G 2
N. Somercotes **45** J 4
North Sound, *inlet* **46** F 2
N. Stradbroke I., *island* **147** K 5
North Taranaki Bight, *bay* **150** F 4
North Truchas Pk., *mt.* **118** F 4
N. Tyne, *river* **45** F 2
North Uist, *island* **38** C 3
Northumberland, *county* **45** F 2
Northumberland, C., *cape* **147** H 7
Northumberland Is., *island group* **147** K 4
Northumberland Str., *channel* **115** L 4
North Vancouver **114** E 4
North Viet Nam **67** G 5
North Walsham **43** J 2
North West Basin, *reg.* **140** B 4
North West C., *cape* **140** B 4
N.W. Christmas Island Ridge, *sea feature* **137** C 2
North Western, *prov.* **104** A 6
North-Western Atlantic Basin, *sea feature* **25** B 3
N.W. Highlands, *mts.* **28** F 3
N.W. Providence Chan., *channel* **123** F 2
North West River **115** L 3
North West Territories, *province* **114** E 2
Northwich **45** F 4
Norton Plains, *region* **146** C 4
Norton Sd., *inlet* **106** B 2
Nort-sur-Erdre **54** D 4
Norvegia, K., *cape* **23** B 2
Norway **28** H 2
Norway House **114** H 3
Norway, Is., *island grp.* **82** E 4
Norwegian Basin, *sea feature* **24** M 2
Norwegian Sea **24** M 2
Norwich, *England* **34** F 3
Norwich, *U.S.A.* **117** F 3
Noshiro **75** R 5
Nossi-Bé, *island* **91** H 7
Nossob, *river* **91** F 8
Nosy-Varika **105** D 4
Noteć, *river* **58** G 2
Nótios Evvoïkós Kólpos, *channel* **63** D 4
Noto **61** E 6
Notodden **51** N 5
Noto Hantō, *peninsula* **80** D 3
Not Ozero, *lake* **50** U 2
Nottingham **28** F 3
Nottingham, *county* **45** G 4
Nottingham I., *island* **115** K 2
Nottoway, *river* **119** M 1
Notre Dame B., *bay* **106** H 3
Notre Dame Mts., *mts.* **106** G 3
Nouakchott **90** B 4
Nouméa **141** G 4
Noupoort **101** E 5
Nova Friburgo **133** E 5
Nova Lima **135** D 1
Nova Lisboa **91** E 7
Nova Lusitânia **101** G 2
Novara **36** D 2
Nova Scotia, *province* **115** L 4
Nova Sofala **101** G 3
Nova Varoš **62** A 2
Nov. Ladoga **35** K 2
Novaya Sibir, O., *island* **75** S 2
Novaya Zemlya, *island group* **66** D 2
Nova Zagora **62** D 2
Novelda **52** E 3
Nové Zamky **64** C 3
Novgorod **51** U 5
Novi **60** E 2
Novi Ligure **60** B 2
Novi Pazar, *Bulgaria* **62** E 2
Novi Pazar, *Yugoslavia* **62** B 2
Novi Sad **37** E 2
Novocherkassk **35** L 4
Novograd Volynskiy **64** E 2
Novogrudok **64** E 2
Novo Hamburgo **135** C 2
Novokuznetsk **75** L 4
N. Mesto **59** F 6
Novomoskovsk **65** C 4
Novo Redondo **91** E 7
Novorossiysk **37** G 2
Novoshaktinsk **37** G 2
Novosibirsk **66** F 3
Novosibirskiye Ostrova, *island group* **67** J 2
Novo Uzensk **74** G 4
Novo-Vyatsk **35** M 2
Novozybkov **35** K 3
Novska **60** F 2
Nový Jicín **64** C 3
Novyy Port **66** E 2
Nowy Sącz **64** D 3
Nowa Sól **64** B 2
Nowe Worowo **58** F 2
Nowgong **86** F 3
Nowogard **58** F 2
Nowra **147** K 6
Noya **52** A 1
Noyon **54** F 3
Noyan Uula, *mountains* **76** D 3
N'riquinha **101** D 1
Nubian Desert, *desert* **90** G 3
Nu Chiang, *river* **82** C 3
Nudo Coropuna, *mt.* **135** A 1
Nuneaton **39** F 5
Nueltin Lake, *lake* **114** H 2
Nueva Rosita **122** C 2
Nueve de Julio **135** B 3
Nuevo Laredo **122** D 2
Nugget Pt., *cape* **151** C 8
Nûgssuaq, *peninsula* **115** M 1
Nui Mang, *mountain* **83** E 5
Nukha **37** H 3
Nukus **74** H 5
Nullagine **152** C 2
Nullarbor Plain, *plain* **140** C 5
Numazu **80** D 4
Nuneaton **43** F 2
Nung-an **76** H 3
Nungwe, Ras, *cape* **104** D 4
Nunivak I., *island* **137** C 1
Nuong, L., *lake* **103** E 2
Nuoro **61** B 4
Nuratau, Khr., *mountains* **86** C 1
Nuremberg, see Nürnberg **59** D 4
Nuristan, *region* **86** C 2
Nürnberg **59** D 4
Nuro **81** F 8
Nurri **61** B 5
Nusa Tenggara, *province* **84** C 4
Nu Shan, *mountains* **79** G 3
Nushki **78** D 3
Nut Mt., *mountain* **118** G 1
Nuweveldreeks, *mts.* **101** D 6
Nuyts Archo., *island group* **146** F 6
Nuyts, Pt., *cape* **147** C 7
Nya Chu, *river* **82** C 2
Nyak Tsho, *lake* **86** D 2
Nyanza, *region* **104** C 3
Nyasa, Lake, *lake* **91** G 7
Nyaungu **82** B 4
Nyazepetrovsk **35** N 3
Nybro **51** P 6
Nyenchentanglha Ra., *mountains* **66** F 4
Nyeri **90** G 6
Nyíregyháza **37** E 2
Nyiri Desert, *desert* **99** G 6
Nyiru, Mt., *mountain* **90** G 5
Nyköbing, *Denmark, Falster* **34** G 3
Nyköbing, *Denmark, Jylland* **51** M 6
Nyköping **51** P 5
Nylstroom **91** F 8
Nymburk **58** F 3
Nymphe Bank, *sea feature* **39** C 6
Nynäshamn **51** P 5
Nyngan **149** D 5
Nyon **57** B 3
Nyons **55** G 5
Nysätra **50** R 3
Nyssa **120** C 3
Nyuk, Oz., *lake* **50** U 3
Nyunzu **104** A 4
n'Zérékoré **98** C 5

Oakdale **120** B 4
Oakey **147** K 5
Oakham **43** G 2
Oakland **118** C 4
Oakover, *river* **152** C 2
Oak Ridge **119** L 4
Oamaru **151** D 7
Oa, Mull of, *cape* **38** C 4
Oas **81** E 5
Oasis Jalo, *oasis* **90** F 3
Oates Land, *region* **23** K 2
Oatman **120** D 5
Oaxaca de Juárez **122** D 3
Ob', *river* **66** E 2
Obama **80** C 4
Oban, *New Zealand* **151** C 8
Oban, *Scotland* **38** D 3

Pacific-Antarctic Ridge, *sea feature* 23 P 3
Pacific Grove 120 B 4
Pacific Ocean 18 B 4
Paclasan 81 D 5
Pactolus Bank, *sea feature* 23 R 3
Padada 81 F 8
Padang 66 G 6
Padang, P., *island* 84 B 3
Padany 50 V 3
Padaran, C., *cape* 83 E 7
Padas, *river* 81 A 9
Paddington 41 D 2
Paddock Wood 41 E 3
Paderborn 58 C 3
Padilla 132 C 4
Padova 36 D 2
Padra 86 C 4
Padre Island, *island* 119 H 6
Padstow 42 C 4
Paducah 121 B 2
Padul 52 D 4
Paengnyŏng-do, *island* 76 G 4
Paeroa 150 F 3
Paete 81 D 4
Pag, *island* 60 E 2
Pagadian 79 K 5
Pagai, Kep., *island group* 84 B 4
Pagan 82 B 4
Pagan, *island* 85 F 2
Pagasitikós Kólpos, *bay* 62 C 4
Pagsangan 81 F 5
Pahang, *river* 84 B 3
Pahia Pt., *cape* 151 B 8
Pahiatua 150 F 5
Pahote Pk., *mountain* 120 C 3
Pahute Mesa, *tableland* 120 C 4
Paignton 42 D 4
Päijänne, *lake* 28 K 2
Paimboeuf 54 C 4
Pai-miao-tzu 82 E 2
Painis 81 G 9
Painted Desert, *desert* 106 E 4
Painter, Mt., *mountain* 149 B 5
Pai-se 79 H 3
Pai-sha-li 79 H 4
Paisley 38 D 4
Paisley Seapeak, *sea feature* 153 B 3
Pai-t'ou Shan, *mountain* 76 H 3
Paitsi Shan, *mountains* 77 F 6
Paiva 52 A 2
Paiyu Shan, *mountains* 76 D 4
Pajala 50 R 2
Pajares, Pto. de, *pass* 52 C 1
Pajaros, I., *island* 134 D 2
Pakaraima Mts., *mts.* 132 C 2
Pakchan, *river* 83 C 7
Pakistan 66 F 4
Pakokku 86 F 4
Paks 60 G 1
Pala 102 C 2
Palafrugell 53 G 2
Palamós 53 G 2
Palana 75 S 4
Palanan Pt., *cape* 81 E 3
Palanges, *region* 55 F 5
Palanpur 86 C 3
Palapag 81 F 5
Palapye 101 E 5
Palar, *river* 87 D 5
Palas de Rey 52 B 1
Palatka, *U.S.A.* 121 D 4
Palatka, *U.S.S.R.* 75 S 3
Palau 60 B 4
Palau Is., *island group* 67 H 5
Palaw 83 C 6
Palawan, *island* 67 G 5
Palawan Passage, *channel* 79 J 5
Paldiski 51 S 5
Palembang 67 G 6
Palencia 52 C 1
Palenque 134 D 1
Palermo 28 H 5
Paletwa 82 A 4
Palghat 87 D 5
Palgrave, Mt., *mountain* 152 B 2
Pali 86 C 3
Palit, K. i, *cape* 62 A 3
Palizada 134 C 2
Palk Bay, *bay* 87 D 5
Palkonda Ra., *mountains* 87 D 5
Palk Str., *strait* 66 F 5
Palla Bianca, *mountain* 57 F 3
Pallanza 57 D 4
Pallars, *region* 53 F 1
Palliser Bay, *bay* 150 F 5
Palliser, C., *cape* 150 F 5
Palma, B. de, *bay* 53 G 3
Palma del Rio 52 G 4
Palma de Mallorca 53 G 3
Palma, *Mozambique* 104 E 5
Palmas, C., *cape* 90 C 5
Palmas, G. di, *gulf* 61 B 5
Palma Soriano 123 F 2
Palm Beach 119 L 6
Palmea, *river* 134 C 2
Palmela 52 A 3
Palmer Archo., *island group* 23 R 2
Palmer Land, *district* 23 S 2
Palmerston 151 D 7
Palmerstone, C., *cape* 148 D 3
Palmerston North 150 F 5
Palmi 61 E 5
Palmira 132 B 2
Palmira, C. de la, *cape* 53 F 3
Palm Is., *island group* 147 J 3
Palm Springs 120 C 5
Palmyra, see 'Tadmur 88 B 3
Palmyras Pt., *cape* 87 E 4
Palni Hills, *mountains* 87 D 5
Palo 81 F 6
Palo Alto 120 B 4
Palomar Mt., *mountain* 118 D 5
Palomas 52 B 3
Palomera, Sa., *mountains* 53 E 2
Palopo 79 K 6
Palos, C. de, *cape* 36 B 3
Pålsboda 51 P 5
Palu 88 C 2
Palu Trench, *sea feature* 67 H 5
Pamekasan 79 J 6
Pa-mieh Shan, *mountains* 77 D 6
Pamiers 55 E 6
Pamirs, *mountains* 66 E 4
Pamlico Sd., *inlet* 119 M 4
Pampa del Tamarugal, *pampas* 132 C 5
Pampas, *region* 127 C 6
Pamplona, *Colombia* 123 F 4
Pamplona, *Spain* 36 B 2
Panagyurishte 62 D 2
Panamá 107 G 5
Panamá, Bahía de, *bay* 134 D 2
Panama Canal, *canal* 107 G 5
Panama Canal Zone 107 G 5
Panama City 119 K 5
Panamá, G. de, *gulf* 107 G 5
Panama, Isthmus of, *region* 123 F 4
Panama, *state* 107 F 5
Pan American Highway 136 B 2
Panamint Ra., *mountains* 118 D 4
Panaon, *island* 81 F 7
Panaro, *river* 60 C 2
Panay, *island* 67 H 5
Panayía, *island* 62 D 3
Pancake Ra., *mountains* 120 C 4
Pančevo 64 D 4
Panda 101 G 4
Pandan, *Philippines, Catanduanes* 81 F 4
Pandan, *Philippines, Panay* 81 E 6
Pandan Roxás 84 D 2
Pandharpur 87 D 4
Panevezhis 64 E 1
Pang, *river* 41 B 3
Pangaíon Óros, *mts.* 62 C 3
Pangani 104 D 4
Pangbourne 43 F 3
Pang-fou 67 G 4
Pangi 104 A 3
Pangi Ra., *mountains* 86 D 2
Pangkalanbrandan 84 A 3
Pangkalpinang 84 B 4
Pangnirtung 115 L 2
Pangong Tso, *lake* 86 D 2
Pangutaran Group, *island group* 81 D 8
Panipat 78 E 3
Panjnad, *river* 86 C 3
Pankshin 102 B 2
Panorama, Mt., *mountain* 148 D 3
Panrango, G., *mountain* 84 B 4
Pantanal do Taquari, *region* 132 D 4
Pantar, *island* 84 D 4
Pantelleria, *island* 28 H 5
Pan, Tierra del, *region* 52 C 2
Pao-chi 79 H 2
Paola 61 F 5
Pao-shan 66 F 4
Pao-t'ou 75 N 5
Pápa 64 C 3
Papakura 150 F 3
Papantla de Olarte 122 D 2
Papar 81 A 9
Paparoa Ra., *mountains* 151 D 6
Pápas, Akr., *Greece, Ikaría, cape* 63 D 5
Pápas, Akr., *Greece, Pelopónnisos, cape* 63 B 4
Papa Stour, *island* 46 G 1
Papatoetoe 150 F 3
Papa Westray, *island* 46 F 2
Pa-pien Chiang, *river* 77 C 7
Paps of Jura, *mountains* 47 C 6
Papua, Gulf of, *gulf* 140 E 2
Papua, Territory of 140 E 2
Papuk, *mountain* 36 E 2
Papun 83 B 5
Papusa, *mountain* 64 E 4
Pará, *river* 133 E 3
Paracale 81 E 4
Paracas, Pena., *peninsula* 132 B 4
Parachinar 86 C 2
Paraćin 62 B 2
Paradise 120 B 4
Paragould 121 B 2
Paraguai, *river* 126 D 4
Paraguaná, Pena. de, *peninsula* 132 B 1
Paraguarí 135 C 2
Paraguay 126 C 5
Paraguay, *river* 126 D 5
Paraíba, *river* 126 E 5
Paraíso 134 D 1
Parakou 102 B 2
Paralímni, *lake* 63 C 4
Paramaribo 126 D 2
Paramillo, *mountain* 132 B 1
Paramo, El, *region* 52 C 1
Paramonga 132 B 4
Paramore I., *island* 121 F 2
Paramushir, O., *island* 75 S 4
Paran, *river* 89 A 4
Paraná 127 C 6
Paraná, *river* 126 D 5
Paranaguá 135 D 2
Paranaíba, *river* 126 E 4
Paranapanema, *river* 126 D 5
Paranapiacaba, Sa., *mts.* 126 E 5
Parapóla, *island* 63 C 5
Parbati, *river* 86 D 3
Parbhani 87 D 4
Parc de la Verendrye, *national park* 116 E 2
Parchim 58 D 2
Parc National de l'Upemba, *national park* 104 A 5
Parc National Albert, *national park* 104 B 3
Parc. Prov. des Laurentides, *national park* 117 F 2
Pardes Hanna 89 A 2
Pardoo 152 B 2
Pardubice 34 G 3
Parece Vela, *island* 85 E 1
Parecis, Chapada dos, *mountains* 132 C 4
Paredes de Nava 52 C 1
Pare Mts., *mountains* 103 E 3
Parengarenga Harbour, *harbour* 150 E 2
Parent, Lac, *lake* 116 E 1
Parepare 79 J 6
Parghat Pass, *pass* 87 C 4
Pargolovo 51 U 4
Paria, G. de, *gulf* 132 C 1
Paria, Pena. de, *peninsula* 132 C 1
Paria Plateau, *plateau* 120 D 4
Parigi 84 D 4
Parima, Sa., *mountains* 126 C 2
Pariñas, Pta., *cape* 126 A 3
Paris 28 G 4
Parita 134 C 3
Parita, Golfo de, *gulf* 134 C 2
Paritilla 134 C 3
Parker 120 D 5
Parker Hill, *mountain* 152 C 4
Parker Pt., *cape* 148 B 2
Parker Ra., *mountains* 146 C 6
Parkersburg 119 L 4
Parkes 147 J 6
Parkhurst Forest, *region* 41 B 4
Park Ra., *mountains* 118 F 3
Parma 36 D 2
Parnaíba 126 E 3
Parnaíba, *river* 126 E 3
Parnassós, *mountains* 63 C 4
Párnis, *mountains* 63 C 4
Párnon Óros, *mountains* 63 C 5
Pärnu 34 J 2
Paro Dz 86 E 3
Paroo, *river* 147 H 5
Paropamisus, *mountains* 78 D 2
Páros, *island* 63 D 5
Parramatta 147 K 6
Parras 122 C 2
Parrett, *river* 42 E 3
Parry Bay, *bay* 114 J 2
Parry, C., *cape* 114 E 1
Parry Islands, *island grp.* 106 E 2
Parry Sound, *inlet* 115 J 4
Parseier Sp., *mountain* 57 F 2
Parsnip Pk., *mountain* 120 D 4
Partabgarh 86 D 3
Partanna 61 D 6
Pårtefjället, *mountain* 50 P 2
Parthenay 55 D 4
Partry Mts., *mountains* 39 B 5
Paru, *river* 133 D 3
Parys 102 D 5
Pasadena 118 D 5
Paşalimani, *island* 62 E 3
Pasaula, *river* 134 B 2
Pasay City 81 D 4
Pasco 120 C 2
Pasewalk 58 F 2
Pasig 81 D 4
Pasley, C., *cape* 140 C 5
P. de los Libres 135 C 2
Paso de los Tores 135 C 3
Paso Robles 120 B 5
Pasquia Hills, *mountains* 118 G 1
Passage West 49 C 5
Passau 59 E 4
Passero, C., *cape* 28 H 5
Passi 81 E 6
Passo Fundo 136 C 1
Passos 135 D 2
Pasto 132 B 2
Pastrana 52 D 2
Pasuquin 81 D 2
Pasuruan 84 C 4
Pasvikelv, *river* 50 T 1
Patagonia, *region* 127 B 7
Patan 86 C 4
Pataudi 86 D 3
Patea 150 F 4
Pateley Bridge 44 G 3
Paterna 53 E 3
Paterno 61 E 6
Paterson 119 N 3
Paterson Inlet, *inlet* 151 C 8
Pati 84 C 4
Patiala 78 E 2
Patience Well, *well* 152 D 2
Patkai Hills, *mountains* 86 F 3
Pátmos, *island* 63 E 5
Patna, *India, Bihar* 66 F 4
Patna, *India, Orissa* 87 E 4
Patnanongan I., *island* 81 E 4
Patomskoye Nagor'ye, *mountains* 66 G 3
Patos, Lagôa dos, *lake* 127 D 6
Pátrai 37 E 3
Patraikós Kólpos, *strait* 63 B 4
Patrington 45 H 4
Patta I., *island* 90 H 6
Patterson 120 B 4
Pau 36 B 2
Pauillac 55 D 5
Paulau Is., *island group* 85 E 3
Paulding Bay, *bay* 23 J 2
Paulis 102 D 2
Paungde 83 B 5
Pavant Mts., *mountains* 120 D 4
Pavia 36 D 2
Pavlodar 74 K 4
Pavlograd 35 K 4
Pavlovsk 35 J 2
Pawn, *river* 82 B 5
Pawtucket 117 F 3
Paximádhia, *island* 63 D 6
Paxoí, *island* 62 B 4
Payerne 57 B 3
Payette 120 C 2
Payette, *river* 120 C 2
Payne, *river* 115 K 3
Payne Bay 115 K 2
Payne L., *lake* 115 K 3
Payne's Find 152 B 3
Payo 81 F 5
Paysandú 127 D 6
Pays Basques, *region* 55 D 6
Pazardzhik 62 D 2
Peace, *river* 106 E 3
Peacehaven 41 E 4
Peace River 114 F 3
Peacock Sound, *inlet* 23 P 2
Peak Hill-Horse Shoe 152 B 3
Peak Ra., *mountains* 148 D 3
Peal de B. 52 D 4
Pearl, *river* 119 J 5
Pearson Is., *island group* 146 F 6
Peary Land 24 Q 1
Pebane 105 A 3
Peć 37 E 2
Pechenga 50 U 1
Pechora 35 N 2
Pechora, *river* 29 N 2
Pechorskaya Guba, *bay* 35 M 1
Pechorskoye More, *sea* 24 J 2
Pechory 51 T 5
Pecos, *river* 106 E 4
Pécs 64 C 3
Pedasí 134 C 3
Pedreiras 133 E 3
Pedro Bank, *sea feature* 107 G 5
Pedroches, Los, *region* 52 C 3
Pedro González, I., *island* 134 D 2
Pedro Miguel 134 D 1
Pedro Muñoz 52 D 3
Pedro, Pt., *cape* 87 D 5
Peebles 38 E 4
Peebles, *county* 47 E 6
Peebles, Mt., *mountain* 149 B 4
Pee Dee, *river* 121 E 3
Peel 44 D 3
Peel Fell, *mountain* 47 F 6
Peel Sd., *inlet* 114 H 1
Peene, *river* 51 O 7
Peera Peera Poolanna L., *lake* 147 G 5
Pegasus Bay, *bay* 151 E 6
Peg Meratus, *mountains* 140 B 2
Pegnitz 58 D 4
Pego 52 E 3
Pegu 83 B 5
Pegu, *province* 83 B 5
Pegunungan Barisan, *mountains* 66 G 6
Pegu Yoma, *mountains* 79 G 4
Pegwell Bay, *bay* 41 G 3
Pehuajó 136 B 2
Pei Chiang, *river* 77 E 7
Pei-feng 76 H 3
Pei-hai 79 H 3
Pei-li-shih 77 D 8
Peilstein, *mountain* 59 F 4
Peine 58 D 2
Pei-pan Chiang, *river* 77 D 6
Pei-p'ing 67 G 4
Pei Shan, *mountains* 75 M 5
Pei-shan Gobi, *desert* 76 C 3
Pei-shuang Lieh-tao, *island* 77 G 6
Pei-ta Ho, *river* 76 B 4
Pei Wan, *bay* 76 G 4
Pekalongan 79 H 6
Peking, see Pei-p'ing 76 F 4
Pekon 82 B 5
Pekul'ney, Khr., *mts.* 75 U 3
Pelabuhan Ratu, Tel., *bay* 84 B 4
Pelado, *mountain* 53 E 3
Pelado, C., *cape* 53 F 3
Pelagie, Isole, *island grp.* 28 H 5
Pélagos, *island* 62 D 4
Pelee I., *island* 121 D 1
Pelée, M., *mountain* 123 G 3
Pelee Pt., *cape* 116 C 3
Peleng, *island* 79 K 6
Pelhřimov 59 F 4
Pelican Harbour, *harbour* 121 E 5
Pelican Pt., *cape* 101 B 3
Pelkosenniemi 50 T 2
Pelleluhu Is., *island grp.* 85 F 4
Pellg i Drinit, *bay* 62 A 3
Pelline, Val., *valley* 57 C 4
Pellworm, *island* 58 C 1
Pelly, *river* 114 D 2
Pelly L., *lake* 114 G 2
Pelly Mts., *mountains* 106 D 2
Pelopónnisos, *peninsula* 28 J 5
Pelotas 136 C 2
Pelsart Group, *island group* 146 B 5
Pelusium, *ancient site* 100 D 1
Pemalang 84 B 4
Pematangsiantar 79 G 5
Pemba, B. de, *bay* 105 B 2
Pemba Channel, *channel* 104 D 4
Pemba I., *island* 91 G 6
Pemberton 146 C 6
Pembridge 42 E 2
Pembroke, *Canada* 116 E 2
Pembroke, *England* 39 D 6
Pembroke, *county* 42 C 3
Peña de Francia, Sa. de, *mountains* 52 B 2
Peña, Emb. de la, *lake* 53 E 1
Penafiel, *Portugal* 52 A 2
Peñafiel, *Spain* 52 C 2
Peñagolosa, *mountain* 53 E 2
Peñalara, Pico de, *mt.* 52 D 2
Penamacor 52 B 2
Penambo Ra., *mountains* 84 C 3
Penampang 81 B 9
Penang, *island* 66 F 5
Peña Prieta, *mountain* 52 C 1
Peñaranda de Bracamonte 52 C 2
Peñarroya, *mountain* 36 B 3
Peñarroya-Pueblonuevo 52 C 3
Penarth 42 D 3
Peña Rubia, *mountain* 52 B 1
Peñas C. de, *cape* 52 C 1
Peña, Sa. de la, *mts.* 52 E 1
Peñas, G. de, *gulf* 127 B 7
Peña Trevinca, *mountain* 52 B 1
Pena Vieja, *mountain* 36 B 2
Pen-ch'i 67 H 3
Pendleton 118 D 2
Pend Oreille Lake, *lake* 120 C 1
Péné, Mt., *mountain* 98 E 5
Peneda, Sa. de, *mountains* 52 A 2
Penedo 133 F 4
Penganga, *river* 87 D 4
Penge 41 D 3
P'eng-hu Tao, *island* 77 F 7
P'eng-lai 76 G 4
Penguin Deeps, *sea feature* 140 C 3
Peniche 52 A 3
Penicuik 47 E 6
Penistone 45 G 4
Penju, Kep., *island grp.* 85 D 4
Penmarch, Pte. de, *cape* 54 B 4
Pennemünde 58 E 1
Penner, *India, Andhra Pradesh, river* 87 D 5
Penner, *India, Madras, river* 87 D 5
Penneshaw 149 B 6
Pennine, Alpi, *mountains* 57 C 4
Pennines, *mountains* 34 E 3
Pennsylvania, *state* 119 M 3
Penny Highlands, *mts.* 115 L 2
Penola 149 C 6
Penonómé 134 C 2
Penrith 44 F 3
Pensacola 119 K 5
Pensacola B., *bay* 121 C 4
Pensacola Cay, *reef* 121 E 5
Pensacola Mts., *mts.* 23 R 1
Pensiangan 81 B 9
Penticton 114 F 4
Pentland 148 D 3
Pentland Firth, *strait* 34 E 3
Pentland Hills, *hills* 38 E 4
Penungah 81 B 9
Penza 29 M 3
Penzance 39 D 6
Penzhinskaya Guba, *gulf* 75 T 3
Penzhinskiy Khr., *mts.* 75 T 3
Peoria 119 K 3
Pepido, *island* 84 C 4
Pequop Mts., *mountains* 120 D 3
Pera Hd., *cape* 148 C 1
Percée, Pte., *mountain* 57 B 4
Perche, Col de la, *pass* 36 C 2
Perche, Coteau du, *reg.* 54 E 3
Percival Lakes, *lakes* 152 C 2
Perdices, Sa. de, *mts.* 52 D 2
Perdido, M., *mountain* 53 F 1
Pereira 132 B 2
Pergamino 136 B 2
Perhon joki, *river* 50 S 3
Peribonca, *river* 117 F 1
Peribonca Lake, *lake* 116 F 1
Périgord, *region* 55 E 5
Perigueux 36 C 2
Perija, Sa. de, *mountains* 126 B 1
Perim I., *island* 90 H 4
Periperi, Sa. do, *mts.* 133 E 4
Perlas, Archo. de las, *island group* 123 F 4
Perlas, Pta. de, *cape* 123 E 3
Perleburg 58 D 2
Perm 29 O 3
Pernik 62 C 2
Péronne 54 F 3
Peron Pena., *peninsula* 152 A 3
Perouse Strait, La., *strait* 137 B 1
Perovo 74 F 4
Perpignan 36 C 2
Perregaux 53 F 5
Perris 120 C 5
Perry River 114 G 2
Persepolis, *ancient site* 158
Persian, *civilisation* 158
Persian Gulf, *gulf* 29 N 6
Perth, *Australia* 140 B 5
Perth, *Canada* 116 E 2
Perth, *Scotland* 38 E 3
Perth, *county* 47 E 5
Perth Amboy 117 E 3
Pertuis Breton, *channel* 55 D 4
Pertuis de Maumusson, *channel* 55 D 5
Peru 126 B 4
Peru-Chile Trench, *sea feature* 126 B 4
Perugia 36 D 2
Pervomaysk 65 B 4
Pervoural'sk 74 H 4
Pesaro 60 D 3
Pescador, Pta. del, *cape* 52 D 1
Pescadores Channel, *channel* 77 F 7

Potomac 119 M 4
Potosí 126 C 4
Pototan 81 E 6
Po-t'ou-chen 76 F 4
Potsdam 58 E 2
Potters Bar 41 D 2
Potton I., *island* 41 F 2
Pou Loung, *mountain* 82 D 4
Poughkeepsie 119 N 3
Poulo Cecir De Mer, *island* 83 E 7
Poulo Condore, Iles de, *island group* 83 E 7
Poulo Obi, *island* 83 D 7
Poulo Panjang, *island* 83 D 7
Poulo Way, *island* 83 D 7
Pouso Alegre 135 D 2
Povenets 50 V 4
Poverty Bay, *bay* 150 G 4
Povlen, *mountain* 62 A 1
Povoa de Varzim 52 A 2
Povorotnyy, Mys., *cape* 80 C 2
Powder, *river* 118 F 2
Powel Cay, *reef* 121 E 5
P'o-yang Hu, *lake* 67 G 4
Poza 52 D 1
Požarevac 64 D 4
Poza Rica 122 D 2
Poznań 28 J 3
Poznań, *province* 64 C 2
Pozoblanco 52 C 3
Pozo, Sa. de, *mountains* 52 D 4
Prachin Buri 83 C 6
Prachuap Khiri Khan 66 F 5
Pradairo, *mountains* 52 B 1
Praděd, *mountain* 64 C 2
Prades 55 F 6
Prague, *see Praha* 58 F 3
Praha 28 H 3
Prasonísi, Akr., *cape* 63 E 6
Prasoúdha, *island* 63 D 4
Pratas, *see Tung-Sha Tao* 77 F 7
Prat del Llobregat 53 G 2
Prätigau, *valley* 57 E 3
Prato 60 C 3
Pratomagno, *mountains* 60 C 3
Pratt 118 H 4
Pravia 52 B 1
Precordillera, *mts.* 136 B 1
Predazzo 60 C 1
Pregolya, *river* 51 Q 6
Premier Downs, *hills* 146 E 6
Prenzlau 58 E 2
Preparis I., *island* 87 F 5
Preparis South Channel, *sea feature* 87 F 5
Přerov 64 C 3
Presanella, *mountain* 51 F 3
Prescot 44 F 4
Prescott, *Canada* 117 E 2
Prescott, *U.S.A.* 118 E 5
Preservation Inlet, *inlet* 151 B 8
Presidente Prudente 136 C 1
Presidencia Roque Sáenz Peña 135 B 2
Preslav 62 E 2
Prešov 64 D 3
Prespansko Jez., *lake* 62 B 3
Presque Isle 119 O 2
Prestatyn 42 D 1
Presteigne 42 D 2
Přeštice 58 E 4
Preston, *England* 39 E 5
Preston, *U.S.A.* 120 E 3
Prestwick 38 D 4
Pretoria 91 F 8
Prévaza 37 E 3
Prey Veng 83 D 7
Pribilof Is., *island group* 67 L 3
Příbram 64 B 3
Price 118 E 4
Price, C., *cape* 83 A 6
Prichernomorskaya Nizmennost', *plain* 37 G 2
Pridneprovskaya Nizmennost, *plain* 28 K 3
Priego 52 D 2
Priego de Córdoba 52 C 4
Prieska 91 F 8
Priest L., *lake* 120 C 1
Priest Rapids Res., *reservoir* 120 C 2
Prijedor 60 F 2
Prikaspiyskaya Nizmennost', *plain* 29 N 4
Prikubanskaya Nizmennost', *plain* 29 L 4
Prilep 62 B 3
Priluki 35 K 3
Primorsk 51 T 4
Prince Albert, *Canada* 114 G 3
Prince Albert, *Rep. of South Africa* 101 D 6
Prince Albert Pena., *peninsula* 114 F 1
Prince Albert Sd., *inlet* 114 F 1
Pr. Alfred C., *cape* 106 D 2
Pr. Charles I., *island* 106 G 2
Prince Edward-Crozet Ridge, *sea feature* 153 A 5
Prince Edward I., *island* 106 G 3
Prince Edward Is., *island group* 153 A 5
Prince George 114 E 3
Pr. of Wales, C., *cape* 106 B 2
Prince of Wales I., *Australia, island* 147 H 2
Prince of Wales I., *Canada, island* 106 E 2
Prince of Wales I., *U.S.A., island* 106 D 3
Prince of Wales Str., *strait* 114 F 1
Pr. Patrick I., *island* 106 D 2
Prince Regent Inlet, *inlet* 114 H 1
Prince Rupert 106 D 3
Princes Highway 147 J 7
Princes Risborough 43 G 3
Princes Risborough Gap, *river gap* 41 C 2
Princess Charlotte Bay, *bay* 147 H 2
Princess Elizabeth Land, *region* 23 G 2
Princetown 42 D 4
Príncipe, *island* 90 D 5
Prinsesse Astrid Kyst, *region* 23 C 2
Prinsesse Ragnhild Kyst, *region* 23 D 2
Prins Harald Kyst, *region* 23 D 2
Prior, C., *cape* 52 A 1
Priozersk 35 J 2
Pripolyarnyy Ural, *mts.* 29 O 2
Pripyat', *river* 28 K 3
Priština 64 D 4
Pritzwalk 58 E 2
Privas 55 G 5
Privolzhskaya Vozvysh., *plateau* 29 M 3
Prizren 62 B 2
Prizzi 61 D 6
Prnjavor 60 F 2
Probolinggo 84 C 4
Progreso 122 E 2
Prokop'yevsk 66 F 3
Prokuplje 62 B 2
Prome 66 F 5
Proserpine 147 J 4
Prosser 120 C 2
Prostéjov 64 C 3
Provadiya 62 E 2
Provence, *province* 55 G 6
Provence, Alpes de, *mountains* 55 H 6
Providence 119 N 3
Providence, C., *cape* 141 G 6
Providence Is., *island group* 91 J 6
Providencia, I. de, *island* 123 E 3
Provideniya 75 V 3
Provins 54 F 3
Provo 118 E 3
Prozor 60 F 3
Prüm 58 B 3
Prüm, *river* 56 E 4
Pruszków 64 D 2
Prut, *river* 28 K 4
Prydz Bay, *bay* 23 F 2
Przemyśl 37 E 2
Przheval'sk 74 K 5
Psará, *island* 63 D 4
Psathoúra, *island* 62 D 4
Psevdhókavos, Akr., *cape* 62 C 4
Pskov 35 J 3
Pskovskoye Oz., *lake* 51 T 5
Ptich', *river* 51 T 7
Ptolemaïs 62 B 3
Ptuj 60 E 1
Pucallpa 132 B 3
Pucarani 135 B 1
Pucio Pt., *cape* 81 D 6
Pudozh 35 K 2
Pudsey 45 G 4
Pudukkottai 87 D 5
Puebla 107 F 5
Puebla de Don F. 52 D 4
Puebla de G. 52 B 4
Puebla de Sanabria 52 B 1
Pueblo, *U.S.A.* 118 G 4
Pueblo, *civilisation* 159
Puentedeume 52 A 1
Puente Genil 52 C 4
Puerto Armuelles 123 E 4
Puerto Ayacucho 132 C 2
Pto. Aysén 136 A 3
Pto. Barrios 123 E 3
Puerto Berrío 123 F 4
Pto. Cabello 123 G 3
Puerto Carreño 132 C 2
Pto. Cortés 123 E 3
Pto. de Sta. Maria 52 B 4
Pto. La Cruz 123 G 3
Puertollano 52 C 3
Puerto Montt 127 B 7
Puerto Natales 136 A 4
Puerto Plata 107 G 5
Puerto Princesa 79 J 5
Puerto Rico 107 G 5
Puerto Rico Trench, *sea feature* 107 G 5
Puerto Santa Cruz 127 C 8
Puerto Suárez 135 C 1
Puisaye, Collines de la, *region* 54 F 4
Pugachev 65 G 3
Puget Sd., *inlet* 118 C 2
Puget-Théniers 60 A 3
Puglia, *province* 61 F 4
Puigcerdá 53 F1
Pugimal, *mountain* 53 G 1
Puig Mayor, *mountain* 53 G 3
Pukaki, L., *lake* 151 D 7
Pukekohe 150 F 3
Puketeraki Ra., *mts.* 151 E 6
Puketoi Ra., *mountains* 150 F 5
Pula 60 D 2
Pulacayo 135 B 2
Pulangi, *river* 81 F 8
P'u-lan-tien 76 G 4
Pulap, *island* 85 F 3
Pulborough 43 G 4
Pulicat L., *lake* 87 D 5
Pullman 118 D 2
Pulo Anna, *island* 85 E 3
Pulog, Mt., *mountain* 81 D 3
Pułtusk 64 D 2
Puluwat, *island* 85 F 3
Pumpsaint 42 D 2
Puna de Atacama, *region* 135 B 2
Puná, I., *island* 126 A 3
Punata 135 B 1
Punakha 66 F 4
Pungsan 80 B 2
Punjab, *province* 86 D 3
Punjab, *region* 66 E 4
Puno 132 B 4
Punta Alta 135 B 3
Punta Arenas 127 B 8
Punta, C. de, *mountain* 123 G 3
Puntarenas 123 E 3
Puntas Negras, Co., *mt.* 135 B 2
Purbeck Downs, *hills* 43 E 4
Purcell Mts., *mountains* 106 E 3
Purchena 52 D 4
Purdy Is., *island group* 85 F 4
Purfleet 41 E 3
Puri 79 F 4
Purley 41 D 3
Purnea 86 E 3
Pursat 79 H 4
Purulia 86 E 4
Purus, *river* 126 C 3
Puruvesi, *lake* 50 T 4
Pŭrvomai 62 D 2
Pusan 67 H 4
Pushkin 35 J 2
Putao 82 B 3
Putaruru 150 F 4
P'u-t'ien 77 F 6
Putorana, Gory, *mts.* 66 F 2
Puttalam 87 D 5
Putumayo, *river* 126 B 3
Puulavesi, *lake* 50 S 4
Puyallup 120 B 2
Puy de Dome, *mountain* 55 F 5
Puy de Sancy, *mountain* 55 F 5
Puy de Sauvagnac, *mt.* 55 E 4
Puy Mary, *mountain* 55 F 5
Pweto 104 B 5
Pwllheli 39 D 5
Pyamalaw, *river* 83 B 6
Pyandzh, *river* 86 C 2
Pya Ozero, *lake* 50 U 2
Pyapon 83 B 5
Pyasina, *river* 75 L 2
Pyatigorsk 37 H 2
Pyhäjärvi, *lake* 51 R 4
Pyinmana 82 B 5
Pyong Yǎng 66 H 4
Pyramid Lake, *lake* 118 D 3
Pyrenees, *mountains* 28 F 4
Pyrzyce 58 F 2
Pytalovo 51 T 5
Qa', Al, *region* 100 E 4
Qa'āmīyāt, Al., *region* 78 B 4
Qabr al Hindī, Ra's, *cape* 78 C 3
Qa'el Hafira, *salt lake* 89 C 3
Qa'el Jinz, *swamp* 89 C 4
Qala'en Nahl 88 A 7
Qalqiliya 89 A 2
Qalyūb 100 C 2
Qalyūbīyah, *province* 100 C 2
Qanţarah, J., *mountain* 100 B 2
Qar'a al Bāgūrīyah, *river* 100 B 2
Qārat al Haddādīn, *mt.* 100 B 2
Qarā', J. al, *mountains* 88 E 6
Qarat Jahannam, *mts.* 100 B 3
Qareh Dagh, *mountain* 65 F 6
Qareh Sū, *river* 88 D 3
Qaşbah, Ra's, *cape* 37 G 4
Qaşbah, Ra's, *cape* 100 F 4
Qash Qai, *mountains* 88 E 3
Qasr 89 B 3
Qaşr al Qaţājī, *ancient site* 100 A 2
Qa'ţabah 88 C 7
Qatana 89 C 1
Qatar 66 D 4
Qatrāna 89 C 3
Qaţrānī, Jabal, *mountains* 100 B 3
Qattara Depression, *region* 90 F 3
Qaysūm, Juzur, *island* 100 E 5
Qazvīn 74 G 6
Qena 90 G 3
Qerkh Bolāgh, *mountain* 88 D 2
Qeshm 78 C 3
Qeshm, *island* 88 F 4
Qeys, J., *island* 88 E 4
Qinā, W., *wadi* 100 D 5
Qiryat Gat 89 A 3
Qiryat Shemona 89 B 1
Qiryat Tiv'on 89 B 2
Qir. Yam 89 B 2
Qishon, *river* 89 B 2
Qīzān 78 B 4
Qom 66 D 4
Quairading 146 C 6
Quakenbrück 58 B 2
Quang Ngai 83 E 6
Quang Tri 83 E 5
Quang Yen 82 E 4
Quantocks, *hills* 42 D 3
Qu'Appelle, *river* 118 G 1
Quarry Hills 41 F 3
Quattervals, P., *mts.* 57 F 3
Qūchān 88 F 2
Queanbeyan 147 J 7
Quebec 106 G 3
Quebec, *province* 115 K 3
Quedlinburg 58 D 3
Queen Alexandra Range, *mountains* 23 L 1
Queen Bess, Mt., *mt.* 114 E 3
Queenborough 41 F 3
Queen Charlotte Is., *island group* 106 D 3
Queen Charlotte Sound, *Canada, inlet* 114 E 3
Queen Charlotte Sd., *New Zealand, inlet* 150 F 5
Queen Charlotte Str., *strait* 118 B 1
Queen Elizabeth Islands, *island group* 106 E 2
Queen Mary Land, *region* 23 G 2
Queen Maud Gulf, *gulf* 114 G 2
Queensland, *state* 140 E 4
Queenscliff 149 C 6
Queenstown, *Rep. of Ireland, see Cobh* 49 C 5
Queenstown, *Australia* 147 J 8
Queenstown, *New Zealand* 151 C 7
Queenstown, *Rep. of South Africa* 91 F 9
Queija, S. de, *mountains* 52 B 1
Quelimane 91 G 7
Que Que 91 F 7
Querétaro 122 C 2
Quetta 66 E 4
Quetta, *province* 86 C 3
Queyras, *region* 55 H 5
Quezaltenango 122 D 3
Quezon 81 E 6
Quezon City 81 D 4
Quibdó 123 F 4
Quiberon 54 C 4
Quilán, C., *cape* 136 A 3
Quillacollo 132 C 4
Quillan 53 G 1
Quill Lakes, *lakes* 114 G 3
Quilmes 136 C 2
Quillota 136 A 2
Quilon 79 E 5
Quilpie 147 H 5
Quimper 54 B 4
Quimperlé 54 C 4
Quinabucasan Pt., *cape* 81 E 4
Quinag, *mountain* 46 C 3
Quincy 119 J 4
Qui Nhon 67 G 5
Quintana de la S. 52 C 3
Quintanar de la Orden 52 D 3
Quionga 104 E 5
Quirimba, Ilhas, *island group* 103 F 4
Quiroga 52 B 1
Quissanga 104 E 6
Quissico 101 G 4
Quita Sueño Bank, *sea feature* 123 E 3
Quito 126 B 3
Qulansiyah 88 E 7
Qulansīyah, Ra's, *cape* 99 J 4
Qumbu 101 F 5
Qumran, *ancient site* 89 B 3
Quoich, L., *lake* 46 C 4
Quorn 147 G 6
Qūr 'As'as, *mountain* 100 B 4
Qurayyah, W., *wadi* 100 F 2
Qus 99 G 3
Quwaysinā 100 C 2
Raahe 34 J 2
Ra'anana 89 A 2
Raasay, *island* 46 C 4
Raasay, Sd. of, *inlet* 38 C 3
Rab, *island* 64 B 4
Raba 67 G 6
Rába, *river* 59 G 5
Rabal 85 E 4
Rabat 90 C 2
Rabaul 141 F 2
Rabba 89 B 3
Rābigh 88 B 5
Raccoon Pt., *cape* 121 B 4
Race, C., *cape* 106 H 3
Race Pt., *cape* 117 F 3
Rach Gia, B. de, *bay* 83 D 7
Racibórz 64 C 2
Racine 119 K 3
Radama, Is., *island* 105 C 2
Radan, *mountain* 62 B 2
Rădăuţi 64 E 3
Radcliffe 45 F 4
Radeburg 58 E 3
Radium Hill 149 C 5
Radkersburg 59 F 5
Radlett 41 D 2
Radnor, *county* 42 D 2
Radnor Forest, *region* 42 D 2
Radolfzell 57 D 2
Radom 34 H 3
Radomir 62 C 2
Radomsko 64 C 2
Radomyshl' 64 F 2
Radstadt 59 E 5
Rae 114 F 2
Rae Bareli 86 D 3
Rae Isthmus, *isthmus* 114 J 2
Raeside, L., *lake* 140 C 4
Raetea, *mountain* 150 E 2
Raetihi 150 F 4
Rafaela 135 B 3
Rafah 89 A 3
Rafsanjān 78 C 2
Raft, *river* 120 D 3
Raft River Mts., *mts.* 120 D 3
Ragay G., *bay* 81 E 5
Ragged Mt., *mountain* 152 C 4
Raglan 150 F 3
Raglan Harb., *harbour* 150 F 3
Raglan Ra., *mountains* 150 E 5
Ragstone Ra., *hills* 41 E 3
Ragusa 36 D 3
Rāḩah, J. ar, *mountains* 100 D 3
Rahaţ, Ḩarrat, *lava flow* 88 C 5
Raheita 88 C 7
Rahuri 87 D 4
Raia, *river* 52 A 3
Raichur 87 D 4
Raigarh, *river* 86 E 4
Raijua, *island* 146 D 2
Railroad Valley, *valley* 120 D 4
Raine Entrance, *channel* 147 H 2
Raine I., *island* 147 H 2
Rainham 41 E 2
Rainier 120 B 2
Rainier, Mt., *mountain* 106 D 3
Rainy L., *lake* 114 H 4
Raipur 78 F 3
Raja, Bt., *mountain* 84 C 4
Rajahmundry 78 F 4
Rajang 79 J 5
Rajapalaiyam 87 D 5
Rajasthan, *state* 86 C 3
Rajgarh 86 D 3
Rajkot 78 E 3
Rajmahal Hills, *mountains* 86 E 3
Raj Nandgaon 86 D 4
Rajshahi, *province* 86 E 3
Rajura 87 D 4
Rakaia, *river* 151 E 6
Rakaposhi, *mountain* 86 D 2
Rakovník 58 E 3
Rakvere 51 S 5
Raleigh 119 M 4
Raleigh Bay, *bay* 121 E 3
Rall Amane, *region* 98 B 3
Ram 89 B 5
Ram, J., *mountain* 89 B 5
Ramallah 89 B 3
Ramapo Deep, *sea feature* 137 B 2
Ramat Gan 89 A 2
Rambouillet 54 E 3
Rambutyo I., *island* 85 F 4
Ramdurg 87 D 5
Rame Head, *cape* 42 C 4
Rāmhormoz 78 B 2
Ramla 89 A 3
Ramlat Dahm, *region* 88 C 6
Ramlat Sab'atayn, *region* 88 D 6
Rämmen 51 O 4
Ramnäs 51 P 5
Râmnicu Sârat 64 E 4
Râmnicu Vâlcea 64 E 4
Ramona 120 C 5
Ramon, H., *mountain* 89 A 4
Rampur 78 E 3
Ramree I., *island* 79 G 4
Rāmsār 88 E 2
Ramsbottom 45 F 4
Ramsele 50 P 3
Ramsey 39 D 4
Ramsey I., *island* 42 B 3
Ramsgate 39 G 6
Ramsjö 50 P 4
Ramtha 89 C 2
Rana, *region* 50 O 2
Rañadoiro, Sa. de, *mt.* 52 B 1
Ranau 81 B 9
Ranau, D., *lake* 84 B 4
Rancagua 136 A 2
Rance, *river* 54 C 3
Ranchería, I., *island* 134 B 3
Ranchi 86 E 4
Randalstown 48 E 2
Randers 34 G 3
Randsburg 120 C 5
Raneå 50 R 3
Ranfurly 151 D 7
Rangiora 151 E 6
Rangitaiki, *river* 150 G 4
Rangitata, *river* 151 D 6
Rangitikei, *river* 150 F 4
Rangitoto Ra., *mts.* 150 F 4
Rangoon 66 F 5
Rangoon, *river* 84 A 2
Rannoch, L., *lake* 46 D 5
Rannoch Moor, *moor* 38 D 3
Ranpur 87 E 4
Rantekombola, Bk., *mt.* 140 B 2
Rao Co., *mountain* 82 D 5
Raoui, Erg er, *sand dunes* 98 C 3
Rapallo 60 B 2
Rapang 84 C 4
Raphoe 48 D 2
Rapid City 118 G 3
Rapperswil 57 D 2
Raqqah 37 G 3
Rasa, Pta., *cape* 127 C 7
Rās Ghārib 100 E 4
Rashādīya 89 B 4
Rashīd 99 G 2
Rasht 66 D 4
Raskam, *river* 86 D 2
Raskoh, *mountains* 78 D 3
Ras Koh, *mountain* 86 B 3
Raso, C., *Brazil, cape* 126 E 2
Raso, C., *Portugal, cape* 52 A 3
Raso del Portillo, *region* 52 C 2
Rason, L., *lake* 146 D 5
Rasskazovo 35 L 3
Ras Tannūrah 88 E 4

San–Sea

196

San Antonio, C., *Cuba, cape* 123 E 2
San Antonio, C. de, *cape* 53 F 3
San Baudilio de L. 53 G 2
S. Beneidcto, *island* 123 B 3
San Bernardino, *Paraguay* 135 C 2
San Bernardino, *U.S.A.* 118 D 5
San Bernardino Mts., *mountains* 118 D 5
San Bernardino Pass, *pass* 57 E 3
San Bernardino Str., *strait* 81 F 5
San Bernardo 136 A 2
San Blas, C., *cape* 119 K 6
San Blas, Cord. de, *mts.* 134 D 1
San Blas, Pena. de, *peninsula* 134 D 1
San Blas, Pta., *cape* 123 F 4
S. Bruno, Serra, *mts.* 61 F 5
San Carlos, *Argentina* 136 A 3
San Carlos, *Chile* 135 A 3
San Carlos, *Panama* 134 D 2
San Carlos, *Philippines, Luzon* 81 D 4
San Carlos, *Philippines, Negros* 79 K 4
San Carlos, *Spain* 53 F 2
San Carlos, *Venezuela* 123 G 4
San Carlos del Zulia 123 F 4
S. Celoni 53 G 2
Sancerre 54 F 4
San-ch'a Ho, *river* 82 D 3
San-chiao Shan, *mt.* 77 D 7
San-chien Shan, *mts.* 77 C 7
San Clemente 52 D 3
San Clemente, *island* 118 D 5
San Cristóbal, *Argentina* 136 B 2
San Cristóbal, *Panama* 134 C 2
San Cristóbal, *Venezuela* 132 B 2
S. Cristóbal de las Casas 122 D 3
San Cristobal I., *island* 141 G 3
S. Cristobal Tr., *sea feature* 141 G 3
Sancti-Spíritus 123 F 2
Sand 51 M 5
Sanda, *island* 47 C 6
Sandakan 67 G 5
Sandanski 62 C 3
Sanday, *island* 38 E 2
Sanday Sound, *gulf* 46 F 2
Sandgate, *Australia* 149 E 4
Sandgate, *England* 43 J 3
Sand Hill Pt., *cape* 151 B 8
Sand Hills, *hills* 119 M 4
San Diego 106 E 4
Sandikli 65 B 6
Sandlings, *region* 43 J 2
Sand Mt., *mountain* 121 C 3
Sandnes 51 L 5
Sandoa 102 D 3
S. Donà di Piave 60 D 2
Sandover, *river* 146 G 4
Sandoway 79 G 4
Sandown 39 F 6
Sandown Bay, *bay* 41 B 4
Sandpoint 120 C 1
Sandras D., *mountains* 63 F 5
Sandray, *island* 38 C 3
Sandstone 152 B 3
Sandur 87 D 5
Sandusky 116 C 3
Sandviken 34 H 2
Sandwich 43 J 3
Sandy Cape, *cape* 141 F 4
Sandy Hd., *cape* 148 B 2
Sandy Lake 114 G 3
Sandy L., *lake* 114 H 3
San Felipe, *Chile* 135 A 3
San Felipe, *Venezuela* 132 C 1
S. Felipe, C. de, *mountain* 36 B 3
San Félix 134 B 2
San Félix, *river* 134 B 2
San Félix-Juan Fernández Ridge, *sea feature* 137 E 3
San Fellíu de Guixols 53 G 2
San Fernando, *Chile* 135 A 3
San Fernando, *Philippines, C. Luzon* 81 D 4
San Fernando, *Philippines, W. Luzon* 81 D 3
San Fernando, *Spain* 52 B 4
San Fernando, *Trinidad* 132 C 1
San Fernando, *U.S.A.* 120 C 5
San Fernando de Apure 132 C 2
Sanford, *U.S.A., Florida* 121 D 4
Sanford, *U.S.A., N. Carolina* 121 E 3
Sanford, *river* 152 B 3
Sanford, Mt., *mountain* 114 C 2
San Francisco, *Argentina* 136 B 2
San Francisco, *Panama* 134 B 2
San Francisco, *U.S.A.* 106 D 4
San Francisco Bay, *bay* 120 B 4
San Francisco del Oro 122 C 2
San Francisco del Rincón 122 C 2
San Francisco de Macoris 123 F 3
San Gabriel 132 B 2
San Gabriel Mts., *mts.* 120 C 5
Sangachō Dz 86 F 3
Sangamon, *river* 121 B 2
Sangboy Is., *island group* 81 D 8
Sangeang, *island* 84 C 4
Sanger 120 C 4
Sangha, *river* 90 E 5
Sangihe, Kep., *island group* 79 K 5
Sangilen, Khr., *mts.* 76 B 1
Sangju 76 H 4
Sangli 87 D 4
San Gorgonio Mt., *mt.* 120 C 5
Sangre de Cristo Ra., *mountains* 106 E 4
Sangüesa 53 E 1
Sanibel, *island* 121 D 5
San Ildefonso Pena., *peninsula* 81 E 3
San Isidro 81 F 6
San Jacinto 81 E 5
San Javier, *Bolivia* 132 C 4
S. Javier, *Chile* 135 A 3
Sanjō 80 D 3
San Joaquin, *river* 120 B 4
San Joaquin Valley, *valley* 118 C 4
San Jorge, G. de, *Argentina, gulf* 127 C 7
San Jorge, G. de, *Spain, gulf* 36 C 3
San José, *Costa Rica* 107 F 5
San Jose, *Philippine Is., Luzon* 81 D 4
San Jose, *Philippine Is., Mindoro* 81 D 5
San José, *Spain* 53 F 3
S. José, *Uruguay* 136 C 2
San Jose, *U.S.A.* 118 C 4
San Jose de Buenavista 81 D 6
San José, I., *island* 134 D 2
San Juan, *Argentina* 136 B 2
San Juan, *Philippines* 81 G 7
San Juan, *Puerto Rico* 107 G 5
San Juan, *mountain* 121 D 6
San Juan, *river* 118 F 4
San Juan, C. de, *cape* 90 D 5
S. Juan de los Morros 132 C 2
San Juan Mts., *mts.* 106 E 4
San Just, Sa. de, *mts.* 53 E 2
Sankt-Gallen 57 E 2
Sankt Wendel 59 B 4
Sankuru, *river* 90 F 6
S. Lazaro, C., *cape* 122 B 2
S. Lázaro, Sa. de, *mts.* 122 C 2
San Lorenzo de El 52 C 2
Sanlúcar de Barrameda 52 B 4
Sanlúcar la Mayor 52 B 4
S. Lucas, C., *cape* 107 E 4
San Luis 136 B 2
San Luis, Lago de, *lake* 132 C 4
San Luis Obispo 118 C 4
S. Luis Obispo Bay, *bay* 120 B 5
San Luis Potosí 122 C 2
San Luis Valley, *valley* 118 F 4
S. Marco, C., *cape* 61 B 5
San Marcos 118 H 6
San Marino 60 D 3
San Marino, *state* 28 H 4
San Martín de V. 52 C 2
San Martín, L., *lake* 127 B 7
San Mateo, *Spain* 53 F 2
San Mateo, *U.S.A.* 118 C 4
San Matías, G., *gulf* 127 C 7
S. Miguel, *El Salvador* 123 E 3
San Miguel, *Panama* 134 E 2
San Miguel, *island* 118 C 5
San Miguel, *river* 132 C 4
San Miguel de Tucumán 126 C 5
San Miguel Is., *island group* 81 C 8
San Nicolás, *Argentina* 136 B 2
San Nicolas, *Philippines, C. Luzon* 81 D 3
San Nicolas, *Philippines, N. Luzon* 81 D 2
San Nicolas, *island* 120 C 5
Sannūr, W., *wadi* 100 C 4
Sano 80 D 3
San Pablo 79 K 4
San Pablo, *river* 134 B 2
San Pedro, *N. Argentina* 135 B 2
San Pedro, *S. Argentina* 135 C 3
San Pedro, *Paraguay* 135 C 2
San Pedro, *river* 134 B 3
San Pedro Chan., *chan.* 120 C 5
San Pedro de las Colonias 122 C 2
San Pedro de Macorís 123 G 3
San Pedro Mártir, Sa., *mountains* 122 B 1
S. Pedro, Pta., *cape* 123 E 4
San Pedro, Sa. de, *mts.* 52 B 3
San Pedro Sula 123 E 3
S. Pietro, *island* 61 B 5
Sanpoil, *river* 120 C 1
Sanquhar 47 E 6
San Rafael 120 B 4
San Rafael Mts., *mts.* 120 B 5
San Raphael 136 B 2
San Remo 60 A 3
San Roque 52 C 4
San Salvador 107 F 5
San Salvador, *island* 107 G 4
San Salvador de Jujuy 132 C 5
San Sebastián 36 B 2
San Sebastian, C. de, *cape* 53 G 2
S. Sebastião, C. de, *cape* 101 G 3
S. Severo 60 E 4
San-shui 79 J 3
S. Vicente de la Barquera 52 C 1
Sta. Ana, *El Salvador* 122 E 3
Santa Ana, *U.S.A.* 118 D 5
Santa Barbara, *Mexico* 122 C 2
Santa Barbara, *U.S.A.* 118 D 5
Santa Barbara, *island* 120 C 5
Sta. Barbara, *mountain* 52 D 4
Santa Barbara Chan., *channel* 118 C 5
Santa Barbara Is., *island group* 106 D 4
Santa Catalina, *island* 118 D 5
Santa Catalina, Gulf of, *gulf* 120 C 5
Sta. Catarina, I., *island* 127 E 5
Santa Clara 123 F 2
Santa Coloma de Farnes 53 G 2
Sta. Comba 52 A 1
Sta. Comba Dão 52 A 2
Santa Cruz, *Bolivia* 132 C 4
Sta. Cruz, *Canary Is., La Palma* 98 B 3
Sta. Cruz, *Canary Is., Tenerife* 98 B 3
Santa Cruz, *Philippines, Luzon* 81 D 4
Santa Cruz, *Philippines, Negros* 81 E 7
Santa Cruz, *Spain* 52 D 3
Santa Cruz, *U.S.A.* 120 B 4
Santa Cruz, *island* 118 D 5
Santa Cruz, *river* 127 B 8
Santa Cruz Basin, *sea feature* 141 G 3
Santa Cruz de Mudela 52 D 3
Santa Cruz Is., *island group* 141 G 3
Santa Cruz Mts., *mts.* 120 B 4
Santa Cruz, Sa. de, *mts.* 52 E 2
Sta. Eugenia de Ribeira 52 A 1
Sta. Eulalia, *Spain, Aragon* 53 E 2
Sta. Eulalia, *Spain, Ibiza* 53 F 3
Santa Fe, *Argentina* 127 C 6
Santa Fe, *Philippines* 81 D 5
Santa Fe, *U.S.A.* 118 F 4
San-tai 79 H 2
Santa Inés, I., *island* 127 B 8
Sta. Isabel 90 D 5
Santa Isabel I., *island* 140 F 2
Santai Shan, *mountains* 77 C 6
Santa Lucia Ra., *mts.* 120 B 4
Santa Maria, *Brazil* 136 C 1
Santa María, *Panama* 134 C 2
Santa Maria, *U.S.A.* 118 C 5
Santa María, *river* 134 C 2
Santa María, C., *cape* 127 D 6
Santa Maria, C. de, *Mozambique, cape* 101 G 4
Sta. Maria, C. de, *Spain, cape* 36 B 3
S. Maria di Leuca, C., *cape* 61 G 5
Santa María, I., *island* 136 A 2
Santa María la Real de Nieva 52 C 2
Santa Maria, Pta., *cape* 126 B 4
Santa Marta, *Colombia* 132 B 1
Sta. Marta, *Spain* 52 B 3
Sta. Marta Grande, C., *cape* 136 D 1
Santa Monica Bay, *bay* 118 D 5
Santander, *Colombia* 123 F 4
Santander, *Spain* 36 B 2
Sant' Angelo Lodigiano 57 E 4
Santañy 53 G 3
Santa Paula 120 C 5
Santa Pola, B. de, *bay* 53 E 3
Santa Pola, C. de, *cape* 53 E 3
Santarém, *Brazil* 126 D 3
Santarém, *Spain* 52 A 3
Santaren Chan., *channel* 119 M 7
Santa Rosa 118 C 4
Santa Rosa, *island* 118 C 5
Sta. Rosa de Toay 136 B 2
Santa Rosa I., *island* 121 C 4
Sta. Rosalia 122 B 2
Santa Rosa Mts., *mts.* 120 C 3
Santa Rosa Pk., *mountain* 114 F 4
Santee, *river* 119 M 5
Sante Fé 134 C 2
S. Telmo, Pta., *cape* 122 C 3
Santhià 57 D 4
Santiago, *Chile* 127 B 6
Santiago, *Dominican Rep.* 123 F 3
Santiago, *Panama* 123 E 4
Santiago, *mountain* 52 B 3
Santiago, Cerro, *mt.* 134 B 2
Santiago de Compostela 36 A 2
Santiago de Cuba 106 G 4
Santiago del Estero 127 C 5
Santiago do Cacem 52 A 3
Santiago, Serr. de, *mts.* 132 D 4
Santillana 52 C 1
Santis, *mountain* 57 E 2
Sto. André 133 E 5
Santo Domingo, *Dominican Rep.* 107 G 5
Sto. Domingo, *Spain* 52 D 1
Santolea, Emb. de, *lake* 53 E 2
Santoña 52 D 1
Santos 126 E 5
Santos Dumont 135 D 2
Santos, Sa. de los, *mts.* 52 C 3
Santo Tirso 52 A 2
Sto. Tomé 135 C 2
San Valentín, C., *mt.* 127 B 7
San Vicente, C., *cape* 127 C 8
San Vicente de A. 52 B 3
S. Vicente, Sa. de, *mts.* 52 C 2
S. Vito, C., *cape* 36 D 3
San-yüan 79 H 2
São Bernardo do Campo 135 D 2
São Borja 135 C 2
S. Braz de Alportel 52 B 4
São Carlos 136 D 1
São Francisco, *river* 126 E 3
São Francisco do Sul 136 D 1
São Francisco, I. de, *island* 126 E 5
S. João del Rei 135 D 2
São José do Rio Prêto 133 E 5
S. José dos Campos 135 D 2
S. Leopoldo 135 C 2
S. Lourenço 135 D 2
São Luís 126 E 3
São Luís, I. de, *island* 133 E 3
São Mamede, Sa. de, *mts.* 52 B 3
São Marcos, B. de, *bay* 126 E 3
Saône, *river* 28 G 4
São Paulo 126 E 5
São Pedro do Sul 52 A 2
São Roque, Cabo de, *cape* 126 F 3
São Sebastião, I. de, *island* 126 E 5
São Tomé, *island* 90 D 5
São Tomé, Cabo de, *cape* 126 E 5
S. Vicente, C. de, *cape* 28 E 5
Sápai 62 D 3
Sapelo I., *island* 121 D 4
Sapocoy, Mt., *mountain* 81 D 3
Sapphire Mts., *mountains* 120 D 2
Sapporo 67 J 3
Sapri 61 E 4
Saqqez 88 D 2
Sarāb 88 D 2
Sarabīt al Khadīm, *ancient site* 100 E 3
Sara Buri 83 C 6
Sarajevo 37 E 2
Sarameti, *mountain* 82 B 3
Sarangani B., *bay* 81 F 9
Sarangani Is., *island group* 81 F 9
Sarangani Str., *strait* 81 F 9
Sarangarh 86 E 4
Saransk 35 L 3
Sarapul 35 M 3
Sarar 88 D 8
Sarasota B., *bay* 121 D 5
Sarāt, Ḩarrat as, *lava flow* 88 C 6
Saratov 29 M 3
Saravan 86 B 3
Saravane 83 E 6
Sarawak, *province* 79 J 5
Saray 62 E 3
Sarayköy 63 F 5
Sardegna, *island* 28 H 5
Sardinia, *see Sardegna* 61 B 4
Sardis, *ancient site* 63 E 4
Sardis Res., *reservoir* 121 B 3
Sardona, Piz, *mountain* 57 E 3
Sarektjakko, *mountain* 50 P 2
Sarenga, *mountain* 99 G 4
Sarentine, Alpi, *mts.* 60 C 1
Sargans 57 E 2
Sarga, Punta, *cape* 98 B 3
Sargasso Sea 25 B 3
Sargodha 78 E 2
Sargodha, *region* 86 C 3
Sarhro, Dj., *mountains* 90 C 2
Sārī 88 E 2
Sariá, *island* 63 E 6
Sarigan, *island* 85 F 2
Sarina 148 D 3
Sariñena 53 E 2
Sar-i-Pul 86 B 2
Sarir Calansho, *region* 90 F 3
Sariwŏn 76 H 4
Sarıyer 62 F 3
Sark, *island* 39 E 7
Sarkişla 65 D 6
Şarköy 62 E 3
Sarlat 55 E 5
Sarmiento 136 B 3
Särna 51 O 4
Sarnau 42 C 2
Sarnen 57 D 3
Sarnersee, *lake* 57 D 3
Sarnia 115 J 4
Sarny 64 E 2
Saronikós Kólpos, *bay* 63 C 5
Saronno 57 E 4
Saros Körfezi, *gulf* 62 E 3
Šar Plan, *mountains* 28 J 4
Sarpsborg 51 N 5
Sarrebourg 54 H 3
Sarreguemines 54 H 3
Sarria 52 B 1
Sartène 60 B 4
Sarthe, *river* 54 D 4
Sarych, Mys, *cape* 37 G 2
Sarzeau 54 C 4
Sasd 60 G 1
Sasebo 67 H 4
Saskatchewan, *province* 114 G 3
Saskatchewan, *river* 114 G 3
Saskatoon 114 G 3
Sassandra 90 C 5
Sassandra, *river* 98 C 5
Sassanid, *civilisation* 159
Sassari 36 D 3
Sassnitz 58 E 1
Sassuolo 60 C 2
Sata-misaki, *cape* 80 B 5
Satara 87 D 4
Säter 51 P 4
Sater Land, *region* 56 F 1
Satka 35 N 3
Satmala Ra., *mountains* 87 D 4
Sátoraljaújhely 64 D 3
Satpura Ra., *mountains* 66 E 4
Satu Mare 37 E 2
Saudhárkrókur 50 C 3
Saudi Arabia 66 D 4
Sauer, *river* 56 E 5
Sauerland, *region* 58 B 3
Sault Ste. Marie, *Canada* 115 J 4
Sault Ste. Marie, *U.S.A.* 116 C 2
Saumarez Reef, *reef* 141 F 4
Saumlaki 85 E 4
Saumur 54 D 4
Saunders, C., *cape* 151 D 7
Saundersfoot 42 C 3
Saunders I., *island* 23 A 3
Sauveterre, Causse de, *limestone region* 55 F 5
Sava, *river* 28 J 4
Savalou 98 D 5
Savannah 119 L 5
Savannah, *river* 106 F 4
Savannakhet 79 H 4
Savantvadi 87 C 5
Savanur 87 D 5
Savaştepe 62 E 4
Savé 90 D 5
Save, *France, river* 53 F 1
Save, *Mozambique, river* 91 G 8
Sāveh 88 E 2
Savernake Forest, *region* 43 F 3
Saverne 54 H 3
Savoie, *province* 55 H 5
Savona 36 D 2
Savonlinna 50 T 4
Savukoski 50 T 2
Sawankhalok 83 C 5
Sawara-dake, *mountain* 80 E 2
Sawatch Mts., *mountains* 106 E 4
Sawbridgeworth 41 E 2
Sawdā, J. as, *mountains* 90 E 3
Sawel, *mountain* 39 C 4
Sawl Haud, *region* 88 D 8
Sawtooth Mts., *mts.* 118 D 3
Sawtooth Ra., *mountains* 120 B 1
Sawu, *island* 67 H 6
Sawu, Laut, *sea* 79 K 6
Saxby, *river* 148 C 2
Saxmundham 43 J 2
Saya de Malha Bank, *sea feature* 153 C 3
Şaydā 37 G 4
Sayb, W., *wadi* 100 E 4
Sayn Shanda 75 O 5
Say'ūn 66 D 5
Sazan, *island* 62 A 3
Sazawá, *river* 58 F 4
Scaër 54 C 3
Scafell Pikes, *mountain* 39 E 4
Scalea 61 E 5
Scalloway 46 G 1
Scalp, *mountain* 49 C 4
Scalpay, *Scotland, Outer Hebrides, island* 46 B 4
Scalpay, *Scotland, Skye, island* 46 C 4
Scandinavia, *region* 66 B 3
Scapa Flow, *inlet* 39 E 2
Scarba, *island* 47 C 5
Scarborough 39 F 4
Scarborough Shoal, *reef* 81 B 4
Scariff, *island* 49 A 5
Scarp, *island* 46 A 3
Scarpe, *river* 54 F 2
Scesaplana, *mountain* 57 E 2
Schaffhausen 57 D 2
Schaffhausen, *canton* 57 D 2
Schagen 56 C 2
Schanfigg, *river* 57 E 3
Schebeschi Mts., *mts.* 90 E 5
Schefferville 106 G 3
Schelde, *river* 56 B 4
Schenectady 119 N 3
Scheveningen 56 C 2
Schichallion, *mountain* 38 D 3
Schiedam 56 C 3
Schiermonnikoog, *island* 56 E 1
Schio 60 C 2
Schleswig 58 C 1
Schleswig-Holstein, *länder* 58 C 1
Schönebeck 58 D 2
Schongau 59 D 5
Schöningen 58 D 2
Schopfheim 57 C 2
Schouten Is., *island group* 85 F 4
Schouten, P-Pa., *island* 67 H 6
Schouwen, *island* 56 B 3
Schouwen-Duiveland, *island* 54 F 2
Schrankogl, *mountain* 57 G 2
Schulpengat, *channel* 56 C 2
Schuls 57 F 3
Schussen, *river* 57 E 2
Schwäbische Alb, *mt.* 36 D 2
Schwandorf 59 E 4
Schwaner Geb., *mts.* 79 J 6
Schwarzer Mann, *mt.* 56 E 4
Schwarzrand, *mountains* 101 C 4
Schwarzwald, *mountains* 28 H 4
Schwarzwalder Hochwald, *mountains* 56 E 5
Schwaz 59 D 5
Schwedt 58 F 2
Schweinfurt 58 D 3
Schwelm 56 F 3
Schwerin 36 D 1
Schwyz 57 D 2
Schwyz, *canton* 57 D 2
Sciacci 61 D 6
Scicli 61 E 6
Scilly, Isles of, *island group* 34 E 4
Scinawa 58 G 3
Scoresby Sd., *inlet* 106 J 2
Scotia Basin, *sea feature* 23 S 3
Scotia Ridge, *sea feature* 23 S 3
Scotia Sea 23 S 3
Scotland 38 E 3
Scott Base, *scientific base* 23 L 2
Scottburgh 101 F 5
Scott, C., *cape* 106 D 3
Scott I., *island* 23 M 2
Scott L., *lake* 114 G 3
Scott Reef, *reef* 146 D 2
Scottsbluff 118 G 3
Scrabster 46 E 3
Scranton 119 M 3
Scridain, L., *lake* 47 B 5
Scunthorpe 39 F 5
Seabrook, L., *lake* 146 C 6
Seaford 43 H 4
Seaham Harbour 45 G 3
Seahorse Pt., *cape* 115 J 2
Seal, *river* 114 H 3

Stack Skerry, *island* 38 D 2
Stack's Mts., *mountains* 49 B 4
Stac Polly, *mountain* 46 C 3
Staffa, *island* 47 B 5
Stafford 39 E 5
Stafford, *county* 43 E 2
Staines 43 G 3
Stalina, Pik, *mountain* 66 E 4
Stalinogorsk 35 K 3
Stalybridge 45 F 4
Stamford, *Australia* 148 C 3
Stamford, *England* 39 F 5
Stamford, *U.S.A.* 117 F 3
Standerton 101 F 4
Standon 41 E 2
Stanford-le-Hope 41 E 2
Stanger 101 F 5
Stanhope 45 F 3
Stanislav 64 E 3
Stanke Dimitrov 62 C 2
Stanley 127 D 8
Stanley, *mountain* 90 F 5
Stanley Falls, *falls* 104 A 2
Stanley Pool 102 C 3
Stanley Res., *reservoir* 87 D 5
Stanleyville 90 F 5
Stanovoy Khr., *mountains* 67 H 3
Stanovoye Nagor'ye, *plateau* 66 G 3
Stans 57 D 3
Stanstead Abbots 41 E 2
Stansted 41 E 2
Stanthorpe 147 K 5
Stanton Banks, *sea feature* 38 C 3
Stara Planina, *mountains* 28 K 4
Staraya Russa 35 J 3
Stara Zagora 37 F 2
Stargard 64 B 2
Stari Dojran 62 C 3
Starnberg 59 D 5
Starogard 64 C 2
Staro-Konstantinov 64 E 3
Star Pk., *mountain* 118 D 3
Start Pt., *cape* 39 E 6
Staryy Oskol 65 D 3
Stassfurt 58 D 3
Statesville 121 D 3
Staunton 121 E 2
Stavanger 34 F 2
Staveley 45 G 4
Stavelot 56 D 4
Staveren 56 D 2
Stavropol', *U.S.S.R., Kuybyshev* 65 G 3
Stavropol', *U.S.S.R., Stavropol'* 37 H 2
Stavropol'skaya Vozyvshennost', *hills* 37 H 2
Stavrós, Akr., *cape* 63 D 6
Stawell 147 H 7
Steens Mt., *mountain* 118 D 3
Steens Mts., *mountains* 120 C 3
Steenwijk 56 E 2
Steep Point, *cape* 152 A 3
Stefanie, L., *lake* 103 E 2
Stefansson I., *island* 114 G 1
Steiermark, *province* 59 F 5
Steinhuder See, *lake* 58 C 2
Steinkjer 50 N 3
Stellenbosch 101 C 6
Stendal 58 D 2
Stenness, L. of, *lake* 46 E 2
Stenón Sérifou, *strait* 63 D 5
Stenón Thérmion, *strait* 63 D 5
Stensele 50 P 3
Stepanakert' 74 G 6
Stephens, C., *cape* 150 E 5
Stephenson I., *island* 150 E 2
Stephenville 117 J 1
Stepnoy 65 F 4
Stepnyak 74 K 4
Stereá, *region* 63 B 4
Sterkstroom 101 E 5
Sterling 118 G 3
Sterlitamak 74 H 4
Steubenville 121 D 1
Stevenage 43 G 3
Stewart I., *island* 141 G 6
Stewarton 47 D 6
Stewart Sound, *strait* 87 F 5
Steyning 43 G 4
Steyr 64 B 3
Stia 60 C 3
Stikine, *river* 106 D 3
Stikine Mts., *mountains* 106 D 3
Stilís 62 C 4
Stillwater 118 H 4
Stillwater Mts., *mts.* 120 C 4
Stilo, C., *cape* 61 F 5
Stimson, Mt., *mountain* 120 D 1
Stinchar, *river* 47 D 6
Štip 62 C 3
Stirling 38 E 3
Stirling, *county* 47 D 5
Stirling Ra., *mountains* 140 B 5
Stjørdal 50 N 3
Stockbridge 43 F 3
Stockerau 64 C 3
Stockholm 28 J 2
Stockhorn, *mountain* 57 C 3
Stockport 39 E 5
Stockton 120 B 4
Stockton-on-Tees 39 F 4
Stoer, Pt. of, *cape* 46 C 3
Stokenchurch 41 C 2
Stoke-on-Trent 28 F 3
Stokesley 44 G 3
Stokes Ra., *mountains* 146 F 3
Stokkseyri 50 B 3
Stolac 60 F 3
Stone 43 E 2
Stonehaven 38 E 3
Stonington I., *island* 23 R 2
Stony Pt., *cape* 117 E 3
Stony Stratford 43 G 2
Stora Lule älv., *river* 50 Q 2
Stora Lulevatten, *lake* 50 Q 2
Storavan, *lake* 28 J 2
Store Bælt, *strait* 51 N 6
Stören 50 N 3
Storfosshei 50 O 2
Storjorm, *lake* 50 O 3
Stornoway 38 C 2
Storr, The, *mountain* 46 B 4
Storsjö 50 O 4
Storsjön, *Sweden, C. Jamtland, lake* 34 G 2
Storsjön, *Sweden, S. Jamtland, lake* 50 O 4
Storrington 41 D 4
Stort, *river* 41 E 2
Storuman, *lake* 50 P 3
Storvindeln, *lake* 50 P 3
Stour, *Dorset, river* 39 E 6
Stour, *Essex, river* 39 G 6
Stour, *Kent, river* 41 G 3
Stour, *Worcester, river* 43 E 2
Stourbridge 39 E 5
Stourport 43 E 2
Stow 47 F 6
Stowmarket 54 E 1
Strabane 39 C 4
Strakonice 59 E 4
Stralsund 58 E 1
Strand 102 C 6
Stranda 50 M 4
Strangford 48 F 2
Strangford L., *lake* 39 D 4
Strängnäs 51 P 5
Stranorlar 48 D 2
Stranraer 39 D 4
Strasbourg 28 G 4
Stratford, *Canada* 116 D 3
Stratford, *New Zealand* 150 F 4
Stratford-upon-Avon 39 F 5
Strathaven 47 D 6
Strathbogie, *valley* 46 F 4
Strath Dearn, *valley* 46 E 4
Strath Errick, *valley* 46 D 4
Strath Farrar, *valley* 46 D 4
Strath Halladale, *valley* 46 E 3
Strathmore, *valley* 38 E 3
Strathpeffer 46 D 4
Strath Spey, *valley* 38 E 3
Strathy Pt., *cape* 46 D 3
Straubing 59 E 4
Streaky B., *bay* 140 D 5
Streatley 41 B 2
Strel'na, *river* 50 W 2
Stresa 57 D 4
Stretford 45 F 4
Stříbro 58 E 4
Strimón, *river* 62 C 3
Strimonikós, K., *bay* 62 C 3
Strofádhes, *island group* 63 B 5
Stromboli, *island* 28 H 5
Strome Ferry 46 C 4
Stromness 46 E 3
Strömstad 51 N 5
Strongoli 61 F 5
Stronsay, *island* 38 E 2
Stronsay Firth, *channel* 46 F 2
Strood 43 H 3
Stroud 43 E 3
Struga 62 B 3
Struma, *river* 62 C 3
Strumble Hd., *cape* 39 D 5
Strumica, *river* 62 C 3
Stryama, *river* 62 D 2
Stryy 37 F 2
Stuart Bluff Ra., *mts.* 146 F 4
Stuart Highway 146 F 3
Stuart Ra., *Australia, mountains* 140 D 4
Stuart Mts., *New Zealand, mountains* 151 B 7
Stubaier A., *mountains* 59 D 5
Stugun 50 P 3
Stung Sen, *river* 83 D 6
Stung Streng, *river* 83 D 6
Stung Treng 83 E 6
Sturgeon Falls 116 D 2
Sturry 41 G 3
Sturt B., *bay* 149 B 6
Sturt Creek, *river* 140 C 3
Sturt Desert, *desert* 140 E 4
Sturt, Mt., *mountain* 147 H 5
Sturt Plain, *plain* 140 D 3
Stutterheim 101 E 6
Stuttgart 28 H 4
Stykkishólmur 50 B 3
Suakin 90 G 4
Subansiri, *river* 82 B 3
Subotica 64 C 4
Suceava 64 E 3
Suchan 80 C 2
Suchet, *mountain* 57 B 3
Su-ch'ien 76 F 5
Su-chien Shan, *island* 77 F 7
Suck, *river* 39 B 5
Sucre 126 C 4
Sudan 90 F 4
Sudbury, *Canada* 115 J 4
Sudbury, *England* 39 G 5
Sudd, *region* 90 G 5
Sudety, *mountains* 28 H 3
Suē, *river* 102 D 2
Sueca 53 E 3
Suehfeng Shan, *mountain* 77 E 6
Suez, *see As Suways* 99 G 3
Suez Canal, *canal* 90 G 2
Suez, G. of, *gulf* 90 G 3
Suffolk 121 E 2
Suffolk, *county* 43 H 2
Su-fu 66 E 4
Sugluk 115 K 2
Sugut, Tg., *cape* 81 B 8
Ṣuḥār 88 F 5
Suhayn Nuur, *lake* 86 F 2
Suhe Bator 76 D 1
Suhr, *river* 57 D 2
Su-hsien 76 F 5
Sui-Ch'i 77 E 7
Suido, Sa. del, *mountains* 52 A 1
Sui-fen-ho 76 J 3
Sui-hua 76 H 2
Sui-lai 86 E 1
Suilven, *mountain* 46 C 3
Suir, *river* 39 C 5
Suita 80 C 4
Sukabumi 79 H 6
Sukarnapura 67 J 6
Sukau 81 C 9
Sukhe Bator 75 N 4
Sukhona, *river* 29 M 2
Sukhumi 37 H 2
Sukkur 66 E 4
Sula, *river* 65 C 3
Sula, Kep., *island group* 67 H 6
Sulabesi, *island* 85 D 4
Sulaiman Ra., *mountains* 66 E 4
Sula Sgeir, *island* 38 C 2
Sulaymānīyah 88 D 2
Sulawesi, *island* 67 G 6
Sulechow 58 F 2
Sule Skerry, *island* 38 D 2
Sulina 37 F 2
Sulitjelma 50 P 2
Sulitjelma, *mountain* 28 J 1
Sulmona 60 D 3
Su-lo Ho, *river* 76 B 3
Su-lo Shan, *mountains* 76 B 4
Sulphur Springs 119 H 5
Sultan D., *mountain* 65 B 6
Sultanpur 86 E 3
Sulu Archo, *island group* 67 H 5
Sulu Sea 67 G 5
Sulzbach 59 D 4
Sulzberger B., *bay* 23 N 2
Sūmār, J., *mountain* 100 E 3
Sumatera Selatan, *prov.* 84 A 3
Sumatera Tengah, *prov.* 84 A 3
Sumatera Utara, *prov.* 84 A 3
Sumatra, *island* 66 F 5
Sumatra Trough, *sea feature* 153 D 2
Sumba, *island* 67 G 6
Sumba, Selat, *strait* 84 C 4
Sumbawa, *island* 67 G 6
Sumbawanga 104 B 4
Sumbing, G., *mountain* 84 C 4
Sumburgh Hd., *cape* 38 F 2
Sumerian, *civilisation* 158
Sumgait 65 G 6
Sumisu-jima, *island* 80 E 5
Summer L., *lake* 120 B 3
Summit 134 D 1
Summit Mt., *mountain* 120 C 4
Sumy 35 K 3
Sunart, Loch, *lake* 46 C 5
Sunchong 77 E 7
Sundarbans, *swamp forest* 78 F 3
Sundargarh 86 E 4
Sunda, Selat., *strait* 67 G 6
Sunda Shelf, *sea feature* 155 H 3
Sunderland 39 F 4
Sundgau, *region* 57 C 2
Sundsvall 34 H 2
Sung, *civilisation* 159
Sungacha, *river* 80 C 1
Sungari, *see Sung-hua Chiang* 76 J 1
Sungari Res., *reservoir* 76 H 3
Sung-chiang 76 G 5
Sungguminasa 84 C 4
Sung-hua Ch., *river* 67 H 3
Sung-p'ing-ling, *mountain* 82 F 3
Sung-p'ing-lung, *mt.* 77 E 6
Sunndalsöra 50 M 4
Sunne 51 O 5
Sunnmør, *region* 34 F 2
Sunnyside 120 B 2
Suō-nada, *sea* 80 B 4
Suonne, *lake* 50 S 4
Suoyarvi 50 U 4
Superior 119 J 2
Superior, L., *lake* 106 F 3
Suphan Buri 83 C 6
Ṣur, *Lebanon* 88 B 3
Ṣūr, *Muscat & Oman* 66 D 4
Sura, *river* 35 L 3
Sura, Ras, *cape* 88 D 7
Surabaja 67 G 6
Surakarta 67 G 6
Surat, *Australia* 149 D 4
Surat, *India* 66 E 4
Surat Thani 66 F 5
Surbiton 41 D 3
Sûre, *river* 56 D 5
Sureibīt, J., *mountain* 100 G 3
Suri 86 E 4
Suria 53 F 2
Surigao 67 H 5
Surigao Str., *strait* 81 F 6
Surin 83 D 6
Surinam 126 D 2
Suriname, *river* 132 D 2
Surnadal 50 M 4
Surnena Gora, *mountain* 62 D 2
Sur, Pt., *cape* 120 B 4
Surrey, *county* 43 G 3
Surr, W. as, *wadi* 100 G 5
Sur-Sari, *island* 51 S 4
Sursee 57 D 2
Surt 98 E 2
Suruga-wan, *bay* 80 D 4
Susa 60 A 2
Sušak 36 D 2
Sušac, *island* 60 F 3
Sūsangerd 88 D 3
Susanville 118 C 3
Sušice 59 E 4
Susquehanna, *river* 119 M 3
Sussex, *county* 43 G 3
Sussex, Vale of, *valley* 43 G 4
Sustenhorn, *mountain* 57 D 3
Sustenpass, *pass* 57 D 3
Susui 81 B 9
Susuman 75 R 3
Susurluk 62 F 4
Sutherland 101 D 6
Sutherland, *county* 46 D 3
Sutlej, *river* 66 E 4
Sutter Cr. 120 B 4
Sutton 41 D 3
Sutton Coldfield 43 F 2
Suttor, *river* 148 D 3
Suva 141 H 3
Suva Pl., *mountains* 62 C 2
Suva Reka 62 B 2
Suvasvesi, *lake* 50 T 4
Suvo Rudiste, *mountain* 62 B 2
Suwa 80 D 3
Suwałki 64 D 1
Suwannee, *river* 121 D 4
Suwannee Sd., *inlet* 121 D 4
Suwŏn 76 H 4
Suzuka 80 D 4
Suzuka san., *mountain* 80 C 4
Suzu-misaki, *cape* 75 Q 6
Svalbard, *island group* 24 L 2
Svärdsjö 51 P 4
Svart, *river* 51 O 5
Sveg 50 O 4
Svenčionis 51 S 6
Svendborg 51 N 6
Svensgrunnen, *island* 50 P 1
Sverdlovsk 29 O 3
Sverdrup Is., *island grp.* 106 E 2
Svetogorsk 35 J 2
Svilengrad 62 E 3
Svir', *river* 35 K 2
Svishtov 62 D 2
Svisloch', *river* 51 T 7
Svitavy 64 C 3
Svolvær 50 O 2
Svratka, *river* 59 G 4
Svrljig, *river* 62 C 2
Svrljiške Pl., *mountains* 62 C 2
Svyatoy Nos, M., *cape* 75 R 2
Swaffham 43 H 2
Swain Reefs, *reefs* 141 F 4
Swakopmund 91 E 8
Swale, *river* 39 F 4
Swan, *river* 140 B 5
Swanage 39 F 6
Swan Hill 147 H 7
Swan Is., *island group* 123 E 3
Swan River 114 G 3
Swansea 34 E 3
Swansea Bay, *bay* 42 D 3
Swartberge, *mountains* 91 F 9
Swatow, *see Shan-t'ou* 77 F 7
Swaziland 91 G 8
Sweden 28 H 2
Swellendam 102 D 6
Swidnica 64 C 2
Świdwin 58 F 2
Swiebodzin 58 F 2
Swift Current 114 G 3
Swilly, L., *inlet* 38 C 4
Swindon 39 F 6
Swineshead 93 G 2
Swinford 48 C 3
Świnoujście 58 F 2
Swire Deep, *sea feature* 155 J 3
Switzerland 28 G 4
Swords 48 E 3
Swords Ra., *mountains* 148 C 3
Syamozero, Oz., *lake* 50 V 4
Syas', *river* 65 C 1
Sydney, *Australia* 140 F 5
Sydney, *Canada* 115 L 4
Syktyvkar 35 M 2
Sylt, *island* 34 G 3
Syracuse, *Italy* 61 E 6
Syracuse, *U S.A.* 119 M 3
Syr-Dar'ya, *river* 66 E 3
Syria 66 C 4
Syriam 83 B 5
Syutkya, *mountain* 62 C 3
Syzran' 35 M 3
Szczecin 28 H 3
Szczecin, *province* 64 B 2
Szczecinek 64 C 2
Szczecinski, Zalew, *bay* 64 B 2
Szechwan, *province* 77 C 5
Sze-fang Shan, *mountains* 79 H 3
Szeged 37 E 2
Székesfehérvár 64 C 3
Szekszárd 64 C 3
Szentes 64 D 3
Szigetvár 60 F 1
Szolnok 64 D 3
Szombathely 36 E 2
Szprotawa 58 F 3
Sztalinvaros 60 G 1
Taal, L., *lake* 81 D 5
Tabaco 81 E 5
Tabankulu 101 F 5
Tabar Is., *island group* 85 G 4
Tabarka 61 B 6
Ṭabas 78 C 2
Tabasará, *river* 134 B 2
Tabasará, Serranía de, *mountain* 134 B 2
Tābask, Kūh-e, *mountain* 88 E 4
Tabayoo, Mt., *mountain* 81 D 3
Tabernas 52 D 4
Tabernes de Valldigna 52 E 3
Tabia 53 E 5
Tablas I., *island* 84 D 2
Tablas Str., *strait* 81 D 5
Table Cape, *cape* 150 H 4
Table Hill, *mountain* 151 B 8
Table, I. de la, *island* 77 D 7
Table Mt., *mountain* 91 E 9
Tabletop, Mt., *mountain* 148 C 2
Taboga 134 D 2
Taboga, I., *island* 134 D 2
Taboguilla, I., *island* 134 D 2
Tábor 59 F 4
Tabora 90 G 6
Tabor, Mt., *mountain* 89 B 2
Tabriz 29 M 5
Tabūk 37 G 4
Ta-ch'ang-shan Tao., *island* 76 G 4
Ta-ch'an Wan, *bay* 77 E 7
Ta-chiao T'ou, *cape* 77 D 8
Ta-ch'ing Shan, *mountain* 67 G 3
Ta-ch'i Yang, *gulf* 76 G 5
Tacloban 79 K 4
Tacna 132 B 4
Tacoma 106 D 3
Tacuarembó 136 C 2
Tadcaster 45 G 4
Tademaït, Pleateau du, *plateau* 28 G 6
Tadmur 37 G 3
Tadzhikskaya S.S.R., *republic* 74 J 6
Taebaek-san, *mountain* 80 B 3
Taedong 76 H 4
Taegu 67 H 4
Taejon 67 H 4
Taf, *river* 42 C 3
Tafalla 53 E 1
Tafas 89 C 2
Ta-feng Shan, *mountain* 77 G 6
Tafersit 52 D 5
Taff, *river* 39 E 6
Tafila 89 B 4
Tafí Viejo 135 B 2
Ta-fung 79 J 1
Taganrog 37 G 2
Taganrogskiy Zaliv, *bay* 37 G 2
Tagawa 80 B 4
Tagaytay City 81 D 4
Tagbilaran 81 E 7
Tage 85 F 4
Tagliamento, *river* 60 D 1
Tagolo Pt., *cape* 81 E 7
Tagomago, I., *island* 53 F 3
Tagremaret 53 F 5
Tagudin 81 D 3
Taguine 53 G 5
Tagula I., *island* 147 K 2
Tagum 81 F 8
Tagus, *see Tejo* 52 B 3
Ta-hai-shan, *mountain* 76 E 3
Tahan, G., *mountain* 79 H 5
Tahat, *mountain* 90 D 3
Tahiti, *island* 137 C 3
Tahoe Lake, *Canada, lake* 114 G 1
Tahoe, Lake, *U.S.A., lake* 118 C 4
Tahoua 98 D 4
Ta-hsing-an-ling Shan-mo, *mountains* 67 G 3
Ta-hsüeh Shan, *mountains* 76 C 4
Ta-hung Shan, *mountains* 76 E 5
T'ai-an 76 F 4
Taibilla, Sa. de, *mts* 52 D 3
Taichow Wan, *bay* 77 G 6
T'ai-chung 67 H 4
Taieri, *river* 151 D 7
T'ai-hang Shan, *mountains* 66 E 4
Taihape 150 F 4
T'ai-hsien 79 J 2
T'ai Hu, *lake* 76 G 5
T'ai-lai 76 G 2
Tailles, *region* 56 D 4
Tain 46 D 4
Tainan 67 H 4
Taínaron, Akr., *cape* 28 J 5
T'ai-pei 66 H 4
Taiping 84 B 3
Taira 80 E 3
Ta-i-shan 76 F 5
Tai Shan, *island* 76 G 5
T'ai-shan Lieh-tao, *island* 77 G 6
T'ai-shun 77 F 6
Taitao, Pena. de, *peninsula* 127 B 7
Taito 77 G 7
Taivaskero, *mountain* 50 S 2
Taiwan, *island* 67 H 4
T'ai-wan Hai-hsia, *strait* 67 G 4
Taíyetos Óros, *mts.* 63 C 5
Taiyība 89 B 4
Taiyuan, *see Yang-ch'ü* 76 E 4
Tai-yün Shan, *mountain* 77 F 6
Ta'izz 66 D 5
Tajo, *river* 28 F 5
Tajumulco Vol. de, *mt.* 107 F 5
Tajuña, *river* 52 D 2
Tak 79 G 4
Takada 80 D 3
Takahe, Mt., *mountain* 23 P 2
Takalar 84 C 4
Takamatsu 80 C 4
Takao 67 H 4
Takaoka 80 D 3
Takapuna 150 F 3
Takasaki 80 D 3
Takaungu 104 D 3
Takayama 80 D 3
Takefu 80 D 4

Venezia, Golfo di, *gulf* 28 H 4
Venice, *see Venezia* 60 D 2
Venlo 56 E 3
Venraij. 56 D 3
Venta, *river* 51 R 6
Ventnor 43 F 4
Ventspils 34 H 3
Ventura 120 C 5
Venus Bay, *bay* 149 D 6
Vera 52 E 4
Veracruz 107 F 5
Veraval 86 C 4
Verbania 57 D 4
Vercelli 60 B 2
Vercors, *region* 55 G 5
Verde, *Paraguay, river* 135 C 2
Verde, *U.S.A., river* 120 E 5
Verde, I., *island* 134 B 3
Verden 58 C 2
Verdinho, Sa. do, *mts.* 133 D 4
Verdun 54 G 3
Vereeniging 91 F 8
Vergara 52 D 1
Vergato 60 C 2
Verín 52 B 2
Verkh. Kuyto, Oz., *lake* 50 U 3
Verkh. Tura 35 N 2
Verkhoyansk 75 Q 3
Verkhoyanskiy Khrebet, *mountains* 67 H 2
Vermilion Cliffs, *cliffs* 120 D 4
Vermilion Ra., *mountains* 119 J 2
Vérmion Óros, *mountains* 62 B 3
Vermont, *state* 119 N 3
Vernon, *Canada* 114 F 3
Vernon, *France* 54 E 3
Vernon, *U.S.A.* 118 H 5
Véroia 62 C 3
Verona 36 D 2
Versailles 34 F 4
Vert, Cap, *Senegal, cape* 90 B 4
Vert, C., *South Viet Nam, cape* 83 E 6
Vertana, C., *mountain* 57 F 3
Verviers 56 D 4
Vervins 56 B 5
Verwall, *mountain* 57 F 2
Vesle, *river* 56 B 5
Vesoul 54 H 4
Vest-Agder, *county* 51 M 5
Vesterålen, *island group* 28 H 1
Vestfjorden, *channel* 28 H 1
Vestfold, *county* 51 N 5
Vestmannaeyjar, *island* 50 C 3
Vestvågøy, *island* 50 O 2
Vesuvio, *mountain* 28 H 5
Veszprém 64 C 3
Vetlanda 51 P 5
Vetluga, *river* 65 F 2
Vetren 62 D 2
Veurne 56 A 3
Vevey 57 B 3
Vézère, *river* 55 E 5
Vezhen, *mountain* 62 D 2
Viacha 132 C 4
Viana do A. 52 A 3
Viana do Castelo 52 A 2
Viareggio 60 C 3
Viborg 34 G 3
Vibo Valentia 61 F 5
Vicente, Pt., *cape* 120 C 5
Vicenza 60 C 2
Vich 53 G 2
Vichuga 35 L 3
Vichy 55 F 4
Vicksburg 119 J 5
Vico 60 B 3
Victor Harb. 147 G 7
Vicor, Sa. de, *mountains* 53 E 2
Victoria, *Argentina* 135 B 3
Victoria, *Cameroun* 90 D 5
Victoria, *Canada* 106 D 3
Victoria, *Chile* 135 A 3
Victoria, *Hong Kong* 79 J 3
Victoria, *Seychelles* 66 D 6
Victoria, *U.S.A.* 119 H 6
Victoria, *province* 101 F 3
Victoria, *river* 140 D 3
Victoria, *state* 140 E 5
Victoria de Durango 107 E 4
Victoria Falls, *falls* 91 F 7
Victoria I., *island* 106 E 2
Victoria, L., *Australia, New South Wales, lake* 149 C 5
Victoria, L., *Australia, Victoria, lake* 149 D 6
Victoria, Lake, *East Africa, lake* 90 G 6
Victoria Land, *district* 23 L 2
Victoria, Mt., *Burma, mountain* 82 A 4
Victoria, Mt., *Terr. of Papua, mountain* 85 F 4
Victoria Nile, *river* 104 B 2
Victoria Point 66 F 5
Victoria Ra., *mountains* 152 A 3
Victoria Str., *strait* 114 G 2
Victoria West 91 F 9
Victorville 120 C 5
Vidigueira 52 B 3
Vidin 37 E 2
Vidio, C., *cape* 52 B 1
Vidzy 64 E 1
Viedma 136 B 3
Viedma, L., *lake* 127 B 7
Viejo, C., *mountain* 134 B 2
Viella 53 F 1
Vienna, *see Wien* 59 G 4
Vienne 55 G 5
Vienne, *river* 55 E 4
Vientiane 67 G 5
Viersen 56 E 3
Vierwaldstättersee, *lake* 57 D 3
Vierzon 54 F 4
Vieste 60 F 4
Vigan 79 K 4
Vigevano 57 D 4
Vigia, *mountain* 52 A 4
Vignemale, P. de, *mt.* 36 B 2
Vigo 36 A 2
Vigo, Ria de, *inlet* 52 A 1
Vigors, Mt., *mountain* 152 B 2
Vijayavada 78 F 4
Vijosë, *river* 62 A 3
Vik 34 C 2
Viking Bank, *sea feature* 34 F 2
Vila 141 G 3
Vila Cabral 91 G 7
Vila Coutinho 104 C 6
Vila de João Belo 91 G 8
Vila do Conde 52 A 2
Vila Fontes 101 G 2
Va. General Machado 91 E 7
Vila Gouveia 101 G 2
Vila Henrique de Carvalho 91 F 6
Vilaine, *river* 54 C 4
Vila Luiza 101 G 4
Vila Luso 91 E 7
Vila Manica 101 G 2
Vilanculos 101 G 3
Vila Nova de F. 52 A 2
Vila Nova de Fozcôa 52 B 2
Vila Nova de Gaia 52 A 2
Vila Nova de O. 52 A 3
Vila Pereira d'Eça 101 B 2
Vila Pery 101 G 2
Vila Real, *North Portugal* 52 B 4
Vila Real, *South Portugal* 52 B 2
Va. Robert Williams 91 E 7
Vilano, C., *cape* 52 D 1
Vila Teixeira da Silva 91 E 7
Vila Velha de Rodão 52 B 3
Vila Viçosa 52 B 3
Vileyka 64 E 1
Vilhelmina 50 P 3
Viljandi 51 S 5
Vil'kitskogo, Proliv, *strait* 66 G 2
Villa Ángela 136 B 1
Villa Bens 98 B 3
Villacañas 52 D 3
Villacarrillo 52 D 3
Villach 59 E 5
Villacidro 61 B 5
Villa Cisneros 90 B 3
Va. Constitución 135 B 3
Villa del Rio 52 C 4
Villadiego 52 C 1
Villa Dolores 136 B 2
Villadossola 57 D 3
Villafamés 53 E 2
Villafranca del Bierzo 52 B 1
Villafranca di Verona 60 C 2
Villafranca de los Barros 52 B 3
Villafranca del Panadés 53 F 2
Villagarcia de A. 52 A 1
Villaggio Duca degli Abruzzi 90 H 5
Villaguay 135 C 3
Villahermosa, *Mexico* 122 D 3
Villahermosa, *Spain* 52 D 3
Villajoyosa 52 E 3
Villaba, *Spain, Galicia* 52 B 1
Villalba, *Spain, Castilla la Vieja* 52 C 2
Villalón de Campos 52 C 1
Villalpando 52 C 2
Villa María 136 B 2
Villamartin 52 C 4
Villa Mercedes 136 B 2
Villa Montes 132 C 5
Villa Nador 52 D 5
Villanueva de Córdoba 52 C 3
Villanueva del A. 52 D 3
Villanueva de la Serena 52 C 3
Villanueva y Geltrú 53 F 2
Villaputzu 61 B 5
Villarcayo 52 D 1
Villar del A. 53 E 3
Villarelho, Sa. de, *mts.* 52 B 2
Villarramiel 52 C 1
Villarreal 53 E 3
Villarrica, *Chile* 135 A 3
Villarrica, *Paraguay* 136 C 1
Villarrobledo 52 D 3
Villa San Giovanni 61 E 5
Villa Sanjurjo, *see Al Hoceima* 52 D 5
Villavicencio 123 F 4
Villaviciosa de C. 52 C 3
Villefranche, *France, Lyonnais* 55 G 5
Villefranche, *France, Provence* 55 H 6
Villefranche-de-Lauragais 55 E 6
Villefranche-de-Rouergue 55 F 5
Villena 52 E 3
Villeneuve-sur-Lot 55 E 5
Villuercas, Las, *region* 52 C 3
Vilnya, *river* 51 T 6
Vil'nyus 28 K 3
Vilshofen 59 E 4
Vilvoorde 56 C 4
Vilyuy, *river* 75 P 3
Vilyuysk 75 P 3
Vimioso 52 B 2
Vimmerby 51 P 5
Viña del Mar 136 A 2
Vinaroz 53 F 2
Vincennes 119 K 4
Vindelälven, *river* 50 Q 3
Vindeln 50 Q 3
Vindhya Range, *mts.* 66 E 4
Vinh 67 G 5
Vinhais 52 B 2
Vinh Long 83 D 7
Vinh Yen 82 D 4
Vinkovci 64 C 4
Vinnitsa 37 F 2
Vino, Tierra del, *region* 52 C 2
Vinson Massif, *mts.* 23 Q 2
Vintar 81 D 2
Virac 81 F 5
Vire 54 D 3
Virgenes, Cabo, *cape* 127 C 8
Virgen, Sa. de la, *mts.* 52 E 2
Virgin, *river* 120 D 4
Virginia, *Rep. of Ireland* 48 D 3
Virginia, *Rep. of South Africa* 101 E 5
Virginia, *U.S.A.* 119 J 2
Virginia, *state* 119 M 4
Virginia Mts., *mountains* 120 C 4
Virgin Is., *island group* 107 G 5
Virgin Mts., *mountains* 120 D 4
Virovitica 64 C 4
Virton 56 D 5
Vis, *island* 64 C 4
Visalia 120 C 4
Visayan Sea 79 K 4
Visby 34 H 3
Viscount Melville Sound, *channel* 106 E 2
Viseu 52 B 2
Vishakhapatnam 78 F 4
Viso, Mt., *mountain* 55 H 5
Visoko 60 G 3
Visoko, *mountain* 63 B 3
Visokoi I., *island* 23 A 3
Visp 57 C 3
Vistonís, L., *lake* 62 D 3
Vit, *river* 62 D 2
Vitava, *river* 64 B 3
Vitebsk 35 J 3
Viterbo 60 D 3
Vitiaz Str., *strait* 85 F 4
Vitichi 135 B 2
Vitigudino 52 B 2
Viti Levu, *island* 141 H 3
Vitim, *river* 67 H 3
Vitimskoye Ploskogor'ye, *tableland* 75 O 4
Vitória, *Brazil* 126 E 5
Vitoria, *Spain* 52 D 1
Vitória da Conquista 133 E 4
Vitré 54 D 3
Vitry-le-François 54 G 3
Vitsi, *mountain* 63 B 3
Vittangi 50 R 2
Vittoria 61 E 6
Vitu Is., *island group* 85 F 4
Vityaz' Deep, *sea feature* 67 J 3
Vivarais, Monts du, *mts.* 55 G 5
Vivero 52 B 1
Viveros, I., *island* 134 D 2
Vize 62 E 3
Vizianagram 87 E 4
Vizzini 61 E 6
Vladičin Han 62 C 2
Vladimir 35 L 3
Vladimir-Volynskiy 64 E 2
Vladivostok 67 H 3
Vlajna, *mountain* 62 B 2
Vlašim 58 F 4
Vlieland, *island* 56 C 1
Vlissingen 56 B 3
Vlonës, G. i, *gulf* 62 A 3
Vlorë 62 A 3
Vöcklabruck 59 E 4
Vodla, *river* 50 W 4
Vodlozero, Oz., *lake* 50 W 4
Vodnany 59 F 4
Vogelkop, *peninsula* 67 H 6
Vogelsberg, *mountain* 58 C 3
Voghera 60 B 2
Vohémar 105 D 2
Vohipeno 105 C 4
Voi 90 G 6
Voiron 55 G 5
Voitsberg 59 F 5
Vojmsjön, *lake* 50 P 3
Volendam 56 D 2
Volga, *river* 29 M 4
Volgo-Donskoy K., *canal* 29 M 4
Volgograd 29 M 4
Volkhov 35 K 2
Volkhov, *river* 65 B 1
Volkovysk 64 E 2
Volksrust 101 F 4
Volissós 63 D 4
Volnovakha 65 D 4
Vologda 35 K 2
Vólos 37 E 3
Volta, *river* 90 D 5
Volta L., *reservoir* 90 C 5
Volta Montovana 57 F 4
Volta Noire, *river* 90 C 4
Volta Redonda 135 D 2
Volta Rouge, *river* 98 C 4
Volturno, *river* 60 E 4
Vol'sk 35 L 3
Vólvi, L., *lake* 62 C 3
Volzhskiy 65 F 4
Voorburg 56 C 2
Vopnafjördhur 50 E 3
Vopnafjördhur, *gulf* 50 E 3
Vorarlberg, *mountains* 59 C 5
Vorderrhein, *river* 57 D 3
Vordingborg 51 N 6
Voríai Sporádhes, *island group* 37 E 3
Vórios Evvoïkós Kólpos, *channel* 62 C 4
Vorkuta 35 O 1
Voronezh 29 L 3
Voronov, Mys, *cape* 50 Y 2
Vöru 51 S 5
Vosges, *mountains* 28 G 4
Voss 51 M 4
Vost. Chink Ustyurta, *mountains* 29 O 4
Vostochnyy Sayan, *mts.* 66 F 3
Vostok 23 Q 2
Votkinsk 35 M 3
Voúrinos, *mountain* 62 B 3
Vouzier 56 C 5
Voxna 51 P 4
Vrakhonisís Kaloyéroi, *island* 63 D 4
Vrangelya, O., *island* 24 B 2
Vranje 64 D 4
Vratsa 64 D 4
Vrbas 64 C 4
Vrede 101 F 4
Vršac 64 D 4
Vryburg 102 D 5
Vryheid 91 G 8
Vŭcha 62 D 3
Vukovar 64 C 4
Vulcano, *island* 61 E 5
Vyal Oz., *lake* 50 V 2
Vyatka, *river* 35 M 3
Vyatskiye Polyany 65 G 2
Vyaz'ma 35 K 3
Vyazniki 65 E 2
Vyborg 35 J 2
Vychegda, *river* 29 N 2
Vygozero, Oz., *lake* 50 V 3
Vyrnwy, *river* 42 D 2
Vyrts'yarv, Oz., *lake* 51 S 5
Vyshniy-Volochek 35 K 3
Vyškov 59 G 4
Vysoké Mýto 58 G 4
Vytegra 35 K 2

Waal, *river* 56 D 3
Waardgronden, *bay* 56 D 1
Wabag 85 F 4
Wabash, *river* 119 K 4
Wabowden 114 H 3
Waccasassa B., *bay* 121 D 4
Waco 118 H 5
Waddenzee, *channel* 34 F 3
Waddington, Mt., *mt.* 106 D 3
Wadebridge 42 C 4
Wadenswil 57 D 2
Wadhurst 41 E 3
Wādī 'Arabah, *valley* 37 G 4
Wadi es Sir 89 B 3
Wadi Halfa 66 C 4
Wādī Mūsā 89 B 4
Wadi Sirhān, *region* 66 C 4
Wādīyan, Al, *region* 29 M 6
Wad Medani 90 G 4
Wager Bay 114 H 2
Wager Bay, *bay* 114 J 2
Wagga Wagga 140 E 5
Wagin 146 C 6
Wągrowiec 58 G 2
Wahai 85 D 4
Wāḥāt al Khārijah, Al, *oasis* 99 G 3
Wahībah Sands, *sand dunes* 88 F 5
Wahong Shan, *mountains* 76 B 4
Wah Wah Mts., *mts.* 120 D 4
Waiau 151 E 6
Waiau, *New Zealand, Nelson, river* 151 E 6
Waiau, *New Zealand, Otago, river* 151 B 7
Waidhofen 59 F 4
Waigeo, *island* 67 H 6
Waiheke I., *island* 150 F 3
Waihi 150 F 3
Waihou, *river* 150 F 3
Waikare L., *lake* 150 F 3
Waikare Moana, *lake* 150 G 4
Waikato, *river* 150 F 4
Waikouaiti 151 D 7
Waikouaiti Downs, *hills* 151 D 7
Waimate 151 D 7
Waimea Plain, *plain* 151 C 7
Wainfleet 45 J 4
Wainganga, *river* 86 D 4
Waingapu 79 K 6
Wainwright, *Canada* 114 F 3
Wainwright, *U.S.A.* 114 B 1
Waipa, *river* 150 F 4
Waipawa 150 G 4
Waipukurau 150 G 4
Wairarapa, L., *lake* 150 F 5
Wairau, *river* 150 E 5
Wairoa 150 G 4
Wairoa, *New Zeaalnd, Auckland, river* 150 E 3
Wairoa, *New Zealand, Hawkes Bay, river* 150 G 4
Wairua, *river* 150 F 2
Waitaki, *river* 151 D 7
Waitaki Plains, *plain* 151 C 7
Waitara 150 F 4
Waitoa 150 F 3
Waiuku 150 F 3
Wajir 104 E 2
Wakamatsu 80 D 3
Wakasa-wan, *bay* 80 C 4
Wakatipu, L., *lake* 151 C 7
Wakayama 75 Q 6
Wakefield 39 F 5
Wake I., *island* 137 B 2
Wakkanai 75 R 5
Wakkerstroom 101 F 4
Wałbrzych 64 C 2
Walbury Hill, *hill* 41 B 3
Walcha 149 E 5
Walcheren, *island* 56 B 3
Wałcz 58 G 2
Waldburg Ra., *mountains* 146 C 4
Waldia 88 B 7
Waldshut 57 D 2
Wales 39 E 5
Wales I., *island* 114 J 2
Walgett 149 D 5
Walgreen Coast, *region* 23 P 2
Wālih, J., *island* 100 G 5
Walikale 104 B 3
Walker B., *bay* 101 C 6
Walker Cay, *reef* 121 E 5
Walker Lake, *lake* 120 C 4
Walker Ra., *mountains* 81 A 9
Walkerville 120 D 2
Wallabi Group, *island group* 146 B 5
Wallaby I., *Australia, C. York Pena., island* 148 C 2
Wallaby I., *Australia, Wellesley Is., island* 147 G 3
Wallal Downs 152 C 1
Walland Marsh, *marsh* 41 F 4
Wallaroo 147 G 6
Wallasey 39 E 5
Walla Walla 118 D 2
Wallel, T., *mountain* 99 G 5
Wallensee, *lake* 57 E 2
Wallenstadt 57 E 2
Wallingford 43 F 3
Wallowa Mts., *mountains* 118 D 2
Wallsend 149 E 5
Walmer 41 G 3
Walney I., *island* 39 E 4
Walpole, *island* 141 G 4
Walsall 39 F 5
Walsh 148 C 2
Walter's Ra., *mountains* 149 C 4
Waltham Abbey 41 E 2
Walthamstow 41 D 2
Walton 43 G 3
Walton on the Naze 43 J 3
Walvis Bay 91 E 8
Walvis Bay, *bay* 101 B 3
Walvis or Cape Basin, *sea feature* 25 F 6
Walvis Ridge, *sea feature* 25 E 6
Wana 86 C 2
Wanaaring 149 C 4
Wanaka, Lake, *lake* 151 C 7
Wanapitei, L., *lake* 116 D 2
Wandels Sea 24 N 1
Wandoan 149 D 4
Wang, *river* 83 C 5
Wanganui 141 H 6
Wanganui, *river* 150 F 4
Wangaratta 147 J 7
Wang-ch'ing 80 B 2
Wan-ch'üan 67 G 3
Wang-chün Shan, *mts.* 82 E 3
Wangen 57 E 2
Wangerooge, *island* 56 F 1
W'ang-p'ing Ling, *mt.* 82 E 4
Wang-yeh-miao 75 P 5
Wan-hsien 77 D 5
Wankie 91 F 7
Wanne-Eickel 58 B 3
Wansbeck, *river* 45 G 2
Wansford 43 G 2
Wanstead 41 E 2
Wantage 43 F 3
Wan-Ta Shan-mo, *mts.* 76 J 2
Wanyang Shan, *mts.* 77 E 6
Wapenamanda 85 F 4
Warangal 78 E 4
Waratah B., *bay* 149 D 6
Warburg 58 C 3
Warburton, *river* 140 D 4
Warburton Ra., *mts.* 146 E 5
Wardha 86 D 4
Ward Hunt Str., *strait* 85 F 4
Ware 43 G 3
Wareham 43 E 4
Waren 58 E 2
Warendorf 56 F 3
Warialda 149 E 4
Warlingham 41 D 3
Warmbad 101 C 5
Warminster 39 E 6
Warnemünde 58 E 1
Warner Ra., *mountains* 118 C 3
Warner Valley, *valley* 120 C 3
Warnham 41 D 3
Warnier 53 F 4
Warning, Mt., *mountain* 149 E 4
Warnow, *river* 58 D 2
Waroona 146 C 6
Warragul 149 D 6
Warrawagine 152 C 2
Warrego, *river* 140 E 4
Warrego Ra., *mountains* 147 J 5
Warren, *Australia* 149 D 5
Warren, *U.S.A.* 116 D 3
Warrenpoint 48 E 2
Warrenton 102 D 5
Warri 98 D 5
Warriners, *river* 149 B 4
Warrington 39 E 5
Warrnambool 147 H 7
Warszawa 28 J 3
Warszawa, *province* 64 D 2
Warta, *river* 28 J 3
Warwick, *Australia* 147 K 5
Warwick, *England* 39 F 5
Warwick, *county* 43 F 2
Wasatch Range, *mts.* 118 E 4
Wasco 120 C 5
Wash, The, *gulf* 34 F 3

Name	Page	Ref
Yalutorovsk	35	O 3
Yalvaç	65	B 6
Yamagata	75	R 6
Yamaguchi	80	B 4
Yamal, P-ov, *peninsula*	66	E 2
Yamalik Dunes, *sand dunes*	76	C 3
Yambi, Mesa de, *tableland*	132	B 2
Yambol	62	E 2
Yamdrok Tso, *lake*	86	F 3
Yamethin	82	B 4
Yamma Yamma, L., *seasonal lake*	147	H 5
Yamsay Mt., *mountain*	120	B 3
Yamuna, *river*	66	E 4
Yana, *river*	75	Q 3
Yanam	87	E 4
Yanbu'al Bahr	66	C 4
Yang-chiang	77	E 7
Yang-ch'ü	67	G 4
Yang-hsiung Shan, *mt.*	77	C 7
Yangi-Yul'	86	C 1
Yang-ting Ho, *river*	76	F 3
Yangtse Kiang, see *Ch'ang Chiang*	77	D 6
Yangtse Gorges, *gorge*	77	D 5
Yanis'yarvi, Oz., *lake*	50	U 4
Yankton	118	H 3
Yano-Indigirskaya Nizmennost', *plain*	67	H 2
Yanskiy	75	Q 3
Yanskiy Zaliv, *bay*	75	Q 2
Yao	80	C 4
Yao Shan, *mountain*	77	E 7
Yaoundé	90	E 5
Yap, *island*	67	H 5
Yap Ridge, *sea feature*	67	H 5
Yap Trench, *sea feature*	67	H 5
Yaqui, *river*	118	F 6
Yar, *river*	41	B 4
Yare, *river*	39	G 5
Yarega	35	M 2
Yarí, *river*	123	F 4
Yariga-take, *mountain*	80	D 3
Yarīm	88	C 7
Yaritagua	123	G 3
Yarkand	66	E 4
Yarm	44	G 3
Yarmouth	41	B 4
Yarmuk, *river*	89	B 2
Yaroslavl'	66	D 3
Yarra, *river*	149	D 6
Yarram	149	D 6
Yarran Ra., *mountains*	148	B 2
Yarri	152	C 3
Yarrow, *river*	47	E 6
Yartsevo	65	C 2
Yarumal	123	F 4
Yass	147	J 6
Yatağan	63	F 5
Yatsushiro	80	B 4
Yatta Plat., *plateau*	103	E 3
Yavarí, *river*	132	B 3
Yaví, Co., *mountain*	132	C 2
Yavne	89	A 3
Yawata	80	B 4
Yawatahama	80	C 4
Yazd	66	D 4
Yazoo, *river*	119	J 5
Yazun Burnu, *cape*	37	G 3
Ydzhid Parma, *mountain*	29	O 2
Ye	83	B 6
Yebala, *region*	28	F 5
Yébenes, Sa. de, *mts.*	52	C 3
Yecla	52	E 3
Yegor'yevsk	35	K 3
Yeguas, Sa. de, *mts.*	52	C 4
Yeh-ma Shan, *mountains*	74	B 4
Yei	104	B 1
Yelets	35	K 3
Yelgava	34	H 3
Yelizavety, M., *cape*	67	J 3
Yell, *island*	38	F 1
Yellowhead Pass, *pass*	114	F 3
Yellowknife	114	F 2
Yellow Mt., *mountain*	149	D 5
Yellow River, see *Huang Ho*	76	C 4
Yellow Sea	67	H 4
Yellowstone, *river*	106	E 3
Yell Sound, *channel*	46	G 1
Yemen	66	D 5
Yemil'chino	64	E 2
Yenakiyevo	35	K 4
Yen Bay	77	C 7
Yen-ch'ang	79	H 2
Yen-ch'eng	75	P 6
Yen-chi	76	H 3
Yen-ch'i	75	L 5
Yenisey, *river*	66	F 2
Yeniseysk	75	M 4
Yeniseyskiy Zaliv, *bay*	75	L 2
Yen-t'ai	79	K 2
Yeo, *river*	42	E 3
Yeo, L., *lake*	146	D 5
Yeotmal	87	D 4
Yeovil	39	E 6
Yeppoon	147	K 4
Yerevan	29	M 5
Yergeni, *mountain*	35	L 4
Yerofey-Pavlovich	75	P 4
Yershov	65	G 3
Yerupaja, *mountain*	126	B 4
Yesa, Emb. de, *lake*	53	E 1
Yesil, *river*	29	L 5
Yes Tor, *mountain*	39	D 6
Yetman	149	E 4
Yeu	82	B 4
Yeu, Î. d', *island*	55	C 4
Yevpatoriya	37	G 2
Yeysk	35	K 4
Yialí, *island*	63	E 5
Yianisádhes, *island*	63	E 6
Yiannitsá	62	C 3
Yin-ch'uan	79	H 2
Ying-chiang	77	B 7
Ying-k'ou	76	G 3
Ying-p'an Chiang, *gulf*	77	D 7
Ying-te	77	E 7
Yin-hsien	67	H 4
Yinmabin	82	B 4
Yioúra, Kikládhes, *island*	63	D 5
Yioúra, Voríai Sporádhes, *island*	62	D 4
Yirga-Alam	99	G 5
Yíthion	63	C 5
Ylikitka, *lake*	50	T 2
Yllästunturi, *mountain*	50	S 2
Yoichi	80	E 2
Yokkaichi	80	D 4
Yokohama	67	H 4
Yokosuka	75	Q 6
Yokote	80	E 3
Yola	90	E 5
Yonago	80	C 4
Yonaguni-jima, *island*	77	G 7
Yŏng-an	80	B 2
Yonne, *river*	54	F 3
York, Australia	146	C 6
York, England	39	F 5
York, U.S.A.	116	L 3
York, *county*	45	G 3
York, C., *cape*	140	E 3
Yorke Pena., *peninsula*	149	B 5
York Factory	114	H 3
York, K., *cape*	106	G 2
York, Vale of, *valley*	39	F 4
Yorkshire Moors, *moors*	39	F 4
Yorkshire Wolds, *reg.*	39	F 4
Yorkton	114	G 3
Yosemite Lodge	120	C 4
Yosemite National Park	120	C 4
Yoshkar Ola	35	L 3
Yotvata	89	B 5
Youanmi	152	B 3
Youghal	39	C 6
Youghal Bay, *bay*	49	D 5
Young	147	J 6
Younghusband Pena., *peninsula*	147	G 7
Young Ra., *mountains*	151	C 7
Youngstown	119	L 3
Yozgat	37	G 3
Yreka	120	B 3
Ysabel Channel, *channel*	85	F 4
Yssingeaux	55	G 5
Ystad	51	O 6
Ystrad	42	C 2
Ystwyth, *river*	42	D 2
Ythan, *river*	46	F 4
Ytterhogdal	50	O 4
Yu'alliq, Jabal, *mountain*	100	E 2
Yüan Chiang, *river*	77	E 6
Yüan-ling	79	J 3
Yuan yang	77	C 7
Yuba City	120	B 4
Yub'a, J., *island*	100	G 5
Yubari	80	E 2
Yucatan, *peninsula*	107	F 5
Yucatan Basin, *sea feature*	107	F 5
Yucatan Channel, *chan.*	107	F 4
Yü Chiang, *river*	82	E 4
Yudomo Mayskoye Nagor'ye, *mountains*	75	Q 4
Yüeh-yang	77	E 6
Yugorskiy P-ov., *peninsula*	29	O 1
Yugorskiy Shar, *bay*	35	N 1
Yugoslavia	28	J 4
Yugo-Vostochnyye Karakumy, *desert*	86	B 2
Yukagirskoye Ploskogor'ye, *tableland*	67	J 2
Yukon, *province*	110	D 2
Yukon, *river*	106	C 2
Yü-lin, China, Hai-nan	67	G 5
Yü-lin, China, Kwantung	77	E 7
Yü-lin, China, Shensi	75	N 6
Yu-lung-Shan, *mountain*	77	C 6
Yuma	118	E 5
Yuma Desert, *desert*	120	D 5
Yü-men	75	M 5
Yumenshih	75	M 6
Yuna	152	B 3
Yün-chao Shan, *mts.*	77	E 6
Yün-feng Shan, *mts.*	76	C 5
Yungas, *region*	126	C 4
Yung-chia	67	H 4
Yung-hsin	77	E 6
Yung-kai-ta Shan	77	E 7
Yün Ho, *river*	76	G 5
Yün-hsien	79	J 2
Yunlin	77	G 7
Yun-ling Shan, *mountains*	66	F 4
Yün-meng Shan, *mts.*	76	F 4
Yunnan, *province*	77	C 6
Yunndaga	152	C 3
Yurimaguas	132	B 3
Yuryuzan'	35	N 3
Yu Shui, *river*	82	E 2
Yuta	89	B 3
Yü-t'ien	76	F 4
Yü-tzu	76	E 4
Yu-yü	76	E 3
Yuzhno-Sakhalinsk	67	J 3
Yuzh. Anysyskiy Khr., *mountain*	75	T 3
Yuzhnyy Bug, *river*	28	K 4
Yuzhnyy, M., *cape*	75	S 4
Yuzh. Ural, *mountains*	29	O 3
Yverdon	57	B 3
Yvetot	54	E 3
Za'faranah, Ra's, *cape*	100	D 3
Zaforas, *island*	63	E 5
Zafra	52	B 3
Zagán	58	F 3
Zaghouan	61	C 6
Zagorsk	35	K 3
Zagreb	28	H 4
Zagros, Kuhhā-ye, *mts.*	65	F 7
Zahd, J., *mountain*	100	G 4
Zāhedān	78	D 3
Zahrez Chergui, *lake*	53	G 5
Zahrez Rharbi, *lake*	53	G 5
Zailiyskiy Alatau, Khr., *mountains*	86	D 1
Zaječar	64	D 4
Zākhō	37	H 3
Zákinthos	63	B 5
Zákinthos, *island*	63	B 5
Zala, *river*	60	F 1
Zalaegerszeg	64	C 3
Zalamea de la S.	52	C 3
Zalamea la Real	52	B 4
Zambales Mts., *mountains*	81	C 3
Zambeze, *river*	91	G 7
Zambezi, *river*	91	F 7
Zambézia, *province*	104	D 7
Zambia	91	F 7
Zamboanga	67	H 5
Zamboanga Pena., *peninsula*	81	E 8
Zamora, Mexico	122	C 3
Zamora, Spain	52	C 2
Zamość	64	D 2
Záncara, *river*	52	D 3
Zanesville	119	L 4
Zanjān	88	D 2
Zanthus	152	C 4
Zanzibar	91	G 6
Zanzibar, *region*	91	G 6
Zanzibar Channel, *chan.*	104	D 4
Zanzibar I., *island*	91	G 6
Zapadana Morava, *river*	62	B 2
Zap. Dvina, *river*	28	K 3
Zapadno-Sibir'skaya Nizmennost', *plain*	66	E 2
Zapadnyy Chink Ustyurta, *escarpment*	29	N 4
Zapadnyy Sayan, *mts.*	66	F 3
Zapata, Pena. de, *peninsula*	121	D 6
Zaporozh'ye	29	L 4
Zapovednik, *mountain*	80	D 1
Zara	65	D 6
Zaragoza, Philippines	81	C 3
Zaragoza, Spain	28	F 5
Zarand, east Iran	88	F 3
Zarand, north Iran	88	E 2
Zārandului, Mtii., *mts.*	64	D 3
Zárate	135	C 3
Zaraza	123	G 4
Zaria	98	D 4
Zarqa	89	C 2
Zarqa, *river*	89	B 2
Zary	58	F 3
Zarzis	98	E 2
Zasheyek	50	U 2
Zaskar Mts., *mountains*	78	E 2
Zastron	101	E 5
Zatec	58	E 3
Zavitinsk	75	P 4
Zawiercie	64	C 2
Zayat, J. az, *mountains*	100	E 5
Zaysan, Oz., *lake*	66	F 3
Zayt, J., *mountain*	100	E 5
Zdolbunov	64	E 2
Zduńska Wola	64	C 2
Zebdāni	89	C 1
Zeeland, *province*	56	B 3
Zeelim	89	A 3
Zeerust	101	E 4
Zehdenick	58	E 2
Zeila	88	C 7
Zeist	56	D 2
Zeitz	58	E 3
Zelenodol'sk	65	G 2
Zelenogorsk	51	T 4
Zell-am-Ziller	59	D 5
Zeluán, see *Selouane*	52	D 5
Zembra, *island*	61	C 6
Zemio	99	F 5
Zemlya Frantsa Iosifa, *island group*	66	D 2
Zemmora	53	F 5
Zemun	64	D 4
Zenica	64	C 4
Zepče	60	G 2
Zerqan	62	B 3
Zetland, *county*	46	G 1
Zevenaar	56	E 3
Zeya	75	P 4
Zeya, *river*	75	P 4
Zêzere, *river*	52	A 3
Zhdanov	29	L 4
Zhelaniya, Mys, *cape*	66	E 2
Zheleznodorozhnyy	35	M 2
Zhigansk	75	P 3
Zhiguli, *mountains*	29	N 3
Zhitomir	35	J 3
Zhlobin	64	F 2
Zhmerinka	37	F 2
Zhob, *river*	86	C 3
Zholkva	64	D 2
Ziarat	86	C 3
Zidani Most	60	E 1
Ziębice	58	G 3
Ziel, Mt., *mountain*	140	D 4
Zielona Góra	64	B 2
Zielona Góra, *province*	64	B 2
Ziesar	58	E 2
Ziftá	100	C 2
Ziguinchor	98	B 4
Zikron Ya'aqov	89	A 2
Zile	37	G 3
Zilina	64	C 3
Zilling Tso, *lake*	79	F 2
Zimbabwe, *civilisation*	159	
Zimniy Bereg, *region*	50	X 3
Zimricea	62	D 2
Zinder	90	D 4
Zin, *river*	89	B 4
Zion Canyon, *gorge*	120	D 4
Zitácuaro	122	C 3
Zittau	64	B 2
Zlatibor	62	A 2
Zlatograd	62	D 3
Zlatoust	35	N 3
Złotoria	58	F 3
Złotow	64	C 2
Znin	58	G 2
Znojmo	64	C 3
Zoco el Tzenin de Yamani	52	C 5
Zofingen	57	C 2
Zomba	91	G 7
Zonguldak	37	F 3
Zonza	60	B 4
Zrenjanin	64	D 4
Zuckerhütl, *mountain*	59	D 5
Zuénoula	98	C 5
Zuera	53	E 2
Zug	57	D 2
Zug, *canton*	57	D 2
Zugersee, *lake*	57	D 2
Zugspitze, *mountain*	57	F 2
Zd. Beveland, *island*	56	B 3
Zuidelijk flevoland, *polder*	56	D 2
Zuiderzee, see *IJsselmeer*	56	D 2
Zuid Holland, *province*	56	C 2
Zújar	52	C 3
Zumbo	104	B 6
Zürich	28	H 4
Zürich, *canton*	57	D 2
Zürichsee, *lake*	57	D 2
Zurrón, Punta, *cape*	134	B 3
Zutphen	56	E 2
Zwai, L., *lake*	99	G 5
Zweibrücken	59	B 4
Zwettl	59	F 4
Zwickau	34	G 3
Zwolle	56	E 2
Zyrardów	64	D 2
Zyryanka	75	S 3
Zyryanovsk	74	L 5